La Nouvelle France

La Nouvelle France

The Making of French Canada—A Cultural History

Peter Moogk

Michigan State University Press

East Lansing

Copyright © 2000 by Peter Moogk

∞ The paper used in this publication meets the minimum requirements
of ANSI/NISO Z39.48–1992 (R 1997) (Permanence of Paper).

Michigan State University Press
East Lansing, Michigan 48823-5202
Printed and bound in the United States of America.

07 06 05 04 03 02   2 3 4 5 6 7 8 9 10

LIBRARY OF CONGRESS CATALOGING-IN-PUBLICATION DATA
Moogk, Peter N., 1943–
La Nouvelle France : the making of French Canada : a cultural history / Peter Moogk.
p. cm.
Includes bibliographical references and index.
ISBN 0-87013-528-7 (alk. paper)
1. Canada—History—To 1763 (New France) 2. Canada—Social conditions—To 1763.
3. French-Canadians—History. 4. Quebec (Province)—History.
5. Canada—English-French relations. I. Title.
F1030 .M793 2000
971.01—dc21

00-008122

Cover design by Ariana Grabec-Dingman
Book design by Sharp Des!gns, Lansing, MI

Visit Michigan State University Press on the World-Wide Web at:
www.msu.edu/unit/msupress

—◆—

This book is dedicated to my father,

Willis John Moogk, who communicated

his enthusiasm for history to me, and

to William John Eccles, who taught

me the historian's craft.

—◆—

Contents

Acknowledgments

I AM THANKFUL TO JOHN F. BOSHER AND RICHARD W. UNGER, WHO READ AN early draft of this manuscript and provided helpful suggestions for its improvement. Bill Eccles, before his death in October 1998, commented on chapter 3, but, as he would probably say, that does not mean that he agreed with it. James Axtell provided an evaluation of an early version of chapters 4 and 5. My wife Susan helped identify those passages in need of clarification and rewriting. The patient staff of the University of British Columbia's Main Library, especially those in the Special Collections Division, produced obscure and rare publications that served me well. I was also greatly assisted by the staff at the Archives départementales de la Charente-Maritime; the Archives nationales du Québec (including the Montreal and Trois-Rivières branches); the Archives du Séminaire de Québec; the National Archives of Canada; the Public Record Office on Chancery Lane, London; and, particularly, the Fortress of Louisbourg National Historic Park, where I spent a happy and productive year. My debt to others, who helped me on particular subjects, is acknowledged in the footnotes. To each one of you, *gratia tibi!*

My Discovery of French Canada

MY FIRST ENCOUNTER WITH THE ORIGINALITY OF CANADA'S FRENCH-SPEAKING cultures came at an early age, when living in Ottawa during the 1950s. It was immediately apparent that the French taught in English-language public schools belonged to a world apart from the everyday French spoken in the streets. Canadian vernacular French had a direct and earthy quality: mashed potatoes were "patates pilées." When a restaurant listed "pommes de terre en purée" on its menu, I knew that I was going to pay well for the proprietor's European pretensions. French Canada savored more of François Rabelais than of Pierre Corneille or Jean Racine, whose affected classical dramas were my fare as an undergraduate university student. When perusing Montreal's telephone directory, I found a listing for nuns which included a "Soeur Sanschagrin." Sister "No Worries" was probably the descendant of a soldier whose nickname this had been. Directories for the Acadian communities of Nova Scotia's south shore, like West Pubnico, were surprising for the small number of surnames, such as *d'Eon* or *Amirault*, with multiple entries. Here were different and unexpected worlds within my own country. Canada's schools and universities had seemed intent on preparing us "les autres" (also known as "les Anglais," for a Canadian who is not French-speaking is an Anglo-Saxon) for a visit to Paris rather than for a sojourn in Montreal or a tour of Acadia.

While living in the Province of Quebec as a graduate student in the late 1960s, I became aware of differences, in addition to language, that distinguished French-speakers from their English-speaking compatriots. The North American veneer over life in Quebec is deceptive because it gives an illusion of continental uniformity. In Quebec I observed that English-speakers were disproportionately active in historical preservation groups, even in predominantly French-speaking regions. It was not because Franco-Quebeckers were indifferent to history; indeed, they were passionately interested in their past. It was evident that self-organization and the lobbying of government came more naturally to the English-speaking Canadians. Here was a visible difference between the two language groups. It was also evident in a graduate student exchange between McGill University and the Université de Montréal that our French-speaking peers were more inclined, during the radical 1960s, to embrace a comprehensive ideology than, as we did, to choose ideas that appealed to us eclectically and without concern for coherence. They were also more likely to believe that a historian could attain a definitive knowledge of the past, despite the fragmentary nature of surviving evidence.

At social events French-speakers behaved with great civility, and yet, when I was a passenger in a car driven by my wife, men made rude, mocking gestures as if to say that any man who let a woman drive for him was no man at all. *Machismo* was not just a trait of Latin American men. I had my last will and testament drawn up by a Pointe Claire notary, and this experience was an introduction to the conceptions of marriage and the family upheld by the Civil Code of Quebec. Upon further investigation, I found much to admire in this system of law, which was unlike that in the other Canadian provinces, whose private law is derived from English Common Law. Marriage contracts, long the practice in Quebec, were finding favor as "prenuptial agreements" among couples in the other provinces. The civil law heritage was important because it not only preserved distinctive social values, it also shaped patterns of thought among the educated. Political arguments by French-speakers frequently began with the enunciation of a principle, such as "Canada was meant to be an equal partnership of two founding nations." This was not so much a historical truth as it was an idealistic statement of what ought to have been. This pattern of reasoning, starting from some general principle, was the preferred mode of argument among well-educated Franco-Quebeckers.

French Canadians are proverbially a family-minded people and there is truth in that preconception. The strength of family ties was evident when a French-speaking friend declined an invitation with the explanation that the day in question was Mother's Day and he felt that he should be at his parents' home then. Sometimes French Canada seemed to be one extended family. The interplay between French-speakers meeting for the first time was intriguing: once the surname was given, inquiries began with something like, "do you belong to the Rainvilles of Beauport or those from Beauce? I have an uncle who married a Louise Rainville. . . ." The genealogical knowledge displayed was impressive, and, more surprisingly, the interlocutors usually found some shared ancestor or a common acquaintance. This happened at a time when Quebec had a population of five million. Few French Canadians are ignorant of their lineage, and family lore includes knowledge of the family's founder in Canada. When I was working in the notarial archives, French-speakers were surprised to find an outsider there and were even more astonished that I was *not* doing research on my ancestors. I do have ancestors from France, but they were German-speaking Alsatians who settled in the Province of Ontario during the early nineteenth century and they did not appear in Quebec's notarial archives.

French Canada's history, as it was written in the 1960s, did not explain the origins of this distinctive culture, save in the most general way. The immigration from France, the foundation of the Roman Catholic Church in North America, and the military and political reasons for the British conquest of New France all were discussed in texts. This explained the presence of an overwhelmingly Roman Catholic, French-speaking people in a former portion of the British Empire, but it did not explain the origins of French-Canadian social values and behavioral patterns. One source of that distinctive character must have been the era of New France, when immigrants from France and elsewhere were transformed into *Acadiens* and *Canadiens*—singular provincial types within the old French empire. Thus, *la Nouvelle France* is the obvious starting point for understanding the origins and nature of French-Canadian distinctiveness; this, however, was not as obvious to scholars as it ought to have been.

Current popular histories of Canada seemed to assume that New France, being so long departed, could have no residual influence upon the present. In twentieth-century Canadian schools, the French Regime was presented as a colorful but inconsequential era of heroic missionaries, valiant warriors, intrepid explorers, and hardy fur traders—an entertaining divertissement before the serious business of achieving political self-rule and democracy began. Textbook histories acquired a clear sense of direction only after New France had been swept aside by the British conquest of 1759–60. The French colony had no useful place in a history designed to train young Canadians in the duties and rights of democratic citizenship.

Because historians are intermediaries between past and present generations, we should provide some explanation for the distinctive cultures of French Canada. A historian's primary task is to explain, in clear prose, how the present came into being. Useful history enlarges the reader's understanding of why things evolved as they did. My notion of a good history book is one that can be read with profit and, when finished, that allows the reader to say, "So that's why that is as it is." Many of the explanations offered about present-day French Canada are superficial and, after mentioning the British conquest, rarely venture back farther than the 1800s in seeking formative experiences. The culture studied was usually that of an educated elite, rather than the world of all social ranks. When the full range of society was considered, scholars tended to apply classifications from other eras rather than seek out the distinctions that were important to people of the seventeenth and eighteenth centuries. Applying to one age templates from another time conveys a certain comparative understanding of the past, but because this approach ignores the imperatives of the period under study, it cannot explain collective human behavior in a bygone era. To find an explanation, one must detach oneself from current concerns, causes, and conflicts. If one is making a connection between past events and current circumstances, that is not an easy task.

Independent scholarship is needed because every human institution and interest group has its own self-serving version of the past, and the public is inundated with a variety of distorted accounts about what happened long ago. The detached historian can serve society by providing a dispassionate interpretation of the evidence that does not justify, glorify, or condemn any one group. For every scholarly writer there is a legion of propagandists seeking or inventing heroic precursors of their cause, magnifying the role of their own group in the past and recasting it as suffering, guiltlessly, at the hands of others. In doing so, a group's moments of aggression and collective misdeeds are expunged from the record. In Canada it is fashionable to build group identity upon the theme of victimization. For descendants of exiled Acadians, of American Loyalist refugees, of Japanese-Canadians removed from the Pacific Coast in 1942, or of Jewish survivors of the Nazi Holocaust, there is a factual basis for this self-image.

Canada is also touched by the currents of cultural nationalism. Nationalism is built upon a selective mythology designed to cultivate pride and an exclusive attachment to one cultural group. Historical research is judged by nationalists for its service to the cause, not for its reliance upon convincing evidence. Nineteenth-century French historian Joseph-Ernest Renan once said, "to forget, I will venture to say, to get one's history wrong, are essential factors in the making of a nation."

An academic historian who yields to partisanship and acts as a self-appointed apologist for those whom we might regard as history's victims abandons the scholar's calling. A distortion of the evidence to serve modern causes, no matter how generous the writer's intentions, is still falsification, and it hinders our understanding of the past. Some subjectivity is inescapable: our judgment of what is probable and reasonable is based, necessarily, upon our own backgrounds and experiences. All written history will be marked by the character of its author. The self-aware writer must wrestle with his or her own biases and refrain from moral judgments of bygone people on the basis of current values. To know one's own biases demands an appreciation of the context for past events. The reading public, however, tends to believe that current values are the only legitimate reference points and it prefers simple dichotomies of good and evil, of oppressors and the oppressed, and of right and wrong.

Abandoning all pretense to neutrality has the blessing of intellectual fashion. The postmodernists' claim that all human knowledge and description are subjective and, therefore, scholarly objectivity is a fraud is a half-truth masquerading as a deep insight. There is a difference between historical fiction and scholarly history. Complete objectivity is unattainable, yet a credible interpretation will appeal to the evidence and allow the reader to verify that there is a foundation for the writer's view. All historical evidence is not of equal value, and the well-trained historian will appraise the veracity of surviving testimony, consider the context of the times, and produce an account that is consistent with the best evidence.

In the years after my all too brief sojourn in Montreal I uncovered the historical origins of some of the cultural traits observed in the 1960s. The preference for political arguments founded upon authoritative principles was a legacy of French civil law and the process of reasoning it fostered. When studying craft organizations among colonial workers, I found an explanation for the French-speakers' reticence to organize locally to promote special interests. I expected that others, more capable than I, would see the same things and put their observations into print within a few years. That did not happen and I became impatient. I also became skeptical about the penchant among contemporary historians for seeing economic determinism in the behavior of generations long dead. In marriage contracts I found patterns of behavior that made no economic sense. People assumed financial obligations without regard for their real resources; social standing compelled them to do this. In French North America the colonists' sense of an individual's social value was detached from personal wealth; the dignity of one's occupation and family were the prime considerations. It was a shock to my own preconceptions to find that status determined economic behavior and that rank was not defined by wealth, yet I had to cede to the evidence of how people behaved and of what they said. Although private letters and personal testimony from this period are rare, the words of people from the era have been quoted liberally in this book to describe their lives and ideas. They were the best witnesses to their own values. For too long, we have relied on the impressions, contained in the readily available government correspondence, of French bureaucrats—who were outsiders—to describe the colonists. The colonists' standards, as expressed in their own letters, in court records, and in notarial deeds, were very different from those we hold dear today. Identifying and comprehending those alien values are the tasks of cultural history.

A historical explanation that assumes all human actions are undertaken to satisfy material needs and that ignores the desire for psychological or emotional gratification, or even cultural imperatives, is an incomplete explanation. Familiar patterns provided comfort in an unfamiliar setting. To the chaste mind cultural history may seem like ethnic stereotyping, which it is not. Shared values and beliefs do predispose us to certain courses of action or modes of understanding, but they do no eliminate individual choice, originality, or nonconformity. Cultural traditions can be remarkably tenacious, and the colonists of French North America were social conservatives who were determined to preserve what they remembered of their homeland's ways. New France, as William J. Eccles observed, was an extension of Old Regime France, and many patterns in the parent state were reproduced in the French colonies. Cultural conservatism is a unifying theme for this study. Some of the values and behavioral patterns established in the French Regime endured into the twentieth century and these are addressed in the conclusion.

When we speak of cultural values, whose standards are at issue? Among university scholars, it has been recognized that the lower ranks of society had a culture apart from that of their literate "betters," yet it is unfashionable to treat popular culture as an independent force. Historians of the French *Annales* school have taught us to believe that once economic cycles and structures of the past have been identified then all coincidental events and human acts are thereby explained. The influence of individual choice is discounted, impersonal forces are emphasized, and material considerations are paramount. There is also a vogue for believing that uneducated and humble folk in earlier times calmly devised economic "survival strategies" and thought of little else. This view of bygone people as cool and materialistic calculators shows a limited appreciation of human nature. The imagined passionless calculating machines have nothing in common with the impatient, proud, and headstrong people encountered in the law courts' records. Concern with acquiring sufficient resources to support life was certainly paramount, but that drive could be deflected by other concerns. This book treats human culture as both a product of experience and a force shaping people's conduct.

History is about people, and each individual's life combines commonly shared elements with those that are unique to that person. Quantitative history helps to distinguish the commonplace from the exceptional by identifying dominant behavioral patterns from several cases. Small samples of authoritative evidence are preferable to large bodies of information from questionable sources. Here, too, there are problems because there is sometimes no quantifiable data on certain aspects of past life, such as the daily diet of farmers or the use of superstitious rituals. There are only incidental references which provide glimpses of these activities. In such cases, one must resort to the older social history technique of constructing a composite picture out of selections from written sources. This is risky because the historian must rely on experience and informed judgment when selecting "representative" examples from the evidence.

The definition of *la Nouvelle France* used in this work is that of the period: the French colony extended west and east beyond the largest settlements in the St. Lawrence Valley. New France included fishing establishments on Terreneuve (Newfoundland) and spread as far west as the Illinois Country, drained by the Mississippi and its northern tributaries. Present-day political boundaries, whether state, provincial, or national, had no bearing on events before 1760 and can be ignored.

Montreal, the last major center held by French forces, was surrendered to the British army in 1760. The British Conquest left a deep imprint on the history that followed this event, but it was not the preordained destiny of New France. Before the publications of William Eccles, English-speaking historians customarily looked upon French North America as a foredoomed empire that was ripe for conquest, whose institutions were an affront to rational and liberal minds. The censorious view of the colony's institutions as backward and repressive was the legacy of nineteenth-century historian Francis Parkman, whose perspective dominated the English-language historiography of French North America for a century. In fact, the French settlements had institutions, laws, and patterns of life with virtues as well as defects and they worked well for the colonists. These institutions and practices, along with popular beliefs and values, are the constituent parts of a human culture and, though later generations may find some features admirable or repugnant, they were parts of a coherent whole. They "made sense" to the people of that time. The same logic and coherence were to be found in pre-1700 aboriginal cultures. The cooperation of Amerindian captives when they were tortured surprised Europeans, who did not comprehend that this horrific ceremony was a man's last opportunity to prove that he had a warrior's indifference to pain, even if he had been captured. The victim had an honorable role to play. It is a historian's duty to understand each culture on its own terms, not to censure or praise it. Only after asking "What was going on here?," can one proceed to the challenging question of "*Why* was this happening?"

The *Canadiens* and colonists of the Atlantic region, like most human groups, were confident of their own superiority over other peoples. They were overwhelmed in the Seven Years' War by an accumulation of external forces; defeat was not the inevitable consequence of moral decay or the result of the presumed backwardness of French colonial society. Without this military calamity, *la Nouvelle France* might have endured and evolved in later decades in ways we cannot imagine. The fact that many legacies of this colony survived, with modifications, until the twentieth century attests to their adaptability and their utility to French-speaking North Americans.

The present account deals with the roots of the *Acadien* and *Canadien* cultures. It is not a comprehensive history of New France; it is a series of exploratory essays on various aspects of French-Canadian culture before 1760. Those seeking an account of military and political events will find plenty of books, written by hands more capable than mine, on these subjects. This is a tentative examination of another world by a person removed from the subject by time and space. As a foreigner to New France, I cannot assume that I understand this departed world by virtue of ancestry, religious convictions, or residence in the historic territory of *la Nouvelle France*. I must work to make sense of the information found. I claim no instinctive understanding of the subject.

Approaching the bygone world of the French colonists as a foreigner restrains that anachronistic human inclination to see past generations as people who thought and acted just as we do, but merely dressed in period costume. Beyond sharing some common human traits, such as self-interest or idealism, we cannot presume to fully know or understand the minds of our own ancestors or of kindred peoples who lived more than two and a half centuries ago. Watching twentieth-century craftsmen "reconstructing" Louisbourg and Quebec's Place Royale showed me how difficult, how impossible, it was for people of my era to duplicate the handiwork of earlier artisans, whose aesthetic values and attitudes were so different from our own. The reconstruction workers could not entirely suppress their own modern concerns for uniformity, symmetry, and precision.

The statements of the long-dead people of the French Regime reveal how remote the colonists were from our secular and materialistic world. In 1743 the plaintiff in a libel case stated that he and his table companions were discussing "the proposition that the skull of a man who had been strangled or hanged was more medicinal than any other [remedy] that physicians used." Another man who was present opined that surgeons collected the fat of hanged men to make their salves.[1] The most inventive modern mind would be hard put to create such a dialogue. Historical reality can be more surprising than fiction. One can enter the mental world of educated folk, such as public officials or priests, by reading the books they read or the private letters they wrote. The thoughts of the more numerous and less literate residents of the colony are difficult to reconstruct because their ideas have survived only in brief, chance references in accounts written by others, like the court record above.

The colonists of New France gave supernatural forces as much weight as material causes when they interpreted the world. Their beliefs were not limited to religious orthodoxy. A bright comet in the night sky was taken as a sure portent of some great event to come. All events, disasters too, answered to the inscrutable will of God. In the seventeenth century even the well educated believed in divine providence and in the power of magic to injure, kill, or protect. The colonists' sense of powerlessness before the forces of nature and unpredictable fortune led them to call upon the supernatural world for help and protection. Patron saints, such as St. Anne, were considered to be especially helpful in averting tragedy.

These French colonists were proud, mutually suspicious, and fearful people living in a dangerously unpredictable world. In time, and involuntarily, they developed French colonial cultures that distinguished them from other peoples. One could not mistake them for British North Americans. Guy Frégault's statement that "between Canada and the British colonies the chief difference was not one of kind but of size"[2] is a polemical extravagance by a historian who knew better. *Canadiens* and *Acadiens* were different from the British Americans, and these differences are the subject of this book. Those differences went deeper than language, which is the focus of present-day ethnic identities in Canada. Given the political turmoil in Canada over language and culture, we should seek to know more about the historic inheritance of French-speaking Canadians.

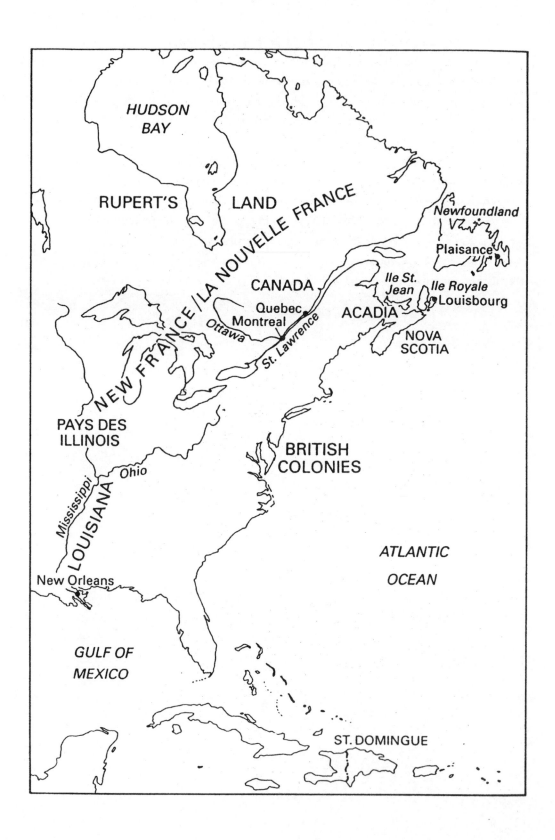

CHAPTER I

Cyrano de Bergerac's Imaginary Voyage to Canada: A Survey of the Colony

IN THE SEVENTEENTH CENTURY SAVINIEN CYRANO DE BERGERAC DESCRIBED A fantastic flight from France to Canada in his book *Histoire . . . de la Lune*. He said that he escaped the pull of gravity by girdling his body with bottles of dew that evaporated in sunlight, lifting him skyward, where a westering wind carried him to the New World. Upon landing near Quebec, Cyrano was rescued from hostile "savages" by the governor-general's guards. What would this aerial traveler have seen on that westward flight to the St. Lawrence Valley, after passing over the gray, foam-flecked waves of the Atlantic Ocean and coming within view of land? First would be the rocky and indented shores of Newfoundland, known to European fishermen since the late fifteenth century. Few friends here, he might have thought while soaring over the Avalon Peninsula's English establishments. From the 1490s European fishermen had been harvesting Newfoundland cod, and some had come ashore to obtain fresh water and firewood. The oldest fishery was the "green fishery," in which the cod were beheaded and gutted on shipboard and packed immediately in the hold with intervening layers of salt to preserve the fish. Cheap salt, obtained from the evaporation of seawater, was abundant in the Iberian Peninsula and in southwestern France, whose seasonal fishermen preferred the green fishery. The English, who had to import solar salt, pioneered the land-based "dry fishery," in which men landed their catch in sheltered coves to prepare and sun-dry the cod fillets. The result was a lighter, more compact, and longer-lasting fillet that could be shipped to Europe at the fishing season's end. The seasonal settlements of England's West Country fishermen were concentrated on the Avalon Peninsula, the easternmost portion of Newfoundland.

To the southwest, near the fish-laden waters of St. Mary's Bay, was Plaisance, now called Placentia, the principal French settlement of southern "Terreneuve." Norman and Breton fishermen, as well as Basques, followed the English example and entered the land-based cod fishery of Newfoundland, making Plaisance their principal location. There, by good fortune and English negligence, these fishermen from France found a haven with deep waters, sheltered by steep, rocky hills. Amid these sheltered waters was a long, flat, pebbled beach, ideal for drying cod fillets after they had been rinsed in brine to draw out the moisture and to kill the bacteria that caused decay. Newfoundland's dried cod found a ready market in France, the Mediterranean countries, and, later, the West Indies.

The town of Plaisance was established in the 1620s to take advantage of the harbor's natural assets. Seventy years later there were no more than 250 permanent residents, augmented during the summer by Basque, Breton, and Norman fishermen.[1] To secure this port, the natural protection of the surrounding hills was supplemented by man-made fortifications. The narrow harbor entrance, which facilitated the defense of Plaisance, was also a liability in a siege because it was easily closed by blockading vessels, forcing the defenders to survive on their limited stores of food. The hinterland was barren and supported few wild animals. Local trees were small and stunted and they were soon cut down for firewood. Because of the destruction of trees within a league or more of the settlement, said one official in 1711, "the hardness of this land" had "become even worse." He suggested moving the troops and settlers from "this miserable land where there are only rocks," possibly to Cape Breton.[2] This was a prophetic suggestion.

Plaisance was admirably situated and well suited for the dry fishery, but for little else. The population was dependent on imported foodstuffs, supplemented by the produce of kitchen gardens and a small number of livestock. The merchants who brought food, clothing, and other necessities to Plaisance charged extortionate prices, keeping the resident population in poverty.[3] With only a score of soldiers under his command, the governor of the fishing settlement could neither defend Plaisance nor impose his will on the unruly population of fishermen and traders.

Louis-Armand de Lom d'Arce, Baron de Lahontan, who had served in Plaisance's small garrison in 1693, described the bay as

> fourteen leagues deep by twelve or fourteen wide. It contains several small harbors . . . in which the largest vessels would be safe. . . . That of Placentia, then, is the largest, the best and the most commodious, for it is surrounded by mountains,

the anchorage marvelous, and in that (whose shape is oval) one could easily draw up eight hundred ships which the smallest cable would be sufficient to hold in any storm. . . . In front of it is a large and fine roadstead which puts the ships under cover from all winds, except those from the northwestern direction.

De Lahontan considered the fort and gun batteries to be "bad and irregular." The governor's "cottage" (*cabane*) was inside the fort while the houses of other permanent residents, including soldiers, "are scattered here and there." There was space to accommodate three times the fifty families already located at Plaisance. The port's economy was depressed by war, but eighty vessels might be expected each year in peacetime.

> The fishery is very prolific in that station, it is carried on at a distance of one league from the harbor. The cod is dried there wonderfully well and any number of ships that may be there are assured of returning well laden; for the fishery never fails there. . . . It begins on the 5th, 10th or the 15th of May and ends at the end of August . . . not that they don't catch fish the whole length of the year but they stop at that time because the sun is failing.[4]

Beyond Plaisance, there were several small French fishing stations scattered along Newfoundland's south shore; a few were located in the far north, and others were on the islands of the Gulf of St. Lawrence, such as Cape Breton Island.

Had Cyrano the gift of foresight as well as of flight, he might have seen the people of Plaisance embarking for Cape Breton after French claims to Newfoundland, including their settlement, were ceded to Britain in 1713. Their destination was "English Harbor" on Cape Breton, not so convenient to the fishing banks as Plaisance, but still ice-free in winter and blessed with an inshore fishery. That harbor became the new focus of the French dry fishery, which, though smaller than the ship-based "green fishery," still produced considerable wealth. Of the many French fishing stations on Cape Breton, it was this haven that was chosen in 1719 to become the administrative center and naval base for French North America's Atlantic Coast.

Havre à l'Anglais on Cape Breton was renamed Louisbourg, while Cape Breton became Ile Royale. The French government spent millions of livres to erect gun batteries and a fortified town worthy of those regal names. The construction of fortifications was an industry in itself, and expenditures on the fixed defenses and upon the large garrison helped sustain the town's economy. After the fishery and maritime trade, government building contracts were Louisbourg's third major industry. Reality fell short of the government's vision, however: over the rising masonry of bastions and batteries there blew an oily, pungent odor of drying fish, as if to remind Louisbourg of its humble origins and the main occupation of its working population. Half of Ile Royale's European residents lived in Louisbourg, and the port's population of fishermen, soldiers, indentured servants, and slaves was dominated by royal officials, military officers, wholesale merchants, and fishing contractors (*habitants pêcheurs*). This dominant social group was possessed by a mercantile spirit that would have been repugnant to the aristocratic sensibilities of French officers and officials elsewhere.

Louisbourg, like Plaisance, had no local agricultural base, which explains the absence of a landed aristocracy. Ungenerous nature had given the town an acidic, swampy, and woody neighborhood unfit for cultivation or grazing. Geography, however, had endowed the fortress town with a location of great commercial potential. Ships from the larger settlements on the St. Lawrence were imprisoned by the ice-bound river until May, and they were hard-pressed to make one voyage to the West Indies or France before winter once again seized the port of Quebec in its frozen grip. Cargoes deposited at ice-free Louisbourg from all sources were ready to be forwarded once the North Atlantic gales had subsided, and so the port became a transfer point between the mother country, the Caribbean colonies, and the mainland settlements of French North America. In peacetime, 150 merchantmen would sail into Louisbourg harbor each year, dwarfing the seaborne trade of Quebec, which occupied a score of vessels. It was the exportation of dried fish and the transshipment of West Indian products that paid for Ile Royale's provisions.

French-speaking Acadians from peninsular Nova Scotia voyaged north with cattle and grain to feed the soldiers, fishermen, merchants, and denizens of Louisbourg. In 1713 the formal cession by France in the Treaty of Utrecht of "all Nova Scotia or Accadie, with its ancient Boundaries" left the French Acadian population within British territory. French government agents, seconded by the Roman Catholic clergy, tried to persuade the 2,500 Acadians in Nova Scotia to remove themselves to areas still subject to the monarch of France. In this they had little success; the Acadians were dismayed by rocky Cape Breton. Just 500 found a living there as fishermen and carpenters. Bay of Fundy's western shore, still held by France, was scarcely more appealing to these tillers of the soil. The settlements on this coast were always small. There were scarcely fifty French colonists on the River Saint John in 1695 and it took forty years to double that number. No fools they, most Acadians refused to leave their rich farmlands in the Annapolis Valley and around the Bay of Fundy's eastern shore.

Their ancestors had established themselves on the Nova Scotian peninsula in the 1630s and were joined by a small number of fishermen, indentured servants, and soldiers. Their descendants had spread northward from Port Royal, up the

Annapolis Valley, and around the Bay of Fundy's head. There settlers found extensive tidal flats suited to their system of diking and draining land for agriculture.
Cutting down trees was a laborious process, and the interior lands, when cleared of
timber, were not as fertile as the reclaimed tidal marshlands. Land reclamation also
avoided a conflict over territory with the Amerindian peoples who exploited the
woody interior. In 1720 Paul Mascarene observed that farming was the Acadians'
"chief employment," yet they lived "hand-to-mouth, and provided they have a good
field of Cabbages and Bread enough for their families, with what fodder is sufficient
for their cattle, they seldom look for much further improvement." Trapping sable
martens and fishing were incidental activities.[5] Though unlettered, the Acadians
shrewdly insisted that the French military garrisons pay for provisions and cattle in
coin.

The big silver écus and Spanish colonial currency were passed on to the equally
canny New England shippers who brought manufactured goods to both Nova Scotia
and Louisbourg. Of 273 trading and fishing vessels that arrived at Louisbourg in
1752, 156 came from the "Coste de Baston" (Boston's shore: Massachusetts Bay).[6]
"Simple refreshments" to satisfy Ile Royale's immediate hunger was how royal officials
described the Yankees' contraband goods flowing into the island. France's American empire was supposed to be a closed trading preserve for the benefit of French
suppliers. Officials concealed the full extent of the illegal commerce from their
superiors and granted extraordinary trading permits to British Americans. The people
of Louisbourg lived in houses whose chimneys were built of New England bricks,
with roofs and wall sheathing made of New England boards, and when the French
colonists drank, it was sometimes from earthenware tankards bearing the British
monarch's royal initials, "G.R." (for Georgius Rex—King George). New England
was a real, though unofficial, partner in Louisbourg's transshipment trade between
Canada, France, and the West Indies.

Louisbourg was at its zenith in 1745 when two Spaniards visited the fortress
town. It had three thousand residents, with an additional, seasonal population of
hundreds of fisherfolk. Yet, to the visitors' eyes, Louisbourg was "of middling size,
the houses [are built] of wood on a foundation of stone to the height of two yards or
two yards and a half from the ground. In some houses the whole ground floor is of
stone. . . ." As for the port, "it is walled, and extreamly [*sic*] well fortified with all
the modern works." One of these modern works was the King's Bastion citadel,
which contained a barracks and the governor's residence. The bastion's military
chapel became the town's parish church, which suited the colonists, who were content to let the king pay for its upkeep and for the clergy. The other chapel, "belonging to the hospital of St. Jean de Dieu . . . is an elegant and spacious structure all of
stone." The visitors admired the harbor's sheltered north end, which contained a

careening basin for overhauling ships, and noted the south end—the principal anchorage—which was open to eastern winds.

"The inhabitants of Louisbourg," noted the two strangers, "consisted of French families, some Europeans and others [are] Creoles [born in the colonies] of the place itself, and from Placentia in the island of Newfoundland. . . . Their principal if not only trade is the cod-fishery, from which also large profits accrued to them, not only on account of the abundance of this fish, but that of the neighboring sea affords the best of any about Newfoundland. The wealth of the inhabitants consisted in their storehouses . . . and in their number of fishing barks. . . . The cod storehouses never failed of being filled against the time the ships resorted hither from most of the ports of France, laden with provisions and other goods, with which the inhabitants provided themselves in exchange for this fish; or consigned it to be sold in France on their account; likewise vessels from the French colonies of St. Domingo and Martinico [Martinique], brought sugar, tobacco, coffee, rum, &c. and returned loaded with cod; and any surplus, after Louisbourg was supplied found a vent [sale] in Canada, where the return was made in beavers' skins and other kinds of fine furs. Thus Louisbourg, with no other fund than the fishery, carried on a continual and large commerce both with Europe and America." The garrison's seven hundred soldiers, "when not on guard, very gladly work" on the repair and improvement of the defenses, "as being a comfortable addition to their pay."[7] Neither walls nor soldiers could prevent the capture of Louisbourg in 1745 and 1758, after seven-week sieges. British engineers leveled the defenses in the 1760s and the site was gradually abandoned, leaving few visible traces of the once-busy, eighteenth-century seaport.

Ile Saint-Jean, later called Prince Edward Island, was a dependency of Louisbourg that supplied some of the farm produce that Ile Royale could not furnish for its chief settlement. In Cyrano de Bergerac's time, this large island in the Gulf of the St. Lawrence was not yet settled by Europeans. In the 1720s colonists were introduced by a French monopoly company, but more came from Acadia. The island's red soil was exceptionally fruitful and the small aboriginal population there cultivated maize. After 1720 there was a French garrison at Port La Joie, on Charlottetown Harbor, to consume the surplus that Acadian farmers produced. The Acadians fed British and French troops, for a price, and once again the happy conjunction of hungry mouths, money, and fertile land served the Acadians well. By 1732 the island had 347 settlers, primarily farming families, while others engaged in fishing and shipbuilding. Each good harvest enticed more mainland Acadians to join them. By 1758 there were some 5,000 European settlers on the island.

Population growth in Nova Scotia and pressure from the administration upon the Acadians to assume the military obligations of British subjects—for that is what they were—encouraged the migration across Northumberland Strait to Ile Saint-Jean. These independent and militarily neutral people did not like imperial governments that demanded submission and an unqualified allegiance. Their neutrality and self-reliance were a result of their history. French Acadia, like Louisbourg, had a troubled past of conquest and destruction. It was located in a war zone between the major French settlements and the colonies of Great Britain, which contested France's title to the region. The oldest establishment, Port-Royal, was destroyed in 1613, and from 1654 to 1670 the area was controlled by the English. This British occupation followed a period of civil war between rival claimants to the governorship of French Acadia. Even when France's authority was exercised from Port-Royal, the isolated colonists had to fend for themselves. French monarchs neglected Acadia and contributed little to its development, colonization, administration, or defense. Because of the colonial government's weakness, the *Acadiens* became accustomed to governing themselves.

Acadians were suspicious of outside governments and did not cooperate with census-takers. Thus, the first reliable population figure does not appear until 1671, and even then it is not certain whether the correct figure is 423 or 441. The Acadian population grew from a small nucleus of indentured servants and soldiers brought out by fur-trading companies. The pioneers were joined by fishermen who had decided to settle in Acadia rather than return to France with the seasonal fishing fleet. Some of the earliest settlers took wives from the local Micmac (Mi-kmaq) Indians, who had been converted to Roman Catholicism. The small number of founder-immigrants is evident from the limited range of surnames among the current Acadian population: there are only about one hundred of them. Brittany and Normandy furnished settlers, but analysis of Acadian French suggests that most colonists came from southwestern France.[8] Certainly, the Acadians' land reclamation techniques, using dikes and sluice gates, resembled the enclosures on tidal flats near La Rochelle that received and contained seawater for making solar salt. Although one system was designed to exclude seawater while the other was to retain it, the resemblance of the diked marshlands to the salt pans of southwestern France favors a link between the two regions. The building and maintenance of these earth and wattle dikes forced Acadians to develop a communal organization that brought different families together for this work. By 1714 the Acadian population had increased to 2,528, largely by natural increase. A French visitor then noted that "men cause themselves no great fatigue by labor in this Land . . . they are free to populate the World; which is, moreover, that which they do best." At Port-Royal he came upon two couples with eighteen children, "which shows a capacity in the business," and then he encountered a third pair with twenty-two children and, more wondrous, "[they] give promise of more."[9]

The attitude of the British and French governments ensured that the Acadians would never enjoy lasting peace. The 1713 Treaty of Utrecht, as French officials saw it, did not include the mainland portions of Acadia, and they confined the British to the Nova Scotian peninsula. Since the French crown could not entice most Acadians to withdraw to its territory, it tried to use the Roman Catholic clergy to maintain the settlers' attachment for France and to weaken British control over peninsular Nova Scotia. Conflict over the limits of Britain's title, the presence of French forts in the neighborhood, and attacks upon British settlements and ships by France's Amerindian allies and a few young Acadians compromised the French-speaking, Roman Catholic colonists within Nova Scotia. In June 1755 three hundred of King George II's French-speaking subjects were found inside Fort Beauséjour when it was captured. That was the justification needed by the colony's governor and council to force all Acadians to prove that they were not their sovereign's enemies. At Halifax the governor and council twice demanded an unqualified oath of allegiance, entailing military service, from representatives of these distrusted subjects. The Acadian delegates assumed that their neutrality was lawful, because one governor had accepted a limited oath of fidelity to King George II in the 1720s, and they offered only their customary acknowledgment of British sovereignty without active support for it. This was insufficient for the governing council, which decided, on 28 July 1755, to expel all Acadians from the British colony. Six thousand of an estimated ten thousand Acadians were forcibly removed and dispersed among the other British North American colonies. A few thousand fled overland to "Canada," that is to say, the St. Lawrence Valley and lower Great Lakes region of *la Nouvelle France*. That inland region had been the real focus of French colonization in the seventeenth century.

Drifting southwesterly from the gulf and above the St. Lawrence River's estuary, Cyrano de Bergerac might have mistaken the river's wide mouth for an arm of the sea. The high banks of either shore converged imperceptibly. Covered with brooding woods, the shorelines would have appeared lifeless to our airborne traveler. Only cresting waves and the white sails of an occasional ship would have enlivened the watery expanse below him. The inland French settlements were isolated by vast expanses of wilderness and dependent upon maritime communication. West of the Saguenay River, signs of human life—fishing stations and scattered farms—became more frequent. A widening shelf of arable land appeared on the rugged north shore, and the climate grew more temperate as one moved southwesterly up the river. Gradually, whitewashed farmhouses appeared along the shoreline in a loose, straggling line—an odd pattern of settlement to Europeans, who expected to see rural villages rather than the isolated farmsteads preferred by rural *Canadiens,* who made up more than three-quarters of the valley's population. The

Beauport shore, on the north bank, was the site of the first intensive farming settlements near Quebec.

Moving farther inland, Ile d'Orléans comes into view, like a great ship permanently moored in the river, shielding Quebec, the capital of New France. A fortified trading post had been placed at Quebec in 1608 because it was the first point where the river was narrow enough to be commanded by a cannon, and the chartered trading company wanted to keep rival traders from ascending the river and reaching those regions that produced the best fur pelts. The name "Quebec" has been traced to the Algonkian word for "the narrowing of the river." Gone was the Iroquoian village of Stadacona, visited by Jacques Cartier in the mid-1500s. The Laurentian Iroquois, populating this and other villages, had disappeared, allowing the French to occupy their lands without facing the issue of aboriginal land title. Administrative functions and a base for Christian missions to the natives were grafted onto the original trading post at Quebec. This community in the St. Lawrence Valley became the core of the largest European settlement in French North America. This expanding settlement was called "Canada" and its colonists became known as *Canadiens*. The colonial administration located at Quebec governed all of New France, although its authority over Acadia and Ile Royale was theoretical rather than real. Their regional governors answered directly to the king and his ministers in France.

Late-seventeenth-century Quebec, Cyrano's landing place, was sited on a headland and was divided into an upper and lower town. The physical division was functional as well. Above was the governor-general's palace, the residence of the colony's bishop, a seminary for training priests, and other ecclesiastical communities. Here, wrote a traveler in 1701, "live all persons of distinction."[10] The upper town was the metaphorical head of *la Nouvelle France*—the continental headquarters of its church, government, and armed forces. The Lower Town was the stomach, where merchants coexisted with butchers, seafarers, metalworkers, and building tradesmen. The royal intendant, who concerned himself with the day-to-day existence of the colony, shared their company. This was stratification without segregation: artisans and tavern-keepers were scattered throughout the town. With nearly eight thousand residents in the 1750s, Quebec was the nearest thing to a city in New France, followed by Louisbourg. Our 1701 tourist struggled up the steep road linking the lower to the upper town in order to view the two-story, governor-general's palace and then to admire the painted windows of the Franciscan chapel opposite. Cyrano's journey ended in the home of the governor-general, the Château St-Louis. His next voyage took him to the moon, a place even more fantastical than Canada in the 1600s.

Had his eyes been able to scan the lands upriver, de Bergerac would have espied Trois-Rivières, at the junction of the St. Maurice and St. Lawrence Rivers. The St.

Maurice was a safer route than the Ottawa River for interior nations bringing furs to the French. The meeting place of the rivers became a place of trade between natives and French. Located on sandy, ill-drained terrain, Trois-Rivières (f. 1634) never developed into more than a village and military post, and its population remained under one thousand throughout the French Regime. A writer in 1709 described the town as "small, little populated, and having only a small trade with the two Abenaki Indian missions." Trois-Rivières contained a royal storehouse, a friary, and an Ursuline hospital and was "surrounded by a palisade . . . [with] most houses . . . only half-timbered or built of squared, wooden logs laid one upon another."[11] The region's poor farmland offered only a mediocre living. Men of the Trois-Rivières district earned extra money by making bark canoes, by serving as voyageurs for fur traders and, after 1737, by working for a local ironworks.

Farther up the St. Lawrence, and at the point where continued navigation of the river was blocked by rapids, was Montreal Island. The flat, arable plains south of Montreal and its warmer climate encouraged an internal migration westward throughout the French Regime. Good farmland in the St. Lawrence Valley is confined to the north by the Laurentian Mountains and on the south by the Adirondacks and Green Mountains. The southern barrier, however, dips down at the western end, leaving a wide, fertile belt below Montreal. Of the 67,000 European inhabitants of the St. Lawrence Valley in 1760, scarcely 10 percent resided in the Trois-Rivières district, while the rest were evenly divided between the Quebec and Montreal districts. The balance, however, was already shifting in favor of the Montreal region.

Founded in 1642 as a missionary settlement for the conversion of Amerindians to Christianity, Ville-Marie de Montréal digressed from its holy vocation to become, as Abbé Vachon de Belmont put it, "a little Babylon which has overwhelmed and intoxicated all the [Amerindian] nations with the wine of its prostitution." Mission villages of Christian "sedentary Indians" were established well outside the town to hamper the spread of drunkenness and prostitution—scourges in all the missions accessible to the French settlers. Montreal's location at the portage leading to the junction of the St. Lawrence and Ottawa Rivers—the most direct passage to the interior—was too convenient for commerce to be neglected by less-devout Europeans. Rapids blocked the movement of European vessels upriver, and travel inland by water depended on bark canoes. Montreal was first a rendezvous for trade with the interior nations and then became the main departure point for fur-trading ventures into the heart of North America. Its merchants outfitted and dispatched trade canoes manned by French-Canadian voyageurs. The large number of canoemen, soldiers, and visiting Indians in Montreal ensured that drunkenness and brawling were common sights in the town's taverns and streets. Because of the rough, frontier character of Montrealers they were called "wolves" by the more sedate residents of Quebec City. With only half Quebec City's population in the 1750s, Montreal's role as the commercial center of nineteenth-century Canada was in the unforeseen future. In the French Regime it was a secondary town at the westernmost edge of European settlement.

The St. Lawrence River and the tributary network of lakes and lesser rivers gave the French access to the continent's interior. Intensive settlement beyond the meeting point with the Ottawa River was prevented by the French Crown's refusal to grant seigneurial estates beyond sixty kilometers west of Montreal Island. A compact, defensible agricultural colony in the St. Lawrence Valley was what the government desired, and it suspected, quite rightly, that settlers along the western rivers would waylay Amerindians coming to Montreal with their furs rather than engage in tillage. After the Iroquois had scattered the original inhabitants of what became southern Ontario in the mid-seventeenth century, the rich land of the region was left to migratory Indians until the arrival of American Loyalist refugees in the 1780s.

Continuous French colonization westward had been forestalled, yet small, isolated communities of settlers grew up next to missions and military posts in the Great Lakes region. Detroit and Michilimackinac became Montreal's commercial outposts, where Europeans worked in the fur trade and intermarried with women from neighboring aboriginal villages. In the 1670s Jesuit missionaries had joined Huron refugees on Mackinac Island, in the straits linking Lakes Huron and Michigan. The mission later moved to a nearby Ottawa (Odawa) village, called St. Ignace by the French. Fur traders used St. Ignace de Michilimackinac as a base for forwarding trade goods into the continent's interior and for gathering furs for dispatch to Montreal. A small fort and French garrison appeared at the site in about 1690. The glut of furs coming out of New France produced a government order in 1698 to abandon the fort, and the natives living there were encouraged to move south to the narrows (*le détroit*) between Lake Erie and Lake St. Clair. The Jesuits, the Ottawas, and some fur traders refused to move. Fort Pontchartrain du Détroit had been promoted in the late 1690s by Antoine Laumet, who called himself de Lamothe Cadillac, with the promise that a French settlement there would bind the Great Lakes nations to the French and bar the British and Iroquois from the region. The proposal won the backing of the minister responsible for overseas colonies. Fort Detroit was augmented by European farms, as *Canadiens* settled there, but the aboriginal peoples who reestablished themselves at Detroit now found it easier to trade with the English, using the Iroquois as intermediaries. They were beyond the control of the small French garrison and the influence of a few hundred settlers. By 1715 Fort Michilimackinac was reestablished on the south side of the Mackinac Straits and the Jesuit mission to the Ottawas was relocated near it.

The other French posts south of the Great Lakes were home to small European garrisons living next to aboriginal villages. By the early 1700s, intrepid *Canadiens* had reached the Illinois Country along the Mississippi River, where small agricultural settlements had sprung up to feed fur traders and military garrisons and to send wheat, flour, pigs, cattle, and tobacco to the people of Louisiana, farther south. Eventually the region was annexed to French Louisiana. As one passed down the Mississippi, below the junction with the Missouri, French farming villages appeared along the banks of the great river: Cahokia, Saint-Philippe, Fort de Chartres, Prairie-du-Rocher, Kaskaskia, and Sainte-Geneviève. In a regression to ancient European patterns, the settlers lived in compact villages, shared pasturelands, and cultivated lots in large, open fields.[12]

These lands had been farmed by the peoples of the Illini Confederacy and the region was known to the French as the "Pays des Illinois." It was the new land of opportunity. In 1729 a Canadian settler at Kaskaskia wrote to his mother, "I am beginning to live comfortably enough; I am doing well in cattle and I now have some slaves. . . . The climate . . . suits my health and temperament better than Canada. Ignore what people say about this land; judge if it can really be said that there is a famine in a land where grain and cattle are found in abundance. The winter hunt alone can feed three times the people who are presently here."[13]

The 1,400 colonists living in the Illinois Country during the 1750s were mostly of Canadian stock, but their world was tied more closely, socially and commercially, to Louisiana's plantation economy than to Canada. This was evident from the hundreds of slaves living in their midst; most white farmers of the Illinois were slave owners. New France's economy had no need of African slave labor, although a few hundred were employed as domestic servants by those who could afford them. Slave ownership was a visible way of displaying one's wealth in the northern settlements. Farming in Canada and Acadia was the domain of European smallholders, whose families worked the land; in Louisiana, tropical crops and slave labor dominated. The Illinois settlements were an intermediate zone between France's southern and boreal colonies in North America, and their way of life was a blend of the two different colonial economies. Here was where *la Nouvelle France* ended and where the northern frontier of *la Louisiane* began.

From this brief aerial survey of *la Nouvelle France,* it is apparent that the colony was not a single entity with a uniform character. New France was a loose chain of isolated establishments, separated from one another by wide expanses of water and wilderness. Each outpost of French culture had its own distinctive character, despite having a common institutional heritage, language, and religious faith. The fishing settlements beside the Atlantic Ocean were tightly linked, commercially and culturally, with France. Louisbourg was a transplanted piece of western France that never had enough time to develop a strong identity before it was destroyed. The *Acadiens* had no identity problem. They were a close-knit people living in near equality in their villages, with the Roman Catholic clergy providing their only reliable link to the French Empire. Acadia, even before it was permanently joined to Britain's possessions in 1713, was a commercial dependency of New England. "Canada," as the St. Lawrence Valley was called, had the largest concentration of European settlers. Here was an agrarian society organized into parishes and seigneuries reminiscent of the homeland. Religious, educational, commercial, and governmental institutions were concentrated in Canada's three towns. Quebec might have passed for a French provincial seaport, but as one moved westward the influence of the frontier and the fur trade pressed in and marked the aspect of Trois-Rivières, Montreal, and Detroit. The admixture of aboriginal cultures became more evident. French government policy for this heterogeneous colony changed and changed again as commercial and strategic interests shifted.

New France, from Cape Breton to the Illinois Country, was France's largest over-seas colony. Like a huge, ungainly child, the colony was difficult to love. Dazzled by the mineral wealth of the Spanish and Portuguese possessions in the Americas, French kings were continually disappointed by the small returns from *la Nouvelle France* in the 1500s. Fish—not diamonds, gold, or silver—came from the new pos-sessions, and the cod fishery did not require settlement of the mainland. *La Nouvelle France* also produced fur pelts and beaver fur, needed for hat-making felt, which became increasingly valuable. At first the task of upholding France's title to the colony was given to trading companies licensed by the king. The grantees were usually Normans or Bretons, whose involvement in the cod fishery had acquainted them with North America. From 1541 to 1627 six fur-trading partnerships succes-sively agreed to govern and protect New France in return for a ten-, twelve-, or fifteen-year trade monopoly. This was French colonialism on the cheap.

Royal interest in North America did not revive until the seventeenth century. When King Louis XIV assumed direct rule over the colony from the charter com-panies in 1663, he intended to remake the sickly dependency into a flourishing and militarily secure extension of France. Hopes and royal funds were invested in colo-nial crops and industries but, apparently, it was all in vain. Ginseng root from Canada promised to be an export that might gratify the Chinese, who generally accepted nothing but silver and gold from Europeans in return for silks, tea, and porcelain. As a revitalizer and aid to the amorous powers, however, Canadian gin-seng was a poor substitute for the oriental product and the Asian market for it failed. French shipbuilders spurned Canadian timber as excessively damp and quick to rot. Apart from fur pelts, New France produced few natural products that could not be obtained in France more cheaply. The West Indian islands were a more profitable field for investment because they supplied exotic, tropical products, such as sugar and indigo, complementing France's natural resources.

A proverb among administrators held that colonies were founded as beneficial dependencies of the parent state, and, to use the words of Jean Frédéric de Maurepas, minister of the navy, "the colony of Canada is only valuable insofar as it can be useful to the kingdom."[14] That utility could be strategic as well as economic. Eighteenth-century strategists valued New France because it confined the British possessions to the Atlantic Coast and prevented Great Britain from dominating the North American continent. The threat of French incursions from the north kept British colonists on the defensive and discouraged attacks on the smaller French settlements to the south. From an economic viewpoint, however, *la Nouvelle France* was judged to be an unprofitable drain on the royal treasury. This was the viewpoint that prevailed. The 1713 Treaty of Utrecht foretold the settlement of the Seven Years' War: overseas territories would be sacrificed to recover lost ground in Europe. Those who negotiated the 1763 Treaty of Paris felt that they had done well to retain access to the Newfoundland fishery; the loss of Canada was not regretted. Voltaire's flippant remark in *Candide* (1759) that the war in North America was being fought for "a few acres of snow" reflected the superficial thinking of his day. Ironically, New France proved to be the most successful effort at overseas colonization undertaken by the French, and its people endured, despite being abandoned by the founder state.

Voltaire's remark reflected a commonly held and unflattering stereotype of the colony. Canada had a fearsome reputation in France: the colony was regarded as the domain of gray-bearded Father Winter, to use Marc Lescarbot's expression. In his history of the giant's son Pantagruel (1533), François Rabelais recalled stories of this icy land when he wrote of a region near "the Glacial Sea" (later located west of Hudson Bay) where words once uttered froze instantly into icicles, "like striped candy of various colors." One had to warm the icicles to hear what had been said.[15] According to Baron de Lahontan, a person needed a body of brass, eyes of glass, and brandy for blood to survive a Canadian winter. For French administrators and officers, Canada was a hard-luck posting. Intendant Jacques de Meulles observed in the 1680s that "Canada has always been regarded as a country at the end of the world, and as an exile that might almost pass for a [sentence] of civil death."[16] The dangers of New France were too well known to French readers to be denied by Pierre Boucher, who, in his 1664 book, acknowledged the colony's drawbacks: long winters, mosquitoes, rattlesnakes, and the threat of "the Iroquois our enemies."[17]

The "savages" from whom Cyrano de Bergerac had to be rescued in his fanciful tale were regarded with curiosity and fear by Europeans. Seventeenth-century readers in France eagerly sought accounts of the North American Indians, whose reputedly free and licentious existence fascinated secular Europeans. To Christian missionaries, indulgence of the flesh was an affront to the ascetic ideal. The Society of Jesus and other religious orders came to New France to educate aboriginal peoples in Christianity. In this enterprise the missionaries were seconded by the crown. Roman Catholicism was expected to unite the native allies to the French and prepare the way for full cultural assimilation of the aborigines. Christian Amerindians and European colonists, it was hoped, would merge into a single Roman Catholic, French-speaking agricultural people.

This program of cultural transformation accorded with the French crown's aims at home. Ruling a culturally diverse and politically divided kingdom, the Bourbon monarchs of France had begun a centralizing program to impose Roman Catholic orthodoxy and to culturally assimilate the kingdom's ethnic minorities. Because religion was regarded as the key to political loyalty in seventeenth-century Europe, the achievement of religious uniformity was given priority as the surest means of ensuring loyal subjects. After the revolution of 1789–92, religion was left to private consciences and it became a government axiom that the loyal citizen must be culturally French. In 1663, when Louis XIV took over the administration of New France from the commercial charter companies that had hitherto governed the colony in the king's name, the sovereign was determined that the colony would live up to its name. "La Nouvelle France" would be the precursor for a unified Kingdom of France: a country whose people professed one religious faith and who spoke French. The plan to assimilate the colony's native peoples would help to achieve this aim, but as will be seen, this plan ran into unexpected resistance.

—◆—

*The mythical Wild Man of North European lore, represented on a
1664 taler of Brunswick-Wolfenbuttel. From the author's collection.*

CHAPTER 2

Europeans and "The Wild People": French-Amerindian Relations

CYRANO'S TALE OF HIS ESCAPE FROM THE ABORIGINES OF CANADA APPEALED TO European readers; they were fascinated by the "Wild People of the Forests," which is what *les Sauvages* meant in French. Originally written as *Saulvages*, the word originated from the Latin *silva,* meaning forest. The French description of Amerindian peoples as "les sauvages" is sometimes taken as evidence of European contempt and racism because, in modern French and English, the term "savage" means fierce and cruel. In its older sense, however, the description was not so hostile. The name predated the Europeans' first encounter with Amerindians and was colored by North European folklore. In late Medieval and Renaissance art and architecture there are many representations of a being whom German-speakers called the *Wildermann*, the English referred to as the "Green Man," and the French termed *l'homme sauvage*. This mythical creature was a hairy, solitary being who lived in the woods and was customarily portrayed wearing a leafy girdle and holding a club or uprooted tree in one hand. Wild people were depicted as physically powerful, yet ignorant of religion, government, and civil society. In 1392—well before Europeans knew about Amerindians—King Charles VI of France and his friends appeared at a masquerade dressed as wild men in canvas and tow suits. Someone set fire to their costumes, and Charles's later insanity was attributed to the fiery experience. Tales of the wild people were known to Europeans during the Age of Discovery and they continued to shape perception of Amerindians in later centuries.

French writers tried to banish the preconception that aboriginal North Americans were the same as the legendary wild men. In *Nouvelle relation de la Gaspésie* (1691), Brother Chrestien Le Clercq described this notion as "one error which is only too common," because, "in our Europe people are persuaded too easily that the peoples of North America, because they have not been raised in the maxims of civility, retain nothing of human nature but the name of wild men [*Hommes Sauvages*], . . . believing them to be all hairy [*velus*] like bears, and more inhumane than tigers and leopards."[1] When Father Joseph-François Lafitau published his book *Moeurs des Sauvages amériquains, comparées aux moeurs des premiers temps* in 1724, he said "the idea formerly held about the savages was of a species of naked man, covered with hair, living like an animal in the forests without social organization."[2] The story of the sylvan wild man was, nonetheless, still alive in Europe. In the French *Encyclopédie* of 1751–65, there is a curious entry for "CANADIANS, Philosophy of." The author, identified only as "C," freely used the term *Sauvages* to refer to the native peoples of the Americas. He cautioned his readers not to mistake these people for the mythical wild men: "Most of those who have never seen or heard about the Savages imagined that they were men covered with hair, living in the woods without society, like beasts, and having an imperfect resemblance to men." The writer quickly added that the *Sauvages* of Canada were free of body hair, were well-proportioned, and possessed many virtues: "they are good, affable, and display a charitable hospitality to strangers and the unfortunate that would confound the nations of Europe."[3]

The struggle to disentangle the actual native Indians from European preconceptions had been going on for centuries. Even sympathetic writers generalized from particular cases and accepted the view that there was a universal Amerindian character, despite the variety of cultures and peoples in North America.[4] The French dealt primarily with the Eastern Woodlands peoples, who, linguistically, were divisible into Algonkians, who were primarily migratory hunters and gatherers, and Iroquoians, who cultivated crops and lived in semipermanent villages. In 1606–7 a world-weary Parisian lawyer, Marc Lescarbot, spent a winter at Port Royal in Acadia. He noted qualities of the heart among Algonkian Micmacs [Mi-kmaqs] that did not fit the stereotype of the antisocial wild men: "they have courage, fidelity, generosity, and humanity, and their hospitality is so innate and praiseworthy that they receive among them every man who is not an enemy. They are not simpletons. . . . So that if we commonly call them Savages, the word is abusive and unmerited."[5]

Sixteenth-century visitors were less charitable in satisfying their curiosity about the peoples of the Americas. In 1535 Jacques Cartier's party kidnapped natives to be exhibited as oddities in Europe. Europeans had wondered if these beings were humans like themselves, with immortal souls and the power of reason. The Bible

and ancient histories were assumed to be comprehensive accounts of human existence, yet here was a hitherto-unacknowledged fourth continent with people not
described in those authoritative works. The problem was resolved in 1493 and 1512
by papal decrees stating that the natives of the Americas were truly the children of
Adam and Eve, as were the peoples of the known world. In this way, the humanity
of the Amerindians was recognized and they became proper subjects for Christian
missionary work to save their souls from eternal damnation. Thereafter, the natives'
humanity was accepted by the clergy and educated laity of France. "Although they
live in the woods," wrote Father Paul Ragueneau, "they are none the less men."[6]

One riddle remained: where had these true people come from? Once again, Europeans resorted to traditional guides to the distant past: the Bible and ancient histories. Since Amerindians were the offspring of the biblical Adam and Eve, they must
have come from the Old World. It was proposed that they were descended from
Noah's third son, or were fugitives from the lost continent of Atlantis, or even were
the lost tribes of Israel. Well-educated writers, such as Marc Lescarbot, looked for
cultural and physical traits that might connect Amerindian peoples with other, known
nations of the past. On the basis of culture, Lescarbot suggested a kinship with
ancient Egyptians. Others perceived a physical resemblance to Mongols, indicating
Asian origins, which shows that one can come up with the right answer, even with
naïve reasoning. This sound suggestion, however, was lost in a sea of speculation.

Another European tradition distorted the newcomers' perceptions of North
America's aboriginal peoples. Readers of the classics and the Holy Bible believed in
a lost world of innocence and plenty, variously called Eden, Arcadia, and Cockayne.
In this golden world, people had been free to do as they pleased and were relieved
from the necessity of labor by a surrounding abundance of edibles. Writers knew
that their readers in Europe yearned to return to that happy era of their imagined
past. Amerindian life was immediately examined for confirmation of the belief that
their long-departed ancestors had lived in primitive innocence before later generations were corrupted by luxury and artificiality. Samuel de Champlain knew the
public appetite for tales about the wild people of the Americas and, accordingly,
titled his first book *DES SAUVAGES, ou voyage de Samuel Champlain de Brouage, fait en
France Nouvelle* (1603). In this publication he promised to tell of "the manners, way
of life, marriages, wars and dwellings of the *Sauvages de Canadas.*" In addition to the
strange plural "Canadas," Champlain's title page referred to the Acadian coast as *la
coste d'Arcadie,*—an allusion to the mythical Arcadia. Champlain's books described
naked dancing among the Algonkians and the sexual promiscuity of unmarried
Hurons (Wendat or Wyandots) and so his works may have provided his Christian
countrymen with erotic fantasies as well as offering partial confirmation of their
belief that humans could live together in a "natural" state of freedom.

Reality intruded on this idyllic picture, however. Champlain's books and the annual *Relations* of Jesuit missionaries, published in 1632–73, horrified readers with eyewitness accounts of the ritualized torture of captives among the Huron-Iroquoians. After prolonged agony by fire and knife, victims were killed and eaten by their captors. Aboriginal North Americans were also criticized by the white outsiders for living "like brute beasts," without religion or law, and for being fickle, devious, and given to revenge.[7] Christian forgiveness made no sense to people for whom revenge was a sacred duty to redress an injury to a kinsman.[8]

Before the French had learned to converse with natives in their aboriginal language, the newcomers relied on their eyes to judge native life. In 1611 Father Pierre Biard had written, speaking of the Micmacs, "they have no temples, sacred edifices, rites, ceremonies or religious teaching, just as they have no laws, arts or government, save certain customs and traditions."[9] The visible absence of churches, law courts, and a public gallows in native villages led the first European visitors to believe that there was no religion, justice, government, or law among Amerindians. These social institutions existed without the visible tokens that seemed essential to French eyes. Huron justice, for example, relied on the public shaming of a wrongdoer and mandatory compensation to a victim's family by the offender's kin to maintain social order. To Europeans, accustomed to government with a coercive power to command, native leadership by persuasion and decisions by consensus seemed to bespeak an absence of authority.

Newcomers from France were culturally self-centered, but they did not see themselves as racially superior. They accepted the Amerindians' humanity. The presence of Mediterranean people with black hair, brown eyes, and dark skin in France's population meant that the physical traits of native Indians were accepted as normal. The aborigines fitted into the range of familiar human types. "They are all of an olive color or, at least, tawny [*bazanez*] like the Spaniards," wrote Marc Lescarbot. Other Frenchmen thought that the natives looked like the Portuguese or said that they might walk the streets of Bordeaux in European dress without provoking comment. Lescarbot added that "our savages are generally as goodly men as they of Europe; . . . They are of good stature, and I have seen no dwarfs there, nor any that were near to it."[10] Most European writers admired the natives' physique and asserted that, if the aborigines shielded themselves from the sun and abstained from greasing their bodies, they would be as white as Europeans.[11] On the matter of intelligence, those who had lengthy dealings with the Amerindians acknowledged their sagacity. Priests, nuns, and royal officials hoped to transform these well-built, intelligent people into French-speaking, Roman Catholic subjects of His Most Christian Majesty, the King of France and Navarre. The 1627 charter of the Company of New France promised every Roman Catholic Amerindian all the rights of a natural-born French subject, such as the right to inherit an estate within the king's dominions. In 1667 the secretary of state for the colonies, Jean-Baptiste Colbert, told the intendant of New France, "you must try to draw these [native] peoples, and especially those who have embraced Christianity, into the neighborhood of our settlements and, if possible, intermingle them there so that, with the passage of time, having but one law and the same master [king], they will form thereby but a single people of the same blood [*ils ne fassent plus ainsy qu'un mesme peuple et un mesme sang*]." [12]

Official approval for intermarriage between the two races is proof that French officials had no racial prejudice against native peoples. Cultural arrogance, however, was evident in the government's assumption that this one, new people would be a French-speaking, Roman Catholic, farming population. Colbert wrote that the king expected the missionaries, whom he subsidized, to "teach [the native allies] our language, and to raise them in the same customs and way of living as the French." [13] A common religion would bind the newcomers and their native allies together, and it would prepare the way for total assimilation of the aborigines to the French way of life. Religious conversion had pride of place because it was axiomatic in this period that one's faith determined political loyalty. Roman Catholic subjects, who adhered to the king's religion, were assumed to be his most trustworthy dependents. From 1632 until the 1660s the Society of Jesus, or Jesuit Order, had an exclusive patent from Cardinal de Richelieu to carry out the transformation of New France's Amerindian peoples.

At first, the task of religious conversion seemed simple enough. When Father Paul Le Jeune recalled his first impression of Canada's natives in 1632, he wrote, "Their natural color is like that of those French beggars who are half-roasted in the Sun, and I have no doubt that the Savages would be very white if they were well covered . . . , they have good figures, their bodies are well made, their limbs very well proportioned, . . . They are fairly intelligent." Two years later, his opinion was unchanged: "as to the mind of the Savage, it is of good quality. I believe that souls are all made from the same stock, and that they do not materially differ; . . . having well-formed bodies and organs well regulated and arranged, their minds ought to work with ease. Education and instruction alone are lacking." [14] During the seventeenth century Father Le Jeune and other Jesuit priests intended to provide that education and instruction. While Christian laymen sometimes placed Amerindians below Europeans in the great Chain of Being, which linked all living creatures, from beasts to angels, Roman Catholic missionaries treated the two peoples as equal in mental and spiritual potential. [15] That potential, however, was not tested in New France before the seventeenth century.

There is no written record of the very first encounter between Europeans and native Indians on North America's Atlantic Coast. Semiliterate fishermen lacked

either the time, inclination, or ability to record their experiences, and the aborigines' first impressions were not preserved in any contemporary document. Men engaged in the dry fishery probably initiated exchanges with Amerindians. The earliest
accounts of French encounters with North America's peoples came from explorers
with royal commissions from King François I. Explorers were required to record
their observations. The Algonkian nations of the Atlantic Coast were familiar with
the European sailors' interests and, when a French vessel under Giovanni da Verrazano
appeared in 1524, the natives refused to let their women board the ship. With the
arrival of Captain Jacques Cartier's 1534 expedition off Gaspé, the Iroquoians also
hid their women in the woods. They already knew what goods would be accepted
by the white strangers in exchange for iron tools and cloth. The chronicler of Cartier's
1534 voyage reported that in Chaleur Bay the Amerindians who saw the French
ships, "set up a great clamor and made frequent signs to us to come on shore, holding up to us some furs on sticks." The fearful Europeans drove off the canoe-borne
natives by firing cannon over their heads. On the following day the aborigines persisted in trying to trade, "making signs to us that they had come to barter with us;
and held up some furs of small value, with which they clothe themselves." At this
date Europeans had little use for furs, except to trim gowns and other garments, but
they eventually accepted the invitation and sent men ashore with iron knives and
hatchets, a cloth cap, and beads. "The savages," noted Cartier's scribe, "showed a
marvelously great pleasure in possessing and obtaining these iron wares and other
commodities. . . . They bartered all they had to such an extent that they all went
back naked without anything on them; and they made signs to us that they would
return on the morrow with more furs." This meeting and subsequent exchanges of
furs and smoked meat for European goods elicited native expressions of joy and
delight. The French were indifferent: "They offered us everything they owned, which
was, all told of little value. We perceived that they are a people who would be easy
to convert [to Christianity]." Captain Cartier and his companions, including a priest,
made no effort to effect that transformation. The captain read the Gospel of St. John
from the Latin Vulgate Bible to the uncomprehending Iroquois of Montreal Island,
"making the sign of the cross over the poor sick people, praying God to give them
knowledge of our holy faith."[16] Thus was responsibility for the conversion of the
Indians transferred from humankind to the Almighty.

In the 1500s the strangers from France were more interested in mineral wealth
and fish than in native souls and fur pelts. The newcomers hoped to repeat the
success of the Spanish, who had discovered astonishing sources of silver and gold in
Mexico and Peru, or, at least, to find a westerly route to Asia, whence might be
drawn spices, silk, tea, and porcelain. When the aboriginal residents of Montreal
Island told the French about the Kingdom of the Saguenay, far up the Ottawa

River, where there was a goldlike metal, the visitors became excited. The Iroquoian informants were probably talking about raw copper from Lake Superior, brought by native traders to the Eastern Woodlands peoples. Cartier's imagination endowed Saguenay with rubies and other riches, as well as gold. The French were determined to find this kingdom where treasures abounded, and, in 1541, an expedition was undertaken to locate it and to establish a settlement in the St. Lawrence Valley.

Greed for instant wealth was the undoing of the short-lived French colony of Charlesbourg-Royal, near the future site of Quebec. The would-be settlers uncovered what they took to be diamonds and gold ore while tilling the soil. They filled barrels with these treasures and, with Cartier leading, abandoned the settlement in 1542 to hasten back to France—even deserting a second party under their nominal commander, La Rocque de Roberval, whom they met in Newfoundland. Alas, their diamonds and gold were nothing but quartz crystals and iron pyrites. "False as a Canadian diamond" entered the armory of French proverbs for specious goods. The French had been deceived by their own cupidity. Such disappointments, accompanied by civil war at home, discouraged further French colonizing ventures in New France during the sixteenth century.

By the 1600s French ambitions in the Americas had changed. Greed, intellectual curiosity, the desire for personal glory as an explorer, and the hope of winning the sovereign's patronage were now supplemented by a sincere desire to bring Christianity to the natives. Hitherto, the professed religious motives of French monarchs, when sanctioning exploration, had been a pretext for ignoring the division of the New World between Spain and Portugal under the 1494 Treaty of Tordesillas, approved by the pope, because they knew that the pontiff would tolerate intruders whose avowed purpose was to spread the Roman Catholic faith. The religious conversion of native North Americans, when seriously undertaken, however, proved more difficult than the Europeans had anticipated.

Superficially, everything seemed to favor the influence of the white men—emissaries from an unknown world—over their aboriginal trading partners. The newcomers had come armed and organized like an Amerindian war party. Naturally, when faced with such a warlike group, the natives were quick to initiate barter, which required a military truce and could be the overture for an alliance. The Europeans had desirable trade goods. Iron cutting tools, whose keen edge could be easily restored, were much more efficient than the fragile and easily-dulled tools of bone, stone, obsidian, or copper. The European copper cooking pot was a miracle for people whose bark or earthenware water vessels could not be heated over a fire and who were obliged to heat up stones that, when deposited in a water-filled container or a stone hollow, would only parboil the maize, meat, and plants it contained. For the Algonkian peoples, wrote Nicolas Denys, "the kettle has seemed . . . and seems still, the most valuable article they can obtain from us."[17] It could be suspended over a fire and the liquid contents kept boiling until they were fully cooked and could be easily digested.

Hurons called the French *Agnonha,* or "iron people," thereby expressing their admiration for the Europeans' iron and steel knives and axes. These new goods accomplished formerly difficult tasks with amazing efficiency. According to Franciscan friar Gabriel Sagard, the Hurons concluded that the king of the French, "being the greatest captain and chief of them all, made the largest [copper] kettles."[18] Woolen blankets, linen shirts, steel strike-a-lights, and firearms were accepted as improved versions of familiar clothes, tools, and weapons. A few European items were modified to suit aboriginal tastes. Archaeological finds from a Neutral Iroquoian burial ground, discovered at Grimsby, Ontario, show that these people took Venetian, layered-glass beads and ground off the outer blue and white layers to expose the red beneath, the color of blood and fire.

European trade goods were acquired for furs that Amerindians reckoned to be of lesser value. Father Paul Le Jeune, who had lived with the Algonkian Montagnais [Innu], reported, "I heard my host say one day, jokingly, *Missi picoutan amiscou*, 'the Beaver does everything perfectly well, it makes kettles, hatchets, swords, knives, bread; and, in short, it makes everything.' He was making sport of us Europeans, who have such a fondness for the skin of this animal and who fight to see who will give the most to these Barbarians, to get it; they carry this to such an extent that my host said to me one day, showing me a very beautiful knife, 'the English have no sense; they give us twenty knives like this for one beaver skin.'"[19] The natives' belief that they were getting the best of the strangers in trade reinforced their self-esteem.

Eastern Woodlands peoples were astonished by lodestones, magnifying glasses, writing on paper, books, and fireworks, but some products of advanced European technology were not so impressive. The thunderous explosion of a cannon, while deafening, could not harm a well-concealed man in the forest. Sailing ships that had crossed the Atlantic were "floating islands," yet they could not ascend the inland rivers, with their shallows and rapids. Native bark canoes were better suited for interior travel. To traverse the land and survive in the wilderness, the earliest arrivals from France depended upon Amerindians for guidance, food, and help. The newcomers were the dependents. In one instance, Hurons perceived that the French could be slaves to their own technical marvels. The natives observed how the Jesuit missionaries regulated their prayers, meals, and actions by the chiming of a clock and correctly deduced that the ticking "Captain of the Day" ruled these Europeans' lives.[20]

The pale-skinned suppliers of iron tools and copper pots were useful trading partners. Because intertribal warfare was endemic, but was suspended when mutually beneficial trade existed, commerce protected the French. A trading partnership could evolve into a military alliance, which was sealed with a reciprocal exchange of hostages. The hostages were a pledge of good faith, and their lives would be forfeited if the alliance were violated by a hostile act. In 1535 the Iroquois near Quebec wanted to bind Cartier's party to them as trading partners and as allies in war. Chief Donnacona presented Jacques Cartier with a child and, when the girl was accepted, the natives gave "three shouts and cries in sign of joy and alliance."[21] Donnacona's people were then offended when the French traveled farther up the St. Lawrence River and supplied inland nations with European goods. Native nations coveted the role of middleman in trade between the Europeans and the inland peoples, who provided furs for secondhand European goods. In bypassing their partners, the French were not behaving like good allies. The Iroquois who lived near Quebec told the newcomers fearful tales of the hazards upriver to dissuade the French from going there, and they demanded that a white hostage remain with Donnacona.

After the first shock of meeting Europeans, natives quickly recovered their confidence, and their customary disdain for strangers reasserted itself. Father Pierre Biard observed that the Micmacs of Acadia "greatly underrate us, regarding themselves as our superiors."[22] Every human group has its own standards of beauty and propriety by which it judges others. We measure the humanity of others by their resemblance to us. Aborigines, being accustomed to their own physical type and culture, usually called themselves "the people," or "true men," with the implication that those who deviated from their norm were lesser beings. They had no moral obligations to strangers unless the outsiders had been taken under their protection. By their physical standards, Europeans were repulsive. In particular, the natives were repelled by the gray, blue, or green, doglike eyes of some Frenchmen, enclosed in folds of flesh, and, especially, by the Europeans' body hair. Facial hair, being rare among Amerindians, was a grotesque deformity. The Hurons, wrote Gabriel Sagard, "have such a horror of a beard that sometimes when they try to insult us they call us *Sascoinronte*, that is to say, Bearded . . . moreover they think it makes people more ugly and weakens their intelligence."[23] In this respect, the newcomers looked more like the legendary wild forest men than did the aborigines.

Curly hair, even if it had the merit of being black, was viewed as bizarre. Even more repulsive were the Europeans' bald pates or their red and blond hair—almost white, like the hair of the very old or ghosts. The Tadoussac Algonkians mocked Father Paul Le Jeune's eyes and hairy face: *"cou attimou,* 'he looks like a dog;' *cou mascoua,* 'he looks like a bear;' *cou ouabouchon ouichtoui,* 'he is bearded like a hare;' *attimonai oukhimau,* 'he is a chief of the dogs;' . . . *matchiriniou,* 'He is deformed, he is ugly.'"[24] For their part, the French admired the Amerindians' stature and strength and marveled at the rarity of deformities among them. Because malformed infants had not been suffered to live and the rigors of native life had eliminated the weak, the Europeans were looking at selected survivors. There is no evidence of Eurocentric prejudices in French observations about the physical appearance of the Eastern Woodlands' peoples—quite the contrary. It was in judgments of aboriginal cultures that European ethnocentrism was most evident. For their part, Amerindians despised both the physical appearance of the French and their ways.

Iroquoian and Algonkian etiquette demanded that men speak, in turn, with gravity, and that true men should neither betray emotion nor acknowledge pain. The French who came among them lacked this manly restraint: they showed their anger, spoke in an agitated manner, and interrupted each other. According to Chrestien Le Clercq, "the Indians never interrupt the one who is speaking, and they condemn, with reason, those dialogues (*entretiens*) and those indiscreet and irregular (*peu réglées*) conversations where each one of the company wishes to give his ideas without having the patience to listen to those of the others. It is, accordingly, for this reason that they compare us to ducks and geese, which cry out, say they, and which talk all together like the French."[25] In addition, Frenchmen performed feminine tasks, such as gathering and carrying firewood, without any shame. Jesuit missionaries who did such things were dismissed as "women." These Amerindians admired oratory and judged people by their range of expression. The first, fumbling efforts of the French in aboriginal tongues brought native ridicule and contempt. Those who had not yet mastered the local Amerindian language were mocked as having no sense. Faulty expression was taken as proof of deficient intellect. The Nipissings complimented a French interpreter who had lived with them for two years: "Well, now that you are beginning to speak our language well, if you had no beard you would be almost as intelligent as such and such a people, naming one that they considered much less intelligent than themselves."[26] The Hurons had no doubt, at first, about their intellectual superiority. Father Charles L'Allemant told his brother in 1626, "they consider the French less intelligent than they [are]."[27]

Pierre Biard was confounded by the Micmacs' belief in their own moral superiority despite, said he, being "extremely lazy, gluttonous, profane, treacherous, cruel in their revenge, and given up to all kinds of lewdness." Nonetheless, "they think they are better, more valiant and more ingenious than the French; and, what is more difficult to believe, richer than we are." They suggested that the failure of the French to take revenge upon them for attacking ships and killing European sailors proved that the French lacked courage. The Micmacs also tasked the outsiders with other failings: "you are always fighting and quarreling among yourselves; we live peaceably. You are envious and are all the time slandering each other; you are thieves and deceivers; you are covetous, and are neither generous nor kind; as for us, if we have a morsel of bread we share it with our neighbor." The vices of some newcomers allowed them to "conclude generally that they are superior to all Christians."[28] Other European practices struck Algonkians as ridiculous as well as reprehensible; according to Le Clercq, "they cannot understand how one can submit to the indissolubility of marriage" when the couple cannot agree, and when they saw the French wipe their noses with fine linen handkerchiefs, which were then folded up and pocketed, "they mock at us and say it is placing excrement in our pockets." One native teased a Frenchman, "if you love that filth [*ordure*], give me your handkerchief and I will soon fill it up."[29]

When French-speakers who had mastered a native language attempted to dazzle Amerindians with tales of the wonders to be found in France, listeners responded with defensive skepticism. Le Clercq claimed that an aboriginal leader at Percé made the following speech in the 1670s:

> You deceive yourself greatly if you think to persuade us that your country is better than ours. For if France, as you say, is a little earthly paradise, are you wise to leave it?; and why abandon wives, children, relatives and friends? Why risk your life and your goods every year, and boldly risk yourself, in whatever season it might be, to the storms and tempests of the sea to come to a foreign and barbarous land, that you consider the poorest and most unfortunate place in the world? . . . We believe, moreover, that you are incomparably poorer than we, . . . all masters and great captains that you may appear to be, since you prize our old tattered [fur] garments and our wretched beaver outfits that are no longer of use to us, and that you come among us for the cod fishery that you undertake in these parts, to ease your misery and the poverty that oppresses you.[30]

This native speaker, it was said, reasoned that when French fishermen asked Amerindians to hunt for wild game, the Europeans did so to escape an everlasting diet of cod, which they were catching in great quantities.

Faced with this invincible disbelief, the French took natives to Europe to let them see its wonders with their own eyes so that they could report their observations to their fellows. When presenting one aboriginal tourist to Indians at Quebec in 1639, Father Le Jeune said, "Reproach me now with falsehood, . . . ask your Countrymen if what I told you about the greatness of our King and of the beauty of our country be not true? And do not any more call into question what I shall hereafter tell you." The son of Chief Iwanchou then told them what he had seen in France: "The great multitude of Paris; the great number of cookshops [*rotisseries*]; the huge statue of Saint Christopher at Notre-Dame [Cathedral], which, at first sight, caused him much terror; the coaches, which he called 'rolling cabins drawn by moose,'" and of the rhythmic drumming to which the king's troops paraded.[31]

The roasting meat of so many animals, with no forest in sight, must have been a mystery to him, and the large Saint Christopher's statue in the cathedral portal, bearing the Christ child, may have been seen as a lifelike representation of a real giant.

When French missions were established in the Upper Mississippi Valley, the Jesuits there encountered the same skepticism and resorted to the same solution: send one of the unbelievers to France. Chief Chikagou of the Illinois people toured Paris and Versailles in 1725. He, too, marveled that there were as many people in Paris "as there were blades of grass on the prairies and mosquitoes in the woods," that the buildings were higher than trees, and of how people "made long journeys in moving cabins of leather." In this case, the traveler was not believed: "everything which *Chikagou* has related to his countrymen, about France, has appeared incredible to them. 'They have paid you,' it was said to him, 'to make us believe all these beautiful fictions.' 'We really want to believe you,' said his relatives and those to whom his sincerity was less suspect, 'that you have really seen all that you tell us, but there must have been a spell that bewitched your eyes, for it is not possible that France can be such as you have painted it.'" Faced with incredulity, Chikagou made matters worse by his exaggerations: "'Hear!' he would say to them in jest, 'if you lack an arm, a leg, an eye, a tooth, a breast, if you are in France, they [hospital surgeons] will provide you with others that match perfectly.'"[32]

It was this protective skepticism, the lamentable appearance of Europeans, their clumsy speech and material dependence upon aboriginal people that left native self-esteem intact. The Amerindians of Percé boldly told Brother Le Clercq, "there is no Indian who does not consider himself infinitely more happy and more powerful than the French."[33] This sense of superiority to the whites was one of several barriers to conversion to the newcomers' religion; why should one adopt the beliefs of an obviously inferior people? The Jesuits' Acadian mission in 1611–13 was also a failure because the wandering Algonkian hunters had little time and no inclination to listen to the missionaries talk about theology. European diseases undid the Jesuits' work by killing off the converts, and liquor gave occasion for violence and sin. The missionaries' efforts were negated by other imported influences, which they did not fully understand.

In 1615 Samuel de Champlain brought four friars of the Observantine or *Récollet* Franciscans from France at the fur-trading company's expense. One of the brothers set off at once for the country of the Hurons, who were trading partners of the French. Being allies of the French, the Hurons tolerated this man's presence and that of two other friars who joined him in 1623. The Franciscans were accepted as the customary hostages who secured alliances. To strengthen this bond, the Hurons invited the friars to intermarry with them. Missionaries were drawn to the nations of the Huron Confederacy because, as agricultural peoples, these natives seemed halfway to becoming Frenchmen, and their sedentary life facilitated instruction. Missionaries blamed their small gains among the itinerant Algonkians on the hunters' wandering life in search of wild game. Gathering together prospective converts in a permanent settlement was seen as a prerequisite for success. The Hurons' central location amid the Great Lakes and their trading network also allowed French missionaries to extend their influence. Once the priests had learned the Huron tongue—the commercial language in the Great Lakes region—they were able to converse with the Hurons' distant trading partners.

The Franciscans limited their work to the Bear Nation, which was the most powerful member of the Huron Confederacy. Although the friars learned much about their hosts' language and religious beliefs, the natives showed no interest in the friars' teachings. Brother Gabriel Sagard blamed native indifference on "those . . . brutal, godless, and sensual" Frenchmen, whose licentious behavior contradicted the Christian morality preached by the brothers. The Franciscans reproached Huron girls for exposing their breasts and for their sexual promiscuity. "The women," wrote Sagard, "received our reproofs in quite good part and finally began to practice modesty and show some shame at their dissoluteness . . . and they were full of admiration & approval of the propriety of girls in France of whom we told them. This gave us hopes of great amendment . . . if the Frenchmen who came up with us, most of them, had not told them the contrary, in order always to be able, like beasts, to enjoy their sensual pleasures to the full. . . . Our Frenchmen had given the women savages to understand that the women in France had beards on their chins, and had also persuaded them of lots of other things which modesty does not allow me to write here."[34] Moreover, some French and native interpreters taught the missionaries obscenities when asked to supply words for everyday objects.

In 1625 the Franciscans gave up the Huron mission and turned to the Jesuits for help. The Society of Jesus had successful Asian missions and a reputation for expertise in converting non-Europeans to Christianity. The society also had greater financial resources and more political support than the Franciscans. The Jesuit "black robes," as natives called the priests, could do no more than reconnoiter Huronia, or the Hurons' Country, before Quebec was captured by the English in 1629, forcing the Roman Catholic missionaries to leave Canada. After New France was restored to the French crown in 1632, the Jesuits had a monopoly of the Canadian missions that lasted until the 1660s. They set about at once to banish the handicaps that had beset their Franciscan predecessors in Huronia.

To ensure that secular Frenchmen living among the Hurons were models of Christian propriety, the Jesuits introduced the *donné* system, by which pious laymen "gave" themselves to the order to serve it as craftsmen and servants without pay for the rest of their lives. The priests were assisted by "coadjutor brothers," yet they still needed men with the strength to carry heavy loads and who were not prevented by religious oaths from using firearms. In a contract the society promised to provide the *donné* with food, clothing, and care when sick, "even to the end of his life," provided "he continue to live in uprightness and fidelity to our service."[35] These pious men replaced the salaried workers employed by the society. The Hurons now saw devout and obedient French laymen whose conduct followed the missionaries' teachings.

In 1639 the Jesuits established a fortified residence, with farm and workshops, in Huronia. Livestock was brought from the St. Lawrence Valley by canoe. The mission complex of Sainte-Marie-aux-Hurons freed missionaries from dependence upon the natives for food while providing priests at four outlying missions with a central base. Sainte-Marie furnished a living example of the European way of life, which the Hurons were expected to embrace. Potential converts were attracted by food, shelter, and a blacksmith's services—essential to people whose iron tools and firearms needed repairs. Thereafter, metalworkers were attached to Jesuit missions throughout North America. The churches at Sainte-Marie dazzled natives and Christian converts were permitted to live in an enclosed village protected by the Jesuits' adjacent fort. The mission employed thirty Europeans, yet, in 1640, there were still only fifty living, native converts from a population of ten to twelve thousand Hurons.

Christianity had little appeal for most Hurons, and they did not see the sense in adopting another people's faith. They believed that each nation had its own particular beliefs, suitable for that people. A universal religion for all nations was an alien concept. According to Father Jean de Brébeuf, Hurons rejected Christianity, saying, "this is good for our Country [France] and not for theirs; that every Country has its own fashions," and "their Country is not like ours, that they have another God, another Paradise, in a word, other customs," or "such is not our custom; your world is different from ours; the God who created yours . . . did not create ours."[36] Precontact ceremonies brought the Hurons together, while Christianity caused division. Rituals, like the Feast of the Dead, in which the bones of villagers who had died of natural causes in the preceding ten to fifteen years were reburied together, served to unite members of the village community. At the ceremony, participants were enjoined to live peaceably together just as their forebears had been united in death. Converts refused to participate in such pagan ceremonies, and the new religion divided Huron communities into Christian and traditionalist camps.

Christianity's social demands conflicted with the realities of native life. Monogamy was ill-suited to a people with a surplus of women, and a Christian marriage to one spouse for a lifetime was regarded as "a servitude full of vexation and bitterness."[37] The Lenten fast from meat came at a time when melting snow aided hunters by slowing down elk, moose, and deer. Abstention from the chase on Sundays was equally impractical. An Algonkin medicine man assured Father Le Jeune, "there are five things that I will not give up,—the love of women, the belief in our dreams [as portents of the future], the eat-all feasts, the desire to kill the Iroquois, the belief in sorcerers, and making feasts for them."[38] The promise of future spiritual rewards in return for abandoning physical pleasures puzzled listeners. Potential converts had to be taught to feel guilty about their carnal desires. They did not see physical self-gratification as a sin—a punishable transgression of Christian moral laws. Moreover, the Heaven of the French did not appeal to most Hurons.

The Huron afterlife was a continuation of the familiar, physical world of the living and it was open to all, except suicides, no matter what their moral conduct had been on earth. In the Huron land of spirits, souls were able to hunt, eat, and dance in the company of friends and relatives. The Christian Heaven offered no comparable pleasures; Hurons asked missionaries if there were blueberries, tobacco, and bear grease in the French land of the dead. Even more dismaying than the absence of earthly comforts was the exclusion of their pagan relations from the Christian paradise. A convert would be denied the company of unbaptized friends and kin in the afterlife. Frustrated missionaries blamed the reluctance of the natives to become Christians upon Satan's influence. The priests saw themselves as engaged in a struggle with the devil to dominate the aboriginal peoples, and each setback was attributed to demonic influence.

The converts' experience of Christianity did not recommend the new faith. Some accepted the new religion to gain the favor of their French trading partners. Baptism was sometimes accepted "as a sort of sacred pledge of friendship and alliance with the French."[39] Brother François du Creux admitted that, at first, Hurons became Christians "for the advantages that they might derive from the French."[40] Jesuits ingratiated themselves with natives by giving them food and gifts, like iron arrowheads or awls, and they presented small rewards, such as beads, rings, and holy medals, to those who had learned religious lessons and who recited answers correctly. In 1643 the colony's governor presented firearms to aboriginal Christians visiting Quebec. Jesus was first understood by natives to be a guardian spirit, and a supernatural patron was expected to provide the devotee with good fortune and to protect him from misfortune. An effective guardian spirit provided tangible benefits. Some expected baptism to cure their sick children.[41] The ability of Europeans to recover from the new sicknesses seemed to testify to their God's protective power. Gabriel Sagard was asked to pray to Jesus during a drought so that his God might bring rain; Jesuit missionaries were entreated to use their magic to summon snow or moose as well as rain. Christian symbols were also seen as propitious. Just as the

Micmacs used crosses in their body painting, Hurons inscribed crosses on round, stone good-luck charms (*askwandi*) they carried, to increase the charms' potency.[42]

The Christian ideal of faith in adversity, of welcoming misfortune as God's test of one's fidelity, was alien to native converts. In the 1640s the Hurons were beset by European diseases, such as smallpox, against which they had no acquired resistance, by famine, and by intensified Iroquois attacks. Their population, estimated to be thirty thousand at the time of first contact, dropped to ten or twelve thousand. Father Jérôme Lalemant complained in 1640 that those who experienced the death of all their kin, "have not had faith enough to endure with courage those blows from the hand of God, but have blasphemed against him" and "abandoned Christianity."[43] A guardian spirit who brought no benefit to his followers was useless and was soon discarded. Christ was a disappointment to many converts and the published Jesuit *Relations* mention several apostates among the Hurons. Paul Le Jeune lamented in 1639 that "all the more prominent persons of the village where we have labored to make Christians either have turned a deaf ear, or, having embraced Christianity, have of themselves abandoned it, or . . . [are] resuming their wicked customs."[44] In desperation, these converts had sought a cure for their sickness in traditional remedies and rituals. Amid these disasters, Christian converts fared no better than religious traditionalists and they occasionally suffered greater misfortunes. One neophyte complained to a Jesuit in 1642, "you tell us that God is full of goodness; and when we give ourselves up to Him, he massacres us. The Iroquois, our mortal enemies, do not believe in God; they do not love the prayers, they are more wicked than the demons—and yet they prosper; and since we have forsaken the usages of our ancestors, . . . they massacre us."[45]

Because missionaries eagerly baptized the dying in order to save souls from the flames of Hell, that sacrament and the subsequent death became linked in the minds of distrustful Hurons. The Jesuits' surreptitious baptism of moribund infants fed this suspicion. When the children died the rite was seen as the cause of extinction. Unfortunately for the missionaries, there was indeed a connection: Europeans were the unknowing bearers of fatal infections, and prolonged contact with them produced smallpox, typhus, and measles epidemics among their aboriginal partners. Neither the priests nor the natives knew about germs. Father Pierre Biard in Acadia reported that the Micmacs there, "often complain that since the French mingle with and carry on trade with them, they are dying fast, and the population is thinning out. . . . Thereupon they . . . sometimes think that the French poison them."[46] Hurons attributed the unfamiliar maladies and resultant deaths to spells cast by the Jesuits. The Ursuline Mother Superior at Quebec reported, at secondhand, the speech of a Huron clan matron in 1640: "it is the Black Robes that make us die by their spells. . . . They lodged in a certain village where everyone was well. As soon as they were established there, everyone was dead except for three or four persons. . . . Do you not see that when they move their lips—what they call prayers—those are spells that come from their mouths? It is the same way when they read in their books." As a consequence, the priests hid their breviaries and dared not pray aloud.[47] It was rumored that the tabernacle above the Jesuits' altar contained a dead child's body that spread the infections—a misinterpretation of the consecrated communion wafers representing the body of Christ. Every object and gesture of the missionaries was suspected of being an evil charm. The priests' ability to survive these new sicknesses suggested that they had the power to direct the epidemics' destructive course.

The natives' initial perception of the priests as medicine men who used magic to bring benefits was displaced by a suspicion that the men in black were really sorcerers who caused harm through supernatural means. By the 1640s the conviction that the priests were dangerous sorcerers was widespread in Huronia. Father Joseph-Marie Chaumonot complained that "when we visit these people; if they do not arrive in time to close the door to our noses, they stop [up] their ears and cover their faces, for fear of being bewitched." Even in the neighboring country of the Neutrals, Chaumonot and Father Brébeuf met closed doors, "for they were looked upon as sorcerers who carried death and misfortune everywhere."[48] Stories of the Jesuits' black magic had spread from one aboriginal nation to another. An Algonkin chief warned the Hurons about the fatal effects of Christianity: "I have been among the French at Quebec and at Trois-Rivières. They taught me the very substance of their doctrine. . . . But, the more I fathomed their mysteries, the less did I see the light of day. They are fables forged to give us real fears of an imaginary fire; and to inspire us with a false hope of good that can never come to us. . . . You saw, years ago, the Algonkians were so numerous that we were the terror of our enemies. Now we are reduced to nothing; diseases have exterminated us; war has depopulated us; famine pursues us wherever we go. It is the Faith that brings us these misfortunes."[49]

Hurons approved of the murder of "those who kill by spells" (*Oki ontatechiata*) because such malefactors endangered everyone. Jesuit missionaries were threatened, harassed, and abused, but not killed because of the military and commercial alliance with the French. The priests had been accepted as the customary hostages who secured a pact between different peoples; murdering the missionaries would end the valuable alliance with the French. Some elders and chiefs realized that the physical threats and harassment were "contrary to the rights of the alliance that they profess with the French," and tried to restrain the young men.[50] Hostility extended to the converts. A "certain unbeliever" from the Huron village of Teanaustayé (St. Joseph) shouted at a Christian chief, "go away you Frenchman, go at once to your own land. Because you are [now] a Frenchman, cross over the sea, for too long a time you have caused us to die here."[51] In 1640 French officials threatened to cut off trade with the Hurons if any harm came to the Roman Catholic missionaries. The priests were spared the fate of native witches, although pagan Hurons still tried to drive them away with threats. In 1649 Father Noël Chabanel was murdered while he was among the neighboring Petuns, who were not allied to the French.

The Jesuits found that, although the Christian Heaven had little appeal to aborigines, the terror of Hell was a powerful inducement to conversion. Missionaries' accounts of the fiery torment of damned souls resembled the torturing of enemy warriors by fire—something most Hurons had witnessed. It was easily imagined. Using techniques pioneered among the unlettered of Brittany, the Jesuits employed pictures to drive their message home. "These sacred pictures," wrote Paul Le Jeune, "are half the instruction that one is able to give the Savages. I had desired some portrayals of hell and of lost souls."[52] In a letter to his brother in France, Father Charles Garnier described the paintings that would be most useful to missionaries in Canada. One was to be of a beardless Christ; others would represent the smiling serenity of a saved soul with a contrasting painting of a tormented sinner. The damned soul's agony in Hell was to be rendered as vividly as possible, "so that it might appear roasted and blackened in the flames . . . the eyes flashing, let the mouth be open like that of a person shouting loudly, . . . the hair bristling, the two hands and the feet bound by burning iron, and another burning iron chain around his middle, with a frightful dragon wound round his body, gnawing upon his ear, . . . let there be two powerful and frightful devils on both sides tearing apart his body with iron spears, with another above trying to lift him by the hair."[53] The pictures and stories of anguished souls in Hell were persuasive to the vacillating. In 1636 Paul Le Jeune admitted that many Hurons "are very glad to die [as] Christians; not, in truth, so much through love as through fear of falling into the fires with which they are threatened. . . . they are beginning to lose the dread they had of Baptism, and the belief that this Sacrament must cause them to die."[54] Just in case, however, some put off baptism until they knew that they were dying and, in that way, their souls escaped the infernal regions, of which the missionaries had told them.

Fear of Hell, material rewards, the *donnés'* example, Sainte-Marie-aux-Hurons mission, the priests' proficiency in the Huron tongue, and the Jesuits' accommodation of Christian beliefs to native cultures aided their work. These missionaries abandoned the royal goal of totally assimilating Amerindians to European culture as they learned more about native beliefs. The first Jesuit missionaries had been intolerant of cultures they did not fully understand. In 1611 Father Pierre Biard wrote that the Jesuits' goal was "to domesticate and civilize" the Amerindians.[55] To Biard, the Algonkians had no religion, just superstitions and errors, and their medicine men were fraudulent tricksters or the devil's agents. His solution was to discredit and uproot these false beliefs and to replace them with Christian truths. Pointing out the inconsistencies of aboriginal ideas about the supernatural was not very effective. Adult Hurons, for example, listened politely to the missionaries' arguments and, because these Iroquoians disliked open conflict, they did not contradict the priests. The Jesuits soon realized, however, that this apparent acceptance of their claims did not prevent the listeners from carrying on their lives as before. Native adults were not impressionable, so, during the 1630s, Father Paul Le Jeune put his hope in "seminaries" for native children who, isolated from their parents and the influence of their own people, would be trained in Christianity and European ways by priests and nuns. These seminaries met with little success. The children sickened and died or they fled back to their families to escape the alien discipline of these boarding schools. By the 1640s Father Jean de Brébeuf was prepared to build Huron Christianity upon existing native beliefs that were similar to Christian articles of faith, such as belief in the power of prayer or in the immortality of souls. This meant reinterpreting aboriginal beliefs rather than entirely supplanting them. Prayers and a catechism in Huron were prepared so that Huron Christians could worship in their own language, and native religious instructors, known as *dogiques,* were used to persuade their own people.

Experience in Canada and a knowledge of African and Asian peoples made some Jesuits more tolerant of cultural differences than other missionary orders. In 1648 Father Paul Ragueneau, Superior of the Huron Mission, wrote, "one must be very careful before condemning a thousand things among their customs, which greatly offend minds brought up and nourished in another world. It is easy to call irreligion what is merely stupidity, and to take for diabolical working something that is nothing more than human; and then, one thinks he is obliged to forbid as impious certain things that are done in all innocence, . . . I have no hesitation in saying that we have been too severe on this point."[56] By the late 1650s a Jesuit in Canada could write, "if one were mounted on a tower high enough to survey at his ease all the nations of the earth, he would find it hard, amid such strange varieties and such a medley, to say who are wrong and who are right, who are fools and who are wise. Verily, God alone is constant."[57] Other Jesuit writers, too, marveled at the contrasting ideas of social decorum and of beauty among foreign peoples. Their position was the reverse of native relativism in spiritual beliefs and disdain for European manners and appearance; it was religious dogmatism combined with flexibility in social behavior when it had no bearing on religion. If morally indifferent, Amerindian customs were not challenged among converts.

The Jesuits now dreamed of native Christian communities that would be morally superior to society in France—an amalgam of the best aspects of both cultures. That Christian Utopia would never exist in Huronia. Huron misfortunes came to a climax in the late 1640s: in 1648 an entire village was destroyed by Iroquois raiders, and in the next year two more villages were taken by surprise during the winter, when warfare usually ceased. In the disintegration that followed, native traditionalists left to join the Iroquois, whose language and culture were close to their own, while 2,700 others embraced Christianity. Diseases, military defeat, and internal divisions created by the new religion shattered many Hurons' confidence in their own culture and made them receptive to evangelization. The Jesuits abandoned Sainte-Marie-aux-Hurons and tried to reestablish the mission and their followers on Christian Island in Lake Huron. They arrived too late to plant crops and the fugitives starved over the winter of 1649–50 and were reduced to eating the flesh of corpses. With three to four hundred survivors, the Jesuits set off for the St. Lawrence Valley, while more Hurons scattered throughout the Great Lakes and beyond. A palisaded Huron village was built on Ile d'Orléans in 1651, but even here the refugees were not safe from the Five Nations Iroquois. Hurons who resisted appeals to join their countrymen among the Mohawks and Onondagas of the Iroquois Confederacy were attacked, and seventy were killed. The battered remnant of the Christian Hurons was moved closer to Quebec, and by 1685 there were a mere 146 left alive. In 1697 they made their home at Nouvelle Lorette, where their French-speaking descendants still live in what is called "le village des Hurons."

There never would be another French religious enterprise in North America as great as the seventeenth-century Jesuit mission to the Hurons. Private donors, who supported these pious ventures, became rarer. The crown became the missions' principal patron. Individual missionary priests were maintained by the king at military posts in frontier areas, and native converts were gathered in segregated mission villages under clerical supervision in the St. Lawrence Valley. Proximity to the French brought a greater risk of epidemics and alcoholism. The Jesuits' first mission village in the valley, St. Joseph de Sillery (f.1637), lost most of its Algonkian residents to smallpox, the effects of liquor, and hunger. These migrant hunters had to be taught farming, and when progressive soil exhaustion reduced the fruits of their labor, they reverted to hunting and fishing.

After the Abenakis along the expanding frontiers of New England were converted by Jesuit missionaries, Abenaki war refugees found a temporary shelter at Sillery in the 1670s. Land grants for Abenaki mission settlements were given to the Society of Jesus along the Chaudière and St. François Rivers above Quebec. An informal Abenaki village also appeared in 1680 on the Bécancour River, opposite Trois-Rivières. Having been driven west by the Protestant New Englanders, Abenaki warriors were firm allies of the French.

The Jesuit seigneury of La Prairie de la Madeleine, opposite Montreal Island, attracted Iroquois Christians. They had been converted by missionaries to the Five

*A drawing by Father Claude Chauchetière of the Sault St. Louis Mission Indians renouncing
the demon of liquor (1680s). From the Archives départementales de la Gironde, Bordeaux.*

Nations Iroquois in 1654–58 and 1667–87. Most of the Roman Catholic converts
came from the Mohawk nation. The Jesuits' success among the Mohawks and
Onondagas was due, in part, to the presence of baptized Hurons among these two
nations. To Five Nations traditionalists, an Iroquois who accepted the French religion was a traitor. Converts escaped persecution by resettling in the St. Lawrence
Valley, where they joined Christian Iroquois from the Oneida nation already living

at La Prairie. In the early seventeenth century, missionaries expected French settlers to act as models for the new Christians. Instead, the colonists' influence was destructive. Despite the governor-general's interdict and clerical condemnation, French settlers traded brandy with the Amerindians and made them drunk, the better to cheat them in trade or to seduce their women. Alcohol ravaged the mission villages and drunkenness had an irresistible appeal for aboriginal men that baffled French observers. By the late 1600s mission priests were trying to isolate aboriginal converts from European colonists.

Chrestien Le Clercq, Paul Le Jeune, François Vachon de Belmont, and Pierre Boucher all observed that native Indians, "only drink . . . in order to get drunk."[58] In 1677 Father Jean Dudouyt of the Quebec Seminary pointed out to the minister responsible for colonies that the Indians "are so fond of becoming intoxicated, that if six or seven are given a bottle, that cannot make them all drunk, they will give it up to two or three, that they may get drunk, whilst the others abstain."[59] It appears that brandy was consumed, in spite of its taste, because the alcoholic delirium approximated a shaman's spirit possession—a coveted experience. At first, natives saw drunkenness as a religious experience. Vachon de Belmont, the Sulpician Superior at Montreal, noted that Iroquoians had "various ceremonies in which they appear possessed by a spirit, outside themselves, and in a passion, whether to do or have what they want without reproach, or to say and do extraordinary things, and make themselves admired." They were "so religious and scrupulous" about the need to get drunk that if there were only a small amount of alcohol, it was given entirely to one person. The favored individual achieved the desired state of intoxication, "that they call 'Ganontiouaratonseri'—complete inebriation—and when they begin to feel the effect of the fumes, they rejoice, saying 'good, good, there is the spirit that spins me [*voila la teste qui me tourne*]' and they begin to sing their Gannonhaoury [death song] into which they put all the evil they want to express," such as maledictions against their enemies.[60] The frenzied behavior of drunkards, who ran about chanting and shouting and tossed burning embers from fires, resembled the conduct of participants in the Huron dream-guessing festivals, described by Gabriel Sagard. The ritual was called *Ononhouaroia,* translated as "turning round the head (the soul's location)" or "upsetting the brain."[61]

Drunkenness may not have been more frequent among Amerindians who associated with Europeans than it was among whites, but the social consequences were greater. Native drunkards set fire to lodges, bit off people's ears and noses, and stabbed others with knives. The alien spirit occupying the inebriated person's head was blamed for these crimes. According to one observer, fellow tribesmen would survey the shattered canoes and smashed contents of a cabin without anger and "laughingly" say of the drunkard responsible for this damage, "he had no mind [*il n'a point d'esprit*]."[62] When an Algonkin killed a Frenchman in the 1630s, his fellows reportedly said, "'it was the brandy and not that Indian who . . . committed this murder. . . . Keep your wine and brandy in prison,' they say, 'it is your drinks that are doing the evil, and not we others.' They believe themselves to be entirely excused from the crimes they commit, when they say they were drunk." If anyone were to be punished, the natives felt, that it ought to be the Frenchman who provided the alcohol: "they say to you 'it is not we who did that, but you who gave us this drink.'"[63] Drunkenness permitted a person to commit crimes with impunity. Although liquor was first accepted for religious reasons, Indians later consumed it for the same reasons as Europeans: to lose their inhibitions and to obtain a momentary escape from life's trials.

The Jesuits asked for a separate mission site upriver from La Prairie, farther from Montreal, to safeguard the aboriginal Christians in their care. In 1676 they were granted a location at the foot of the Lachine Rapids. This settlement became the scene of religious excesses as converts, without worthy secular role models, emulated zealous priests and nuns who punished their bodies with penitential whips, hair shirts, and iron-studded belts. Native Christians flogged themselves with thorns and willow shoots. A pregnant woman stood naked in the falling snow, while two others "made a hole in the ice, in the depth of winter, and threw themselves into the water, where they remained during the time it would take to say a Rosary slowly and sedately." Iroquoian women, who were accustomed to having political influence and personal independence, were being pressed by missionaries to conform to the Christian ideal of the wife as man's obedient helpmate. This pressure may explain why women were foremost in these penitential excesses. Married couples renounced sexual relations. This religious frenzy coexisted with "liquor and drunkenness, which make a Hell of all the Iroquois [mission] villages, wherein life is a continual suffering. The French [settlers] are the cause of its giving us much trouble here; for, in order to strip the Savages of their very shirts, they follow them everywhere, to make them drink and become intoxicated."[64]

From 1660 onward the bishops of Quebec had repeatedly threatened those who sold alcohol to the Indians with excommunication. An excommunicated Christian who died without priestly absolution and the sacraments would suffer eternal damnation. Despite this powerful sanction, the traffic in liquor continued. The king's officials accused the clergy of excessive zeal and an indifference to the interests of trade. They were content to restrict liquor sales to Indians to the towns, where that commerce might be supervised. By the eighteenth century there were special taverns in Montreal for different native nations, to avert conflicts between them. These establishments sold watered-down brandy, beer, and cider. More intoxicating drinks, however, were being sold to Amerindians by unlicensed vendors outside the town.

Amerindian alcoholism and physical self-abuse suggest that the attempt to reconcile Christianity's demands with native culture was psychologically stressful for converts. Observers agreed that aboriginal Christians outdid French colonists in acts of piety. Natives interpreted the missionaries' teachings literally and they carefully imitated the rituals and visible actions of the clergy. Missionaries disagreed on their own ability to communicate Christian beliefs in native tongues, and it does appear that abstract concepts, such as the Holy Trinity, were difficult to express in perceptual languages that dealt with tangible and visible realities. The explanation that Heaven was somewhere above the earth raised a natural fear that souls would fall from so high a place. The first converts did not understand Christianity as Europeans comprehended the faith.

In 1696 the Jesuits moved their spiritual charges farther west to separate them from European settlers and to obtain fresh sources of farmland and firewood. Traditionally, Iroquoian villages were relocated every fifteen years or so, when the soil's fertility was exhausted by corn (maize) crops and firewood could not be found within convenient walking distance, and to escape the accumulated debris of the old site. The Christian Iroquois moved twice more before settling above the rapids at Sault St-Louis, or Kahnawaké, in 1716. Their population grew by natural increase and by adoptions. Prisoners, especially children and women taken in war, were given to families that had lost members to the enemy. Even a few captured men were spared and adopted. Having escaped death, the captives were expected to take on the role and duties of the dead relative they had replaced. To the surprise of European observers, most aboriginal prisoners accepted this exchange of identity and would even go to war against their former countrymen. Young captives from the British colonies also were accepted into native families, as were the French colonists' illegitimate children. By the 1700s the Indians were now accustomed to the Europeans' strange appearance and received them as members of their nation. When dealing with a bastard given to a native woman of Lorette in 1717, the crown attorney of Quebec's *Prévôté* court asked the Maritime Council in France to empower him and the other crown attorneys to place all foundlings in European families, to put an end to "this abuse." He pointed out that the practice of allowing native adoptions of French children was contrary to the king's intention to Frenchify the Amerindians and it increased the number of potential enemies of the French.[65] The council sympathized with his complaint and, by the 1720s, court attorneys were placing foundlings and illegitimate children in French homes as servants or apprentices.

Visitors to New France, such as Peter Kalm, were surprised to encounter "white Indians" in the mission villages of the St. Lawrence Valley.[66] The adoption of Europeans, as well as the fact that natives with a white ancestor were more likely to survive the epidemics that cut through their population, meant that the aboriginal peoples of the Atlantic Coast and St. Lawrence Valley were increasingly of mixed ancestry. Culturally, however, they were still Amerindians. Native descendants of some British captives still bore their names, such as *Hill*, *Williams*, and *Tarbell*. In 1707 John, Zachariah, and Sarah Tarbell were captured by Indians at Groton, Massachusetts, and taken back to Canada. They were all under the age of fifteen. The boys were adopted into the Kahnawaké (Caughnawaga) Iroquois, whose mission village was at Sault St. Louis, close to Montreal, and were said to have married daughters of chiefs and to have become chiefs themselves. Their sister was raised by the ladies of the *Congrégation de Notre-Dame* in Montreal.[67] Some descendants of earlier native converts bore variants of their French godparents' surnames: those descended from a Mohawk sponsored by Sieur d'Ailleboust are called "Diabo," and the "Peltiers" go back to the godchild of a Monsieur Pelletier. These surnames were symbolic of the hybrid culture that developed in the mission villages. In 1752, or later, thirty families from Kahnawaké, including two Tarbells and a part-African Abenaki named Louis Cook, moved to St. Regis-Akwesasné on Lake St. Francis, one hundred miles upriver, and closer to the Iroquois of New York Province.

Native assimilation of Europeans was entirely opposed to the French government's aim, which was to absorb converted natives into the transplanted white population of *la Nouvelle France*. Minister Colbert and Governor-General Buade de Frontenac clung to the dream of totally assimilating the Christian Indians and they criticized the Jesuits, who ran most of Canada's Christian missions, for keeping aboriginal converts apart from the white colonists. Colbert told Intendant Talon in 1668 that "the Jesuit Fathers never worked hard enough to civilize the Amerindians at the same time they were converting them, whether by joining them to the French by marriage, or by drawing entire families to live like ours, or by obliging them to abandon their idle and lazy way of life to cultivate land in the neighborhood of our settlements or, finally, by making them learn our language."[68] The mission Indians retained their own languages and governed themselves, despite the presence of missionary priests. The Sulpician Fathers, who had a fortified mission village on Montreal Mountain for Christian Algonkins, Hurons, Iroquois, Nipissings, and Western Plains Amerindians, were praised by the colonial authorities for adhering to the French crown's original policy.

The Sulpicians, however, eventually learned what the Jesuits already knew: rapid acculturation of the natives was impossible, and proximity to white settlers corrupted their charges. Each group was more likely to acquire the other group's vices than its virtues.[69] In 1696 the Gentlemen of St. Sulpice began moving their Christian converts away from Montreal, north to Sault-au-Récollet on Rivière des Prairies. This was still not far enough, alas, to escape white liquor peddlers. A second exodus, to Oka-Kanesataké, on the north shore of Lac des Deux Montagnes, occurred in 1717–22. Some Christian Nipissings and Ottawas (Odawas) had already resettled in this location. Two seigneuries were given to the religious order as trustee for the aboriginal Christians; it was customary for the government to treat converted Indians as irresponsible dependents under clerical guardianship. The Sulpicians wanted absolute proprietorship of the seigneuries, which they obtained after the British conquest. They were then free to concede or sell land to white settlers, which they did, to the detriment of their native wards. This left the Oka Indians with a truncated reservation, and in 1990 they used firearms to resist any further alienation of land they regarded as their inheritance. The Jesuits, too, began to treat Sault St. Louis seigneury as their own property, and granted land to white settlers despite the order's obligations as trustee of the Christian Iroquois. British hostility to the Jesuits finally allowed the Kahnawaké Iroquois to assume title to what remained of the mission lands in the 1760s.

Native Christians in the St. Lawrence Valley's seven mission villages had a strained relationship with French colonists. These Amerindians lived in European dwellings, wore imported clothes, and farmed, yet they continued to speak their own languages and insisted on their own autonomy. In 1709 an intendant noted, "it is surprising that of so many nations, there is still not one that has taken on our ways and, despite being among us and in daily contact with the French, they still govern themselves in the same manner as they have always governed themselves. . . . They prefer their hard and idle life, their free and self-indulgent existence to the most agreeable [alternatives] one can offer them. . . . It will require labor and an infinite amount of time . . . to compel them to accept our ways and our customs. . . . It is, I assure you, the work of several centuries."[70]

In 1710 there were 1,750 mission Indians in the St. Lawrence Valley, who could supply 600 warriors.[71] This number may seem small, but it equaled the number of French regular troops, and these native allies were experts in forest warfare, to which few colonists, apart from professional canoemen and fur traders, were accustomed. The military support of the "domiciled Indians" for the French was qualified. Aboriginal warriors joined French expeditions to obtain prestige, acquire trophies, take captives, and avenge their dead. Their objectives in warfare were personal or familial, rather than political. When these limited objectives had been achieved, they went home. Prolonged wars, territorial conquest, and the goal of a decisive, total victory—the reasons why Europeans fought—were alien to native warriors. When it seemed likely that the French would be defeated, their native allies faded away rather than be caught on the losing side. Pierre Pouchot, a French officer, complained that when Amerindian allies were needed most, they were not there. Indians would not attack without the advantage of surprise and the assurance that few casualties were likely. Dubois Berthelot, another officer, described the Abenakis' refusal to pursue a retreating enemy raiding party as "friponnerie"(rascality).[72] The Kahnawaké Iroquois refused to fight against their kin of the Five Nations Confederacy, and French authorities had to resign themselves to their allies' military independence. In criminal and legal matters they were equally powerless.

The French failed to impose their criminal law upon the mission Indians. In principle, these natives were subject to the king's justice; in practice, it was otherwise. In 1664 Quebec's Sovereign Council had decreed that "the Indians will be subject to the penalties specified by the laws and ordinances of France for murder and rape." Native accountability was extended to crimes of theft, "drunkenness and other wrongs [*fautes*]" in 1676.[73] Intoxicated aborigines returning from Montreal to their villages sometimes stole goods, killed livestock, murdered settlers, and destroyed whatever came to hand. According to Father Vachon de Belmont, "some kill the cattle they meet, others ravage houses on the way to Sault [St. Louis] causing the inhabitants to flee as though from the Iroquois, while others chase and rape French women." When Tegaraoueron raped and murdered a little girl who was tending livestock in the 1690s, the killer was not punished, wrote Vachon de Belmont, "for fear of angering the Sault [St. Louis] Indians during a dangerous war" against the British.[74] Given the French need for native auxiliaries in wartime, this provisional immunity of allies from punishment for criminal acts made sense, yet this indulgence continued after the restoration of peace.

Of seventy-six Indians accused of disorderly conduct, assault, or murder in the Montreal District from 1669 to 1760, only one native offender was prosecuted; the rest were released from detention without a charge being laid.[75] It was not want of evidence that caused the crown attorneys to abandon these cases. Because almost all of these offenses involved liquor, and the local Amerindians took the view that drunkenness exculpated the violator, they did not accept the right of French criminal courts to punish the offender. They made it clear that judicial retribution would be regarded as a hostile act. An episode in 1719, recorded in the Montreal court records, followed a typical pattern. In February three Iroquois from Sault St. Louis bought spirits from Jacques Detaillis of La Prairie, who was licensed to serve alcoholic drinks only to Europeans. Thouatakouisee paid for one and a quarter pints of brandy with a silver presentation medal he had received from the French and then, between five and six in the evening, he and his companions set off for the mission village. En route, Thouatakouisee entered a settler's home and struck a two-year-old child in the stomach, killing him. When a posse of colonists caught up with the murderer in a native lodge, the Amerindians said, in consternation, "it was the liquor that was the cause of this child's death," and identified Detaillis as the one who had provided the brandy. The chiefs' council refused to hand over the killer. The crown prosecutor of Montreal investigated the matter, obtaining the testimony of five witnesses, and then initiated a charge against the liquor seller, *but not against the murderer*.[76] Colonial officials already had limited the sale of cider, beer, and diluted brandy to Indians to selected taverns in Montreal. In May 1721, following a particularly horrendous crime, Intendant Michel Bégon imposed a 500 *livres* fine on anyone who sold liquor or intoxicating spirits to Indians.

In effect, French court officers accepted the aboriginal view that the vendor of alcohol was ultimately responsible for a native drunkard's misdeeds. Even the suspicion that liquor was involved was sufficient cause to terminate an investigation. European defendants were not allowed the same defense of innocence because of intoxication; their crimes against natives were punished. This double standard for crimes committed while drunk galled some white residents of New France, who wanted to see Amerindian offenders chastised as the settlers would be. When the children of one victim of a native murderer asked for mercy for the culprit, a Quebec merchant wrote, "if I were the master on a similar occasion, no Savage would receive mercy. Instead of making oneself feared by these scoundrels, it is giving them a license to kill and massacre the French whenever it pleases them."[77]

A royal dispatch to the governor-general and intendant of New France in March 1714 proposed a gradual imposition of French laws upon the mission Indians: "With regard to the claims made by the Indians that one cannot imprison them without their consent and that they are not subject at all to the laws of the country [of New France], it is an extremely delicate matter and must be handled gently because they have only agreed that those found inebriated in Montreal's streets may be put in prison [until they are sober] and they did consent to pay the damages set by [Montreal's governor] Sieur de Ramezay to one Nafrechou, whom they had assaulted. One may hope that they can be accustomed to submitting to the [French] laws. This must be done, little by little, with prudence and care. One can begin by trying to induce them to submit to military justice and then, little by little, we will induce them to accept the same justice as the French inhabitants."[78]

One application of military justice revealed the weakness of French authority over native allies. In 1720, when a drunken man from Kahnawaké village killed a white farmer's wife and a servant, Montreal's town major—who was responsible for military discipline—treated the native warrior as a soldier. The Christian Iroquois chiefs, who reserved judgment of their people to themselves and who preferred their own practice of having the aggressor compensate the victim's family, consented to a French trial for this culprit. With their approval, the offender was found guilty by court-martial and was publicly hanged before an audience of his own people. It was said that the chiefs of Sault St. Louis Mission used this example "to contain their restless youths." The colony's governor-general boasted that the affair showed "that it is not impossible to subject the settled Amerindians [*les sauvages domiciliées*] to military justice on certain occasions."[79] It was not impossible, but it clearly required the cooperation of the aboriginal chiefs, who seem to have found this malefactor so obnoxious that they waived the customary exemption from punishment for a crime committed while intoxicated. His execution served their purposes. Without the chiefs' approval, French officials would not have been able to try and execute the offender.

The reason for official forbearance was strategic; it was not because French officers and courts accepted the legitimacy of native beliefs. Colonial officials feared that application of the harsh penalties required by French criminal justice would alienate the Christian Indians and cause them to defect to the Iroquois Confederacy or to ally themselves with the British. The desire to retain the goodwill of Amerindian partners, who were needed in war, also forced French administrators to tolerate the smuggling of furs by mission Indians into the adjacent British colony of New York and the natives' return with foreign goods. This trade violated the export monopoly granted to the French fur company, and smuggling contravened imperial laws. Governor-General Buade de Frontenac told the king in 1681 that "I did not believe it my duty, until now, to oppose it [contraband trade by natives] otherwise than by reprimands for fear that arresting them with their [imported] goods would cause a rift that the country would not be able to endure."[80] A later governor-general, Philippe de Rigaud de Vaudreuil, merely tried to prevent aborigines from acting as couriers for white merchants and to limit Amerindian fur smugglers to the skins of animals that they had caught and to illicit goods for their own use.[81] He, too, was convinced that the use of force against native smugglers would cause the resident Amerindians to desert the French.

The partial assimilation of the Christian aborigines made it hard to accept their persistent independence and qualified allegiance to the French. The mission Indians of the St. Lawrence Valley remained on the edge of French colonial society, never becoming a part of it. Beyond the settlements, the cultural difference of aboriginal partners in the fur trade had to be accepted, and French traders, military officers, and missionaries cultivated their goodwill. These Europeans had to accommodate themselves to native ways. This was more a matter of needing the Amerindians as commercial partners and as allies in war than a consequence of mutual affection.

The mission Indians' retention of a separate identity and special legal status conflicted with the French monarchy's goal of complete assimilation of the converted natives. What was even worse, in the eyes of royal officials, was the acculturation of young European men to aboriginal ways. The appeal of native life enticed men from the farming population. "I could not express sufficiently to you," wrote a governor-general to the minister of maritime affairs in 1685, "the attraction that this savage life of doing nothing, of being constrained by nothing, of following every whim, and being beyond correction has for the young men."[82] Frenchmen who lived with aboriginal people dressed in native garments, greased their hair, and had their bodies tattooed as did the Indians, and, to the horror of the clergy, participated in aboriginal ceremonies and performed pagan rituals.[83] The French crown had always favored intermarriage as a way of merging the two populations, and a dispatch from Louis XIV expressed his astonishment upon hearing that in 1706, Governor-General Rigaud de Vaudreuil had forbidden marriages between the French and natives at Detroit. When pressed for an explanation, the governor-general and intendant replied in 1709 that the order was given because "one must never mix bad blood with good. The experience in this land is that all the Frenchmen who have married native women have become libertines and idlers with an intolerable independence, and that their children are possessed of an idleness as great as that of the Amerindians themselves."[84] Intermarriage in the western posts was more likely to convert Europeans to native ways than to achieve the king's intention of producing French-speaking, Roman Catholic subjects of mixed ancestry. Now royal officials had joined the missionaries in trying to keep the aborigines and French colonists apart. The licit intermixture of the European and native populations was slight. In the St. Lawrence Valley during the seventeenth century thirty-three interracial marriages were sanctified by the clergy. In the eighteenth century, as women began to outnumber men in the white population of *la Nouvelle France*, 116 colonists took aboriginal wives, most in the colony's borderlands, where European women were scarce.[85]

In New France white colonists had an uneasy relationship with the neighboring mission Indians, whom they exploited, feared, and appeased. The settlers would have been astonished at the conception of the Amerindians that was taking hold among their literate countrymen in France. In Europe the old preconception of the wild man of the forests was yielding to a new stereotype that was nearly as fanciful. The second characterization had its roots in the European myth of a lost golden age of innocence and simplicity. In the early 1600s Marc Lescarbot, who had been disillusioned by the chicanery of French law courts, observed the Micmacs in Acadia and wrote, "I consider all these poor savages, whom we commiserate [*deplore*], to be very happy; for pale Envy does not emaciate them, neither do they feel the inhumanity of those who serve God hypocritically; harassing their fellow-creatures under this mask: nor are they subject to the artifices of those who, lacking virtue and goodness, wrap themselves up in a mantle of false piety to nourish their ambition. If they do not know God, at least they do not blaspheme him, as the greater number of Christians do."[86] Roman Catholic missionaries, such as Jean de Brébeuf and Paul Le Jeune, who disdained materialism and worldliness, unwittingly contributed to this favorable picture, which was damaging to the church. Priests admired native fortitude in adversity and the Indians' contentment in what was, by French standards, poverty. Life in the North American forests, wrote missionaries, had given Amerindians a "truly wonderful innocence," because they were not exposed to "luxury, ambition, avarice, or delights."[87] They knew nothing of the inheritances and legacies which perturbed the French. Father Le Jeune intended to reproach his readers in France when he said that he preferred aboriginal "sincerity" to flowery European compliments, which were "wind and smoke, under offers of service that are full of falsehood."[88] Like the Roman historian Cornelius Tacitus, who used the German barbarians' simplicity as a foil for the moral and civic failings of his fellow Romans, missionaries in Canada wrote of the natives' "noble moral virtues" to shame those bearing the name of Christian for their shortcomings. Readers in Europe could not plead a lack of religious instruction to excuse their sins. The existence among uncatechized aborigines of "Christian" virtues, such as a concern for the souls of the dead or a patient acceptance of deprivation and hardship, also suggested that the natives' conversion to the Christian faith would be easily accomplished, if readers supported the missions with their prayers and money.

Skeptical lay readers did not see these aboriginal virtues as the missionaries saw them. The presence of social morality without the benefit of a Christian education suggested that mankind was not innately evil, as pious Europeans believed. Evidence that pagans could be morally superior, in some respects, to Christians revived belief in an age of primitive innocence. Secular writers contrasted the undeniable faults of Europeans with the admirable traits of Amerindians, as reported from *la Nouvelle France*. Social critics, such as Baron de Lahontan and Claude LeBeau, went beyond selective truth and exaggerated the merits of aboriginal life in order to show that primitive peoples were morally superior because they had *not* been subjected to Christian, European civilization. Cynical authors exploited the Europeans' curiosity about alien cultures, as well as their readers' yearning to experience the lost Golden Age—a world removed from the flawed existence that they knew too well. These writers had grasped a principle of publishing success: it is more profitable to feed public delusions than to challenge them.

Press censorship in France made it dangerous to disparage public institutions openly, so liberal authors used fictitious Amerindians or other foreigners to express the writers' criticisms of church and state. This tactic was suggested by the candid and surprising observations of North American Indians who were brought to France. Their remarks revealed a fresh, critical perspective on the Europeans' world and led readers to question practices that they had formerly taken for granted. Natives were startled to see adult courtiers bow down to a juvenile monarch, for was it not more logical for the young to defer to the old? In the 1700s François Arouet (Voltaire) and Charles-Louis de Secondat, Baron de Montesquieu, invented ingenious Hurons and Persians to voice their own irreverent views about contemporary France. Their model was Adario, a crafty and perceptive Huron devised by Louis Armand de Lom d'Arce, Baron de Lahontan, to appeal to his anticlerical and cynical readers. Lahontan was a French officer who had deserted his post on Newfoundland and became a wandering exile in northwestern Europe, enjoying the patronage of princes and intellectuals. One edition of Lahontan's *Nouveaux Voyages dans l'Amérique septentrionale* (1703) described the imaginary Huron as "a Savage of good sense who has traveled." Adario was clearly modeled on the aboriginal tourists brought to France and described in the Jesuits' annual *Relations*. In the published dialogue between Lahontan and Adario, the baron put up an ineffectual defense against the Huron's systematic exposure of the hypocrisy of French life. Adario argued that every one of the biblical Ten Commandments was routinely violated in France: "to touch upon the head of Murder; 'tis such a common thing among you, that upon the least accident, you clap your hands to your Swords, and butcher one another. I remember when I was at *Paris,* People were run thro' in the Streets every night; . . . Lying and Slandering your Brethren, is a thing that you can as little refrain from as Eating and Drinking. I never hear four *French-men* Converse together, without speaking ill of some body." Adario went on to mock the Roman Catholic faith, whose Latin masses were "spoke in an unknown language" and whose fasts permitted gluttony upon fish and eggs.

In contrast to the French, whom Adario characterized as liars, hypocrites, and "downright infidels," the imaginary native presented a radiant picture of Huron life:

> thou shalt never see the good Country of Souls, unless thou turn'st *Huron.* The Innocence of our Lives, the Love we tender to our Brethren, and the Tranquility of Mind we injoy in contemning the measures of [self-] Interest: These, I say, are three things that the Great Spirit requires of all Men in General. We practise all these Duties in our Villages, naturally; while the *Europeans* defame, kill, rob, and pull one another to pieces in their Towns.

The real Hurons, who tortured and ate captives, committed suicide, and engaged in endless blood feuds with other nations, were transformed by Lahontan into innocent children of nature, living in harmony, uncorrupted by wealth and social affectations. The new *Sauvage* of the libertines was a free man, a deist, naturally virtuous and happy, whereas Europeans were said to be enslaved by governmental institutions, organized religion, and private property. "You see," says Adario, "we have no Judges; and what's the reason for that? Why? We neither quarrel nor sue one another. . . . Because we are resolved neither to receive nor to know Silver [money]."

Personal property was said to be the origin of social inequality among the French; Amerindians were alleged to be strangers to private possessions and, reputedly, owned all things in common. In reality, Huron-Iroquoian families had hereditary privileges, and, although natural resources were owned collectively, these peoples had a concept of private property applicable to personal effects. Favorite private possessions were buried with their owner, and were often broken to release the objects' spirits so that they could be used by the owner's soul in the afterlife.[89]

Lahontan's Adario was a rationalist missionary intent on converting eighteenth-century Europeans to what was said to be a Huron morality—one based on nature, reason, and social equality:

> We content our selves with denying all manner of Dependance, excepting that upon the Great Spirit, as being born free and joint Brethren, who are all equally Masters; Whereas you are all Slaves to one Man. . . . What Authority or Right is the pretended Superiority of your great Captain [king] grounded upon? . . . Take my advice, and turn *Huron* for I plainly see a vast difference between thy Condition and mine. I am the Master of my own Body, . . . I do what I please, . . . I fear no Man, . . . thou'art affraid of Robbers, false Witnesses, Assassins, &c. and thou dependest upon an infinity of Persons whose Places have rais'd 'em above thee. . . . Ah! my dear Brother, thou seest plainly that I am in the right of it; and yet thou choosest rather to be a *French* Slave than a free *Huron*.[90]

Baron de Lahontan's *Nouveaux Voyages dans l'Amérique septentrionale,* with the accompanying *Mémoires* and *Suite du Voyage,* were enormously popular: from 1703 to 1758 the books went through twenty-five editions and various translations. European readers were seduced by the picture of Natural Man who was benevolent, rational, born equal, and free from the weight of inherited institutions. Prussian philosopher Gottfried Wilhelm von Leibnitz credited Lahontan with adding to the evidence "that the Americans [Indians] of these regions live together without any government but in peace; they know nothing of struggles, hatreds, battles, or very little, except of those against men of different nations and languages." Conversations with the baron convinced Leibnitz that "there are peoples [in North America] who live in society without government and who are not tormented by the spur of cupidity; . . . ambition is a stranger to them."[91] Lahontan's conclusion was that Europeans were the real savages, but their situation could be remedied: did not the good Hurons prove that there could be a society based on reason, social equality, and justice?

The fictitious, noble, and virtuous "bon Sauvage" of the Americas was the foundation for Jean-Jacques Rousseau's vision of humankind before it was degraded by "civilization." In his *Discours sur l'Origine de l'Inégalité* (Discourse on the origin of inequality among men) (1755), humans "in a state of nature" were portrayed as socially equal, happy, compassionate, and self-sufficient. Echoing Lahontan, Rousseau saw private property as the great disrupter, the source of competition and conflict. Thence came the institutions of civil society to regulate the consequent discord. These institutions and personal property led to pride, war, and subjection. For political revolutionaries who yearned to "restore" humankind to "natural liberty," Rousseau's *Le Contrat social* (1762) provided the slogan "Man is born free, but is everywhere in chains." It was this watchword and Rousseau's claim that property and government were the source of Europe's social ills which nourished anarchist and communist political theories. In this way, the seed of Western revolutionary creeds originated in the forests of *la Nouvelle France* and, in particular, from romanticized accounts of the colony's native peoples.

From the sixteenth to the eighteenth century, the view of Amerindians as kin of the mythical wild people of the forests was gradually eclipsed by the stereotype of Native Americans as the unspoiled children of benign Nature. The two perspectives coexisted for a long time, with a slow shift in favor of the romantic conception of aboriginal peoples. The fiction of Amerindians as "natural men" contributed to the French Revolution of 1789–93; it helped destroy the descendants of those seventeenth-century Bourbon monarchs who wanted to reshape the natives of New France. Royal policy had been to merge European immigrants and Christian aborigines into a single race. Instead, religious missions and social contact produced four new peoples: partly Christian Amerindians dependent upon European trade goods; *Canadiens* and *Acadiens,* who had a small admixture of native culture and blood; and, eventually, the prairie *Métis,* who were equally the heirs of their native and European parents, without belonging to either ancestral group. The royal policy of assimilating aboriginal people to French, Christian culture was supposed to be an alternative to continued emigration of the king's subjects from France. The policy's failure meant that the colony's population was going to depend on white newcomers and their reproduction for its growth. To help retain travelers who had come to North America from France, King Louis XIV and his ministers tried to create a perfected form of government and justice in *la Nouvelle France*—a divine-right monarchy's Utopia. That project had more success than the Jesuits' plan for creating an aboriginal, Christian Utopia in New France.

The scepter and main de justice, *representing the king's power as ruler and law-giver, underneath the intersecting initials of Louis XIV, appear on the walls of the royal apartments in the Palace of Versailles. Photograph by the author.*

Scepter and *Main de Justice:* Government Ambitions to Create a Renewed France in North America

MID-SEVENTEENTH-CENTURY FRANCE WAS NOT YET A NATION AND SCARCELY A unified kingdom. Ideals express aspirations, not realities, and King Louis XIV's dream of a Roman Catholic France under an unquestioned, divinely sanctioned monarch was still far from reality in the late 1600s. His ancestors, the kings of Ile-de-France, had pieced together this patchwork realm, and he extended it in his reign. The kingdom's heterogeneous nature was reflected in the diversity of languages spoken by his subjects. As one moved outward from the Paris region, Parisian *français*—the language of government—gave way to provincial dialects and, on France's frontiers, to alien tongues such as Flemish, Breton, Basque, and Provençal. The annexation of Alsace, including the free city of Strassburg, after the Thirty Years' War (1618–48) added German to the many languages spoken within France. Louis XII made French the language for all criminal trials in 1512. In 1539, five years after Jacques Cartier's first voyage to North America, the royal ordinance of Villers-Cotterets required that all legal acts, both public and private, be written in *français*. It took another three centuries to extend the use of this language to the entire population by universal, elementary schooling in French and by conscripting all young men into a national army. Without a common tongue, Louis XIV's twenty million subjects were united only by a vague fealty to their distant ruler; they did not see themselves as a single people. When residents of France wrote of their homeland, or "patrie," they meant the provincial region surrounding their birthplace. Without a sense of nationhood, France's unification, perforce, had to be built around the person of the king and his religion. The Roman Catholic Church and the sovereign were the two symbols to which most of France's disparate peoples could rally.

Regionalism was evident in the institutions of Old Regime France. The king presided over a hodgepodge of local jurisdictions, each with its own civil laws, social customs, weights, and measures. When Louis XIV recalled his assumption of effective rule in 1661, he wrote that "everywhere was disorder." Typical of the administrative confusion was the lack of a single body of private law for the entire kingdom; only the procedure for dealing with civil cases had been standardized in 1667. A century later Voltaire observed that a traveler crossing France by coach changed civil codes more often than his driver changed horses. The administrative, political, and legal unification of France was achieved, finally, after the French Revolution of 1789–93. It was Emperor Napoleon Bonaparte, a military dictator, who imposed a single code of civil law upon France in 1804—the revolution's child had achieved the dream of the Bourbon kings. Before the revolution royal reformers had looked to the legal usages of the Paris region and to Justinian's Roman Law Code, which held that that the king's will was law, as models for standardizing the diverse laws of provincial France. The Germanic origins of customary law and even of France, as the kingdom of the Franks, were ignored; the Ancient World of the Mediterranean was the preferred source of examples to justify the centralization of political power. As in imperial Rome, "si veut le Roi, si veut la loi [the king's will is law]" became a maxim of government, but this regal claim to unlimited legislative power was one of those aspirations that was far from reality.

Standardization of laws and the centralization of governmental power were impeded by a respect for local privileges, customary exemptions, and existing institutions. Abolition of these established rights and bodies would have been too provocative. Reduction of the nobility's rights, new royal taxes upon the peasantry, and the attempted subordination of the regional law courts known as *parlements* had provoked rebellions against Louis XIV's predecessors. Rather than risk more direct confrontations with defenders of the inherited, medieval institutions, the royal government superimposed its own officials, such as the Intendants of Justice, Public Order and Finance, upon existing bodies. By giving intendants the power to judge legal cases in the first instance and to hear appeals from regional courts, the older jurisdictions were bypassed or undermined. The intendant also had the power to enact regulatory laws, and this mandate encroached on the legislative power of provincial assemblies. The French crown also sapped the independence of self-governing regional bodies by devices such as the royal edict of August 1692, which declared that the mayor's office in all French towns, hitherto an elected position, could be bought from the king. This measure forced townsfolk to buy back the mayoralty if they wanted to fill it with someone of their choice. The king also declared the executive offices of merchants' and craftsmen's corporations to be venal, compelling members to purchase them as well. Positions not bought by the burghers or guild members could be sold by the crown to strangers or be filled by its appointees, so that if an institution wanted to retain some autonomy, it had to contribute to the royal treasury. Aristocrats, likewise, had to pay new royal taxes to confirm their nobility and retain their exemption from the head tax (*taille*).

The kings of France exacted tribute from those who wished to preserve their ancient rights because money was needed to pay for the monarch's expanding bureaucracy and for the armed forces. From 1661 to 1690, the army (on paper) increased from 48,900 men to 388,000 and the strength of the royal fleet grew from twenty to around two hundred ships. The cost of this expansion in military strength and administrative services perpetuated a practice that frustrated the achievement of absolute power by the king. The sale of public offices had begun under King François I as an emergency measure to pay for his wars in Europe. Judicial and governmental offices continued to be sold by the government, thus weakening the monarch's ability to select, remove, or control those who had purchased their positions. This was not the only sacrifice made for immediate revenue. By "farming out" to private contractors the king's right to collect certain taxes, the crown obtained a single payment at once, but the government received only a fraction of the taxes levied in its name. Pursuit of short-term fiscal gains worked against the accumulation of secular power in the monarch's hands or the acquisition of sufficient revenue to support the administrative personnel and military forces required to assert Louis XIV's political and territorial claims.

Quite apart from the self-defeating fiscal policies of the French crown, there was domestic resistance to the centralizing revolution of France's Bourbon kings. Provincial assemblies, municipal governments, the nobility, and Protestants fought back as their rights were chipped away systematically from the 1620s onward. Uniformity of religion was imposed at great human cost. Having brought the Roman Catholic Church in France under royal control and having purged it of deviants such as the Jansenists, Louis XIV wanted all of his subjects to embrace his faith, that of the Holy, Catholic, Apostolic, and Roman Church. This, he imagined, would be a thing pleasing to God and admirable to his devout second wife, the Marquise de Maintenon. Spain's monarchs might call themselves "their Catholic Majesties," but Louis was determined to outshine them as "His Most Christian Majesty." The shrinking official tolerance for French Protestants, or "Huguenots," ended in 1685 when the king made membership in the Roman church compulsory. Protestants were harassed and their children were taken from them to be raised as "new Catholics." As a consequence, France lost nearly 200,000 of its most valuable residents, engaged in commerce and in skilled trades, who went into exile rather than conform to the king's imposed religious uniformity. These French Protestant refugees enriched neighboring states with their talent and proved articulate critics of royal tyranny. In London Huguenot silversmiths introduced new designs and raised the standard of workmanship for their trade. One of the exiled critics was Pastor Pierre Jurieu, who had fled from the Orléanais to Rotterdam, and who defended Protestant theology in books that found their way into France.

Association with religious heresy may have damaged the case for popular participation in government, but the times favored royal absolutism in France. Decades of civil war, in which Protestants, nobles, and *parlements* fought against the crown, discredited the medieval constitution, which had divided civil authority among several bodies. Disorder was blamed upon dissidents' claims that they had their own source of legitimacy, apart from the crown. Jurist Charles Loyseau argued, in opposition, that authority conferred by the king must always take precedence over power derived from the populace. All levels of government within France existed by the monarch's sufferance, it was said, and he could revoke their power at will. In a book about the jurisprudence of public offices, Loyseau wrote, "in France it is very true that people give as much honor as one can to town officials . . . and elevate them, if possible, above royal magistrates. This tends to democracy, even anarchy, and, in truth, their excessive authority has been, on infinite occasions, the cause of popular sedition and, even, of rebellions, as history testifies and, only too recently, is proven by example."[1] Seventeenth-century French jurists looked upon democracy as something close to mob rule—as an evil to be avoided. Public elections were described by royal officials as riotous assemblies involving the lowest elements of society, who were incapable of discerning the public good.[2] Appointment by the king, under these circumstances, would be better than selection by popular suffrage.

Popular sovereignty and self-rule were out of the question because educated people believed that common folk were unreasonable. Christianity, too, taught that humans without the assistance of God's grace were inclined to evil. A moral and intellectual education was necessary to teach people to respond to the call of duty, religion, and honor. It therefore followed that most of humankind, uneducated and, by nature, irrational and depraved, was unfit for self-government. The lower ranks, their betters *knew*, were motivated only by greed and fear. The preamble of the Louis XIV's 1670 *Ordonnance criminelle* stated that criminal justice "restrains by fear of punishment those who are not restrained by a consideration of their duty." Human selfishness and the natural propensity for disorder were arguments for a strong, external force to control the populace. To make a monarch answerable to the fickle and disorderly multitude was reckoned to be madness. The king, asserted his champions, answered only to God and his sword of divine retribution.

Chevalier d'Arcq expressed the conventional wisdom of France's ruling elite when he wrote that "if the governmental organization that allows the greatest ferment is most perfect, then Republican government is superior to Monarchy, but if public tranquillity and the security of citizens constitutes the virtue of government, then monarchy is preferable to all other forms of government."[3] Advocates of divine-right monarchy presented royal absolutism as a cure for civil disorder, and the peoples of France had experienced enough chaos to make this promise of internal peace irresistible. Challenges to royal sovereignty had produced bloodshed and anarchy. Popular yearning for civil peace facilitated acceptance of the king's supremacy. For intellectuals, a theory that made the sovereign the source of all earthly authority and placed no limit on the crown's jurisdiction—apart from the spiritual realm—gave it a logic and simplicity that was appealing. A single, central authority appointed by God was admirably straightforward when compared with the medieval tangle of self-governing institutions inherited from the past. The promise of domestic peace and order was probably more persuasive to most of Louis XIV's subjects. Order was a civic ideal and this was reflected in the administrators' constant reference to the goal of "bon ordre." Good order was a clear social hierarchy, with the king at its apex, and the visible subordination of his subjects, from the highest to the lowest rank.

Despite the promise of peace, Louis XIV's government undertook a series of wars, both to expand the kingdom's frontiers in Europe and, incidentally, to maintain an empire overseas. The young monarch's desire for conquests and military glory frustrated the attempts of his chief minister, Jean-Baptiste Colbert, to create a financially solvent and efficient royal government. Colbert had quadrupled the king's income from indirect taxes and he increased yearly revenue from the royal domains and forests from 248,000 *livres* to 6,500,000 *livres*. Attempts to wring more money from the population by taxes to support an aggressive foreign policy exacerbated the effect of natural calamities, such as the general crop failure of 1709–10. The later years of Louis XIV's reign were scarred by popular revolts against the crown. Royal absolutism had produced the very unrest that it had promised to end.

In contemporary iconography, France's monarchy was represented by a crown above a crossed scepter and *main de justice*. This motif appeared on French coins and it decorated the royal apartment's wall panels in the Palace of Versailles. The scepter was emblematic of sovereign's power to rule. The hand of justice spoke of the king's role as supreme lawgiver, judge, and protector of his people. He was reckoned the fountainhead of all justice and he alone could grant pardons and remissions from court sentences. Although all criminal trials were conducted in the king's name, his active intervention in the process of justice usually was limited to granting letters of remission to convicted offenders.

In his book *Politique tirée de l'Ecriture sainte* (1709) Bishop Jacques-Bénigne Bossuet wrote that "the prince is, by his office, the father of his people." The concept of the monarch as father of his subjects was not an original idea. The family was the model for all social relationships: priests were addressed as "father" and nuns were called "sister" or "mother." Members of lay associations, such as guilds, were "brethren." The bishop of Quebec addressed the faithful as his "children"—the same term was used by royal officers to describe the king's native allies. The claim to a paternal role was not to be taken literally, as Louis XIV himself acknowledged. A 1665 royal memorandum to Intendant Jean Talon in Canada stated, "the King, considering all his Canadian subjects, from the highest to the lowest, *almost as his own children* and wishing to satisfy his obligation to make them feel the sweetness and joy of his reign . . . Sieur Talon will strive solely to make them comfortable in all things and to stimulate them to work . . . even going into their petty concerns and their household matters . . . so that, in doing his duty like a good father, he might help provide them with the means of making some profits and of bringing wild lands into cultivation."[4]

In this document Louis XIV admitted that a true father-child relationship could not be reproduced between monarch and subject, but it was the standard by which secular and religious authorities were judged. In his Easter sermon of 1674, Abbé François Salignac de la Mothe-Fénélon reproached the colony's governor-general for his impositions upon the people of Montreal, saying, "he who is endowed with authority must not disturb the people who are his dependents, but rather he is obliged to look upon them as his children and to treat them as a father would do."[5]

The model family in question was not a conventional, modern North American family. From the government's viewpoint, the ideal family was a patriarchal one. A stern paterfamilias who ruled his dependents with unquestioned authority rather than an indulgent "Dad" within a companionate family was what the colonial administrators had in mind. A monarch was obliged to feed and to protect his subjects, and this the king's government attempted to do by regulating the food trades and by sending troops to the colony, as Louis XIV did in 1665. In 1672 the viceroy of New France was told that the highest court, the *Conseil souverain* at Quebec, was established in 1663 "solely to prevent the oppression of the poor by the most powerful and comfortable residents."[6] In 1714 members of this court defended their right to pass public order regulations, in addition to those issued by the intendant, "because the interest of God and his church, of the King, of the public, of the widow and the orphan reside in the person of the king's officials."[7] In a blend of compassion and authoritarianism, which was characteristic of government in *la*

Nouvelle France, concern for the weak was coupled with a stern approach to the able-bodied poor. Local poor boards were established in the late seventeenth century to suppress public begging, to aid the indigent, and to find work for healthy and strong beggars on terms that could not be refused.[8] In return for protection and aid, dependents owed their superiors submission and obedience. Everyone, except the king, had a natural superior on earth and anyone who claimed to be free from authority was a threat to public order.

While Lutheran Protestants believed that faith alone could achieve a person's spiritual salvation, Roman Catholics were more mindful of James the Apostle's words that "faith, if it does not lead to action, is in itself a lifeless thing. . . . Can you not see . . . faith divorced from deeds is barren?" The Roman church encouraged practical acts of charity. Bishop Saint-Vallier's 1702 catechism for the Diocese of Quebec stated, "it is not sufficient for a Christian to spurn evil and to avoid sin; he must still undertake good works, not only before God but also in the eyes of men." The bishop reminded readers of the Beatitude "Blessed are the merciful; for they shall obtain [God's] mercy."[9] The traditional seven acts of Christian charity included feeding the hungry, clothing the naked, and visiting the sick. Earlier, the bishop had directed his priests to "represent to the great and to magistrates . . . that they do not forget the orphan's interest and the widow's case," because, at the end, "God will demand an accounting from them for the oppression of the weak, the scorned poor, and those abandoned to the power of the rich."[10]

The need for good works to attain personal salvation was as important as royal paternalism in shaping government policies. Roman Catholicism made the French colonies more humane in caring for the sick, the aged, the abandoned, and the poor than the neighboring Protestant colonies of Great Britain. *Canadiens* were provided with hospitals and shelters from 1639 onward, whereas the more populous British colonies lacked comparable institutions until the 1713 foundation of the Philadelphia Almshouse. Charitable institutions run by personnel of the Roman Catholic Church made New France a welfare state, and in Spanish and Portuguese America, the same religious heritage produced hospitals and shelters for the unfortunate. In *la Nouvelle France* the French crown subsidized these benevolent religious foundations, but to thank the sovereign for their existence would be to place the cart before the horse. Solicitude for the unfortunate was inspired by religion, and the French monarchs, to their credit, supported the charitable work of priests, nuns, and brothers.

Louis XIV's real achievement was in administrative reform. France's American colonies were ideal subjects for the royal government's centralizing zeal. The colonies were almost a blank page on which the king could inscribe his ideals. There were no long-standing traditions to be confronted. Among the small number of established European residents there were, apart from the clergy, few entrenched interest groups, like France's old nobility or municipal corporations, to resist a central royal government. Before 1663, when the power of government was delegated to chartered trading companies, the concession holder paid for administration, defense, and, after 1627, for Christian missionaries to the aborigines. Although the monarch of France assumed responsibility for these services in 1663, the legal fiction of company rule continued for a few more years. Real political power in the colony belonged to a governor-general, representing the king's person, who handled military and diplomatic matters, and to the king's intendant, who attended to civilian matters, including justice and public finances. The senior court was the Sovereign Council, whose members were appointed by the monarch. Because French government in the Old Regime did not divide powers strictly and the senior officials and court could legislate, judge, and administer, jurisdictions overlapped and internal conflicts between institutions and officials occurred.

La Nouvelle France was intended to be the fulfillment of Louis XIV's dreams for France. Even before he came to the throne, the colony was declared to be the exclusive domain of the Roman Catholic Church. It would not be sullied by the presence of heretics, even if Protestants had been prominent in the charter companies that had maintained the colony for the French crown. Under its 1627 charter, the Company of One Hundred Associates was obliged to populate the colony only with "natural-born, French and Catholic subjects."[11] Protestants and foreigners were not welcome in New France and they were denied the right to acquire land or to settle permanently in the colony. The 1676 public order regulations of the Sovereign Council at Quebec forbade "people of the so-called reformed religion to gather together to practice their religion" anywhere in the colony, and if, by special permission, they were allowed to spend a winter in Canada, they were to "live like Catholics without scandal."[12] Even Protestant sailors visiting Canada were forbidden to sing their vernacular psalms. In 1677 a priest of the Quebec Seminary told the minister responsible for colonies, "that it was important that the Huguenots should not settle nor winter in Canada, because we are placed between three English [and Protestant] colonies and that, if war should occur, the Huguenots would not fail to side with their party; that it was not suitable to have a mixture of Huguenots among the Catholics in so remote a place." The minister agreed with this argument that the military security of New France still required the exclusion of Protestants, who were regarded as untrustworthy subjects.[13]

Protestants managed to enter the colony, especially in the casually recruited levies of workers sent out from France in the 1660s. The two hundred or so Huguenots who managed to stay in New France were converted to Catholicism before marriage or death. A priest's endorsement was required to occupy a public office or to exercise the professions of notary or midwife. The merchant Gédéon Petit from La Rochelle was baptized a Roman Catholic at Quebec in 1673 and was granted the right to acquire land in Canada in 1677. His father Alexandre was already an established merchant at Quebec and he too had abjured Protestantism. Their motive in converting seems to have been a desire to remain permanently in Canada to engage in trade. Gédéon was not comfortable in his new faith and fled to the Huguenot settlement of New Rochelle in New York, where his will was probated in April 1687.[14] Another one hundred former Protestants had come as soldiers. At Louisbourg public abjurations by Swiss soldiers, "formerly of Calvin's religion which he detests," confirmed the population's conviction that Roman Catholicism was the only true faith. The convert took a vow, with his hand upon the New Testament, to be a good Roman Catholic, and was then rebaptized and given a priest's absolution from excommunication.[15] Captives and fugitives from the British colonies supplied a few hundred more converts. Marc-André Bédard estimates that 542 Protestants settled in the St. Lawrence Valley, although those who resisted conversion may be unrecorded.[16] By the 1740s a few French Protestant merchants, despite the bishop of Quebec's protest, were permitted tacitly to live at Quebec, where they acquired dominance in that port's import-export trade. These men remained outsiders and did not become permanent residents of Canada.

Returning to heresy after embracing Roman Catholicism, as Gédéon Petit had done, was the crime of apostasy. That was only one of the offenses committed by a Dutch-speaking New Yorker. John Hendricks Lijdius (1699–1791) was the son of a Calvinist minister at Schenectady. John appeared at Montreal in 1725. Intendant Claude-Thomas Dupuy was alarmed by the number of English-speaking craftsmen and merchants at Montreal, whom he suspected of contraband trading. John, however, accepted Roman Catholicism and, with the permission of Montreal's governor, he married a *Canadienne* in February 1727. He even obtained a ministerial exemption from the royal edict of October 1727, which excluded naturalized subjects of foreign birth from commerce. The trade in which he was really interested was smuggling goods from Albany, using Indians of the Sault Saint-Louis mission as his carriers.

What was worse was that Lijdius's conversion had been a sham. His parish priest affirmed that in six months the New Yorker had not entered Montreal's church, nor had he performed any act of faith. Another Sulpician, Jean-Gabriel de Lescoat, testified in 1730 that "the said Lidius . . . has not, since his abjuration, given any proofs of Catholicity, but [has shown] many utterly repugnant to the Catholic religion; firstly, in objecting to present his child in the church to have it baptised; secondly, in having exhorted an Englishman on the point of death, to persist in his heretical opinions; and thirdly, in having assisted at his interment, and [having] performed the service according to the manner of English Ministers."[17] The missionaries to the Indians at Sault Saint-Louis and Lac des Deux Montagnes also complained that Lijdius bribed natives, encouraged their warlike spirit, and had ridiculed Catholicism. Apostasy on top of smuggling was too much, and in September 1730 Quebec's Superior Council fined Lijdius three thousand livres and ordered him to be exiled to France. At Rochefort the New Yorker obtained his release from prison after convincing French authorities that he had left an estate worth twelve thousand livres—more than enough surety for his fine—in Canada. It was a lie: he had left no assets in the colony. He also convinced the Maritime Council that he was Dutch, and he and his wife were allowed to go to the Netherlands. They reappeared in New York in 1732, back in the smuggling trade with Canada, but from the safety of British territory.[18]

The number of Jews who tested New France's religious orthodoxy was very small. In October 1738 Mother de Sainte-Hélène of Quebec's hospital reported that "a young Jewish girl arrived in Canada this year disguised as a sailor. She was suspected of being a woman on the ship but she would not admit it. Monsieur the Intendant interviewed her and she told him the truth and said that she had fled her parents' home because she was not as well loved as her sister. She has been traveling in every country in this [men's] clothing for five years."[19] The girl was Esther Brandeau. She was sent back to France in 1739, after exhausting the patience of the priests and nuns who tried to instruct her in Christianity.[20] Marianne Perious, another Jewish woman, arrived a decade later and submitted to Christian baptism in order to stay and to be able to marry.[21]

Humane the colony might have been in helping those with physical afflictions or material needs, but it was intolerant of religious diversity. The legacy of enforced religious conformity during the French Regime was the later assumption that a French-Canadian or an Acadian was, necessarily, a French-speaking Roman Catholic. Religion, as much as language, was the defining trait of Franco-Canadian identity for more than two centuries. French-speakers were also accustomed to an ideological homogeneity among themselves. This was the legacy of the French government's policy of maintaining religious orthodoxy.

In keeping with the crown's inclination to make the usages of Paris a standard for legal reforms, the 1580 text of the Customary Civil Laws of the Paris *Prévôté* and Viscounty, succinctly called *la Coutume de Paris,* was declared to be the basis of New France's private law in May 1664. All other regional bodies of law, such as the *Coutume de Normandie,* henceforth, were excluded, and the mixture of provincial laws that had existed in the colony was ended. The Parisian laws were supplemented, from time to time, by royal ordinances on matters such as commercial transactions (1673) and wills (1735). The 1664 ordinance had enduring consequences, particularly in the future Province of Quebec, because civil law reinforces certain social values and molds the way people trained in law think.

Like all legal regulations, the *Coutume de Paris* incorporated norms for social behavior and for the conduct of family members. Society was assumed to be aristocratic, patriarchal, agricultural, and Roman Catholic. Seigneurial estates and noble lands were the concern of 87 of the 362 articles of the *Coutume*. Commercial transactions, apart from those involving real estate, are scarcely mentioned. In New France some portions of this law code were discarded as being inapplicable to the colony's condition. Section 12, for example, which dealt with "la garde noble et bourgeoise," entitling legal guardians within Paris to use revenues from a minor's estate for their own benefit, was ignored. According to François-Joseph Cugnet, twenty other articles were "retrenched . . . as being of no use."[22] These dealt primarily with the privileges, duties, and real estate of Parisian burghers, with venal offices, which were almost unknown in the colony, and with annuities sold by the City of Paris.

Rural values pervaded the *coutume*. A typically agrarian desire to have blood kin retain family lands was aided by *retrait lignager,* which permitted a blood relation to recover a landed property within a year and a day of its sale to a stranger by repaying the buyer for the original purchase price and associated expenses. Lineal retrocession discouraged the sale of land to non-kin and it hindered commercial speculation in land because the buyer's title was precarious in the first year after purchase.

Since the French crown defended Roman Catholicism and, in return, the church upheld the Bourbon monarchy, there was no separation of the sacred and profane realms. Blasphemy, sacrilege, atheism, and apostasy were criminal offenses. Religious standards were expressed in the *coutume*'s refusal to acknowledge de facto unions without the rite of marriage or bastardy. Children born outside wedlock had no legal claim on their parents' estate. Debts for alcoholic drinks consumed and for gambling could not be pursued in law. The civil law disavowed activities condemned by the clergy and supported marriages blessed by the church and the families that resulted from these sanctified unions.

The approved family was a patriarchal one in which wife and children were subordinates of the husband and father. Legal culture does not exist independently of the wider culture, and the monarch, bishop, priests, and fathers all were expected to deal with their dependents as a stern, protective paterfamilias. A wife was placed firmly under her husband's tutelage. Legally, he was the sovereign of his family. Article 223, about a married couple's Community of Goods, stated, "a married woman cannot sell, alienate or mortgage her estate without the authority and written consent of her husband; and if she makes any contract without the authority and consent of her husband, that contract is void."[23] The husband, by contrast, could dispose of their joint property, as well as his own personal effects, without his wife's consent. He was the supreme governor of their community of goods.

The legal assumption that women were irresponsible by nature and could be dominated by men had compensatory benefits. Protection was the corollary of subjection. There were safeguards against a man who abused his powers to the detriment of his dependents. A married woman could petition for a legal separation from or an interdict against an insane, brutal, habitually drunk, or profligate husband who might squander their property. An interdict deprived him of power over their goods. Minors could also protest against the management of their inheritance by a legal guardian. To judge from the court records of New France, however, these dependents' rights were rarely exercised. In the St. Lawrence Valley settlements, where most of the population lived, there were just 150 surviving petitions for legal separation—submitted by women in almost every case. Four-fifths of the petitioners sought a legal division of property, without physical separation from their spouse, so they were not protected from a husband's physical abuse.[24] Magistrates, for their part, were reluctant to undermine a husband's authority, which was seen as essential to "bon ordre."

Because of the assumption of feminine irresponsibility, women who participated in crimes were considered to be less culpable than their male partners, who were suspected of leading the women astray. Unauthorized assemblies and collective public protests were serious offenses in *la Nouvelle France,* but in December 1757 Montreal's womenfolk publicly protested against the substitution of horse meat for half of their beef ration, because, "they had an aversion to eating horse flesh; [saying] that he was the friend of man; that religion forbade the killing of horses." The governor-general belittled their complaint and blustered about imprisoning all of them and hanging half the protesters.[25] The women, however, were allowed to disperse and go home, unpunished.

French civil law encouraged values unlike those embodied in English Common Law, which prevailed in the British American colonies. The *coutume* enforced family obligations; it did not deal with individual rights beyond a dependent's right to food, shelter, or protection. When making bequests, there was no absolute personal freedom, as in English law. One's legitimate progeny could be disinherited only for "just cause," such as conviction for a capital crime, heresy, high treason, or for injuring or spurning a parent.[26] The division of a commoner's property after death was predetermined by the law. All children, except for those of noble birth, were equal as heirs and, by the *droit de légitime,* were entitled to at least one half of an equal share of the parental estate. Customary dower gave the widow the enjoyment of one half of her husband's possessions, as they were at the time of their marriage, for her lifetime, in addition to other benefits to assure her a decent living. The provisions of the *coutume* made last wills and testaments redundant, save for single people without natural heirs and those who wished to make a special bequest to the church. Thus, few wills are to be found in the notarial archives of New France.

There is evidence that, in this family-centered society, people had to be forced to respect the needs and interests of strangers or non-kin. Dividing walls between properties were minutely regulated by the *coutume,* as if neighbors would be unable to resolve such matters between themselves. Statutes forbade damming or diverting rivers and streams from their natural course to the detriment of those downstream. Civil law buttressed the view that the family, and not the individual, was the basic unit of society. This was, of course, a patriarchal family in which wife and children were subject to the *"puissance paternelle* [paternal authority]" of the husband and father. As a consequence of the law and cultural values, individualism in this frontier society was family individualism, it was a drive for family self-sufficiency and not for personal autonomy.

Male authority, family duties, retention of landed property, and the Roman Catholic moral values inherent in the *coutume* were secondary to two other features of this law code. First was the implicit assumption that there were universally valid principles for human behavior and social relationships. The 362 articles were general rules for what humans ought to do; they did not acknowledge exceptions or nonconforming practices. Magistrates, guided by the king's attorney (*procureur du roi*), identified the general principle pertinent to the case and then applied it. The law had a unitary view of society that rejected the right of dissent or cultural pluralism within the European population. This is a fundamental difference from the English Common Law tradition, which refers to legal precedents and to current practice as guides for present-day judgments. Common Law takes a historical approach that is indifferent to the ideal of a single, consistent system of rules. For example, lawful matrimony was best, yet when an unwed couple lived together, they were deemed to have a "Common Law marriage." French civil law did not acknowledge unhallowed cohabitation or the children resulting from such extralegal relationships. To do so would have been immoral. Deviant behavior, even if it were widespread, was not recognized by civil law.

The legal heritage of *la Nouvelle France,* which survived the British conquest in 1759–60, encouraged an idealistic rather than a pragmatic view of life. Put another way, it assumed that there was only one right way to deal with a situation and that the rules were known. Those universal principles were written down in the simplified *Coutume de Paris* used in the French North American colonies. A judge's role was to apply the appropriate general rule to a particular case.

Dogmatic idealism also was encouraged by Roman Catholic education—the church had a near monopoly of formal instruction in New France. In religion there was only one truth; it was contained in sanctioned dogma which was authoritatively explained by the clergy. The laity had only to memorize the approved responses to every question. That was how Christian catechism was taught. This indoctrination was similar to contemporary Protestant instruction, but the attitude to speculative inquiry was different. Catholic lay people were discouraged from reading and interpreting the Bible for themselves; only the ordained clergy had the authority to interpret Scripture. Those who owned books read biblical digests called "holy histories," and, for practical examples of how individuals applied Christian precepts, they consulted the biographies of saints. The Protestant insistence on an individual's duty to read the Bible to effect a personal reformation had produced a diversity of sects based on different constructions of God's revealed Word. This result of intellectual freedom was held up by Bishop Bossuet's *Histoire des Variations des Églises Protestantes* (1688) and by other Roman Catholic writers as proof of the dangers of personal interpretation of Scripture.[27]

Given this legal and religious background, educated French colonists favored argument from unquestioned principles rather than pragmatic appeals to what had been tried and found to work. An argument from a general rule was, intellectually, more respectable than a reference to experience. This did not prevent pragmatic decisions or the granting of exceptions, but these government actions had to be presented as acts of principle. French civil law reinforced this deductive predilection. For a person raised in this intellectual tradition, compromise was akin to a betrayal of principle; it was not an admirable course of action, as it tended to be for English-speakers.

The law's impact may seem overrated in a colony from which barristers were excluded, yet its influence spread well beyond court personnel and notaries. Legal training or knowledge of the law was a prerequisite for an administrative appointment in New France, and in 1733 the Quebec *Conseil supérieur*'s attorney general began giving lectures in law to help *Canadiens*—especially officials' sons—qualify for a government post. In *la Nouvelle France,* not only public officials, but military officers, merchants, clerics, and building contractors revealed their knowledge of the law in their transactions. Their estate inventories sometimes listed the legal manuals they consulted. As one might expect, Guillaume Gaillard, who sat on the Superior Council, had twenty-three law books in his library.[28] The 1699 postmortem listing of assets belonging to Claude Baillif, Quebec builder-architect, noted that his library contained "La Coutume de Paris" and an "abrégé de la Coutume de Paris." An army officer, Joseph Fournerie de Vezon, owned 130 books, including legal works such as "Ordonnances de Louis XIV . . . Histoire du droit public . . . Conférences [des Ordonnances de Louis XIV] de Bornier" and one called "Les causes célèbres."[29] In commerce and public affairs, a little legal knowledge was a good thing.

A bias for deductive rather than inductive reasoning distinguished educated *Canadiens* from the British newcomers who entered the colony after 1760. The new arrivals, steeped in the Common Law, were inclined to favor pragmatic, inductive arguments. After the formal acquisition of *la Nouvelle France* by Britain in 1763, British government policy assumed, logically, that a British colony should be endowed with English legal and political institutions, like those in the older American possessions of Britain. In the next decade that policy underwent a radical reversal, and parliament decided, instead, to preserve the *Coutume de Paris* in Canada. After the introduction of representative government in 1791, lawyers' and notaries' offices were preparatory schools for generations of provincial politicians. Legal professionals dominated the politics of French Canada. French jurisprudence continued to shape the values of French-speakers and to influence the way people thought, long after the conquest of New France. Idealism and deductive reasoning remained the preferred modes of thought.

An example of the educated elite's preference for doctrine over experience in eighteenth-century New France was the enthusiasm of military engineers and army officers for the theories of Sébastien Le Prestre de Vauban (1633–1707), who wrote treatises on methods for attacking and defending towns. He was a master of siegecraft. Vauban's integrated system of angled slopes, covered ways, ditches, projecting bastions, and curtain walls provided an admirable, interlocking defense against a frontal assault by infantry from the landward sides. His defensive system was logical, comprehensive, and geometrically beautiful and therein lay its appeal. Enemy actions were expected to follow a predictable pattern that would give all advantages to the defenders. In North America, however, attackers did not play by Vauban's rules or follow a predictable script. Ignorant amateurs confounded professional soldiers with their unpredictability. At Louisbourg in May 1745 New Englanders, untutored in the finer points of warfare, dragged guns and mortars over "impassable" bogs with improvised wooden sledges to place the weapons on rises southwest of the town. French defenders here and elsewhere had left terrain within artillery range of the towns unoccupied, and British forces were allowed to erect siege batteries, with which they breached walls and lobbed mortar bombs into the fortifications. The French garrison guns were usually sited in embrasures on bastion cheeks to fire in enfilade upon enemy troops as they attempted to scale the intervening curtain walls. British regulars and colonial soldiers did not rush into this trap; they used artillery, from a distance, to blow gaps in the defenses, rather than assaulting them immediately. The defenders' garrison guns had to be redeployed to fire outward against the siege batteries.

In New France potential locations for siege guns, across bodies of water, were left unprotected not once, but *four times* during King George's War (1744–48) and

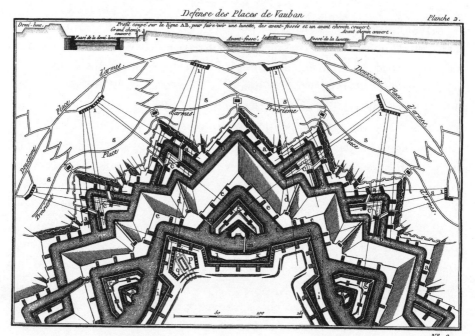

Vauban's designs for defenses were logical and geometrically beautiful.
From Traité de la Défense des Places *(Paris, 1795).*

in the French and Indian War (1755–63). This happened at Louisbourg in 1745 and 1758; it occurred at Fort Niagara and at Quebec in 1759. Captain Pierre Pouchot, commandant of Fort Niagara, learned of the enemy gun battery on Mississauga Point "on the other side of the river" when a cannon ball struck the chimney of his quarters and "the ball rolled beside his bed upon which he had just lain down to rest."[30] In each case, the enemy occupied elevated ground across a body of water, where guns were emplaced to fire upon the lightly protected flanks of the fortifications, and, on every occasion, the French defenders were surprised. Montreal capitulated in 1760 when the town was surrounded by a vastly superior force; its walls were also overlooked by the undefended heights of Mount Royal—a prime location for siege guns. The French military officers' preference for a logical, comprehensive, and authoritative system of thought did not entirely exclude pragmatism. In 1758 the defenders of Louisbourg and Fort Carillon (Ticonderoga) recognized their fortifications' deficiencies and they built improvised defensive works outside the permanent, masonry-and-rubblestone walls.

Lesser examples of doctrinaire idealism are the views and maps of Louisbourg produced by French royal engineers and sent back to France in the eighteenth century. A 1731 view by Chief Engineer Étienne Verrier shows a parish church, in a central place as it ought to be, on the port's harborside. The building's roof, the chapel's outline, or the site marked with a cross and, sometimes, with the notation

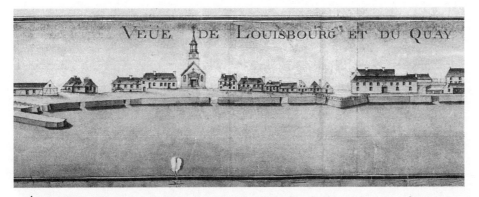

*Étienne Verrier's portrayal of the nonexistent parish church of Louisbourg in this 1731
view was repeated in other maps and views for three decades. From the Archives du Génie,
Service historique de l'Armée de Terre, Ministère de la Défense (France).*

"la paroisse" (the parish church) appeared repeatedly on maps by Verrier and others
over the next three decades.[31] This would lead one to believe that there was a parish
church on St. Louis Street, next to the Récollet Franciscans' friary. In fact, the parish
chapel did not exist and construction of it never began, yet so strong was the conviction that a proper town had to have a parish church that the proposed place of
worship was shown along with existing structures. Louisbourg's townsfolk actually
worshipped in the King's Bastion Chapel. When reality conflicted with propriety,
it was sometimes ignored or denied.

Government compromises were not acknowledged as a violation of the principle that the sovereign acted of his own volition and answered only to God. A legal
fiction of absolute sovereignty was upheld. The setting of prices for essential foods
was pragmatic. Occasional urban, consultative assemblies (*assemblées de police*) of the
leading townsmen, identified as "les plus notables bourgeois," were called to furnish information on current commodity prices, upon which the authorized rates for
bread and beef were based. Sometimes, test loaves were baked to assess the yield
from a given amount of flour. The local magistrate then decreed what prices might
be charged, allowing a small profit to the licensed bakers and butchers. This regulatory system was supposed to furnish townspeople with basic foodstuffs at the
lowest possible price.

In the eighteenth century, the magistrates relied less and less upon these advisory gatherings and used their own judgment to set the authorized prices for bread
and meat. This unilateral process occasionally lost touch with current costs. In
1710 Quebec's butchers petitioned the *Conseil supérieur* to have their price scale
raised because the cost of livestock and of the forage needed to feed animals awaiting slaughter had increased. The sanctioned prices were raised, the butchers were
told, "without any regard for their petition [*ayant aucunement Egard a leur demande*]."

The same formal disclaimer was used by the Quebec Prévôté court in 1749, when yielding to complaints from the city's licensed bakers.[32] Collective petitions from social inferiors were illegal, and a monarch or his agents were not accountable to his subjects. The verbal disclaimer maintained the illusion of the sovereign's absolute supremacy, despite a practical concession. When condemned prisoners escaped custody or a military deserter evaded capture, the death sentence was carried out upon an effigy and the absent victim was declared to be legally dead. Suicides were also tried, postmortem, for the crime of self-murder, and their corpses were then punished. The point of these rituals was to show that the king's justice was inescapable; his authority remained inviolate, in theory at least.

When shaping the institutions of New France, the French crown eliminated potential rivals for secular power. Having disposed of the threat of religious heresy, the royal government wished to ensure that seigneurs in Canada would never become the leaders of their armed tenants, in the manner of France's nobility during the previous century. The crown had claimed a monopoly of armed force within the realm. Command of the rural militia, under the governor-general, was entrusted to a senior tenant-farmer called the Captain of the Militia, and militia companies were organized according to parish, not by seigneury. Officers of the regular garrison troops became seigneurs, yet the troops they commanded were never their vassals. These officers led the king's troops by virtue of a royal commission; they could not pretend to exercise an independent authority.

Elections for officials would have suggested that the population had some right to participate in government or had the power to approve of administrative measures. This was anathema to a divine-right monarchy. As a result of the ideological incompatibility of royal absolutism with representative government, the colonial population's modest share in government was eliminated by the crown after *la Nouvelle France* became a royal province in 1663. An administrative council had been established at Quebec in 1647, advised by five elected syndics, or spokesmen, representing the colonists in the St. Lawrence Valley's three towns. The franchise seems to have been limited to a few leading men.[33] The old council was officially replaced in 1663 by a wholly appointed *Conseil souverain,* as part of the new royal administration. The colonists, however, continued to elect syndics.

In 1673 Governor-General Buade de Frontenac was told to prevent any further elections for these advisors; he was also obliged to destroy his own creation, a municipal council at Quebec. Under Frontenac's March 1673 regulations, Quebec was to have a municipal government of three elected aldermen—the senior man was the mayor. Elections were held for this body. Quebec was the only colonial town in French North America to have a nascent corporation. Because city governments hampered royal authority in France, the king disapproved of Frontenac's creation and ordered that there be no more elections of aldermen. The internal regulation of towns, was thereafter exercised by royally appointed court officers, such as the *lieu-tenants-généraux*, except on Montreal Island, where the Sulpician Fathers retained a seigneurial right to their own *bailliage,* or bailiff's court, until 1693. Their magistrate acted as Montreal's lawgiver and civil administrator.

Governor-General Buade de Frontenac had also failed to grasp Louis XIV's intentions when Frontenac summoned representatives of the Three Estates—the legal categories for social ranks—in 1672 to hear his inaugural address and to take an oath of fidelity to the king. Frontenac had not seen a conflict between assemblies or corporations and the centralizing monarchy's ambition to rule alone. The new governor-general had simply seen this event in 1672 as an impressive ceremony in which he would be the centerpiece.[34] Although this colonial assembly had no deliberative or legislative functions, like an Estates-General in France, Frontenac was reprimanded by the minister responsible for colonies for convoking such a gathering:

> In the government and direction of that land [New France] you must always follow the forms used here and [realize] that our kings have decided some time ago, for the good of their service, never to summon the Estates-General of their realm in order, perhaps, to quietly do away with that ancient usage. You also must not give . . . a corporate form to the said country's inhabitants and it will be necessary shortly, when the colony is stronger than it presently is, to gradually suppress the office of *syndic,* who presents requests in the name of all the residents, it being good that each person speaks for himself alone and that no one speaks on behalf of all.[35]

Montrealers would not accept the loss of their elected representative in government. They had enjoyed a small measure of popular government, apart from the syndic. When the Holy Family Militia was established in 1663, each seven-man squad chose its own corporal. The next year the local governor summoned the residents of Montreal Island to meet in a barn on the common field to elect five *juges* to set commodity prices, hear public order cases, and pass on their recommendations to the seigneurial judge for enforcement. Elections for an "attorney and spokesman for Montreal Island [*procureur syndic de l'Ile de Montréal*]" also occurred until 1672. This officer managed community-owned assets and relayed complaints to the seigneurial judge. In 1674, for example, the *procureur syndic* recommended punitive action against owners of straying cattle. When told that such agents were now illegal, fourteen Montrealers, who claimed to represent their "community," protested against the suppression of elected spokesmen and petitioned the intendant in 1675 "to re-establish their syndic . . . or [grant] that they be permitted to elect [a new] one."[36] It was a futile request; the institution was dead and the royal administration was not going to revive it. The name "syndic" continued to be used for elected managers of common lands and for coordinators of local, public works projects, but such men had no right to present collective grievances or requests to those in authority.

Governor-General Buade de Frontenac complied with the royal directives and put an end to popular representatives. Collective action by commoners was declared to be illegal. In 1677 Frontenac issued a decree forbidding unauthorized, private assemblies and the circulation of petitions, "since there is nothing more strictly forbidden . . . than gatherings and conventicles held without [royal] permission, which can only provide an easy pretext for all sorts of monopolies, secret associations, and plots that ill-intentioned individuals might wish to form."[37] A Montreal surgeon was prosecuted in 1693 for soliciting signatures for a petition, "in contempt of the King's ordinances forbidding all assemblies and popular cabals . . . [and] in contempt for His justice and authority."[38] The assumption was that, if there were a problem, the king's officers would know about it and would provide the remedy. A collective petition was seditious because it cast doubt on the royal officials' ability to determine the public good and to undertake the necessary action. There was an element of social bias in this hostility to public gatherings, elected spokesmen, and group petitions; the upper ranks of colonial society were treated with more indulgence. From 1717 onward, merchants were authorized to gather together to discuss trade and to elect their own spokesman, who could present collective requests to government—activities forbidden to their social inferiors. Selected leading townsmen, too, were invited to advise local magistrates in public order matters, such as the pricing of bread, but the colony's population had no right to share in government, except as royal appointees, like those notables selected for the *Conseil souverain/supérieur.*

To avoid the problem of irresponsibility created by venal offices in France, the sale of public positions—with one exception—was excluded from *la Nouvelle France.*[39] For a time, lifetime appointees in New France enjoyed one of the rights given to purchasers of offices in France: the right of succession. In the 1680s the crown seemed to accept the principle that a qualified son had the right to succeed his father in a public post. This right of inheritance (*survivance*) was automatic with a venal office, provided the owner paid a yearly tax known as the *droit annuel,* or *paulette.* On Quebec's *Conseil souverain,* François-Madeleine-Fortuné Ruette d'Auteuil became attorney-general in 1680 by right of succession, and, in 1689, Pierre-Noel LeGardeur de Tilly and Mathieu Damours de Freneuse inherited their fathers' council seats. The positions were treated as private property: in 1695 LeGardeur de Tilly gave his councilorship to Charles Aubert de la Chesnaye as payment for a debt. In the early eighteenth century, however, the French crown shattered the councilors' belief that they owned their positions. Ruette d'Auteuil was dismissed from the council in 1707. When Charles de Monseignat repeatedly asked that his eldest son be assured of inheriting his seat on this high court, as had been done for a previous occupant's son, the minister of maritime affairs and colonies replied in 1714 that "the King is absolutely determined never to grant any [right of] succession for the offices [*les Charges*] of la Nouvelle France."[40] Thus did the sovereign reassert his control over colonial offices.

Few colonists had the legal qualifications to act as judges, and so the colonial bench was occupied primarily by trained men from France. This ensured conformity with metropolitan judicial standards. The judges' different origins and their superior education gave them some independence from popular opinion. They could dismiss colonists' accusations of witchcraft, which occasionally arose when an inexplicable misfortune, such as the sudden death of livestock, occurred. In dealing with common superstitions, the social gap between magistrates and populace was beneficial; on other issues, it could produce unnecessary conflict. In 1741 Jacques-Joseph Guiton de Monrepos from Guyenne was dispatched to Montreal to serve as *lieutenant-général* (royal judge) for civil and criminal matters. De Monrepos was a lawyer of noble birth and the epitome of metropolitan pomposity. Canadian ways were alien to him, and twice, in 1741 and 1753, he tried to outlaw the throwing of snowballs in Montreal's streets.[41]

Residents of the colony were appointed to the *Conseil supérieur,* successor to the *Conseil souverain* of Quebec, yet in the 1700s immigrants from France were preferred as candidates, in part because many were personally connected to a senior official and, possibly, because they were more pliant than *Canadiens* from influential, local families. Men whose position was due to a great man's patronage were more attached to their benefactor's interest. Immigrants would also be free of the pressures exerted by a kinship network in the colony. Twenty-eight of the thirty-eight lay appointees to the council after 1700—excluding clerks—were born in France. Canadians played a junior role in New France's administration and they had no institutionalized right to pass judgment on its actions.

The only, durable, popularly elected bodies in the St. Lawrence Valley were the vestry boards, or *fabriques,* which managed parish property. Even here, the oldest and most respected men of the parish dominated proceedings and priests approved the candidates, so this was not rural democracy in action. Parish residents had to be prodded by the church or crown to hold assemblies to apportion individual contributions for providing or maintaining a public facility, such as a cemetery or a bridge. In Acadia, where the government's hand was scarcely present, villagers developed a form of self-government in which male elders spoke for the community and settled internal disputes, as did their priests. Villagers in the Illinois

Country had collectively administered common fields, whereas, in Canada, the common lands were simply everyone's pasture, sometimes requiring an annual payment to the seigneur. The Illinois colonists and the Acadians had more experience with self-rule than their Canadian cousins. This situation resulted from their geographic isolation and the local weakness of the royal government. In the St. Lawrence Valley the king's agents were active and they were hostile to self-constituted groups and collective petitions. Inexperienced in self-government and deprived of a political voice outside the parish, the *Canadiens'* primary allegiance was to family and parish. Their higher, though less distinct, duty was to God and the king, which is exactly what Louis XIV had desired.

The crown's administrative reforms in the colony were not all self-serving. Lawyers, as a profession, were excluded from New France in the hope that this would make justice more speedy and less costly than litigation in France. Fixed tariffs of notarial and legal fees were published by the crown in May 1678 and April 1749. Despite these measures, however, the duration and cost of trials was only modestly reduced. Legal expenses in the colony were 10 to 20 percent lower than in France, mainly because documents did not have to bear a tax stamp. Civil actions—usually about a debt—seldom extended beyond three days.[42] The place of barristers was taken by notaries and private attorneys (*praticiens*) versed in law and legal procedures who spoke for litigants in civil cases, so that little was gained from the ban on lawyers. In criminal justice the accused was never permitted legal representation, whether in the colonies or in France.

Government self-interest and concern for the unfortunate merged in the regulation of the food trades in the towns of *la Nouvelle France*. In Paris a shortage of affordable bread provoked riots among the poor, so an ample supply of this staple food helped to maintain public order. "Give us this day our daily bread" in the *Paternoster* was a plea for the means of survival. Adults ate from one-and-a-half to two pounds of wheaten bread a day. In Canada the price of wheat had been set periodically since 1653, and bread price legislation began in the 1670s. The close connection between bread supplies and public tranquillity was acknowledged in 1710 when the *Conseil supérieur* at Quebec increased the number of licensed bakers, to quiet "the murmuring of the people who often cannot find some [bread] when they have the greatest need of it."[43] When grain was dear in 1714, the council received complaints from eight wives of "poor day-laborers" in Quebec. At the same time, rural folk gathered to march to town in protest against the rising price of imported goods.[44] At least eight public demonstrations occurred in New France over the price of grain, of salt, and of trade goods, and over the supply of beef. The demonstrators usually threatened the retailers and demanded that the king's officers intercede to reduce prices. This was an acknowledgment of the crown's prerogative

to regulate the economy. Government officials did not feel threatened by these out-
bursts, and, recognizing that poor colonists had no other outlet for their economic
grievances, punished the leaders with only a fine or a verbal admonition not to
repeat the offense.[45] Protests against a *government* measure or in which the demonstrators were armed were more serious affairs and the participants risked imprisonment and physical punishment. By comparison with France, the colony was a
peaceable place that was seldom disturbed by public displays of discontent.

To avert protest demonstrations and to provide townspeople with an abundance
of wholesome food at the lowest price, the colonial magistrates in each town gathered food retailers in an open market and forbade the sale of foodstuffs elsewhere.
The concentration of vendors facilitated inspection of their wares by royal officials,
and it encouraged competition in quality and price. Laws made it difficult for middlemen to buy up foodstuffs. Ideally, the consumer bought directly from the producer.
Market laws enacted by Quebec's *Conseil souverain* on 11 May 1676 embodied these
objectives. Food sales by farmers and butchers in a designated public market were
to occur on Tuesdays and Fridays. To give town residents first choice, farmers could
not deliver produce to private homes before eleven in the morning. Resellers, such
as innkeepers, were excluded from the market until 8 A.M. in the summer and until
9 A.M. in the winter. All butchers had to operate from rented market stalls, but
bakers were permitted to sell bread from their own shops, which were visited by
court-appointed inspectors. Later, supplementary laws forbade the hoarding of food
supplies by speculators and purchases by resellers from farmers on their way to
market.[46] Similar laws against "engrossers, forestallers," and "regratters" of foodstuffs existed in contemporary England. The difference was that in New France
officials set maximum prices for grain, bread, and beef, whereas in England, justices
of the peace regulated the making and selling of an Englishman's staple foods, to
wit: bread and ale.[47]

The increasing attention given to the butchers' trade at the end of the seventeenth century corresponded with the growing consumption of beef in *la Nouvelle
France*. The colonists ate more meat than their cousins in France. In the 1600s much
of the meat came from wild game, but, as time passed, the colonists relied increasingly on domestic animals for their diet.[48] By the eighteenth century not only was
commercial baking restricted to licensed town bakers, but the butchering of steers
and calves for retail sale within towns was confined to a few authorized butchers,
who agreed to sell meat under prescribed conditions and at officially set prices.
Rural millers were also subject to public-order regulations because their trade involved grain and flour.

The milling fee (*droit de mouture*) to which a Canadian miller was entitled was
one-fourteenth part of the grain ground; this was generous by French standards.

Most flour millers were tenants of seigneurial mills that had to be used by the *censitaires,* or tenants, of that estate. On the other hand, few seigneuries in the St. Lawrence Valley had enough residents to make a mill profitable.[49] A miller's lease, moreover, obliged him to make minor repairs to the gristmill so that it remained "turning and working." Until flour was produced for export, as it was in the second quarter of the 1700s, millers struggled to make a living.

The temptation to take more than a fourteenth in weight as payment must have been irresistible to some millers. Stolen grain could be fed to fowl, and purloined flour might be made into bread for the miller's family. The *Conseil souverain*'s May 1676 and March 1689 regulations stipulated that each milling order was to be ground separately, and insisted that mills have scales and weights so that clients could weigh the grain delivered and the flour received in the miller's presence. Local magistrates were to inspect mills to ensure compliance. In 1700 Quebec's lower court, or *Prévôté*, summoned millers to remind them of the rules. Nonetheless, authorities continued to hear complaints of millers giving short weight in flour, and officials, in turn, threatened seigneurs with forfeiture of their mill right, in addition to a fine, for these infractions.[50] In 1690 a Montreal Island miller who had stolen eighty-four *minots* (bushels) of grain was publicly flogged and branded with a hot iron as an example to others who might do likewise.[51] Inventories made when a new tenant took over a mill show that volume measures were more likely to be present than scales for measuring out the miller's portion, which permitted cheating in the looseness or density of packing.[52] The high social standing of most seigneurs may have discouraged strict enforcement of the laws on mill scales, which would explain the persistent complaints about their absence or of a miller's deception.

After 1676 town retailers were required to bring their measures to the local court for verification and stamping with the royal fleur-de-lis. In the 1680s law courts were to have model weights as well as linear and volume measures, usually conforming to Parisian standards, for an annual certification of private measures.[53] A 1746 letter from the governor-general and intendant of New France said that, until then, law court officials had made the tests using matrices or standards kept in the court registry.[54] Restatement of the laws indicates that testing was not done with the regularity or zeal desired by the Sovereign/Superior Council at Quebec.[55]

When superintending colonists' lives, administrators from France had marked prejudices. They tended to believe that there was a legislative solution for every social problem. Pass a new law, they thought, and the difficulty would be overcome. For example, Intendant Jean Talon attributed the low fertility of aboriginal women to their heavy tasks and to the extended nursing of infants; he then observed that these practices "could be overcome by some public order regulation."[56] Officials were more adept at issuing regulations than at enforcement of existing laws. Numerous laws, ordinances, and decrees were published on a variety of subjects. The duplication of rules on the same subject shows that application was inconsistent and that some laws had passed into oblivion without being officially rescinded. In 1685 the newly arrived governor-general, the Marquis de Denonville, reported that "nothing is finer or better conceived than all the regulations in this country, but I assure you that nothing is so badly observed."[57] One gets the impression that each law expressed the momentary enthusiasm of an administrator or a group of legislators, whose successors, if they did not have the same priorities, would ignore. At one stage Cartesian rationalism determined the laws relating to manual trades.

The legislators' ideal of "good order" was mechanistic as well as hierarchic. Learned officials were influenced by the philosopher René Descartes, who believed that nature consisted of classes of creatures and organs, each of which was designed for a specific function. To Descartes, the spider was nature's spinning and weaving machine. Cartesians saw human society as a mechanism; each person had a predetermined role, much like a cog or wheel, that contributed to the harmonious working of the whole. It followed that, if society were to operate well, people should have a well-defined function and be confined to the duties proper to that role. They also should be kept in the subordination determined by their rank. Cardinal de Richelieu's *Testament Politique* (c.1638) argued that most people could be held to their duty by fear of punishment, which should be exercised liberally. One definition of the purpose of justice in New France was "to contain each person in his duty."[58] With skilled workers, this meant restricting each person to one trade. Intendant Jacques Raudot applied this principle to butchers and leatherworkers in New France during his term of office, from 1705 to 1711.

Butchers produced hides as a byproduct of their trade, and animal skins were sold to tanners, who converted the raw hides into durable, tanned leather, which ought to have been available to the saddlers and shoemakers who needed it. Tanners, however, were entrepreneurs untouched by the tight regulation of the food trades and they saw the financial advantage of an integrated system in which they made the finished leather products as well as controlling the supply of raw material. Canadian tanners hoarded their leather and hired their own shoemakers to use it, cutting out the self-employed cobblers. When four Quebec shoemakers complained about this practice in 1674, the *Conseil souverain* and governor-general issued a decree forbidding tanner Étienne Charest of Pointe-de-Lévy to hire shoemakers and ordering him, "for the public good," to deliver sufficient leather to Quebec for local craftsmen.[59] This was not the end of the matter. In the winter of 1691–92, Quebec shoemakers again lamented that Charest was withholding leather from them.[60] When this tanner died in 1699 his tannery still had an attached shoemaking shop. The

1734 inventory of the estate of his son and heir listed eighty-four pairs of shoes among the items in his tannery, so it appears that the family's little economic empire, combining tanning with shoemaking, was never broken up.[61] Montreal's two tanners played the same game, and there even butchers ventured into tanning and shoemaking, taking the hides from hoofed beasts and, after they had been suitably transformed, putting them on human feet.

In July 1706 Intendant Jacques Raudot issued a comprehensive ordinance to limit butchers, tanners, and shoemakers to their respective trades, "until it might please His Majesty to establish trade corporations," because it would be "useful to all residents, by stimulating rivalry among workers in their craft, at the same time giving each of them the means to subsist by reducing them . . . to the activities suitable to their profession." The town's butchers were to supply each tanner with an equal number of skins, and were not to make French shoes (moccasins excepted) themselves. Butchers were not to buy skins from rural folk, thereby preventing the open sale of hides in the town's marketplace. As a concession to tannery owner Charles Delaunay, "in consideration of the [large] establishment he has made," and, "until we might make a ruling that reduces each of the said workers to the work that pertains to his trade," Delaunay was permitted to employ three journeymen shoemakers and an apprentice cobbler.[62] A year later, Delaunay was allowed to hire an additional shoemaker and, in 1707 and 1710, the number of approved tanners in Montreal was increased.[63] Five tanners were sanctioned in the Quebec district in 1707, "in view of the bad quality of the hides tanned by the country people who do not know the [tanner's] craft or who do not leave the hides long enough in the [tanning] pits."[64] Leather making, evidently, was very profitable, and because tannery owners were often merchants of social standing, administrators were indulgent toward them. Even Intendant Michel Bégon had a tannery on his own seigneury.

Jacques Raudot was exceptional among lawmakers in providing a theoretical justification for his public order regulations beyond the conventional preamble of "it being necessary," or, "having being informed that . . ." Raudot's 1706 ordinance for the leather trades stated his belief that each occupation had a distinct role to play and that craftsmen worked best for the public good when confined to that role. He tried to achieve this division of labor by licensing tradesmen and by encouraging competition among them. During his administration, Raudot restored closely supervised food markets and limited commercial baking and butchering to a fixed number of approved tradesmen. He also made tanning a closed trade and thought about adding brewing to the controlled occupations. There were no craft guilds in *la Nouvelle France,* and every skilled worker was free to pursue his trade, unless the occupation affected public health, such as surgery or butchering. In 1710 Raudot established a second brewer at Quebec, "it being necessary that there be more than one person engaged in the same profession for the good of everyone as much as for the stimulus it will give to contractors and workers to improve their goods in order to sell them, because in future . . . they will charge a more reasonable price. That would never happen when these goods are controlled by the same hand."[65] In the same year he authorized a third tanner for Montreal and encouraged the *Conseil supérieur* to sanction a fifth baker for Quebec because of the others' negligence. Raudot saw the benefits of competition for consumers and encouraged rivalry among producers.

After Raudot's departure in 1711, his system started to fall apart. The next year the Superior Council reprimanded Montreal's crown attorney for challenging a brewer's right to work without official authorization.[66] The attorney's action was consistent with the former intendant's policy of licensing brewers. The next intendant continued to regulate tanners, but in 1729, when twenty-three Montreal shoemakers petitioned the royal *lieutenant-général* to enforce the 1706 ordinance against a butcher who was also engaged in tanning and shoemaking, they seem to have been rebuffed.[67] The magistrate did not share the enthusiasms of Intendant Raudot and did not feel obliged to uphold this law, certainly not at the wish of common shoemakers. After this date, courts did not enforce Raudot's ordinances on tanners, butchers, and shoemakers. Later intendants may have shared his belief in the social benefits of a strict division of labor, but they were not prepared to confine butchers and tanners to just one trade.

This cycle of close economic regulation, associated with an energetic administrator, followed by a period of lassitude when a new man came to power had occurred before. Governor-General Buade de Frontenac, as we have seen, initiated a flurry of public order regulations in the 1670s which, after his departure in 1682, fell into neglect. When Governor-General de Denonville arrived in 1685 he reported, "I had the former police [public order] ordinances examined," and then he tried "to compel the councilors to republish the good ones and, if necessary, add to them," especially those regulations to prevent accidental fires at Quebec.[68] Laws were not formally rescinded; they lapsed for want of enforcement. One cannot assume that a law was continuously applied after enactment, and this uncertainty leaves the colony's administrative history in a fog. New France's government was more fickle and class-conscious in regulating tanners than it was in dealing with the food trades. Inconsistent application of laws was commonplace, and this fact, as well as the inefficiency of the small colonial administration, makes the charge of tyrannical government, raised by Francis Parkman and other historians, unbelievable.

The occasional impulse of legislators to maintain trade specialization was opposed by the colonial tendency toward occupational versatility. The typical colonist was a jack-of-all-trades and called on an artisan's services only when a task was beyond a farmer's resources, such as the manufacture of wheels and iron fittings for a homemade plow. Given this situation and the small colonial population, specialists could not make a living as they might in France. Toolmakers, nailsmiths, and farriers became general blacksmiths who would shoe horses or make door hinges—whatever the client required. A Montreal "coppersmith [*chaudronnier*]" provided the parish church with locks, candelabra, and two fleurs-de-lis for the beadle's staff.[69] At the end of his term of office, Intendant Jacques Raudot wrote that his ambition had always been "to give to all the towns . . . the facilities they might need by making all the establishments we believed were necessary there."[70] His plan to reproduce the institutional order and amenities of urban France in North America was compromised during his intendancy and it was abandoned after his departure. The frequently predicted era, when legislation would confine all colonial craftsmen to their proper functions and when "it might please His Majesty" to establish trade guilds and sworn craft inspectors, never came.

The administrative passion for classifying each social role and for ordering society hierarchically appeared in other fields as well. Governor-General the Marquis de la Galissonière impressed a visiting scientist with his scholarly interest in natural history. The governor-general applied the classification system of Karl Linnaeus, which assumed that every living thing had a discrete and fixed form and could be precisely labeled. According to the foreign visitor, Galissonière "told me of several ways of applying natural history to the purpose of politics, [to] the science of government."[71] The truth was that the prevailing mechanistic view of society predisposed French administrators to accept the Linnean system, and they already regulated civil society with the assumption that there was a category for everything and that each person had a specific role and ought to be kept in his or her place.

Legislative attempts to bring order to the leather trades reveal the officials' abhorrence for unsanctioned monopolies. Like many French adminstrators, Raudot thought that the natural tendency of an unregulated economy was to create private monopolies, and he believed that government intervention was required to prevent this development. Commercial monopolies, he felt, would inflate the price of necessities. Government-approved trade monopolies, such as the Canadian fur-trade concession, were created to entice private entrepreneurs to undertake risky and expensive ventures, or to accept burdensome responsibilities, like the fur companies' duty to subsidize the colony's administration. Thus, a government-granted, limited monopoly could serve the public good, whereas an unrestrained, privately contrived one would be injurious to the population.

Given the dark view of human nature in this Christian society, commercial motives could only be selfish and dangerous. In 1692 the king instructed his representatives in *la Nouvelle France*, when supervising the sale of farmers' produce or merchants' imported goods, to consider "the public interest and His Majesty's service" and to correct "the abuses of inflated cost when it only originates from the greed and usury of the said residents [*habitans*] and merchants."[72] The words "greed and usury" expressed a moralistic distaste for mercantile values. Like the Scottish economist Adam Smith, colonial administrators recognized the social benefits of economic competition. Unlike Smith, they did not consider the market capable of self-regulation. Natural human depravity necessitated government supervision and corrective intervention to maintain fair trade; morality had to be imposed on the marketplace. Nicolas de La Mare's *Traité de la Police* (1705), which guided court officers in New France, affirmed that "the desire for profit is the soul of all kinds of commerce and the mainspring animating all those engaged in trade . . . It is, therefore, in their interest to hide, as it were, from the magistrates' vigilance and from the public eye when buying" or selling.[73] The pursuit of private gain, in this pre-laissez-faire age, would not serve the public good unless the vigilant magistrate forced it to do so.

The greed of the tanners Étienne Charest and Charles Delaunay had confounded economic functions and threatened the free marketing of tanned hides. Butchers, too, were trying to control the supply of raw skins by buying them from countryfolk. This undermined the free sale of hides. Government hostility to commercial middlemen and potential monopolists was evident in the regulation of the food trades, which favored direct purchases by the consumer from the producer. The Cartesian prejudice for restricting people to their "natural" role was beneficial to the populace because it sustained competition and hindered vertical integration of the economy by ambitious entrepreneurs. The colony's administrators appeared at their best when trying to assure a supply of wholesome and cheap bread and beef in the towns, even if they were not always successful in achieving that end.

Far more debatable are the practical consequences of the administrators' economic ideas, commonly called "mercantilism," although not as coherent or as uniform as that label suggests. The fixed objective was to make the parent state economically self-sufficient. Self-sufficiency would stem the outflow of silver and gold—esteemed the only true form of wealth—in payment for imported goods. In Louis XIV's reign the crown assisted the establishment of new industries in France to replace foreign products with domestic manufactures. With official encouragement, French manufacturers produced alternatives for such imports as Flemish tapestries, German tinware, Venetian glass, and Chinese silk. Colonies would contribute to the favorable trade balance by being a reliable source of raw materials and by being a captive market for metropolitan products. The most valuable colonies complemented the parent state's range of natural products and reduced the need for supplies from other kingdoms. There was disagreement over the extent to which colonists would be allowed to process their own raw materials.

Jérôme de Pontchartrain, minister of the navy from 1699 to 1715, was—on paper—an inflexible mercantilist. He drafted the 1704 royal instructions to New France's governor-general and intendant, which stated that

> Whatever can compete with the manufactures of France must never be produced in the colonies. Colonies must act as suppliers of raw materials to enable the manufactories of the kingdom to do without imports from foreign states. . . . Colonies are established solely for the benefit of the mother country and never to be independent of the parent country. . . . Anything that might compete with the kingdom's manufactories must never be made in the colonies.[74]

The rigid mercantilism enunciated by de Pontchartrain would have precluded any industries in the colonies. This 1704 statement was made when rejecting a request that textile weavers be sent to New France, and concluded with a firm assertion that the French crown never intended "that cloth be made in Canada."

As in other areas of stated government ideology, de Pontchartrain's stand was qualified in practice. Three years after the interdict on cloth making in Canada, the crown gave a two-hundred-livre annuity to Agathe Legardeur de Repentigny for having established a weaving shop at Montreal. De Pontchartrain told the intendant that "it is time that this colony supported itself," and he praised the cultivation of flax and hemp as well as sheep raising by the colonists, which would have furnished raw materials for cloth making. Not only did the government foster the colony's self-sufficiency in clothing and food; it subsidized economic diversification. The minister offered government aid to colonial producers of pine pitch and porpoise oil. The porpoise fishery was undertaken by two Quebec merchants, François Hazeur and Pierre Peire. De Pontchartrain told the intendant of New France "to entice other merchants into different enterprises that will be useful to the country, avoiding, above all, any [financial] burden to His Majesty." The colony's raw materials, the minister stated, were supposed to go to France for further processing, but "His Majesty does not wish to absolutely prevent the establishment of any [manufacturing] in Canada, especially when it involves poor people."[75] This 1707 letter was a truer reflection of French economic policy than de Pontchartrain's categorical statement in 1704, which seemed to rule out any manufacturing in New France.

The one case usually cited to prove that economic centralism stifled colonial economic development, the suppression of hat making in *la Nouvelle France* in 1736 upon royal instructions,[76] was really an aberration. The initiative for this act came, not from the crown, but from the *Compagnie des Indes,* whose export monopoly for beaver fur was being bypassed by the exportation of finished and half-finished beaver hats made in Canada. The first order in 1735 for the suppression of colonial hat making also spoke of the need to protect French hatmakers. New France's officials protested that Canada's three hatters were not a serious challenge to France's industry and merely forbade hat exports. The protectionist argument may have been copied from the 1732 English act against hat making in the British colonies. A subsequent dispatch in 1736 ordered New France's officials to close down the colonial hat shops immediately and to destroy their equipment, and this was done. The belief that protection of an export monopoly, rather than of an industry in France, was paramount comes from an earlier refusal of the Maritime Council to assist a Parisian hatter who offered to establish a manufactory in Canada: "denied; the Mississippi Company [or *Compagnie des Indes*] has the exclusive privilege for beaver [fur exports]."[77]

For most of its history as a crown colony, New France benefited from a policy of decentralized mercantilism. The ministers Jean-Baptiste Colbert (fl.1666–83) and Jean Frédéric de Maurepas (fl.1723–48) hoped to make the colony into a strong ally of the parent state, self-sufficient in necessities. Given the weakness of the French navy, overseas possessions had to be capable of surviving an enemy blockade. They could not do this if they remained dependent upon France for foodstuffs or other essentials. Agriculture was to be the foundation of the colony's economy, which was also allowed some basic industries. Colbert's agent in Canada, Intendant Jean Talon, was told in 1665 "that one of the greatest of Canada's needs is to establish manufactures and to attract craftsmen there for [making] those things necessary for life." To this end, the king "will contribute by opening his coffers."[78] Assistance to new ventures took the form of direct grants, advance purchase orders at favorable prices, subsidies, free transportation of men and materials, and expert advice. Had it not been for royal aid, many industrial enterprises in *la Nouvelle France,* such as large-scale shipbuilding, would never have existed. Colbert believed that the establishment of primary and extractive industries in Canada would hold the colony's population in the St. Lawrence Valley settlements, curtailing the loss of manpower to the fur trade, and it would stimulate intercolonial commerce.

Royal help was given generously to entrepreneurs in pitch extraction, soap making, beer brewing, potash production, slate quarrying, hemp cultivation, fishing, and ironworking. Direct subsidies went to undertakings that required a large capital expenditure, as in the case of the St. Maurice ironworks. After a Montreal merchant, François Poulin de Francheville, communicated his plan to mine iron ore near Trois-Rivières to Intendant Gilles Hocquart in 1729, the royal administration gave Francheville and his associates a land grant, a twenty-year mining monopoly, and free transportation for the workers and tools from France needed to build his smelter, and agreed to advance him ten thousand livres for this project. The intendant and governor-general were enthusiastic about the St. Maurice ironworks because the furnace and foundry could produce the iron fittings needed by ship-builders and satisfy de Maurepas's desire to make New France self-reliant in essential goods, such as the bar iron used by blacksmiths. At this time all iron had to be imported from France. The government paid experts to assess the operation and to provide advice. Competing ironworks were forbidden. More money was lent to bring the works to completion. The entrepreneurs were pushed into developing, not just a simple puddling furnace, but a charcoal-fed, blast furnace with water-powered bellows and two forges. Production began in 1738, after de Francheville's death. A new private company under François-Etienne Cugnet was running the enterprise when it failed in 1741. By then the crown's investment had surpassed 190,000 livres in loans, not to speak of help in kind and in services. Because the government was the principal investor, it assumed control of the works. As a state-owned industry, the St. Maurice ironworks barely paid for its costs. With a workforce of about 120 men, the foundry and associated forges manufactured cauldrons, cannonballs, stoves, bar iron, and ship fittings.[79] Without government encouragement and aid, the St. Maurice Ironworks would not have existed. It and the shipyards at Quebec were the largest manufacturing industries in New France.

Under Intendants Jean Talon (fl.1665–68, 1670–72) and Gilles Hocquart (fl.1729–48), government-assisted shipbuilding at Quebec City was to be pivotal in the development of a diversified economy that would free Canada from dependence on fur exports for revenue. Talon gave contracts to shipwrights and offered buyers of locally built ships a cash bonus, based on the vessel's tonnage. In 1671, forty thousand livres were allocated for these government incentives. Hocquart paid bounties to private shipbuilders and established a second shipyard at Quebec to construct large vessels for the king. The shipbuilders' needs would encourage the extraction of timber, iron, and pitch, while fostering flax and hemp production for the making of sails and ropes. Other secondary industries, such as sawmills and metalworking shops, would be needed to process raw materials for the shipbuilders. Ultimately, vessels built in New France could be used for a colonial fishery and for trade with the French West Indies, for whom *Canadiens* would produce barrel staves, livestock, flour, and peas. The logic of this scheme to use shipbuilding to stimulate primary and secondary industries and then to facilitate deep-water fishing and intercolonial trade was impeccable. The scheme had some success: the value of goods exported from Canada rose to exceed the cost of the settlement's imports—mainly French manufactured goods and liquor—in 1731, 1739, and 1741. Intendant Hocquart's valuation of Canadian exports in 1739 laid bare the St. Lawrence Valley's persistent dependence on an old staple: 70 percent in furs, only 18 percent in farm produce, and 9 percent in fish and fishery byproducts, such as oil. Iron and wood products accounted for another 2 percent of Canada's exports.[80] So many vessels from Canada arrived at the French port of La Rochelle in ballast, because of their small return cargoes, that it was possible to pave one entire city street there, *rue de l'Escale,* with Canadian ballast stones.

Explanations for Canada's poor performance as a net exporter have encompassed a shortage of skilled labor, the high cost of colonial workers, a small domestic market, distance from potential markets, competition from cheaper suppliers, a lack of local capital for industrial investment, and managerial incompetence.[81] There is a possibility that the construction of large warships and transports in the king's shipyard after 1740 diverted manpower and resources from private shipbuilding, which nearly ceased thereafter. Wartime conditions also deterred maritime activities. On the whole, however, the French government's economic policies were more helpful than restrictive. The diversification of the economy was the result of government aid and incentives. Without the crown's intervention, New France would have been a more primitive and fragile colony, dependent upon the mother country for its basic needs. Apart from the suppression of hat making, the only other activity forbidden to *Canadiens* was the cultivation of tobacco for export—that was reserved for the Caribbean colonists. Laws against direct trade with foreign possessions were frequently evaded. Scholars' preoccupation with exports and overseas commerce have led to a gloomy verdict on the colony's economy, yet there was internal activity not evident in trade figures, and the domestic economy had its successes.

Royal aid was given to individual tradesmen and was as fruitful as the subsidies to major ventures, such as the St. Maurice ironworks. Enlistment in the *Troupes de la Marine,* the colonial garrison troops, provided many skilled workers with an assisted passage to North America. In 1685, soldiers with a manual trade were given leave to work for civilian employers for low wages set by the administration. Some craftsmen were discharged from the garrison troops to marry and to settle in the colony. In 1727, for example, Jacques Armand, the son of a Parisian pewterer, was released from the colonial troops to work at his craft. His father sent him copper molds for casting pewterware, and they were transported *gratis* on the king's ships. In the following year the crown offered a free passage to Canada to any cutlers and wood sawyers wishing to emigrate from France.[82] This was similar to French government policy in the previous century of sending out specialist-tradesmen to expand the range of crafts available to the colonists.[83] Thanks to such small-scale beneficence, *la Nouvelle France* developed a sturdy domestic economy that met the colonists' needs in food, clothing, metalwork, and housing.

Even if the French government's economic ambitions for New France were not fully realized, the colony fulfilled the government's administrative goals. It was more culturally homogenous and more thoroughly Roman Catholic than France itself; there was a uniformity in civil laws, weights and measures; and political authority was concentrated in the hands of a centralized, royal administration. Colonists, as individuals, were admitted into government as the king's appointees; they had no collective right to participate, even as advisers. No private institutions, not even the church, were capable of resisting the king's writ or will. True, the ideal of a static hierarchy of well-delineated occupations had not been achieved and, given human ambition and vanity, it would never be attained. The royal doctrine of the king's supreme and unquestioned paternal authority was shared, in a fashion, by the colony's other principal institutions. Family, church, and state were imbued with compassionate authoritarianism. Like the monarch, the bishop of Quebec and family heads were to conduct themselves as stern father figures. The French crown, by its institutional reforms, had remade the colony into a truly renewed version of France. That institutional legacy was not seriously challenged before the British Conquest and, moreover, the nature of the immigrants who came from Europe to *la Nouvelle France* ensured that they would submit to the king's imposed order as they found it and not attempt to change it.

CHAPTER 4

The Difficulty of Finding Settlers
for New France and the Reluctant Exile
of Manon Lescaut's Countrymen

ABBÉ ANTOINE-FRANÇOIS PRÉVOST'S *HISTOIRE DU CHEVALIER DES GRIEUX ET DE Manon Lescaut* (1731) is the story of a young gentleman whose passion for a courtesan led him into a series of misfortunes. Des Grieux sacrificed reputation and fortune, even a religious calling, to be with the faithless Manon. Their plan to cheat an aged patron of Manon led to their arrest and confinement in Paris. The chevalier's father arranged for the liberation of his son, but the *lieutenant-général de police* offered Manon only lifelong imprisonment or deportation to Louisiana. Abbé Prévost described her sentence as "cruel." When Des Grieux's plan to rescue her miscarried, he begged her guards to let him accompany her to Havre-de-Grace, there to embark together for the Americas. He assured Manon "that I was disposed to follow her to the end of the world, to care for her, to serve her, to love her, and to bind my miserable destiny inseparably to hers." "I had lost," he said, "all that mankind values, but I was master of Manon's heart."[1]

The author described New Orleans, Louisiana's capital, as a cluster of poor huts in a plain of reeds and leafless trees, where inhabitants shared "their misery and their solitude" with the exiled newcomers. The author knew little of New Orleans or the Lower Mississippi's delta, which is verdant, low-lying, and swampy. The lovers set up house in a rude cabin, but Manon died after Des Grieux had fled, thinking he had killed the governor's nephew in a duel over her. The mistake was corrected, alas, too late, and the ruined chevalier returned to France alone. Abbé Prévost claimed that he had written down the entire tragic tale at Calais as he heard it from the pale and careworn exile's own lips.

The story of Manon and Des Grieux confirmed French readers' prejudices about colonists in French America. While the eighteenth-century European view of the native peoples was increasingly sympathetic, the white settlers there were painted in contrastingly dark hues. There was an unshakeable and widespread conviction that France's overseas possessions had been colonized by deported criminals, prostitutes, and social outcasts. The preconception was an old one. Jacques Cartier had been empowered in 1540 to draw fifty men from prisons to take them to Canada, yet such forced emigrants were rare in the European settlement of French North America. The shipment to Louisiana of vagabonds, deserters, Gypsies, and *filles publiques,* such as Manon Lescaut, took place only in 1717–21 and these outcasts accounted for less than a fifth of the 7,020 European colonists dispatched to the southern colony during those years. Most settlers in Louisiana were voluntary migrants, often arriving with families. From 1721 to 1749 some 720 poachers, sellers of untaxed salt, or petty offenders were transported to New France—a small fraction of the 27,000 who embarked for the northern colony.

No matter, people in France were convinced that the American colonies were a dumping ground for Europe's human refuse. In 1641 Father Paul Le Jeune complained about a false rumor in Paris that "a vessel had sailed to Canada laden with girls whose virtue did not have the approval of any doctor."[2] That was certainly the expectation of Marc-Antoine de Gérard, Sieur de Saint-Amant, whose poem "Le Poète crotté" (1649) foretold the fate of the Parisian demimonde:

Adieu, maquerelles et garces	*Farewell pimps and whores*
Je vous prevoy bien d'autres farces . . .	*I forsee many other comic interludes for you . . .*
Dans peu vous et vos protecteurs	*In a little time, you and your protectors*
Serez hors de France bannies	*Will be banished from France*
Pour aller planter colonies	*To go and establish colonies*
En quelque Canada loingtain	*In some distant Canada*[3]

In the 1660s, during a visit to the mother country, *Canadien* Pierre Boucher was asked, "if justice reigns there [in Canada]; if there is no debauchery since, it is said, a quantity of ne'er-do-wells [*garnemens*] and loose women [*filles mal-vivantes*] are sent there?"[4] This unjustified conviction about the Canadians' ancestors was shared by English-speakers. When the Quebec prison-house, in which British captives were held, caught fire in 1746, local townsfolk shouted that the prisoners in the yard ought to have been left in the burning building to fry, because they, undoubtedly, had set the fire. A British-American colonist among the prisoners wrote, "what else could be Expected of the Canadians, when

> *Hither from all parts of France they come*
> *The Spew and Vomit of their Jayls at home."*[5]

The widespread belief in France that the American colonies had been settled by the dregs of European society and by their descendants strengthened a repugnance to emigrate overseas. The New World was a place of cruel exile to which few would freely consent. Transatlantic migration was never accepted as a common solution to unemployment and hunger at home. There was a frequently cited belief, too, that France's peasants were afraid of losing sight of their parish church's steeple to earn their bread elsewhere.[6] On the contrary, the kingdom's peoples were surprisingly mobile, within limits. There was a constant interchange of residents between neighboring towns and contiguous parishes through marriage. One spouse would move a few kilometers to the other's home community to establish a new household. The smaller one's home village, the more unavoidable such moves were, since suitable partners were scarce in one's birthplace. This perpetual, short-range movement within a region did not disrupt the stability of agricultural villages. In fertile regions, without population pressure on the available resources, only a tenth of the families ever left their home region permanently. Rural life was stable as long as famine and war remained at a distance.

People living on infertile land were forced to travel beyond a fifty-kilometer radius to find work to supplement their meager returns from the land, rather than abandon their home permanently. The forest dwellers of Perche Province brought in the crops of the Beauce, while mountain folk of south-central France worked seasonally as harvesters on the rich plains of Languedoc and Aquitaine. Similar to these migratory farm laborers were the fishermen and whalers from Brittany and Gascony who harvested the cod and whales in North American waters for a season or even for a few years. These periodic and extended absences represented a higher level of emigration, beyond the matrimonial interchange between villages. These migrants, however, always intended to return home, and their earnings helped to maintain relatives left behind on the unproductive land of the absentees' birthplace. In France this was the accepted pattern against which overseas migration was judged.

Seasonal departures could evolve into permanent resettlement outside France. Population pressure in the southwest during the sixteenth century impelled French subjects to move across the Pyrenees to Spanish Catalonia and from the Auvergne to Valencia on Spain's Mediterranean coast. Up to 20 percent of Catalonia's adult male population in 1570–1620 was of French origin.[7] Such masssive population shifts were precipitated by prolonged hunger or a calamity, such as the passage of a plundering army.

Less dramatic was the steady movement of countryfolk and villagers into France's cities. Farmers' sons were sent to learn a manual trade from urban craftsmen and country girls went there to work as household servants. Towns and cities, which always lost more people than the countryside to epidemics, replenished their population with rural newcomers, and they would not have grown without this constant infusion of new people. In the seventeenth and eighteenth centuries the French provinces of Flanders and Normandy, as well as the Massif Central region, contributed heavily to this flow into the towns; their people had long before outgrown the soil's capacity to feed all. The surplus people hoped to find work in towns as servants and semiskilled laborers or, at least, to survive as beggars. The greater the city, the more powerful was its magnetism for wanderers seeking a living. Bordeaux and Lyon exerted a strong pull. Jean-Pierre Poussou found that 40 percent of the grooms and 25 percent of the brides married at Bordeaux in 1731–91 had been born outside this metropolis.[8] Paris, the largest city of the realm, drew migrants from the entire kingdom and beyond. There it was proverbial that construction workers were from Limousin, while Savoy supplied the best chimney sweeps. In the 1770s Louis-Sébastien Mercier wrote that in Paris, "the Savoyards are shoe-cleaners, floor polishers, and wood sawyers; those from Auvergne are almost all water-carriers; the Limousins are masons; people from Lyon are usually porters and sedan-chair carriers; Normans [are] stone-cutters, pavers, and thread-peddlers."[9] The migrants from each region of provincial France had an occupational niche to fill in Paris. Regional craft specialization was also evident in the migration to *la Nouvelle France*. Colonial recruiters reached beyond the western coastal provinces and Ile-de-France, which supplied most of Canada's immigrants, to obtain stonemasons from Limousin and Marche or metalworkers from Gascony. Normandy supplied a disproportionate number of immigrant timber-framers in the seventeenth century.[10]

One-way emigration to another state was a step beyond the resettlement of provincials in the great cities of France. Contemporaries noted the diffusion of French craftsmen and servants into the Netherlands the German and Italian states, as well as into Spain. The eighteenth-century European passion for French fashions, manners, and speech ensured employment for musicians, governesses, wigmakers, dancing masters, gentlemen's tailors, and lackeys from France. Mass migrations out of the kingdom, however, were exceptional. The flight of some two hundred thousand Huguenots into nearby Protestant territories at the end of the seventeenth century was an aberration. Subsequent migrations carried the French Protestants from the Netherlands and Britain to South Africa and to the British North American colonies, especially New York. In the late 1600s there were probably more French-speakers in New York Province than in the neighboring colony of New France. These refugees were not welcome in Canada and they had every reason to fear Louis XIV, who had outlawed their religion. Thus, French Calvinists had a small role in the settlement of French North America.

Migration within France affected all social classes, although mobility was tempered by occupation. Landowning peasants were least likely to undertake long voyages,[11] while merchants were accustomed to long-distance travel. Young journeymen-craftsmen often made a tour of the realm before establishing themselves in a town. The kingdom's roads were traveled by a floating population, both skilled and unskilled. Unemployed textile and clothing workers were especially numerous among those seeking work away from home; they provided volunteers for the army. Then there were the distrusted beggars, Gypsies, and vagabonds (*gens sans aveu*) who were harried out of towns during food shortages. Among the "foreign" beggars who died at La Rochelle, there were some who had traveled more than five hundred kilometers, from Mons Diocese and from Arles.[12] Some vagabonds were forcibly dispatched to the colonies,[13] while others, including tradesmen without work, willingly agreed to go to the Americas to serve as indentured workers. Men enrolled in French ports for the colonies were drawn from the internal migrants who had sought work in the coastal cities.

The connection between existing migration patterns within France and emigration to the overseas possessions is evident in the nature of those people recruited as contract workers or as soldiers for the colonies. Townsfolk were disproportionately represented in the net migration to seventeenth-century New France. Over half of the migrants going to the St. Lawrence Valley were from towns, at a time when France's urban residents constituted just 15 percent of the kingdom's population. From a sample of 454 people who made a permanent home in *la Nouvelle France,* Richard Colebrook Harris observed that "about half of the immigrants were artisans, whereas agricultural people were not more than a quarter, and may have been less than one fifth of the total."[14] Larger samples yielded similar results: two-thirds of the French emigrants came from cities and large towns; a third or less came from rural villages or the countryside.[15] Most recruits came from the cities because townsfolk were more loosely attached to their birthplace than were farming people, because recruiters worked within seaports, and because the cities were already full of internal migrants, for whom an American colony was but one more stop on the journey from home in search of paid work.

Atlantic seaports, as cities, took in a part of the kingdom's floating population, and recruiters of emigrants drew from this transient element; hiring agents seldom ventured inland to find candidates. For example, of 106 men enlisted for the marine soldiers' companies on Ile Royale in 1748–49, 103 were enrolled in the seaports of Rochefort, La Rochelle, and Bordeaux.[16] A study of the geographic origins of the immigrants show that most came from Atlantic ports serving the Americas (Dieppe, Rouen, St. Malo, Granville, Nantes, La Rochelle, Bordeaux, and Bayonne) or their immediate hinterland. Two-thirds of the men indentured at La Rochelle came from the town, the surrounding province of Aunis, and the adjoining province of Saintonge. Aunis and Saintonge belonged to one distinct region served by the ports of La Rochelle and Rochefort. In the early seventeenth century the coastal province of Normandy, long an exporter of people, provided nearly a fifth of the emigrants for Canada. The two principal ports of embarkation for the American colonies were La Rochelle and Bordeaux. From 1634 to 1715 the Rochelais dominated French trade with the Americas, and 6,100 indentured workers (*engagés*) for the colonies were signed up before local notaries. The number registered in 1715–72 had dropped to 1,200.[17] By this time La Rochelle was being eclipsed by Bordeaux, where 6,500 workers were enrolled for the Americas in 1698–1771.[18]

Despite being inland, Paris and surrounding Ile-de-France provided a tenth of all the colonists for the St. Lawrence Valley.[19] This was because the kingdom's metropolis was itself a destination for internal migrants. Paris' role was also inflated by the fact that nearly a third of the eight hundred women sent by the crown to New France in 1663–73 as potential brides—the so-called "daughters of the king" (*filles du roi*)—were drawn from a Paris hospice (*hôpital-général*) for orphans.[20] These women bore no resemblance to Manon Lescaut. To sum up, the long-established internal migration to the cities was the main source of voluntary passengers for France's American colonies.

The distinctive character of Acadia is evident from the indentures made at La Rochelle for this part of New France before the British occupied Acadia in 1654. Trading companies and patent holders were the principal recruiters, and they hired men for commercial outposts that were also concerned with fishing. The 104 men they enrolled in 1634–54 can be compared with 141 men also signed up at La Rochelle for the St. Lawrence Valley [Canada] in 1641–54:

	ACADIA	CANADA
Building trades	31%	18%
Soldiers/Sailors	15%	17%
Food preparers	8%	2.2%
Farm workers	6.7%	37.5%
Clothing trades	6.7%	1.6%

The difference in the proportion of agricultural workers, or *laboureurs,* hired under-lined the minor role of farming in Acadia at this time. By comparison, agriculture was the prime concern of recruiters seeking contract laborers for the St. Lawrence Valley.[21] In both cases, military insecurity produced a need for soldiers as well as for manual workers.

In the 1640s and 1650s colonial recruiters from the St. Lawrence Valley en-rolled groups from the interior of Poitou and Perche Provinces. The presence of Poitevins and Percherons—16.5 percent of the pre-1700 emigrants to the St. Lawrence Valley—draws our attention to the influence of recruiting methods upon emigration.[22] Under its 1627 charter, the Company of One Hundred Associates was obliged to bring out four thousand immigrants to New France over the next fifteen years. English attacks upon company vessels and the temporary loss of Quebec in 1629–32 so weakened the enterprise that it alone could not meet its obligations as a colonizer. The company then transferred part of its colonizing duty to recipients of estates, who were landless gentlemen or religious groups. In 1634 Beauport Seigneury was granted to Robert Giffard, a gentleman-surgeon, with the proviso that every person that he or his heirs brought out from France would be counted as part of the total that the company was bound to deliver. Giffard returned to his home at Mortagne in Perche and arranged to have forty-three people join his family and settle on his Canadian seigneury. A surviving contract with a stonemason and a carpenter shows the high price he had to pay to obtain colonists. Giffard agreed to transport the two to Canada and to provide them with food, lodging, and mainte-nance, "in all their necessities," for three years while they helped him clear and cultivate his estate. In addition, they would receive half of the land they cleared, not as tenants but as subseigneurs, plus one thousand acres of wild land near the river. Giffard was to bring out their families two years later and to provide each family with two cows. He kept his part of the bargain, but the ungrateful workers argued that all the lands they had received were noble estates and that they did not owe him tenants' dues.[23] Noël Juchereau Des Chatelets, a member of the Company of One Hundred Associates, and his brothers were also Percheron gentlemen who re-cruited some forty colonists in their home province—primarily at Tourouvre—during the 1640s. Land-clearers were needed in Canada and three-quarters of those recruits whose trades were identified (twenty-three out of thirty-one) were described as "laborers" (*manoeuvres*) or "plowmen" (*laboureurs*). Three made advance arrange-ments for their return to France and one asked that his salary be paid to his wife at home. All had been promised a paid passage back to Europe, and two-thirds of them took this option and left New France.[24]

In the next decade, agents of *la Société de Notre-Dame,* which had received Montreal Island as a seigneury, returned to La Flèche in Anjou, home of the company's business manager, Jérôme Le Royer de la Dauversière, to sign up indentured workers, families, unmarried girls, and some nuns. 119 men were enrolled in 1653, and two-thirds of them were hired to clear and cultivate the land. Eleven of the artisans were employed "en qualité de défricheurs," showing that their skills were of less account in a pioneer settlement.[25] In 1659 a contingent of 109 people, including forty women, was gathered for Montreal at La Flèche. Residents of this French city were convinced that these respectable women were being taken by force to Canada—for what decent person would go there willingly?—and rioters prevented the emigrants' departure until men escorting the group drew their swords to scatter the crowd.[26] Even in places where they were well known, recruiters had to offer extraordinary benefits to attract workers. Merchants who speculated in service contracts for resale in the Americas seldom ventured so far inland, and they were not as generous to their recruits.

In the decade after 1655 direct contracts with colonial employers were outnumbered by impersonal, speculative indentures that were made for resale to an unidentified buyer in New France. The servant was bound "to go and serve him [the recruiter] or others assigned his authority at Quebec." Merchant-traders in the French seaports hired men, sometimes in groups, with one standard agreement made before a notary. Speculative recruiters were not as selective as colonial employers, and the terms they offered were more uniform and less advantageous to the worker. Most of the recruits were young men. A land-clearer (*défricheur*) or manual laborer commanded from sixty to seventy-five livres a year in the 1650s. If a special skill were desired, building tradesmen, millers, and experienced farmhands were preferred, and they received up to one hundred livres annually.[27] No Frenchman would work for three years in a colony for just his upkeep and a passage across the ocean. The promise of a prepaid return passage faded away for the unskilled men. The return passage became conditional in 1655: "if the custom of the land is that masters are obliged to return their servants [to France] at their expense," and then it disappeared for most workers. Because the merchants offered less, the men they obtained were of lower quality: a few were very young or very old, and many had no trade that would be useful in North America.

The growing impersonality of recruitment is evident in the contracts registered with Pierre Moreau, a La Rochelle notary. In 1656 he noted the occupation of most contact workers and the age of a few. In 1657 the age was given and the occupation, if there were one, ignored. Men were needed, no matter what their background, and the speculators' criteria for employment were age and physique. A robust man was given a premium of ten to twenty livres over the minimum salary of sixty livres a year. Many deeds were drafted in advance, with blank spaces that were sometimes not filled in.[28] A score or more men were hired each year to fill the trading ships of

La Rochelle. Men had become a commodity to be sold with the rest of the cargo for a profit. Typical of the speculative contracts made by French merchants is this deed of 27 March 1656:

> Be it known to all that before Pierre Moreau, notary, royal scrivener, and hereditary keeper of records in the town and jurisdiction of La Rochelle, here resident, [appeared] Jean Chauveau called La Fleur from St. Pierre on Oléron [Island] and Jacques Jouin called l'Aiguille [the needle] from Chéré on the said island, [acting] for their part, and Sieur Jacques Pepin, merchant of this town acting for himself and for his associates [*ses consors*], on the other part. The said parties have freely made [this agreement] between themselves, as follows—That is to say, that the said Chauveau and Jouin have hired themselves to Pepin to go and serve him or others bearing his authority at Quebec in New France for the period of three consecutive years, beginning on the day they arrive at the said place. To this end, Pepin in his [partners'] name will embark them on a vessel, feed them during the voyage and during the said three years. The servants will be bound to well and duly serve and obey in all that may be commanded of them. This [indenture of] servitude is made in consideration of 84 *livres tournois* [payable] every year to each of said servants, who separately acknowledge having received 84 livres, 13 sols as an advance [*pour le parsus*] on their salary, which will be paid by Pepin or the others at Quebec designated by him as each year passes. . . . Concluded at La Rochelle in the study of the said notary, on the morning of the 27th day of March 1656 in the presence of Jean Combaud and François Gillois, clerks living in La Rochelle, and the said Chauveau declared that he did not know how to sign [his name] upon being summoned to do so.[29]

The enthusiasm of French merchants and shipowners for enrolling contract workers for resale in the Americas was confined to the decade of 1655–65. The surge in contracting initiated by the merchants, evident in table 1: "Indentures at La Rochelle," was sustained in the 1660s by the French government. The crown entered the business of shipping *engagés* to New France in 1662 and paid for their transportation and for any advances up to 35 livres. This lowered the cost of the workers' indentures in the colony to 30 to 35 livres. The hiring and delivery of the men was subcontracted to merchants who had some experience in this line of commerce. The crown paid about 100 livres for each man: ten for recruiting, thirty for a clothing allowance advanced, and sixty for the sea voyage.[30] The king's transportation subsidy continued until 1671. Because the French crown did not recover Acadia until 1670, the Atlantic region benefited from only one shipment of about sixty people before the program of government-assisted migration ended. At La Rochelle

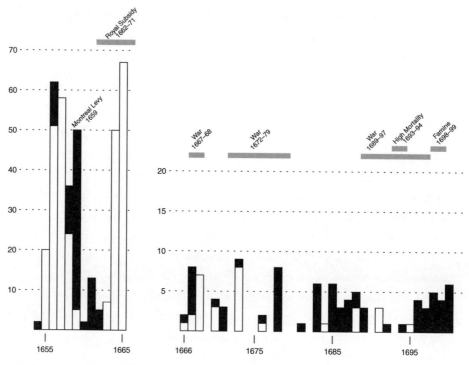

Indentures at La Rochelle for the St. Lawrence Valley, 1654–1760.

private employers hired only thirty men—half of them mariners—for Acadia during the rest of the century.

The royal program subsidizing the transportation of contract workers to New France in 1662–71 encountered the resistance of healthy adults to overseas travel, yet it was also restrained by the government's unreasonable fear that overseas migration would weaken France. The kingdom's population of some twenty million was regarded as the foundation of its great military power. In 1661 Louis XIV promised to send three hundred men a year to Canada for the next ten years. A few thousand French subjects were to be added to the colony's population, which was then to grow by natural increase and absorption of Amerindian Christians. The government feared a reduction in France's population by mass emigration, even to its own colonies. When Intendant Jean Talon suggested that more families be encouraged to come to Canada, the minister responsible for colonies, Jean-Baptiste Colbert, replied bluntly in 1666, "the King cannot agree. . . . He could not employ his power to that end. It would not be prudent to depopulate his kingdom, as it would do, to populate Canada," and, moreover, there was not enough cleared land in the colony to feed a host of new arrivals. "The country will become populated gradually," concluded the minister. The skeptical intendant acknowledged the

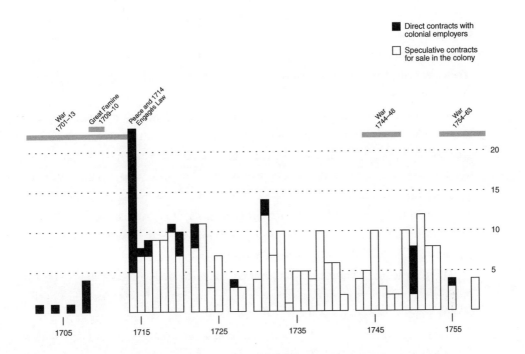

minister's surprising belief "that there are not enough superfluous and useless subjects in old France to populate the new [France]."[31] At that time the king was paying for the transportation of about two hundred men to Canada each year. At first the navy's transport ships were used as carriers, but the high death rate on board them led the crown to pay merchants to convey servants on privately owned vessels.

At Quebec the Sovereign Council took charge of distributing the people delivered at the king's expense and used this power to supply its members and their friends with cheap labor.[32] The councilors complained that the first contingent sent out in 1662–63 contained "several persons unsuited for work or the clearing of land, whether because of their advanced age, infirmities, illnesses or because of ill-usage and misconduct [*a cause de leurs sévices et mauvais déportemens*] while coming on the said vessels. Among their number are some discharged soldiers, all of whom are now public charges. . . . It would be appropriate to send them back to France." The healthy and well-inclined servants were mostly "young clerks, schoolchildren, or [people] of that nature; the best part of whom have never worked."[33] These complaints had some effect: the three hundred men delivered in 1664 were healthy and ready to work upon landing. Quality lapsed again, and in 1667 the intendant bemoaned the levy delivered by the *Compagnie des Indes occidentales*: "Instead of four hundred good men . . . I have received only 127, very weak, or low age, and of little service."[34] He asked that "passengers for Canada" be between sixteen and forty years of age and that "no idiot, cripple, chronically ill person or wayward sons under arrest" be sent; that was a clue to the nature of the people who had disembarked at Quebec in 1667.[35]

In 1682, a decade after the royal subsidy for transporting migrants to New France had lapsed, Intendant Jacques de Meulles asked for a restoration of the program because, "we have an acute need for workers and day-laborers."[36] The result was disappointing: the sixty workers who arrived in 1684 were "little children," aged twelve to fourteen, "fit, at most, to tend cows." The intendant permitted an extension of their period of service to four or five years to entice colonists to buy up their contracts.[37] In France few mature and vigorous men, it appears, would volunteer to work for an unknown master in a distant colony.

The recruiting of volunteers was carried out with little advertising. Merchant shipowners publicized emigration opportunities by having priests include a notice with the public announcements read out in church or by having a public crier read out their offer of employment in the Americas, after summoning listeners with a drum roll or a trumpet call. Those interested in the offer were directed to a well-known tavern or inn to be enrolled. Alluring accounts of Louisiana appeared in the *Nouveau Mercure* and in German-language gazettes. Posters and flyers were used to obtain *engagés* for Cayenne (French Guiana) and the French West Indies; none promoting travel to New France have ever been found. Still, this does not mean that they never existed; a 1664 poster of the *Compagnie des Indes occidentales* inviting workers to come to the southern colonies has survived, and the same company enrolled people for Canada.[38]

At the recruiter's announced rendezvous, a local merchant, sometimes representing the crown or an employer in the colony, enrolled all comers. A service contract was drawn up by a notary and each worker's particulars were noted. Colonists seeking only a few servants in particular trades conducted their business in the notary's home. *Engagés* were usually given a cash advance of thirty to thirty-five livres, to buy clothes and small necessities, and were quartered in a quayside inn until embarkation on the ship. The shorter the waiting period the better because invariably a few men regretted their accord and fled with the advance on their pay.

Colonial employers and their agents were always more discriminating than the merchant-recruiters or the king's agents. Employers from New France wanted to see what they were getting, and they sought skilled specialists and mature men. As an illustration, a Quebec surgeon, Gabriel Baudouin, had his wife hire an assistant when she was in France. In 1692 she found a thirty-eight-year-old surgeon-pharmacist from Dauphiné willing to serve her husband for three years in return for transportation, food, lodging, laundry services, and the payment of one hundred livres a year. The employee stipulated that he would have "the liberty of returning to France at his own expense, . . . or of quitting [*de se retirer*] whenever he wished."[39] In the late 1600s the Quebec Seminary hired building and clothing craftsmen in France, relying on correspondents or visitors to the homeland to find the men needed. In 1707 a priest in Paris, who had been asked to hire a brickmaker for the seminary, lamented, "I did not want one from the provinces, such as Normandy or elsewhere, but no one wanted to go to Canada. . . . It is no small difficulty to find a faithful and industrious man who is not immoral and who has the fear of God." These sounded more like the specifications for a *donné*. A visiting builder-architect from Quebec, who thought himself "too great a lord," refused to help the priest in his search.[40]

In the eighteenth century, the flow of contract workers was directed to new settlements on Cape Breton (*Ile Royale*) and Prince Edward Island (*Ile St. Jean*). Ile St. Jean had been a French fishing station until 1719, when it was granted as a commercial concession and seigneury to Louis-Hyacinthe Castel, Comte de Saint-Pierre. The company he and his associates formed was a short-lived enterprise. The *Compagnie de l'ile Saint-Jean* was responsible for colonizing Prince Edward Island, and in 1720–23 it hired 116 men and several women at La Rochelle. This was a pioneering effort: 30 percent of the workers were destined to clear and break land and 14 percent provided a full range of building trades. Upon the agricultural foundations, the company established a cod and seal fishery. It had coopers and cask sealers to pack seal oil and green cod as well as sawyers and carpenters to erect houses and fishing platforms. This was a well-conceived venture that brought out twenty married couples and three brides-to-be in the 1720 levy. Marriage fever was fanned by the company's promise to release any contract servant who might marry on Ile St. Jean. To show its sincerity, the company paid for the passage of nine daughters and unattached women, as well as of a venerable midwife.[41] Despite this, the farming and fishing colony on Prince Edward Island foundered. Colonists were caught between the company's trade monopoly and competition from interlopers in the fishery. The company's bankruptcy and a famine in 1724 forced many settlers to move to Ile Royale. The French crown revoked the concession. In the end, Acadians from Nova Scotia provided more colonists than did the immigrants from France. The service indentures made for Ile St. Jean were direct, personal contracts, whereas most of the workers arriving at Quebec after 1713 had been enrolled by French merchants under speculative indentures. No speculative contracts had been made at La Rochelle from 1696 to 1713 and if the government had not intervened, this impersonal form of hiring people in France might have disappeared.

Large-volume speculative recruiting of contract workers for the St. Lawrence Valley settlements had almost ceased at La Rochelle after 1673 (See table 1: "Indentures at La Rochelle"). The cheaper workers whose passage was paid for by the crown had undermined private commerce in bond laborers, but that was not the whole story. The speculative trade in bond servants with New France was a junior branch of the larger business with the Caribbean islands.[42] For every man hired at La Rochelle in 1634–1718 for New France, five were enrolled for the French West Indies. Traffic in men for the West Indies did not fall off so abruptly, although it followed the same pattern. Wars from 1689 to 1713, which left French merchant vessels at the mercy of enemy warships and privateers, are a partial explanation for this decline. West Indian plantation owners preferred African slaves to European laborers as agricultural workers. On Saint-Domingue (now Haiti), France's greatest Caribbean colony, there were 27,000 black slaves as opposed to 18,888 whites and 1,484 mulattoes in 1687. Revolts occurred on slave ships sailing from West Africa, and the French government was increasingly concerned about the danger of slave insurrections against the European minority in the Caribbean colonies. White migration had to be sustained by legislation so that the outnumbered Europeans would not be overwhelmed.

After 1699 every ship sailing from France to the French West Indies was required by law to carry a small, minimum quota of indentured workers proportionate to the vessel's tonnage. This law and a 1707 royal ordinance set standards for the age and height of these workers. Under a 1706 wartime ordinance, there was a sixty-livre fine for each man short of the legal quota. There was pressure to apply the same rules to trade with New France. King William's War (1689–97) and Queen Anne's War (1702–13)—the War of the Spanish Succession in Europe—cut off the flow of *engagés* to Canada, and the colony's gentry complained about the resulting shortage of farmworkers and servants.[43] The colony's worthies were hoping for a restoration of the royal subsidy for transporting contract workers, which provided these grandees with cheap labor, and such appeals had produced a special shipment of sixty servants in 1684. In the eighteenth century the French crown's poverty meant that laws alone were used to revive the speculative trade in *engagés*. "His Majesty, . . . being informed that the residents of New France, like those of the islands, needed indentured workers to aid them in their work, whether for the cultivation of the land or for other tasks," extended the regulations for West Indies-bound vessels to all merchant ships destined for New France by the royal ordinance of 20 March 1714. Henceforth, passports would be issued to trading ships bound for North America only on condition "that three indentured workers are carried there on those vessels of sixty tons or less; four for those ships of sixty to one hundred tons; and six for those over one hundred tons." The required workers were to be "at least eighteen years old, and they cannot be older than forty, and they will be, at least, four pieds [four feet, four inches] tall." Port officials were to inspect these men to see that they met the prescribed standards and were "of good complexion."[44] The Ministry of Maritime and Colonial Affairs naively expected shipowners to consider carrying two recruits for the garrison troops in place of each required worker— giving the vessels' owners no profit at all. The alternative that caught the shippers' eyes was the law's proviso that one skilled craftsman would count as two unskilled workers in view of an artisan's greater value to the colony. Thus, the required passengers became skilled tradesmen, in name at least.

Indentures made at La Rochelle and government correspondence indicate that the 1714 ordinance was enforced and obeyed in that year and in the following six years. The merchant shipowners' compliance was deceptively gratifying. The captains of their ships did most of the hiring. When peace returned in 1713, the colonists had been denied a regular supply of contract workers because the war had interrupted maritime commerce and there was, as a result, a brisk market for workers until 1720. After that year, however, merchants tried to evade the 1714 regulations. No contracts, apparently, were made at La Rochelle in 1721, and the government's plan to ensure a continuing flow of men to New France was endangered by the merchants' opposition. This was not the first time overseas traders had frustrated an unpopular law. In 1670, to overcome the reluctance of workers in France to go to remote lands in the Americas, Minister Jean-Baptiste Colbert had ordered that the duration of unskilled emigrant workers' contracts be reduced to eighteen months. When recruiters ignored the new law and had notaries draw up three-year indentures, as before, the administration backed down, and in 1672 it reinstated the customary thirty-six-month term.

The first clue that the ship captains taking workers to New France in the 1720s were doing so unwillingly was provided by their declarations that all the *engagés* on board were qualified artisans, which halved their quota. Merchants, familiar with their impecunious and extortionate government, treated the sixty-livre fine for each missing indentured worker as one more new tax. Since the mandatory passengers had been introduced into the West Indian trade as an alternative to certain goods they must carry, such as flour and muskets, they claimed that their obligation to transport *engagés* ended when a February 1716 regulation lifted the requirement to carry the enumerated commodities. A 16 November 1716 ruling banished this misconception and listed the craftsmen who would be accepted in place of two unskilled men: "mason, stonecutter, blacksmith, locksmith, joiner, cooper, carpenter, caulker, and other trades that can be useful in the colonies."[45] Textile workers were not included, either because they were too numerous or because their products might reduce the colonial market for French cloth.

Merchants of Nantes, La Rochelle, and Bordeaux said that it was difficult to find potential recruits and explained that they sometimes failed to meet their quota because hired men jumped ship before it sailed. The government took them at their word and came up with an ingenious solution that would make up the deficiency and empty the prisons in France. To ship outfitters (*armateurs*), a royal ordinance of January 1721 offered imprisoned "defrauders of the king's [fiscal] rights, vagabonds, and others" to replace voluntary bond servants. These petty criminals would be sold to colonial employers for the cost of their passage. The malefactors' exile would not end after their three or five years of service; it was meant to be permanent. As for the alleged escapes, a ship's crew was believed to be capable of preventing them, and now, for every prisoner who fled, the shipowner would take on *two* more convicts as well as paying the sixty-livre fine.[46] A supplementary ordinance of 20 May 1721 exempted ships of the *Compagnie des Indes* and fishing vessels, while allowing other ships unable to meet the quota, when no prisoners were available, to sail after the prescribed fines were paid.

French merchants were no more willing to transport petty criminals than they were to deliver the required contract workers. In July 1721 the Maritime Council offered to *pay* shipowners sixty livres a head, as well as a daily allowance of seven sols for each prisoner carried in excess of the legal quota. These extra men would cost the carriers nothing, and their services could be sold in the colonies like those of the indentured servants. La Rochelle's merchants promptly rejected this generous proposition.[47] Even with a convenient supply of involuntary recruits, merchants still evaded the laws. In 1722 Louisbourg's senior administrators reported that "of all the [merchant] ships that came last year . . . there was just one from Nantes that brought *engagés*." The other ships' captains pleaded ignorance of the 1721 ordinance.[48] A circular letter to port officials reminded them of the merchants' duties. There was no excuse in 1723, when only eight of thirty-five trading vessels from France brought contract workers to Ile Royale.

The king's ordinance of 15 February 1724 chronicled the deceptions used in France to escape the obligation to transport workers to the Americas. "Most of the outfitters," it said, presented for the mandatory review by port officials, "individuals they would pass off as *engagés* . . . and whom they dismiss after having presented them for inspection. To discharge themselves [from responsibility], they content themselves with bringing back certificates of desertion." As a result, "not even a third of the indentured workers who were embarked in any one port of France went to the colonies last year." Moreover, "some of these outfitters presented people they said were craftsmen, even though they had no trade." Thereafter, documentary proof of desertions was not accepted; there was to be an automatic fine for each worker for whom there was no "certificate of delivery" issued by admiralty officials in the colonies. The fine for each absentee was raised to 120 livres, and those presented as artisans had to have a certificate of competence from a master craftsman chosen by the government.[49] By default, the royal supply ships were the principal carriers of exiled prisoners, because private shipowners and merchants disliked such passengers.

Enforcement became haphazard as port officials lost heart or were bribed to ignore violations. Exemptions were granted and fines accepted to allow ships to sail without any *engagés* on board. In 1742 Louisbourg's senior civil administrator, the *commissaire ordonnateur,* reported that only vessels from Havre de Grace brought the required complement of workers; "those of Bordeaux and Nantes sometimes carry some, and those coming from other ports do not carry any at all."[50] Unfortunately, Quebec's admiralty court records have been lost and, to judge from the surviving correspondence, officials in Canada showed less interest in the observation of these laws than did Louisbourg's administrators. For 1713–43, yearly arrivals from France at Quebec averaged nine or ten ships, and so the number of imported workers would never have been great. This is confirmed by the 1744 town census for Quebec, which listed 27 adult (age nineteen or older) manservants, compared to 226 female and juvenile domestics.[51] Maritime traffic to Quebec doubled and trebled in the next two decades, yet even with full compliance, this would have delivered fewer than one hundred men annually.

War in 1744–48 led to a suspension of laws requiring transportation of contract workers, and when peace returned, merchants acted as though the regulations were still suspended. New France's intendant had to ask for their formal reinstatement. In 1749 he wrote that "the king's ordinance requiring captains of ships coming to the colony to bring *trente-six mois* [three-year bond servants] is not enforced at all: the captains use every sort of pretext to excuse themselves [from compliance] and the commissioners [*Commissaires*] of their ports of origin [in France] do nothing at all about it."[52] Direct personal contracts with colonial employers were now rare, and speculative indentures for resale in *la Nouvelle France* were barely kept alive by these laws. It was the shipowners' reluctance to transport contract workers that prevented a substantial migration to North America in the 1700s. The profit in carrying European servants to New France was small in comparison with the gains from delivering manufactured goods and African slaves to the West Indies. British and Dutch merchants, who profited by carrying a large number of European passengers, both free and indentured, were not imitated. They had grasped the fact that volume could compensate for the small profit on each person or item delivered. The British employed agents to advertise their services and to sign up passengers to fill their vessels. French traders considered themselves carriers of goods, not of people. Ile Royale's governor wrote in 1751 that "most of the outfitters coming here from

France greatly neglect the obligation they are under to bring us indentured workers or *'trente-six-mois.'* Nevertheless, we have great need of them in this colony."[53]

Embarkation lists for passengers departing from some French ports do exist, and they seem to offer a comprehensive picture of people migrating to the American colonies. The lists usually date from the second half of the eighteenth century and they do give the impression that, despite official complaints, there was a steady flow of passengers, including *engagés,* to French North America. The lists are plausible documents. For example, the 1749–58 register for Bayonne, a major port for Ile Royale and the Newfoundland fishery, names seventy-four indentured workers who—if we may believe it—went to Ile Royale and Quebec. Their names, trades, and ages were carefully inscribed. In March 1757 the ledger recorded that, in conformity with the king's regulations, a blacksmith and joiner were taken on board the schooner *La Louise* as contract workers sailing for the colonies.[54] This document is a fraud and we know it. Chance has preserved one private letter about these two men; it was found among the correspondence taken off French prizes-of-war by the British and forwarded to the admiralty for examination. These letters are now at the Public Record Office in London, England. In the letter a Bayonne merchant wrote to his partner on Ile Royale about *La Louise*'s cargo, which was to be sold for their joint profit. "Observe," wrote the merchant, "that there are two *Engagés* with trades on the crew list who will not be making the voyage at all. Do not fail to have them discharged on the roll as having been disembarked, to avoid paying the fine of 80 écus." Another captain in their employ had returned to France without delivery receipts for his mythical workers, and, the writer complained, "I was obliged to pay that [fine] on your behalf."[55] Clearly, deception had become routine and admiralty officers could be counted upon to aid in evading the laws for a consideration. A comparison of ships' rolls with the people actually found on French vessels when they were captured by British warships and privateers in the mid-eighteenth century reveals that these lists, as well as the port registers of passengers, were frequently falsified. Even false, notarized indentures were drawn up to make it appear that maritime regulations were being obeyed.[56] Up to a quarter of the surviving notarial service contracts may be fraudulent. Whoever attempts to reconstruct the history of emigration from French ports during the 1700s from embarkation lists, ships' rolls, and notarial deeds, as though they were firm evidence, is walking into quicksand.

Even if it were possible to find the notarial records of all the French ports serving the Americas, and even if each deed for a contract worker represented a real departure, the total number of contract workers thus delivered would not exceed thirty-five thousand. This is about half the number of eighteenth-century German migrants who arrived in Philadelphia before the American Revolution. Redemption contracts, which were known to the French but seldom used, and service indentures brought only a few thousand people to New France. The same system delivered hundreds of thousands from Europe to British North America. Tempting as it is to lay the blame for the paucity of migrants to New France on merchants who preferred to carry goods or slaves instead of white passengers, the resistance of France's population to overseas resettlement was an older hindrance to a mass movement across the Atlantic. Because the peacetime strength of the French army increased from fifty thousand in the 1660s to three hundred thousand by 1710, able-bodied men had an alternative to emigration abroad. They could enroll as soldiers, which, if unpleasant, was still a known evil, unlike the mysteries of colonial servitude.

From 1662 to 1672 subsidized emigration cost the crown about twenty-five thousand livres a year and, on average, brought two hundred workingmen to Canada annually. None arrived in some years. The *Compagnie des Indes occidentales* delivered 978 people of both sexes in 1665–68. Assuming that a third of the 2,500 or more "persons" delivered by the crown and company were women, the king's settlement program should have added 1,700 men to the colony's population.

The French crown had been subsidizing the transportation of men to New France under the illusion that it was sending future colonists to this land. A worker delivered, however, was not a settler established. When the first nominal census of the colony was undertaken early in 1666, the royal program had transported 460 men to Canada. Just 401 indentured workers were enumerated. That total included men brought out by private recruiters and by religious orders. What had happened? Colbert was astonished when the 1668 census of Canada listed only 1,568 men capable of bearing arms. In 1676 the king ordered the head count to be redone, "being unable to persuade myself that there are but 7,832 people . . . in the entire country, and having transported a larger number in the fifteen or sixteen years since I took charge."[57] This was a regal exaggeration, yet the small number was remarkable because it included the native-born as well as settlers from other sources, such as the garrison troops. Over a third of the earlier emigrants had reembarked for France, and that proportion was increasing in the 1660s. More than two-thirds of the king's *engagés* had gone home to Europe rather than remain in New France.

The exiles' flight back to France resulted from a shortsighted economy. Royal levies were mainly made up of single men. In 1669 a government official described the transportation of families to Canada as "a bad practice," because, "one hundred people, comprising twenty-five families, will cost as much to the king as one hundred bachelors," who, presumably, would all be productive workers.[58] It certainly would be easier to sell single men's indentures than contracts for entire families. No more than 250 families emigrated to Canada—most before 1663. In the seventeenth century unmarried *engagés* resisted settlement, whereas those who had come with families almost always stayed in the colony. Even the presence of a brother or a cousin could affect a person's decision to come and to remain.[59] The administration hoped that marriage *after* emancipation would convert single migrant workers into settlers. Discriminatory measures against bachelors, such as Intendant Jean Talon's 1670 interdict on trading and hunting by single men, were taken to compel men to wed and to make a home in New France.

Free workers had trouble finding wives within the colony's European population. The migration from France had largely been a movement of men. Less than a fifth of all of the known immigrants were women. In Canada during the 1660s there were twelve single men, aged sixteen to thirty, for every eligible woman in the same age group. Eight hundred orphan girls and widows were sent to the colony by the crown in 1663–73 to provide brides for the surplus bachelors. Jean-Baptiste Colbert regarded the women being sent as breeding stock so that the colony's population would grow without extensive emigration from France. He specified that they be "of an age suitable for reproduction," healthy, strong, and not "outwardly repulsive."[60] In 1667 Colbert wrote, "the king will send . . . four hundred good men, fifty girls, twelve mares, and two stallions . . . and next year, I will ensure that a larger number of girls will be sent so that the soldiers who had settled in the country and the new colonists may marry, and thus give rise to the multiplication of people."[61] Because more than half of these women had lost a parent, a quarter were over the age of twenty-five—an age when most women would have been married and none had a dowry to make a good marriage in France, emigration and the royal gratuity given to a third of the female emigrants offered them a chance for an honorable marriage. Their lower fertility, compared with women born in New France, suggests that they were malnourished in France and had accepted emigration as an escape from harsh circumstances.[62] Canada was chosen as the least of many evils. These women were true *immigrants,* in the sense that they had come to North America to wed an established colonist and to stay. Single men retained the outlook of migrant workers; they had no attachment to their place of employment. They had accepted temporary exile from France as a condition of their work. Without a wife and land in New France, they went home. The plan of the crown and the church for producing Roman Catholic, native brides for the colony's restless bachelors, as we have seen, was an illusion. Only the achievement of numerical equality between the sexes in the white population by 1698 solved the problem of involuntary bachelorhood.

The shortage of marriageable women in *la Nouvelle France,* added to the Iroquois threat and the harsh climate, persuaded former contract workers to sail back to Europe. A governor's permit was required to leave the colony, and in 1658 Governor Voyer d'Argenson wrote that even those former servants whose skills were in demand were asking for departure permits.[63] Quebec's Sovereign Council observed in 1663 that "many working men," whose contracts had expired, "ask for the right to return to France."[64] Intendant Talon opposed the liberal distribution of permits, warning Colbert that "while people return, this colony will scarcely grow stronger, whatever pains you take to increase it. . . . Several people returned this year [1671], but a much larger number is waiting to leave next year."[65] Talon proposed that only prominent people and those with an established home and family in Canada be allowed to embark "without difficulty." Single men who had just completed their indentured service ought to be charged a fee equal to a transatlantic fare as a deterrent to departure. An absolute denial, Talon warned the minister, would "dishearten those who might wish to come here . . . with the thought . . . that one never leaves once one is here." In the meantime, Talon was endeavoring "to fix the single men and, by marriage, attach them to some community and so oblige them to work at the cultivation of the land."[66] The irony was that this intendant, at the same time, was begging the king's chief minister to let *him* return home to France.[67]

Talon's proposal of an informal barrier to departures was accepted by his superiors in France. A dispatch in the king's name, sent in 1672, told the governor-general that "my intention is that you do not permit any Frenchman to return to my kingdom if he does not have a wife and children, and a firm establishment in the said land of New France that will ensure his immediate return to the colony." The order was to be kept secret because, if widely known, it might discourage travel to Canada.[68] When the intendant was informed of this directive, he was advised to apply it discreetly, "it being important that the French should not feel themselves detained by force in the said country."[69] Gentle firmness was recommended to the governor-general in 1673 when dealing with the persistent problem of people who wanted to leave the colony. "It would appear to me," wrote the king, "that a rather large number of residents, men and women, return to France. It is something you must prevent, as much as possible, by gentleness and by persuasion." Yet only those "who could never be suspected of deserting" should be allowed to leave New France.[70] Unauthorized departures, especially those to the British colonies, were treated like military desertions. When one fugitive was sentenced to hang, the minister of maritime affairs reprimanded the governor-general for his excessive zeal.[71] If there had been no barriers, fewer than four out of every ten European immigrants would have remained in *la Nouvelle France*. The 40 percent who did remain often had no choice in the matter.

Of the 27,000 people who embarked for the St. Lawrence Valley settlements, about 10,820 remained in Canada. More than half of these migrants came to North America by accident or by compulsion. Perhaps 7,000 people from France arrived in Acadia,—many were transients, such as fishermen. One writer, drawing on genealogical research to establish the number of those who became permanent residents, concluded, "one can say without fear that it was under 600 individuals."[72] Unlike passengers sailing to British North America, most of the people going to French North America were not daring adventurers in search of a different life; chance and misfortune brought them to this alien, brutal land, and they usually had no intention of staying after their service contract or term of military service had ended. These people did not share the ideological commitment of the Roman Catholic clergy to remain in spite of hardships. Fewer than three hundred of those who had settled in the St. Lawrence Valley had paid for their own passage to North America. Independent emigrants who paid their own way were always rare. In the second half of the seventeenth century, the fare—rations included—was sixty to eighty French livres. That was nearly a year's earnings for a French artisan, without deducting living expenses. It was expensive for working people. The colonization of New France, perforce, depended upon sponsored passengers, such as indentured workers. From the 1640s to the 1670s commercial companies, seigneurs, religious groups, merchant-outfitters, and the French crown brought out about four thousand people of both sexes.

Seventeenth-century recruiters in France met popular resistance to overseas emigration, and they seldom spread their nets to catch more than those who were already uprooted from their home communities. Would-be employers had to offer annual wages, a three-year term of service, and even prepaid return passages in order to obtain volunteers. Three years became the standard period of servitude in French North America, and contract workers from Europe were popularly known as "trente-six-mois." By comparison, indentured workers going to British North America were prepared to serve from four to seven years—four being customary for men. Indentured servants from Britain also received no salary beyond "meat, drink, apparel, and lodging." "Freedom dues" were a rare privilege which consisted of clothes, tools, perhaps some land, and, occasionally, a small amount of money at the end of their service.[73] Such deferred rewards were offered to discourage the servant's flight before the contractual period ended. *Engagés* from France were better off than indentured workers in the British colonies, but they did not know it.

Free emigrants, apart from women, were still reluctant to make a permanent home in Canada. As Pierre Boucher found out, his questioners in France were interested in emigration only if they could carry on their old way of life in greater comfort. They had to be assured that familiar religious institutions would be present, and asked, "is wine dear there? . . . Are there horses in the country?" and, most often, "What profit can be made there?"[74] Rough living conditions, the Iroquois threat, the shortage of marriageable European women, and strong ties to family and place of birth led most arrivals to abandon the colony. More than two-thirds of the single men hired en masse and brought out by merchant-speculators and by the king returned home, and more would have gone if colonial officials had not hindered departures. Recall, too, that religious dissenters were not welcome in New France. Only a few hundred arrivals after 1673 were contract workers; the rest were mostly involuntary or unwitting immigrants.

The shipowners' and outfitters' declining interest in *engagés* meant that few real workers' contracts were made for resale in New France after the 1670s. Speculative indentures for the Americas were kept alive from 1699 onward by the force of law. The less-generous terms of later indentures show that popular resistance to overseas employment was waning in the 1700s. Seventeenth-century merchants may have had trouble finding recruits, yet now men were willing to sign up for salaries of fifty livres a year or less, showing that the poor had lost their fear of Canada. Craftsmen hired for Louisiana and Acadia at the end of the century demanded higher salaries.[75] Peace had been made in 1701 with the Five Nations Iroquois, removing their threat, and the colony had passed through the pioneering phase. In the eighteenth century, life there was more comfortable and secure. The merchants' disdain for the traffic in white workers was now the major obstruction, but the traders never explained their dislike for the legal obligation to carry contract workers to *la Nouvelle France*. In 1723 Bordeaux's Chamber of Commerce conveyed the merchants' objection to the legal requirement to take on board *engagés* for the West Indies, because "the *engagés* are no longer useful in any way whatsoever; the country is sufficiently populated and we can no longer find employment for them."[76] In short, the traders claimed that there was no worthwhile market for European workers. *La Nouvelle France* was a poor colony which did not offer indenture sellers a good profit, and the buyers no longer wanted so many unskilled land-clearers. Family-operated farms, which dominated in the St. Lawrence Valley, did not need additional hands once the land had been cleared of trees and brought into cultivation. Exiled petty criminals provided owners of large estates with the agricultural workers they needed. Colonial employers still looked to France for skilled specialists who were not available in New France, but they wanted to know the nature of these workers in advance. Direct personal contracts with skilled tradesmen continued to be made, as table 1 shows, despite the sharp decline in speculative hiring after 1673. Faced with a small, selective market in Canada, French merchants trading with the American colonies evaded the laws that required the delivery of contract workers for resale.

Eighteenth-century immigration to *la Nouvelle France* included a large number of involuntary newcomers. About twelve hundred slaves joined New France's settled population; 55 percent of these were native Indians called "panis," because many were originally Pawnees captured in intertribal wars and then sold to the French. Some came from friendly nations, such as the Montagnais. Most slaves, aboriginal or African, were employed as domestic servants in the homes of the well-to-do, including the households of the Roman Catholic clergy. Representative of this group, but not necessarily typical, is Marie-Marguerite Rose, whose life can be reconstructed from the Louisbourg parish registers. She came from Africa's Guinea coast, certainly via the French West Indies, to Ile Royale. In 1736 she was baptized a Christian at the age of nineteen. Her master was Jean-Chrysostome Loppinot, an officer in the marine troops. Marie-Marguerite gave birth to a bastard son in October 1738, but the circumstances of conception are unknown. With her master as a witness, in November 1755 she married Jean-Baptiste Laurent, who was described as "Indien [Amerindian]." Emancipation seems to have been her owner or future husband's wedding gift, because, when she and her husband rented a house on St. Louis Street, they were described as "both free." Their home was a tavern and boarding house. Her freedom was brief: she died at the age of forty in 1757.[77]

Intendant Michel Bégon hoped that slaves would free aged Canadians from dependence upon their ungrateful, disrespectful children and impudent servants.[78] Although the 540 identified Africans had farming experience, there were no single-crop plantations in New France requiring gangs of field hands. Thus, slavery was of slight economic importance to Canada. Most aboriginal and black slaves were domestic servants in the households of officials, nobles, leading merchants, and high clerics. They were an expensive and visible sign of their owner's wealth and standing.[79] Because most slaves arrived in the 1700s, long after the decline of French workers' indentures, there is no clear cause-and-effect link between the scarcity of white bond servants and the appearance of enslaved workers.

The men who came closest to the French stereotype of colonists in the Americas were some 720 poachers, smugglers, sellers of untaxed salt, and other minor offenders who were exiled to New France from 1721 to 1749. They were all called "faux-sauniers" after the men convicted of transporting and selling salt that evaded the *gabelle* tax. To the colonists, who did not pay the *gabelle* and who were free to hunt where they pleased, these were trifling offenses. Only healthy men with useful skills were to be dispatched, and most were countryfolk suited to farm work.[80] The French system came on the heels of a British law of 1718 that ensured the regular transportation of convicts to the colonies by private contractors, who also sold the felons as indentured workers.[81] In 1735 fifty-four convicts arrived at Quebec, and, of these, four went into the marine troops and the rest were distributed to colonists to work for one hundred livres a year.[82] The offenders were readily accepted as three-year, contract workers in Canada and Louisiana, while enthusiasm for them waned on Ile Royale in the 1740s. Two or three dozen arrived there each year. The exiles were to be agricultural workers on fertile Ile St. Jean and those remaining at Louisbourg were used as manual laborers and domestic servants.

These convicts were not permitted to leave the colony, even after emancipation, yet most managed to flee from New France. In 1741 two on Ile Royale were discovered to be plotting a mass escape to the British possessions; the presence of so many New England ships at Louisbourg facilitated flight. The two culprits were sentenced to serve on the Mediterranean galleys. When no prisoners arrived in 1742, local officials were relieved: "all the residents told us that they would not take any, being dissatisfied with those they had received to date."[83] The minister of the navy was surprised by this cold response and said that the men had done well in Canada and Louisiana, "where the residents use them productively to open and cultivate their land, . . . The *faux-sauniers,* for their part, are animated by a desire to leave domestic service, to which they had been compelled, . . . and are eager to form their own establishments."[84] In 1743 the officials at Louisbourg pointed out that, without much fertile land on Ile Royale to cultivate, the convicts were used to collect firewood from distant forests or to help fishermen—disagreeable tasks. On verdant Ile St. Jean the men were "employed as much in the fishery as on the land." Only three or four had taken up market gardening on Cape Breton, and others, disheartened by the island's "ungrateful" climate and soil, had fled elsewhere.[85] That seems to have ended the matter, as far as Ile Royale was concerned.

During the 1720s seventy exiles were "fils de famille"—a general term for debauched sons sent abroad to save their worthy families further embarrassment. Influential families could obtain a royal *lettre de cachet* to send the offending child to prison or into exile without a trial. This is as close as we come to Chevalier Des Grieux. In 1721 Nicolas Cabot of Rouen obtained an order from the local *parlement*'s attorney-general to have his nephews, François and Vincent Cabot, then in Le Havre's prison, transported to the colonies, "to save their family the ignominy that would ensue if they were tried [in court]." A trial for "their irregular conduct," it was said, would dishonor the family and hurt their sisters, whose marriage prospects, it seems, might be destroyed by their brothers' infamy. The uncle agreed to pay for their food until they were indentured in a colony, and the attorney-general at Rouen verified that this was not just a scheme to deprive the nephews of their patrimony. On 2 September 1721, an order was issued in the king's name, stating that, "having regard for the very humble supplications made by the family of François and Vincent Cabot . . . , two young men accused of crimes and now detained in Le Havre's prisons," they would be "transferred by the first vessel to the American colonies, there to serve as indentured servants."[86] This was the notorious *lettre de cachet* that bypassed the law courts.

One exile of humbler rank described the crime that had brought him to Ile Royale in 1725. Jean Legouel was a short, dark-haired, eighteen-year-old when he was interrogated by two members of Louisbourg's Superior Council after being caught with some stolen white cloth that had been left out in a garden to be sun bleached. Jean admitted to the theft, saying that he had intended to sell the cloth to buy some bread. When asked how he had come to Louisbourg and where he had lived since his arrival, Legouel answered:

> While working at his trade of joiner and turner at his father's house—his father being a [shipyard] foreman for the King at Brest—he unfortunately took from an adjoining storehouse . . . two cotton handkerchiefs that belonged to a merchant. The maidservant saw him and stopped him and, after having taken back the hand-kerchiefs, she and the merchant complained to the father of the accused. The father was outraged by this act [of thievery]. Since he [the son] was a wastrel, his father had him put on board the king's ship *Le Jason* to send him to this island. He arrived in July of this year and was delivered by the ship's captain . . . to Mr. de Bourville, the Town Major, to be employed at his trade for three years, and to be kept longer if he did not become well-behaved.

The councilors then inquired, if Jean had an employer who would have fed him, why did he want to buy food? Legouel replied that the major "only gave him Canadian biscuits and some soup" for his meals.[87]

In 1725 the bishop of Quebec warned the minister of maritime affairs that the continued transportation of these petty criminals to Canada would "destroy the faith of its inhabitants and reduce them to the level of the [Protestant] English, and even of the infidels."[88] Claude Le Beau, who was one of these miscreants, admitted that "the young libertines sent from Paris do not present [the Canadians with] a very good example, amusing themselves by caressing their wives and daughters, singing abominable songs and, in a word, taking their evil debaucheries to the limit." Some, he said, presented themselves to the rural population as schoolteachers, "doing more harm than good."[89] Immoral young men sent abroad by *lettre de cachet* were rare in the later transports of petty criminals.

Like the seventeenth-century contract workers, most exiled convicts left the colony: some fled to the English colonies, while others stowed away on ships returning to France. Gérard Malchelosse, who made a careful study of the transported prisoners in the St. Lawrence Valley, concluded that "like the prisoners and *fils de famille* of 1723–29, a very small number of the *faux sauniers* who came to Canada from 1730 to 1743 became established colonists." Of 648 *faux-sauniers* sent out in 1730–49, only 106 appeared in the colony's parish registers for marriages and burials.[90] Most of the others seem to have escaped from the colony.

Acadian fugitives from Nova Scotia and territories conquered by the British were the largest group of reluctant immigrants to Canada. When Nova Scotia's administration began to round up and expel the French-speaking and Roman Catholic Acadians in 1755 as a menace to the colony's military security, many fled overland to the St. Lawrence Valley settlements of New France. Lieutenant-Governor Charles Lawrence's improvised policy of mass deportation from Nova Scotia became official British policy and was extended to the French islands of Ile Royale (Cape Breton) and Ile Saint-Jean (Prince Edward Island) after their capture in 1758. Almost two thousand Acadians found a refuge in Canada in the late 1750s, and when, at the capitulation of Montreal in 1760, General Jeffrey Amherst refused to suspend the policy of expelling Acadians, the fugitives wisely submerged themselves in the *Canadien* population.

The neighboring British colonies provided several hundred involuntary European settlers for Canada. After the 1680s nearly a thousand British subjects who had been seized by French and Indian raiding parties or who were taken off captured vessels came to New France. Half were repatriated and several hundred chose to remain in the French colony. The Roman Catholic clergy labored to redeem Protestant captives from heresy and succeeded with the children. A clue to the origins of the adults comes from 126 who received letters of naturalization from the king from 1710 to 1714: most had come from New England and New York, some were Irish, and a few had German or Dutch surnames.[91] Hundreds more were brought to the St. Lawrence Valley during King George's War (1744–48). More than five hundred former captives elected to stay in New France, while another one hundred British subjects willingly removed to the French colony. Since Canada's European population was over forty-five thousand in 1750, these foreigners would have had little impact upon the colony's character.

A probable breakdown of the estimated 10,825 immigrants who made a permanent home in the St. Lawrence Valley before 1760 would be:

Soldiers	3,300
Acadians	1,800
Women from France	1,500
Indentured workers	1,200
Slaves	900
British subjects	650
Other European foreigners	525
Male clergy	500
Self-financed migrants	250
Transported prisoners	200[92]

If most British subjects who came to *la Nouvelle France* were unwilling and un-witting immigrants, the largest group, the 3,300 soldiers from France, were set-tlers by choice. When they enlisted in Europe, they did not know where they would be stationed, or even that they would be sent overseas. The French crown, however, saw the colonial garrison troops as potential colonists. Beginning with the Carignan-Salières Regiment and attached companies, which were sent to the colony in 1665, almost 400 soldiers who volunteered to become permanent residents of New France were released from military service and were given some money and land grants.[93] Over a thousand soldier-settlers made a home in New France during the seven-teenth century, and more followed their example in the next century. From 1683 onward, the independent companies of marine troops (*les compagnies franches de la marine*) recruited by the Ministry of the Navy for service on warships and at naval establishments were used to garrison the North American colonies. In the early eighteenth century there were twenty-eight companies, comprising two thousand men, scattered throughout the length of New France. These soldiers, in turn, pro-vided settlers. Quartering soldiers in private homes—a common practice in Canada until the 1740s—and allowing them to work for civilian employers integrated new-comers into colonial society. After 1698, soldiers marrying a woman of the colony with the intention of making a home there were entitled to a discharge, a suit of clothing, land, and, "to give them the means of establishing themselves and of subsisting" until their first harvest, an entire year's pay.[94] The garrison had to be kept up to strength, so the number of settlement discharges granted depended upon the number of replacements arriving from France. If there were no reinforcements, no releases were to be given.

The typical marine soldier who applied to marry in the 1750s was thirty or thirty-one and had lived in the colony from four to seven years. The applicant had to prove that he was truly a bachelor (*garçon*) and a Roman Catholic before he could marry, because married immigrants without local kin or long acquaintances could commit bigamy. "Testimony on the freedom to marry" was recorded by a priest, who interviewed witnesses to a man's marital status in Europe. In June 1757, Jo-seph Poulin, nicknamed "La Brie," appeared before Father Briand, secretary to the bishop of Quebec, who wrote:

> Joseph Poulin called LaBrie, native of Brie-Comte-Robert in the Bishopric of Sens, eighteen leagues from that city and six from Paris, soldier in Cabanac's company, aged 31, and resident for seven years in this land, a pastrycook [*patisssier*] by trade, produced, as witnesses of his freedom to wed, one Floch, a marine soldier, and Garon, soldier of the colony['s garrison] whom he says he has known for sixteen years. Asked where he had learned his trade, he replied "at Paris in the Rue aux Ourses

with [Monsieur] Ozou." [When asked] how long he lived there he replied "four years and [I had] lived in Paris for eight years in all, of which two were at Mr. Clermont's and eighteen months with [Judge] L'Anglois." Asked where he had known the two men [acting as witnesses], he replied that he had known them when he was [a servant] in the house of M. Le Comte de Charolais, on the Rue des Francs-Bourgeois, and Floch, as an apprentice-upholsterer [*tapissier*], in Rue Ste-Avoye. He did not know the name of the master [upholsterer].

On June 11th, 1757, appeared before us Jacques Floch called Beausoleil, marine soldier of St. Vincent['s company], native of Paris, upholsterer on Place Royal, who, after having promised us to tell the truth, assured us that the above-named, whom he called "St. Jean" in Paris and whose surname he did not know, was not married in France and that he had known him for five years in Paris, after he had left Ozou['s service] and [was living] with M. [le] Président opposite the Comte de Charolais, [adding that] they had enlisted together at Belle Isle-en-Mer. . . .

Private Jean-Marie Garon, aged thirty, affirmed that he, too, had known the applicant as "St. Jean" in Paris when Poulin was living "at the home of M. le Président l'Anglois in 1743" and in the following year, when Poulin went off to learn his trade as "upholsterer" [*sic*], and, yes, he was unmarried. The contradictory accounts about when Poulin had learned his craft, whatever it was, made the priest suspicious, and Poulin's use of the alias "St. Jean" may have raised doubts too. Father Briand asked Poulin "if he had learned his trade before joining the judge's household?" The soldier answered "yes, and that he was living with him when he was indentured, or, at least, within three weeks or a month of leaving" the judge's service. This story and, especially, the questionable testimony of Private Garon, caused the priest to reject Poulin's application for marriage. Father Briand preferred witnesses who had known the petitioner since childhood, who had lived in the same village or had attended the same school, and who knew the applicant's family. Poulin reappeared a month later with Sergeant Jean La Serre, who swore that he had known the applicant for ten years, three of them in Paris, when Poulin was employed by M. Clermont ,and then for two and a half years, by Judge l'Anglois, "where he was when he enlisted for Canada." The sergeant's statement and an officer's certificate finally persuaded the priest to authorize the publication of banns for Poulin's marriage in Canada.[95] On 22 July Poulin married a twenty-six-year-old *Canadienne* at Cap de la Madeleine, and they eventually had five children.[96] The officer's help was surprising because military officers and governors disliked the king's settlement policy, since it deprived them of seasoned soldiers and produced few capable farmers.[97]

The same reluctance to enroll as a contract worker for the colonies bedeviled the navy's recruiters in France. The fact that marine troops could serve in the overseas territories, according to one official, troubled people. A popular belief that these men never came home again, he said, hindered recruiting.[98] The royal army and the marine troops drew men from a wider geographic range than the civilian newcomers; there were soldiers whose native tongue was German, Spanish, Flemish, or Italian. Numerous unemployed textile and clothing makers had to be enlisted, for want of better candidates, and, to fill up the ranks, physical standards were lowered, prisoners were conscripted, and deception was used.[99] A plowman who arrived with a levy of troops on Ile Royale in 1750 protested that he had never enlisted but had only accepted three livres from an officer, "to drink to the king's health." That gesture was taken as a commitment to serve with the marine troops for six years.[100]

Many soldiers were social outcasts in France, yet they, too, responded to the siren call of their homeland. In 1698 an intendant wrote of "the ardor that the greater part have to return to France in the hope of greater freedom."[101] A later memorialist regretted that too many soldiers were allowed to go home "under various specious pretexts."[102] This echoed earlier complaints about former indentured servants, who eagerly sought exit permits to leave Canada.

Soldiers were New France's principal source of immigrants in the eighteenth century. Their exact number is open to conjecture. Yves Landry estimates that the six battalions of French regular troops sent out in the 1750s supplied five hundred to seven hundred military colonists.[103] That was about 15 percent of the battalions' personnel. Soldiers provided almost a third of the estimated 10,825 newcomers who settled in the St. Lawrence Valley. Their prominence as progenitors of the Canadians was recognized by a writer in 1709 who boldly asserted that "soldiers populated this country," along with the women sent out by the crown in the previous century. This martial ancestry, he wrote, explained the "excessive pride and idleness" of the *Canadiens*.[104]

Life in *la Nouvelle France* had advantages for soldiers and for people from the mother country's lower social ranks. Land was readily obtainable, material independence was possible, and no direct taxes were paid to the crown—a wondrous situation for a French peasant. Uncleared land on seigneuries could be had for the asking; the tenant would then labor to convert the grant into a secure foundation for his family. Almost as marvelous was the right of commoners to hunt wild game in the colony—a privilege of nobles at home. Seventeenth-century authors, from Samuel de Champlain to the Jesuit missionaries, extolled the St. Lawrence Valley's fertility and the opportunities it presented to humble folk. The same writers wondered why rural people preferred a miserable and precarious existence in France to material security in the New World. After a famine in the 1630s, Father Paul Le Jeune marveled that "there are so many strong and robust peasants in France who have no bread to put in their mouths; is it possible that they are so afraid of losing sight of the village steeple . . . that they would rather languish in their misery and poverty, than to place themselves some day at their ease among the inhabitants of New France?" The reason for this, as we have seen, was that what little the poor had heard about the colony was disheartening: there were horror stories of Iroquois attacks and, possibly, of the six- to nine-week sea voyage to North America, which could be fatal to voyagers.

Stories of how the Iroquois had killed or captured settlers had spread to France. The Jesuits' published accounts may have reached the unlettered through martyr sermons describing the Christ-like agonies of missionaries who were tortured and put to death by the Iroquois. In 1657 a curate at La Rochelle, who was performing the marriage of a merchant, recorded the prior testimony of local witnesses that the man's first wife "had been killed by the Iroquois one league above Quebec."[105] Another man sold his land in 1661 to return to France because in Canada he was "without security from Iroquois incursions."[106] Apart from these horrifying bits of hearsay, however, the semiliterate working population knew little about the colony.

Father Le Jeune admitted that ambitious peasants without land and servants were not his readers: "But to whom to do I speak? To people who cannot know what I am writing, unless more capable ones than they tell it to them. These I beg to do so, in the name of God and of the King, for the interests of both are involved in peopling this Country."[107] His appeal to pious and prosperous readers to pass on the word to their subordinates was no substitute for a vigorous publicity campaign in favor of emigration, if France's government would have sanctioned it. Propaganda to encourage European settlement in the French colonies was rare, irregular, and done on a small scale. Extensive distribution of pro-emigration publications was needed to combat the colonies' low reputation in France, as reflected in Abbé Prévost's novel. The recruitment of contract labor was also sporadic; a would-be volunteer did not know for certain if men were going to be hired for the colonies that year. There was no permanent organization to seek out and sign up indentured servants. The problem with the French recruiting system for contract workers was that it was not a system, just disconnected and improvised attempts to hire men from those who happened to be available. Without continuity, the flow of migrants to New France was fitful and, after the 1670s, small. In peacetime, it was a rare year when more than 150 newcomers arrived in the colony.

British and German overseas emigration from Europe was spurred on by a small army of pamphleteers and professional recruiters, and the movement became a chain migration, thanks to an extensive private correspondence of colonists in British North America with their kin or friends at home. Two-thirds of the Scottish emigrants bound for the Carolinas, when interviewed by Lerwick's customs officials in 1774, said that they were induced to go by letters from friends and relatives in North America.[108] By this transatlantic flow of letters, the hesitant were informed, reassured, and encouraged to follow those who had gone ahead. As for the potential impact of private letters on the colonization of French North America, the surviving correspondence between France and the colonies was primarily between merchants and their overseas agents, with official communications to and from administrators following far behind. Even if a poor emigrant could write, getting a missive delivered was a problem. Without a regular postal service, letters depended on the good will of travelers or of ships' crews for delivery, and these carriers were not as obliging to social inferiors as they were to prominent letter writers. After the 1670s, merchants' letters showed no interest in commercial passenger traffic to New France and eighteenth-century shippers evaded their legal duty to carry a small quota of *engagés*. French ship captains and outfitters were no longer willing to provide a bridge for emigrants from France. As carriers of humans, some, particularly those of Nantes, found greater profits in the slave trade. Most saw themselves as shippers of goods and declined to go beyond the confines of this familiar trade.

Within France there was always internal migration, some of it from the countryside to the cities. The personal information on indentured workers shows that they usually were recruited from these uprooted wanderers. Skilled men among the displaced found work in adjoining European countries. Father Le Jeune drew Cardinal de Richelieu's attention to the loss of valuable subjects: "I have been told," he wrote, "that a large part of the artisans in Spain are Frenchmen. . . . must we give men to our enemies to make war upon us . . . ? The son of a French artisan born in Spain is a Spaniard; but, if he is born in New France, he will be a Frenchman."[109] This argument bore little fruit. The royal army, as well, took in many of the unemployed. There were thus alternatives for the rootless to resettlement across the Atlantic Ocean, which, evidently, was regarded as a last desperate gamble.

Despite unemployment, severe famines, oppressive taxation, and social conflict in France during the reign of Louis XIV (1643–1715), his subjects balked at overseas migration and those who sailed for New France seldom intended to relocate there permanently. There is nothing uniquely French in this unwillingness to travel to distant lands. Remember that the diverse subjects of His Most Christian Majesty were not yet a cultural nation. At this time, most people would have rejected emigration as an escape route from misery at home. The reputation of the France's North American colonies as frightful places of exile for Europe's outcasts would have fortified that resolution. Mass migrations are usually selective: they come from well-defined regions that already have a pattern of seasonal migration. The communities in these areas can become resigned to the continual and permanent departure of residents, who willingly accept settlement abroad. The French provinces that furnished colonists for French North America never produced a sustained flow of departures for Canada.

The lack of favorable propaganda about the colonies and the indifference of shippers to passenger traffic have been emphasized, because publicity, dynamic recruiters, and cheap transportation were essential to a voluntary mass migration. As a positive incentive, the activities of would-be employers were more influential than conditions in France. Looking at the data on workers indentured for the colonies at La Rochelle in 1634–1714, historian Robert Mandrou thought he saw an exact correlation between peaks in enlistment and periods of famine, hunger, and rioting in western France. He concluded that "the emigration from La Rochelle is, therefore, largely due to misery . . . The indentured workers were only willing [to sign up] in the port . . . during difficult years. In ordinary times, it was necessary to appeal to them, to go out and seek them, and often from very far away."[110] Table 1, however, shows that, although famines assisted colonial recruiters, there was not an exact correspondence between acute distress in France and the number of people enrolled for Canada. Colonial recruiters were responsible for the peaks in 1644 and 1659 and the royal subsidies for emigrants underlay the mass of contracts made in 1664–65. If any impersonal force affected the volume of servants going to the overseas colonies, it was war, which reduced and even terminated the hiring of workers in some years. That effect corresponded with the reduction in transatlantic shipping.

The final, decisive force in the colonization of New France was in the minds of those who ventured overseas, despite all of the hazards. The men who came to *la Nouvelle France,* whether as soldiers or contract workers, retained the outlook of temporary exiles from the homeland. European emigrants to New France left very few accounts of their thoughts, yet their behavior makes it plain that most were reluctant expatriates from their provincial homeland, or *patrie*. Single men left France unwillingly and had no intention of staying abroad. The high rate of returns confirms this view. Unlike the indentured servants going to British North America, French *engagés* were migrant workers rather than intending colonists. Soldiers stationed in France's colonies had the same outlook; they, too, were reluctant exiles. Nothing need be said about the intentions of transported prisoners and slaves; they had no choice in their fate. Only the handful of families that came before 1663, most of "the king's daughters," and a few self-financed, independent arrivals were true immigrants who had come to establish a new home overseas. The rest—the majority of Manon Lescaut's countrymen—saw absence from their birthplace as a banishment and they yearned to return to their families in France. Because of the modest number of immigrants and the high proportion that returned to Europe, New France's population grew primarily by natural reproduction after the 1670s.

A gang of convicts, like those dispatched to the colonies, in 1716. From Paul Lacroix,
XVIIIe Siècle: Institutions, Usages et Costumes *(Paris, 1875), p. 303.*

Sea Voyagers and Bonnehomme Terreneuve: The Newcomers' Reception and Appeals to Come Home

OVERSEAS EMIGRATION WAS VIEWED, JUSTIFIABLY, WITH APPREHENSION, AND knowing this, those in charge of people destined for North America took precautions to hold on to their charges. For most emigrants to New France, the voyage began in a French seaport. Men recruited at inland locations, whether contract workers, soldiers, or convicts, might escape along the dusty roads leading to the coast. In the eighteenth century the *faux-sauniers* were tied together and escorted by armed guards to forestall escapes. In 1653 the *Société de Montréal* enticed 153 men to sign up for five years in the colony in return for good pay and a cash advance. Most came from the neighborhood of La Flèche in Anjou, 130 kilometers from the port of embarkation. Before the recruits boarded ship at St-Nazaire, 49 had fled with their advance payment and one had annulled his contract. The hulk bearing the remaining 103 took on so much seawater that it was forced back to France. The expedition's commander placed the migrant workers on an island off the French coast, "from which it was impossible to escape because, otherwise, none of them would have remained." According to the same eyewitness, some passengers were now so desperate to get away that they jumped into the ocean to swim to the mainland, "to save themselves, for they were like madmen and believed that they were being led to destruction."[1] The six to nine week voyage to Canada was hazardous enough without this unfortunate beginning. While crossing in a second ship, 8 voyagers went to a watery grave. The colony's bad reputation was borne out when another 24 were killed by Amerindians. Unlike the clergy of the 1600s, who welcomed the chance to suffer, even to die gloriously for the faith in foreign lands, these lay recruits lacked an ideological motive to endure danger. They were not religious rebels or political innovators intent on creating a New Jerusalem in the North America. They were terrified, humble folk who had accepted indentured service or a military posting overseas to escape unemployment, poverty, or starvation in France.

The *Société de Montréal* was desperately anxious to keep the survivors of the 1653 levy in Canada; it offered them free land and settlement bounties to become colonists. Those who accepted the offer had their service contracts annulled in 1654 and were given credit and wages to assist their establishment. Only forty workers accepted this generous proposal. Immediate land grants and family ties were seen to be effective in keeping former indentured servants in the colony. The Montreal associates applied the lesson in 1659 when they enrolled 109 people in France: 40 were women (12 wives accompanied by single women and a few nuns). Eight families had their passage paid in turn for accepting a redemption bond that required repayment in two years. Thanks to the presence of relatives and marriageable women, most of the people brought out in 1659 became settlers.[2] The value of bringing out entire families, as a sure way of fixing emigrants to the new land, had been demonstrated. That lesson, alas, was ignored by later recruiters. They did, however, take care to avert escapes like those that had occurred in 1653.

In 1720, Jean-Antoine, Comte d'Agrain, was commissioned to hire forty-eight masons, carpenters, and stonecutters to work on the fortifications of Ile Royale and those on the Windward Islands. D'Agrain was obliged to travel more than three hundred kilometers from Rochefort to the Auvergne, where, even with some help, he obtained only twenty-five artisans—of these, two were limeburners, accepted only for want of the desired tradesmen. The workers insisted on a yearly salary, rather than payment by piecework, and they demanded a free return passage to France. All were given an advance of money and a travel allowance to reach the port of embarkation. One ungrateful wretch then tried to desert.[3] The modest results of this costly venture led the Maritime Council to observe that it was still very hard to find craftsmen for the colonies. It directed the intendant at Rochefort to keep all workers subsequently hired on Oléron Island, off the coast, "so they cannot escape."[4] Soldiers enlisted for the Naval Ministry's marine troops were routinely transported to the Ile de Ré, offshore from La Rochelle, to frustrate desertions. They were later ferried to ships at Rochefort and La Rochelle to make the sea voyage to French America.

For many voyagers sailing to New France, their last sight of Europe was of the two stone towers—the Chain and St. Nicholas towers— flanking La Rochelle's harbor entrance. The Tour de la Chaine once held a great chain to close the inner harbor to attackers. Sixteenth-century writer François Rabelais claimed that this iron chain had been used to secure his imagined, giant infant Pantagruel in the cradle. A wall linked this tower to the Tour de la Lanterne, whose beacon guided nighttime mariners to the haven. Some passengers to the colonies knew this structure and the nearby Tour St. Nicolas too well because, as prisoners, they had been confined in them while awaiting transportation to the Americas. The prisoners carved their initials or names, human figures, and religious symbols upon the Tour de la Lanterne's interior walls. The graffiti are the only documentation of their passage left by the captives.

Unlettered soldiers and craftsmen left no record of their feelings upon departing for *la Nouvelle France,* that unknown land across the broad Atlantic Ocean. Their fears and wonder at what awaited them can be imagined. One *fils de famille* exiled to New France in the 1720s left an amusing account of his banishment. Claude Le Beau's *Avantures . . . ou Voyage Curieux,* published in Amsterdam in 1737, was written for the amusement of European salon society. Le Beau's experiences were the conventional memories of gentleman-travelers: banter at supper, watching for porpoises and whales while on the upper deck, catching fresh cod on the Grand Banks, and of a mock baptism by Bonhomme Terreneuve and his sailor-acolytes. Le Beau's voyage could have been passed off as an amusing lark if his ship had not been driven aground in the St. Lawrence River's estuary.

An eighteen-year-old recruit for the colonial garrison left a less picturesque narrative of the sea voyage to Canada. One suspects that he, too, was a rogue whose journey was not a matter of free choice. "J. C. B." asserted that he had accompanied a party of military recruits from La Rochelle to the Ile de Ré in 1751 as a free man seeking a clerical job with the governor of the island's citadel at St. Martin.

April 2nd, we crossed in two small sailboats to the Ile de Ré. As soon as we arrived, I followed the officer, who led his recruits to the citadel and handed them over to the governor. He spoke so favorably of me that I was employed at once in the governor's office. . . . I had worked [there] for about two months after which I was tormented with a desire to travel. As a consequence, I sought information about the best country to live in; about Louisiana or Canada, the only places to which recruits were transported from the Ile de Ré. The sailors told me that Canada was more healthy, although its climate was colder. I resolved to follow their advice and to take advantage of the first sailing. . . . The orders had come to have a number of selected recruits embark for the colonies of Louisiana and Canada. The first sailing was to Louisiana, and took two hundred men, some of whom had been my companions on the road [from Paris]. The second sailing was not delayed. . . . On June 12th [1751] I left the Ile de Ré, five leagues from La Rochelle, in one of the two small vessels which took three hundred recruits to the Charente River, which is two leagues from Rochefort [Naval Arsenal]. There a ship was anchored, waiting to take us to Canada. The vessel was called the *Chariot Royal*. It was a frigate used as a transport vessel [*montée en flûte*] and, although pierced for thirty-six guns, carried only eight. . . . The 27th of the same month of June, we set sail with a good wind from the northeast.[5]

Passengers sailing to New France in the eighteenth century generally fared much better than those borne westward in the 1660s, when crowding spread shipboard fevers and other maladies. Thirty-three percent of the indentured workers carried on the king's ships in 1662 died; 20 percent of the passengers expired in the following year. In that decade one of every fifteen voyagers was buried at sea. A prolonged voyage exhausted the vessel's store of water and rations and raised the chances for an epidemic. Such was the fate of those packed on board the royal transport *Le Rubis* in May 1734. Two Jesuits chronicled the horrors of the trip. A third missionary had surveyed the travelers' living quarters and, after one day on board awaiting departure, had fled the ship. The respectable passengers were given hinged cots in the gun stores room, called the "Sainte Barbe" after the gunners' patron, Saint Barbara. "It is a room," wrote Father Luc François Nau, "about the size of the Rhetoric classroom at Bordeaux, where a double row of frames [*cadres*] was swung up, . . . to serve as beds for the passengers, subaltern officers, and gunners. We were packed into this dark and foul place like sardines in a barrel. We could not reach our beds without hitting our heads and limbs twenty times. Decency did not permit us to undress there. The pitching about of my roof dislodged our bed frames, and entangled them. Once I was thrown with my bed upon a poor officer from Canada . . . It was twelve minutes before I was able to extricate myself from my bed, however, the officer was so out of breath that he scarcely had the strength to swear."

The priests' low-ranking companions, who slept in hammocks on the gun deck, were the origin of the stench below decks, infections, and vermin. "We had on board a hundred newly-raised soldiers, each one of whom had a whole Picardy regiment upon his person." Father Nau's pun referred to fleas as "bold prickers" [*les piques-hardis*]. "In less than eight days these ravenous Picards spread everywhere. No one was exempt from their bites, not even the bishop or the ship's captain. Every time we emerged from below decks we found that we were covered with fleas. I even found them in my bed-socks [*chaussons*]. Another hive of fleas and a source of infection were the eighty *faux-sauniers,* who had languished in prison for a year. These wretches would have aroused the pity of the most barbarous Turk. They were half-naked, covered in ulcers, and some even were being eaten alive by worms. We banded together and took up a collection throughout the vessel to buy shirts for them from sailors who had some to spare. Our care for them did not prevent them from infecting the ship with a sort of plague which attacked everyone and killed off twenty men at a stroke, so that the officers and passengers who were still well were obliged to work the ship in place of the [diseased] sailors." More died and the priests tended the two hundred sick. A gale split the fore topmast. Contrary winds extended their sea voyage to seventy-five days and the ship's tossing meant that the galley fire was extinguished as a safety measure. There could be no hot food. "Our rations on those days," wrote Father Pierre Aulneau, "were biscuits and dry bread," and eventually, "we had scarcely any water and provisions left." The priests were subsisting on the last of the salt beef and helping to haul ropes and make sails taut as the *Rubis* tacked slowly into the mouth of the St. Lawrence River. A boat was sent out to scour the shore for water and wild game and it brought back some. "We reached Quebec only on the 16th of August," concluded Father Nau, "the eightieth day since we embarked. It was one of the longest voyages made from France to Canada."[6]

Le Rubis experienced another disastrous voyage to New France in 1740. The ship sailed in June with a complement of 270, including military recruits, exiled prisoners, and workers for the royal shipyard at Quebec. Forty-two died of fever en route and only 81 reached Quebec in good health that August. In the next year a priest reported that the king's *flûte* had a good crossing: "we did not have many sick . . . only four men were cast into the sea; that was regarded as a small price for a voyage of 85 days."[7] A transatlantic passage without any deaths was reckoned a miracle.

All passengers, whatever their rank, endured the vessel's rolling and the groaning of timbers in their dark, damp living quarters. They welcomed a breath of fresh air above deck and, perhaps, the chance to drop a fishing line over the side. There people speculated on the distance traveled and watched the sea for signs of aquatic life. J. C. B. espied seals and walruses in the Gulf of St. Lawrence. Icebergs, provided they were not too numerous, were an additional diversion. Opposing winds, windless days, violent storms, seasickness, water damage to clothes and luggage, a tedious diet, putrid drinking water, and ship fevers were the commonplace miseries of shipboard travelers. In 1751 *Le Chariot Royal* had to tack against the winds and was delayed by two fierce tempests, when J. C. B. "paid tribute to the sea with a great sickness of the heart . . . [and] I could not eat." In a thunderstorm the lightning, "struck near the vessel with a din like several artillery pieces. We were all terrified of it . . . we seemed to be in the trenches. I was ready at any moment to become food for the codfish on which we planned to dine. . . . [We were caught between] worry and fear, between life and death."[8]

In stormy weather, passengers clung to their swinging hammocks and cots while seawater spurted through seams and loose gun-ports to slosh about with the passengers' vomit on the gun deck. The waves crashing against the straining and tossing hull brought forth cries of despair and prayers for divine protection. During a storm in 1758 one crew made a collective vow and donated money to celebrate a solemn, high mass once they reached land if God would still the tempest.[9] Religious vows in times of distress had been made since the Middle Ages, and probably earlier. St. Anne was often appealed to as the protectress of those in peril at sea. In wartime, a sailing ship on the horizon produced panic because the French navy could not contain foreign warships and privateers. "An Englishman or pirate would have made short work of us," wrote Father Nau, "if they had attacked when we had so many sick" on board. He was amused that the appearance of *Le Rubis* caused other French vessels encountered on the Grand Banks to sheer off in fright.[10] Those who had survived enemy attack, shipwreck, or ocean storms said prayers of thanksgiving, and sometimes had a painting made to attest to St. Anne's saving intervention, which would be exhibited at her shrine near Quebec. Votive paintings of the period can still be seen in Canadian and French churches. Some crews left a model of their ship hanging in a church nave to secure divine protection for their vessel.

J. C. B., like Claude Le Beau, encountered Goodfellow Newfoundland on his transatlantic journey and was "baptized." This ritual, like the ceremonial "crossing of the line" endured by those sailing across the equator, welcomed newcomers to North-American waters.

The 14th of September, we arrived at the Grand Banks of Newfoundland, in eighty fathoms of water. Immediately, the sailors cried 'Vive le Roi' [long live the king]. This is a custom among the sailors when they find the bottom. . . . The weather continued to be calm, the crew amused themselves with a baptismal ceremony that is customarily performed by the sailors upon those passing over the Grand Banks for the first time. This ritual consists of disguising an old sailor with a large, fur-lined, hooded coat, a pair of high boots, a white wig on the head [topped off] with a helmet and stocking cap, and a large white, false beard. The sailor thus attired descends from the main topmast, where he dressed himself, and, with the aid of ropes and pulleys, he slides down to the foot of the foremast, where other sailors receive him and [then] lead him to the base of the mainmast. Near the mainmast the initiate is held in a sitting position on the edge of a tub filled with water. There Bonhomme Terreneuve makes the candidate swear an oath to keep the secret [of this ritual] from those who have not yet passed this latitude, with a [further] promise to never touch any sailor's wife. This must be promised instantly for, if the initiate has not taken the precaution of giving a coin for a drink, he is at once tipped over into the tub by the two men holding him, and from which he promptly emerges to go [below deck] and change clothes. During this time

Goodfellow Newfoundland is sent up [the rigging] where he undresses and then reappears, so that the person who was ducked in the water cannot recognize him. Thus ends this ceremony, which is somewhat disagreeable in cold weather and is only a sailor's game for getting money.[11]

Le Chariot Royal took four months to reach Quebec; it was November 3rd when the ship rounded Ile d'Orléans and anchored below the city, to await high tide on the following day so that the vessels could enter the roadstead under the protection of Quebec's gun batteries. Then the soldiers were marched off to their quarters, passengers with money found lodgings in private homes and inns, and the indentured servants had their contracts sold to colonial employers. J. C. B. appeared at a muster parade in Quebec's Place d'Armes, where the new military recruits from France were inspected by the governor-general before their incorporation into the independent companies of marine troops stationed in the colony.

All the troops were under arms in three ranks, for a total of eighteen companies. The recruits standing opposite were unarmed and were formed up in two ranks. The governor, accompanied by the staff major, arrived about noon. . . . I was placed behind the two artillery companies, which perform the duties of grenadiers. The inspection began with them. . . . Each captain, according to his seniority, beginning with the gunners, took the number of men assigned to him. The commander of the gunners chose ten, without counting me, and the other captains followed. This selection finished, each company withdrew with its recruits. I was one of five taken into the second company, which was lodged over the St. Jean Gate. The next day we were given our clothing and arms.

As is usual during a review, a great many persons, even the most distinguished people of the city, were attracted by curiosity. I saw there with pleasure my three patronesses [wives or widows of officers who had taken an interest in his fate] who greeted me and gave me eighteen francs [livres] in silver. . . . When I joined the company, I gave the eighteen francs I had just received to pay for my initiation [*ma bienvenue*], as was the usual custom. It secured me friends in the manner of soldiers, but I only relied on them when it might serve my interests and without making a habit of frequenting taverns [with them].

They gave me as a bedfellow—for they slept double—a Parisian with a handsome face made to please, who had the vices of gambling and drink. He was also cruel and quarrelsome, often drawing his sword without heed or restraint. . . . Before breakfast he was good-natured and amiable, and especially toward women, whom he studied in order to deceive. He was extremely fond of dancing, at which he was very good. He gave me a taste for it, by taking me to balls with him. . . .

Because of my indulgence, he became accustomed to wearing my clothes and taking everything so that he often prevented me from going out because he had taken my money and my best clothes.

A gunner's pay, wrote J. C. B., was sixteen to eighteen livres a month—twice that of an infantryman, but he was allowed to work as a merchant's clerk. In 1685, when the government was unable to pay the colonial troops, Intendant Jacques de Meulles had allowed soldiers to work for civilians. This emergency measure became an established practice in New France. Soldiers with useful skills, such as bakers and stonemasons, easily found paid employment; less-gifted men earned something by washing clothes and performing guard duty for the artisan-soldiers or by doing menial tasks for civilians. The extra money allowed the men to amuse themselves in the colony's numerous taverns, often run by retired servicemen, and to play cards for small wagers. Hunting was an escape from the tedium of a soldier's daily routine and it provided wild fowl to supplement rations. Spruce boughs were gathered in the woods for making a sweet beer that soldiers brewed for themselves. The men cooked their own food. As was customary in New France, J. C. B. would have given up a portion of his civilian earnings to his company commander so as to be excused from garrison duties, apart from muster parades, which confirmed that he had not deserted. Most of a soldier's military pay was appropriated to pay for necessities, such as clothing. Officers kept their men in debt servitude by giving soldiers goods and liquor on credit. In 1695, on the advice of theologians of the Sorbonne University, the bishop of Quebec directed priests to deny absolution to officers who withheld soldiers' pay and who demanded a share of the men's earnings.[12] On Ile Royale the marine officers' exploitation of their men was worse than elsewhere, and the soldiers' hostility to their superiors produced a mutiny in 1744.[13]

Like other soldiers, J. C. B. had received a nickname, "Jolicoeur," meaning light-hearted. He said nothing about his military training, and it seemed as though, after learning how to fire a musket, wear a uniform, march in order, and perform sentry duty, the marine troops had no further instruction, save by experience.[14] In the same year in which J. C. B. arrived at Quebec, the Count de Raymond sailed from France to become Ile Royale's new governor. He was accompanied by Colonel Michel Le Courtois de Surlaville, a veteran of France's regular army, who described the lamentable review put on by the Louisbourg garrison: "the ranks were misaligned and several soldiers did not even know how to handle their muskets and, moreover, they could not keep quiet. They marched without any fixed spacing, ranks poorly dressed and arms badly borne, their hair loose or ill-tied; their accoutrements [*l'équipment*] and arms were in great disorder, and also their gaiters, garters, collars, with filthy, worn-out uniforms."[15] Some had missed the roll call because they were at their civilian jobs, cutting hay or out hunting. The married soldiers lived in the town and their sergeants ate and lived outside the barracks, paying others to do their duties. Colonel de Surlaville, as town major, immediately ordered regular drills and inspections to restore discipline and to train the men in military skills. A corporal who was intoxicated while on duty was reduced in rank and a court-martial was held for a sentry who was found sleeping at his post.

Colonel de Surlaville blamed the slovenly state of the garrison troops on their officers, who were often out of uniform and busy with private matters. The marine officers came from the colony's landed aristocracy and were distracted by their commercial interests. Those in the St. Lawrence Valley also had estates to occupy their attention and, because there were no barracks in Canadian towns until the 1740s, their men were scattered about in private homes. "The Canadian officers," wrote a professional soldier from France, "although courageous, knew hardly anything of their profession. . . . They hardly knew their own troops, who were always billeted with the *habitants* [settlers]."[16]

Officers commanding military posts were closer to their subordinates, who lived together, yet those in the western territories traded with Amerindians—another distraction from their command responsibilities. One testy informant told de Surlaville in 1754 that the Canadian commandants owed their positions to favoritism rather than to rank or seniority and that they stole most of the gifts intended for the native allies to sell them for their own profit. In truth, officers negotiated with merchants who supplied goods to the commandants for private trade at the posts. Not only was the king being cheated by these men, said the informant, but the commanders' preoccupation with selling goods and buying furs meant that they did not acquire useful intelligence, or the local knowledge and authority needed to influence Amerindian allies, who were being courted by British traders and officers. The hostile commentator concluded, with considerable exaggeration, "all those who, four or five years ago, did not have shoes on their feet, are today millionaires who build palaces and own several ships, who order silverware from France for considerable sums."[17]

Father Étienne de Carheil at Michilimackinac felt that God and the king were badly served by the officers and men stationed in the western posts. There were a few dozen soldiers in each of these establishments. In 1702 the Jesuit told the governor-general of New France that the service

they render to the king is reduced to four principal occupations, of which we beg you to inform His Majesty. The first consists in keeping a public tavern for the sale of brandy, wherein they trade it continually to the savages, who do not fail to become intoxicated, whatever opposition we make to it. The second occupation of the soldiers is to be sent from one post to another by the commandants in order to carry their goods and liquor there. . . . Their third occupation is to make their fort a place that I am ashamed to call by its true name, where the [native] women have learned that their bodies might take the place of merchandise and they would be even better received than beaver-skins; . . . The fourth occupation of the soldiers is that of gaming which, when the traders assemble here sometimes goes to such excess that, not being content to spend the day [in gambling], they also spend the whole night thus. . . . If these sorts of occupations can be called the king's service, I confess that they have always rendered him one of those four services, but I have never seen any others than those four.

Father Carheil concluded that the posts were of no military value and that their garrisons and commandants undermined the missionaries' work and corrupted the aboriginal peoples.[18]

In 1753 J. C. B. was posted to Fort de la Presqu'Ile on Lake Erie, where, because of his clerical and bookkeeping experience, he was made assistant keeper (*commis du garde magasin*) of the rations and trade goods in the king's storehouse. Imitating his superiors, he made the most of this position, eating well and engaging in private trade. He could use the government stores as trading capital. As long as he replaced what he had borrowed and his accounts were in order when he departed, he could safely pocket the profits. He was appointed keeper of the king's stores at Fort Duquesne in 1756. "This position put me in an even better position to improve my affluence [*mon aisance*] without any fear." He made four thousand livres by buying and selling two tons of tobacco in 1758 and, like the commandants, he had a partnership with a trader. He amassed more than thirty-two thousand livres in two years. He was recalled to the St. Lawrence Valley in 1759 and was made secretary to a military engineer and inspector of government building workers at Montreal. The two positions entitled him to a monthly salary of two hundred "dollars" (*piastres*), say, eight hundred livres. He refused a promotion to the rank of sergeant in an artillery company, "since it would be more troublesome than profitable for me, [as one] who was earning so much more in my trips without being rigorously subjected [to an officer]."[19] By then, he had forty-five thousand livres in assets and, amidst the confusion of war, was still engaged in business transactions. If true, J. C. B.'s profitable career set him apart from most private soldiers, who remained close to the bottom of colonial society and in debt to their officers. Although desertion was a hanging offense, there were always a few who risked execution and fled military service.

It might appear that the indentured workers from France were better off than the soldier-recruits, being exempt from military discipline and having been promised good salaries. The difference, however, was slight and not always to the *engagés'* advantage. In August 1715 "Claude Viton," a twenty-four-year-old silkworker out of Amsterdam, arrived from La Rochelle aboard *l'Heureux Retour.* He had been indentured before two notaries in May to Jacques LeClerc, a La Rochelle merchant, to depart with Captain Gaillard for "Quebecq in Canada." "Viton" (Witte?) was bound to three years of service, as of his departure, for three hundred pounds of sugar payable at the end of his term. This West Indian salary was later converted to fifty Canadian livres—a pitiful reward. After their arrival in Canada, Captain Gaillard sold the silkworker's contract to Father Jean-Baptiste Gaulthier de Varennes, representing the Quebec Seminary, for 150 livres, French currency.[20] Some transported petty criminals, surprisingly, fared better than this Dutch servant. In August 1739 two *faux-sauniers,* Pierre Laborde of Bayonne and Gabriel Larchet from Normandy, who had arrived on the king's infamous transport vessel *Le Rubis,* were hired by a Quebec baker, Pierre Joly, to serve him "well and faithfully . . . in all that he might command . . . whether in the bakery or in other things," with "a salary [for each one] of 100 livres currency for each of the said three years." Half of their wages would be paid "in goods suitable for their upkeep and at the best conditions or lowest retail price for goods in this town [of Quebec]." Joly promised them food, laundry services, care, and medicines while sick, "without loss to their salary," and the day off on feast days and on Sundays so that they might attend Mass.[21] The salary was the same as that received by other transported offenders, but, because there are so few records about the disposition of other convicts in the colony, one cannot say that these humane terms were typical.

The workers' salaries that looked so enticing in France were a disappointment in the colony, where goods, especially clothing, were expensive. The contract workers' pay was further whittled down by paying them in kind. The yearly wages were often a credit against which the employer advanced liquor, clothes, personal articles, and services to the indentured men. The Quebec Seminary (*le Séminaire des Missions etrangères*), founded by Bishop François de Montmorency Laval in 1663, hired men to work at Quebec, at Sillery, and on its three country estates. The seminary's account book for 1674–87 shows that, of fifteen *engagés* employed by the seminary, seven were owed nothing at the end of their service, while three were *indebted* to the institution. It appears that the seminary tried to avoid cash payments and preferred to offer the men goods from its storehouse or from merchant-suppliers as remuneration. Julien Brûlé, a shoemaker entitled to 150 livres a year, had a credit of only 6 livres, 3 sols at the end of his first year of service, having accepted the balance in shoes, winter clothing, tobacco, beer, stockings, combs, fine shirts, a crucifix, laundering, and a tailor's services.[22]

The considerable advantages of the "trente-six-mois" in New France, in comparison with indentured workers in British North America, did not exempt him from legal subjection. Servitude was his lot. One governor-general defined an indentured worker in Canada as "a man obliged to go everywhere and to do whatever his master commanded, like a slave."[23] Of course, he was not really a slave because there was a time limit on his bondage, which Quebec's Sovereign Council kept at a minimum of three years.[24] If he failed to obey and submit to his employer or attempted to escape, the law courts would recall him to his duty. Magistrates took the side of the master and would tolerate the physical punishment of servants, provided no blood was shed or bones broken. Brutally hard tasks, such as land clearing, wood-cutting, and hauling water from the river, fell to bond servants. They worked as long as there was sunlight, and sometimes longer. In 1654 Sieur du Hérisson's workers complained to the Trois-Rivières court that their master made them get up from bed "too early" (*trop matin*) and that he fed them "scantily" (*escharsement*). The judge ruled that, by turns, one servant would arise before daybreak to light the fire and that the remainder would be expected to begin work only a quarter hour before dawn. In autumn and summer they labored until a quarter hour after sunset. As for their food, the magistrate ruled that they be given a jug of broth daily and, per week, sixteen pounds of bread, six tablespoons of peas (?), and one pound of meat or, in Lent, nine eels.[25]

A scanty diet and long hours of work were not the sole grievances of *engagés*. To explain the discontent of the Jesuits' indentured workers at Quebec, Father Paul Le Jeune wrote in 1634 that:

1st—It is the nature of working people to complain and grumble.

2nd—The difference in wages makes them complain; a carpenter, a brickmaker, and others will earn more than the laborers, and yet they do not work so much; . . .

3rd—The greater part do not follow their trades, except for a short time; a tailor, a shoemaker, a gardener, and others, are amazed when required to drag some wood over the snow; besides they complain that they will forget their trades.

4th—It must be confessed that the work is great in these beginnings; the men are the horses and oxen; they carry or drag wood, trees, or stones; they till the soil, they harrow it. The insects in summer, the snows in winter, and a thousand other inconveniences, are very troublesome. . . .

5th—They all lodge in one room; and as they have not all learned to control their passions, and are of dispositions altogether different, they have occasions for causeless quarrels.

6th—As we are more or less dependent upon them, not being able to send them back when they fail to do right, and as they see that a stick for the purpose of chastising them is of little use in our hands, they are much more arrogant than they would be with laymen, who would urge them with severity and firmness.[26]

Servants commonly lodged in the attic or apart from their employer if the master were a priest. It was improper for an employer and social inferiors, especially those of a different sex, to share the same living quarters. The issue was not privacy; it was a matter of maintaining social distinctions. In religious institutions workers ate in a separate dining room. Nor could a servant expect to be dressed in clothing of the same quality as worn by his employer. A clue to the rough attire of indentured workers comes from the identification of a frozen body found near Louisbourg in 1737. The corpse was judged to be that of "a sailor or an *engagé*" because it was dressed in a brown vest and pants, gray outer vest, mittens, worn-out stockings, and sealskin moccasins.[27] In the brutal and exploited world of bond servants, the lot of men in *la Nouvelle France* was preferable to the fate of contract workers in the French West Indies, where a white laborer's life was sickly and short. Workers in New France knew little of conditions in other places; they knew their own circumstances and, as Father Le Jeune observed, they were mighty grumblers.

The contract workers employed by religious institutions were subject to rules inspired by the routine of the *donnés,* those unpaid and pious servants-for-life kept by the Jesuits and other orders. The Quebec Seminary had a dozen *donnés* and an equal number of indentured servants in 1686 when Fathers Charles de Glandelet and Louis Ango Des Maizerets drew up their "Regles Communes Pour Les Domestiques & Engagés Du Séminaire" (general rules for the seminary's servants and indentured workers). The regimen prescribed for the hired workers was morally and physically demanding; it stated:

1. There will be no toleration for anyone who is scandalous, quarrelsome, a drunkard, a curser, or free with his words.

2. Taverns will be forbidden to them as well as excursions at night.

3. They will go to confession at least once a month, on every work-day they will attend the first mass, at the beginning of which they will recite the morning prayer together, as well as the common evening prayer, . . .

4. They will begin their work in winter at six in the morning and will continue until mid-day. . . . Their breakfast time [*Le tems de leur déjeuner*] will be after the first mass and until six. At one in the afternoon they will resume their work and continue until seven in the evening, when it can be done by candlelight. In summer they will begin their work by five in the morning and then breakfast time [*Le tems du déjeuner*] will be from seven until eight.

5. They will admit no one to the seminary to eat or sleep there without [our] expressed permission.

6. On feast days and Sundays they will attend high mass, the sermon, vespers, and the benediction [*salut*] unless they have some legitimate impediment.

7. After evening prayers each one will retire [to bed] and they will take care not to make any noise.

8. They will remember that they are obliged to work faithfully and treat the house's [i.e., seminary's] interests as their own.[28]

Within a year, the two priests had produced a more detailed version of the rules, called "ordre journalier pour les Domestiques" (daily order for the servants), which described the prayers to be recited, the times when workers should cross themselves, and the thoughts that the workers should entertain after rising from bed at four A.M. As in a monastery, supper was to be eaten in silence while someone read aloud from "the lives of the saints, the Sinner's Guide, or from some other good book." For recreation, the men were advised to consider "some worthy readings," and, after supper, to avoid "immoderate laughter." The authors appended five pages of religious instructions and twelve more explaining how the grateful, devout, humble, and obedient life, full of self-examination, prescribed for the workers would achieve their spiritual salvation. The servants, "by obedience and submission . . . to those God gave them to serve," would be placed upon "the road to paradise."[29] This saintly life, perhaps, was more than most contract laborers from France had bargained for and may explain why a few servants ran away.

We know a great deal about employers' expectations of servants and their complaints over workers because they wrote most of the surviving accounts of master-servant relations in New France. Securing an indentured worker was troublesome and costly, and, if the man proved to be unreliable or incompetent, the master in North America suffered a great loss. Qualified craftsmen, apart from textile workers and shoemakers, commanded yearly salaries of 75 to 120 livres. There was the initial 70 livres required to recruit and transport a worker from France. In addition, the worker's food and lodgings could cost the employer another 90 to 180 livres a year. A contract worker's master or mistress counted on three years of productive labor to repay this investment. Unfortunately, that expectation was confounded from time to time. A self-styled artisan might not possess the skills for which he was hired. In 1634 a Jesuit priest at Quebec complained that "last year they sent us a man as a carpenter who was not one; and for this reason there has been no building this year, which has done us great harm."[30]

The sad experience of the Quebec Seminary with indentured workers from France led that institution to change its hiring policy. Some of its recruits had turned out to be idlers, incompetents, drunkards, and runaways. Of thirty-two workers hired in France in 1671–76, seven had to be sent back before completing their term of service.[31] A gardener enrolled in 1673 for seventy-five livres a year was given clothing, a knife, and a comb on credit. After seven and a half months at the seminary in

Quebec, he ran away. When he returned, he was sent to a new master on a distant estate, making escape more difficult. After his second flight, the seminary's account book recorded that the gardener was "sent back to France after five months in prison, where he was fed [by the seminary] out of charity."[32]

Experiences of this sort led the Quebec Seminary's proctor to recommend in 1682 that, henceforth, colonial workers be hired, "even if they are more costly . . . since one is often deceived in those who are sent from France," and because the value of the French *engagés'* work in the first year barely covered the cost of acquiring them.[33] Indeed, from 1675 onward, the seminary had relied increasingly upon local workers employed by the year or by the month. Experienced, specialist tradesmen still had to be brought from the mother country. Bishop de Montmorency Laval, who participated in the hiring of men when he was in France, agreed with the proctor that "it is very difficult to judge the character of all these people who want to be employed" at the Quebec Seminary. As a result, some of the French recruits were kept in Paris for a probationary period to assess their nature before they were forwarded to Canada.[34]

Some of the workers' "causeless quarrels," referred to by Father Le Jeune, were inspired by their notions about the different ranking of occupations and by mutual suspicion among the newcomers, who wondered about their companions' origins. This was one of the strains of forming a new community out of strangers. In addition to the prisoners exiled to the colony in the 1720s, there were miscreants who had emigrated to find anonymity abroad. The Ursuline mother-superior at Quebec noted in 1669 that "among the decent folk who come here, there are many rogues of one or the other sex who create a great deal of scandal."[35] Elsewhere, she described them as "terrible riff-raff." In 1683 an intendant observed that the colonists in Canada, "comprise all sorts of people, and villainy has obliged most to seek asylum in this land, and to put a veil over their former crimes."[36] A scandal at home would help overcome the reluctance to emigrate. While visiting France, Bishop de Montmorency Laval accepted a joiner as a contract worker and forwarded him to the Quebec Seminary with the explanation that the man was obliged to leave France, "because of an accident when he struck a tax farmer [*un monopolier*] with a stone and caused his death."[37] Apart from this one offense, the bishop considered the artisan a decent family man.

The surest way to defame residents of New France was to suggest that they, like some notorious emigrants, had a dark past in the parent country. The suggestion was plausible among people who migrated only under duress, and it was nearly impossible to refute this calumny since the same anonymity that protected the guilty few meant that there were also no witnesses to one's innocence. In the 1660s two sisters spread a shocking account about a farmer's wife living at Petit-Auvergne near Quebec. It was recorded that "maliciously and falsely, the sisters accused the said wife of having borne and having disposed of a child while on board the ship that brought her to this land and they had called her a slut [*putain*]."[38]

A remarkably similar exchange occurred at the newer settlement of Louisbourg in July 1744 when a butcher's wife, Servanne Bonnier, tried to prevent Angélique Butel from beating her own daughter, who was blamed for breaking a window pane. The mother resented this intrusion and the two women shouted insults at each other. Bonnier asserted that Butel "had borne two children in France, whose fathers were not her husband, and that she had already killed one child and wished to do the same to her only remaining one," and, moreover, that Butel was "a cheap whore who liked the act but not the [resultant] children." Angélique Butel replied that Bonnier's entire family deserved to be hanged and that Bonnier dared not return to France because of the bastard she had given birth to a decade ago.[39] Attacking a woman by impugning her chastity was standard fare for insults in New France, and the charge of infanticide added a heinous crime to the barrage of insults. In an immigrant population of strangers, such allegations were credible because they were hard to refute. Accusations of having a criminal past in France appeared on other occasions.

Marriage is the ultimate test of social acceptability, and those resisting a proposed union found an armory of reasons in their suspicions about other newcomers' origins. On a Sunday evening in 1672 Pierre de Lugerat, a miller, was drinking wine at a friend's house. While in his cups, the miller told his host and the others present that he, de Lugerat, would never consent to the marriage of his son to the daughter of a Montreal tailor, Nicolas Hubert. The needle trades ranked low among craftsmen. The tailor's family was described as a gang of illicit fur traders (*chasseurs & Coureurs de bois*). The miller went on to say that, in France, the tailor's father and father-in-law "had been hanged, one by the neck and the other by the feet." The crimes which merited such punishment were not identified. The story was surely the miller's own invention because he later changed it and claimed that one of the tailor's parents had been shot by a highway constable.[40] The vilification of the tailor's family as gallow's birds was echoed by other *Canadiens* who labeled people "gens de sac et de corde,"[41] "des races de pendus,"[42] or "reste de gibbet." Settlers were vilified as fugitive murderers, banished criminals, and as having a grandfather who was a malefactor.[43] Among the colonists, the dark myth about those who had populated France's American colonies was alive.

The emigrants' relatives in France were certain that no moral or reasonable person would settle permanently in North America. None of them inquired about the possibility of moving there. Because a third of the immigrant men were illiterate and there was no established and reliable postal service, the original number of private letters to and from low-ranking people must have been small. Add to these considerations the hazards of travel in the seventeenth and eighteenth centuries and the destruction of private documents over time. The survival of any written communication to the present is a miracle, yet a few hundred letters to and from expatriate colonists from France do exist. The theme of letters to emigrants in French America is consistent: those left behind in Europe looked upon resettlement abroad as unnatural, even as selfish and immoral. Family obligations, the writers believed, should bring the exiles home. This sentiment was an additional force that pulled emigrants back to France.

A worker hired in 1653 by the Montreal associates acquired land with the evident intention of becoming a colonist. In 1669 his distressed father wrote to remind his son that filial duty and his material interests called him home. "I find it strange," wrote the father, "to have a child whom I have cherished more than myself and who has no desire at all for me. I believed that I would have the happiness of seeing him within four or five years of his departure." Clearly, the former indentured worker's sojourn in Canada was meant to be a temporary expedient, not a prelude to resettlement there. In just three months, the exile was told, he could be "in your good town of La Flèche, from which you come," and in possession of eight hundred livres from his mother's estate, as well as of "many other things that you only have to ask for." Every lawful child was assured of a share in the parental estate, and this right may have enticed the letter's recipient and others to return home. As a final, persuasive flourish, the man's father conveyed the best wishes of the exile's kin, "and all your good friends in this fine land of Anjou, where we drink good wine for a sou." After receiving this letter, the son did return to France for a decade, but then reappeared in Canada, where he married and died.[44]

Memories of home and friends were also skillfully evoked in 1756 for a Bayonne merchant living on Ile Royale (Cape Breton). "Come back to your homeland [*Patrie*]," he was told, "here fine grapes are eaten. . . . Come and let us see if you have not lost your taste for them as well as for peaches, pears, and so on." The writer in France listed the daily amusements at Bayonne: skittles, the ball game of *pelota,* and playing cards for money. "This game, which will last all winter, will not ruin you," and, the writer added teasingly, "you might even win 800 livres for your bastard children while amusing yourself." The recipient in North America was addressed as "libertine" and "old sinner," and was advised that the "young lasses" (*des jeunes tendrons*) of Gascony would take his mind off commercial profits.[45]

One of the "king's daughters" who had been sent to Canada to marry a colonist and thereby keep him in New France did the opposite. Madeleine-Thérèse Sallé, a Parisian, had married a Montreal carpenter-joiner, who, in 1680, unwisely let her depart with three of their children to visit her home in Paris. Once there, she wrote letters asking him to join her with their other children. "It is something absolutely necessary; that is why I beg you in God's name, my dearest husband, not to delay in coming as soon as you can." He was told to sell their house and all their possessions in Canada and to smuggle, among their clothing, large fur muffs, because "beaver and marten fur are extremely valuable in Paris." The joiner was assured of employment in France and was counseled to eat heartily on the sea voyage to forestall sickness. Church registers testify that the entire family, less one grown-up son, left New France and returned to the homeland.[46]

In a society built upon networks of kinship and patronage, successful and well-connected individuals were expected to help their less-fortunate relatives. Female kin expected succor as a natural right. There are numerous letters from women that pray for the emigrant's good health and express hopes for his early return to France or, failing that, a cash remittance to aid family members in Europe. The aid expected of a good family man was best provided when the giver was back in his birthplace,where he belonged. Transatlantic communications were too uncertain to be a reliable way of conveying assistance.

It was made emphatically clear to one absentee that the welfare of his widowed mother and an unmarried sister demanded his return from New France; sending them money was not enough. Saint-Martin Duronea, a ship's captain, had been living on Ile Royale since 1754 and he had married a Mlle. Dupont at Louisbourg in 1756, suggesting that he might stay permanently in North America. This marriage and its possible consequence caused an uproar at his former home in Gascony. According to the parish priest there, the captain's mother, "was excessively afflicted to the point of dissolving into tears and of shrieking [*a jetter des hauts cris*] when she was given the news of your marriage at Louisbourg, but her pain ebbed slightly after receiving your two letters that inform her of your reasons binding you to establish yourself in this land [Gascony] and, finally, she was almost entirely consoled upon learning that you had married a young lady of merit." In short, the bride had property and respectable parents known to the groom's uncle. Now that the captain and his new wife had told his mother of their wish to come back to his birthplace, "and live with her [the mother], she gives you both her blessing." The priest assured the newlyweds that the mother "only sighs . . . to see you and embrace you. Therefore, come . . . as soon as you can; come to console her and give her the satisfaction of spending her last days with you. Natural impulses, sentiments of honor and religion, gratitude for all the kind acts and for all the pains she took for your education—all cry out for that. All of them call you to her side."[47] By corollary, settlement in North America, far from one's family, would be dishonorable, impious, ungrateful, and immoral.

In 1757, from nearby Saint-Jean de Luz, the mother of a sailor on Ile Royale issued a similar appeal to her absent child: "I am very sorrowful because of you. . . .

As you know, I am old. The grace that I ask of you is that you return home, my dear son, for love of me, whatever your present condition. The favor that I beg for is that, before my death, I might see you once more. After I have seen you that one time, I would be content to die."[48] Here was a mother who knew how to play upon her son's conscience and to exploit his guilt!

The errant Captain Duronea at Louisbourg received appeals from his family, too, in addition to the priest's letter, imploring him to come home. The curate had suggested that Duronea send money at once to his mother and sister, "to ease thereby their discomfort." The expatriate's uncle seconded the priest's suggestion, adding that the captain's mother had been tormented for aid by a sister who had wasted her *légitime* (rightful inheritance), and he proposed that his nephew send a remittance of at least one thousand livres to make amends for his indifference to his "poor, afflicted mother and [to] your sister who is almost always sick. . . . Try to come [home] as soon as possible." Pointedly, the uncle added, "if God gives you children, you will know the love one has for children, and [know] that you would wish to be treated with much love, tenderness and respect by your own children."[49] If this were not enough, the ailing sister sent a letter to add her voice to the chorus calling the emigrant home. She told her "most dear brother" that the news of his wedding overseas, "at first caused us various stirrings of opposition [*divers mouvemens oposez*]," but that his subsequent letters explaining his motives and expressing his intention to return had mollified his family. Now, she wrote, they had "every reason to expect that this union will turn to our advantage [and] that my poor mother will have a tranquil and secure old age and I [will have] all the help and advantages that I should expect from a brother I love tenderly."[50] Faced with this consensus of opposition to his possible settlement in New France, the exile knew that there was only one course open to him: to return to France. If this were typical of the social pressure exerted upon emigrants in French North America, one can readily understand their urge to return home.

The one-third or so of emigrants who remained in *la Nouvelle France* had severed the bonds with family and birthplace and, once freed, they did not give up their wandering ways. Applying to a seigneur for a land concession was only a tentative commitment to the land. Richard Colebrook Harris found that, during the late seventeenth century, "a third of all routures [inheritable leaseholds] on the Ile d'Orléans had been sold within ten years of their concession, and there is evidence that land sales were equally rapid in many other areas. In 1678 only half of the ninety-two rotures in the Jesuits' seigneurie of Notre Dame des Anges were in the hands of the original owners. . . . The turnover of land [titles] was most rapid during the 1660s and 1670s. New settlers were arriving almost every year, and after a man had spent a year or two in one spot he often left for another."[51] The

French-Iroquois War in 1687–1700 discouraged land buyers, but sales resumed after the 1701 peace treaty. Transactions were more frequent in the newer seigneuries and they slowed down on the longer-established estates. Later generations of *Canadiens*—especially families from the Montreal district—produced eighteenth-century settlers for Detroit and, farther west, for the distant Pays des Illinois. Overland travel was not as risky as an ocean voyage, and there was no bribe to be paid to Bonhomme Terreneuve. The royal government also encouraged migration to Detroit, to give this military and commercial outpost an agricultural base. New settlers there were offered land grants and, in 1749–50, material aid to help them establish themselves as farmers.[52] In retrospect, it appears that the children of immigrants who made a home in North America, even rural dwellers, were more mobile than their cousins in France. They were not so firmly attached to their birthplace and would move hundreds of kilometers if it seemed advantageous.

The colonists of *la Nouvelle France,* however mobile, were not willing innovators. Most tried to reproduce the world that they had known in France. The country folk continued to make chairs, tables, and chests in the Louis XIII style (1610–43) right up to the end of the eighteenth century. The insults that colonists hurled at each other revealed their tenacious desire to preserve metropolitan standards of behavior; they rarely formulated fresh epithets based on the exiles' new home and their peculiarly North American experiences. Just as in France, women were charged with sexual misconduct and men were accused of dishonesty in their dealings with others. *Putain,* meaning slut or whore, led all other insults when a woman was the target of verbal abuse. There was more variety in the names hurled at a man: *voleur, larron, filou, coquin*, and *fripon* all were used. They all meant the same thing: the recipient was a thief and a swindler. Taken as an inverse expression of social ideals, the epithets meant that chastity was the virtue most admired in women, while a man was valued for his honesty in dealings with others. These moral standards were exactly the same as those revered in the homeland.[53]

This conservative attachment to the homeland's traditions was also evident in folk songs, another oral tradition. Writing about French-Canadian folksingers in the early twentieth century, Charles Marius Barbeau observed that they "never gave free rein to improvisation, never ventured into new paths. They did not compose poems and melodies, but simply repeated what they had learned in childhood. . . . They plodded over their task and matched their lines to a familiar tune. The result was uncouth and commonplace. There was nowhere a fresh source of inspiration, only imitation, crude and slavish."[54] As in the world of invective, there was little innovation, just a simplified perpetuation of the repertoire remembered by the immigrants.

Royal policies helped screen out religious dissidents and political rebels from the migration to New France. Recruiting from France's semiliterate lower ranks meant that the newcomers were untouched by new and unorthodox ideas about society or politics contained in contemporary books. Liberal works might sometimes appear in the libraries of their betters, yet the merchants and officers who owned these seditious publications were too dependent upon the old order to entertain a proposal to upset it.

Most newcomers were young, single men. In the seventeenth century, these bachelors were bound to serve in a manual trade or in a menial capacity for three years. In the 1660s Pierre Boucher wrote, "most of our settlers here [in Canada] are people who came as servants and, after serving a master for three years, set up for themselves. . . . Ordinarily, they have little of anything and they later marry a woman who has nothing more. However, in less than four or five years you will see them at their ease, if they are fairly hard-working people."[55] For those who remained in the colony to marry and settle, the three years of servitude had acclimatized them to their new environment. In 1664 Quebec's Sovereign Council claimed that this period was "a sort of apprenticeship," by which, "we give the established settlers the means to advance their work and [it allows] the newly-arrived to instruct themselves in the nature of the work which even the best men from France would need to know."[56] The council's former attorney-general repeated this justification in 1715, while adding that "these [indentured] servants would be trained in the work on the land, and begin the dwelling places [*habitations*] upon which they would settle, after their service, and marry."[57] The council refused to countenance any reduction in the three years of service and forbade anyone who had received one of the king's subsidized *engagés* to release him prematurely. Such discharged servants would revert to the council's control.[58] The argument that the three-year term was an essential introduction to colonial husbandry was a self-interested justification by men who were the employers of *engagés* from France. When a man who had already lived in Canada for four years returned on one of the king's ships, the council rejected an appeal on his behalf, made by a Sulpician priest, "that it would not be reasonable" to compel him to serve as long as the other servants, as he had no need of an apprenticeship in colonial ways.[59] Moreover, 40 percent of the men distributed by the council in 1664–65 were employed in the colony's towns, where life was not so different from life in France.

The mandatory three years of servitude did induct workers into the colony's ways, even if they were not spent in learning how to fell trees and clear and cultivate virgin land. Likewise, the four or more years served by soldiers in New France, their quartering in private homes, and their employment at civilian jobs after 1685 helped in assimilating them to colonial life. After the 1670s the bachelors who chose to stay, whether former contract workers or discharged soldiers, usually married women of the colony and were absorbed into established families. They fitted into *la Nouvelle France* and did not alter the society that had been established in North America.

Apart from some Basque-speaking enclaves on Newfoundland and on Ile Royale and the German-speaking soldiers of the Swiss Karrer Regiment at Louisbourg, there were no ethnic communities within the European population of *la Nouvelle France*. There was always a scattering of Irish, Italian, Portuguese, German, and English newcomers. About 11 percent of the migrants to New France came from outside the French empire. Like the Protestants, foreigners were assimilated quickly. Only a surname, such as Schmid, Spagniolini, Feltz, Lopez, or Etcheverry, or a nickname like "le Portugais," identified the bearer's non-French origins, and even that trace could be erased. In Acadia the Mallinson brothers from Boston became progenitors of the numerous Melanson clan. The Gallicization of surnames occurred in Canada, too: Spennert became "Spénard," Leahy was soon "Lahé," Schwinhardt became "Chouinard," Willitt evolved into "Ouellet," and Sullivan emerged as "Sylvain."

Most miraculous was the transformation of Matt Farnsworth, who was captured near Groton, Massachusetts, by a war party of mission Indians from Sault-au-Récollet in August 1704. He was then fourteen years of age. Matt was taken back to Canada, instructed in the Roman Catholic faith, and baptized in January 1706 as "Claude-Mathias," with the local governor, Claude de Ramezay, as his godfather. Farnsworth became a naturalized subject of France and was given a land grant in 1711. Two years later he married Catherine Charpentier, the daughter of a neighboring farmer. A witness to their marriage contract was an Englishman, Joseph Daniel Maddox, who worked as a joiner in Montreal. The bride's father, Jean Charpentier, presented the couple with two bulls, a cow, a pig, two goats, and two acres of land. Farnsworth signed the agreement as "m c farnef." Matt Farnsworth had become "Claude-Mathias Farnef," Canadian farmer.[60] His many descendants, who bore the surname "Fanef" as well as "Phaneuf," could be excused for not knowing of their New England ancestry.

Esther Wheelwright, captured at Wells, Maine, became Mother Superior of the Quebec Ursulines in 1760.[61] She, too, was now a Canadian. Cultural homogenization of the white population in the St. Lawrence Valley was complete by 1700, when writers spoke confidently about the "Canadiens" and their distinctive ways. In spite of their parents' conservative reflexes, these children of displaced provincials from different regions of France and from elsewhere had evolved into *Canadiens* and *Acadiens,* distinguishable peoples with their own traits. As we will see in the next chapter, it had been a painful gestation, full of hardship and conflict.

CHAPTER 6

Proud as a *Canadien*, Stubborn as an *Acadien:* The Emergence of New Peoples

VISITORS' OBSERVATIONS

By the early eighteenth century, French writers spoke of definable Canadian traits and of the archetypal Acadian. Observers were no longer dealing with transplanted Frenchmen or French women, but with distinct regional types within the French Empire, like the Normans or West Indian Creoles. Visitors from France agreed that the Canadians—residents of the St. Lawrence Valley and its westerly extensions—were well built, polite, self-reliant, improvident, unruly, proud, and easily offended. A classic description from about 1737 is attributed to Intendant Gilles Hocquart. Even if he were not the author, the view is certainly that of a French administrator in *la Nouvelle France*.

> The Canadians are naturally big, well-built, and have a robust constitution. Since the crafts are not hindered here by formal masterships and because artisans were rare at the beginning of the colony, necessity has made the Canadians industrious from one generation to the next. The rural folk all handle an axe with skill; they make the greater part of their own farming tools and implements. They also build their own houses and barns. . . . They love honors and flattery, pride themselves on their bravery, and are extremely sensitive to scorn or the slightest punishments. They are self-interested, vindictive, and subject to drunkenness. . . . Those of the towns are less depraved [*moins vicieux*]. All are attached to religion and one sees few criminals here.

Canadians are fickle, have too high an opinion of themselves, which prevents them from succeeding as they might in the crafts, farming and in commerce.

Typical of a metropolitan official's social concern was the writer's recommendation to "enforce . . . the clear subordination that ought to exist among all levels [*ordres*] of society, [especially] among the countryfolk." In the writer's opinion, the best solution would be to increase the number of garrison troops from France, since the five hundred soldiers in Canada's three towns were "not enough to keep the populace of the towns and countryside in good order [*dans le bon ordre*]."[1]

The *Canadiens'* insubordination and saucy familiarity offended haughty gentlemen from Europe. Pierre-Herman Dosquet, the newly arrived coadjutor-bishop of Quebec, was outraged in 1731 when the governor-general denied him the right to lock the gate leading to a terrace beside the bishop's palace. The terrace commanded a fine view of the river and became a popular gathering place for Quebeckers on warm, summer nights. This high ecclesiastic complained

> I am unable to walk around the terrace side [of the palace], without being obliged to salute the passers-by or to reply to the compliments of those I know. It is under my windows that the low class of people of both sexes assemble after supper, where they sing and have licentious conversations that I hear as though they were in my room. I do not speak of their indecent actions. There drunkards come to sleep off their wine and mischief-makers have stripped them naked of their clothes. . . . On holidays and Sundays, one's head is split with the din they make when playing skittles or bowling. . . . If I go into my garden, everyone stops at the post fence to watch me. . . . It is hardly suitable that clergy in recreation find themselves mixed, helter-skelter, with persons of the opposite sex and with the populace.

Royal officials yielded to this complaint and allowed the coadjutor-bishop to have the gate locked, as he had wished, but some unknown townsfolk picked the lock at night and then, as a gesture of defiance, carried off the gate.[2] They were not going to give up their popular rendezvous, whatever Monsignor Dosquet might wish.

The Canadian traits that French administrators felt were most in need of correction were idleness, indiscipline, and insubordination. King Louis XIV instructed Intendant Jean Talon to urge Canadian fathers to see to their children's education, cultivating a veneration for religion and for the king's person, "and afterward to accustom them to work from an early age because we certainly know from experience that idleness in the first years of life is the true source of all the disorders that befall a person."[3] Bishop Saint-Vallier, too, reminded priests of their duty to advise parishioners, "on ruling their family well, [and] to teach them the respect and obe-dience that they must render to their spiritual and temporal superiors."[4]

To judge from other commentators' accounts, nothing came from these pious injunctions. According to Governor-General de Denonville in 1685, "the great lib-erty of long standing which the parents and governors [in Canada] have given the youth, permitting them to dally in the woods under the pretext of hunting and trading . . . has reached such an excess that from the time children are able to carry a gun, fathers are not able to restrain them and dare not anger them."[5] Intendant Jacques Raudot was inclined to blame Canadian parents for the deplorable traits of the colonists: "the residents of this country have never had a proper education be-cause of the over-indulgence [*la foiblesse*] shown to them by their mothers and fa-thers during their infancy. In this, they imitate the Amerindians. It prevents them from disciplining their children and forming their character." The young were as-sumed to be naturally self-indulgent, and, to counter this inclination, physical pun-ishment was reckoned the best cure. As a result of this alleged Canadian leniency, the unruly children showed no respect for their parents, "as well as toward their superiors and parish priests." In 1707 Raudot proposed that resident schoolmasters be established in each parish to end the license of Canadian youngsters.[6] Schooling involved social regimentation as well as learning knowledge, but there were few permanent schools outside the colony's towns. French officials believed implicitly in this unruliness; in the same year a military engineer advised against imposing a head tax, or *taille,* in the colony because, he believed, it would certainly cause a revolt.[7] Sincere though these beliefs might have been, they reflected the outsiders' authoritarian values as much as they corresponded to colonial reality.

EVIDENCE OF A DISTINCTIVE COLONIAL IDENTITY

A language's evolution, as well as distinctive social traits, can signal the emergence of a new identity. Considering the modern debate over the legitimacy of Canadian French as a language, the favorable consensus of French visitors about colonial speech comes as a surprise. The visitors praised the quality of French spoken in New France. Father Pierre-François-Xavier de Charlevoix could have been speaking for all of them when he wrote in the 1720s, "nowhere else do they speak our language more purely [than the Canadians]; one cannot even notice any [provincial] accent here."[8] The fusion of regional dialects of French and the disappearance of other European tongues into a language close to the standard of the educated classes, that of Ile-de-France, was remarkable because it happened so quickly. The Canadians' vocabulary was not entirely free of provincial expressions: they spoke of a tap or faucet as a "champlure" rather than a *robinet* and used "jaspiner" for chatting instead of *causer*.

In the 1740s Father Pierre-Philippe Potier made notes on the peculiarities of Canadian French as it was spoken near Quebec and Detroit. The colonists had borrowed Amerindian terms for many North American novelties: a bullfrog was a "ouaouaron," cranberries were "atoca," a wolverine or badger was a "carcajou," and the annoying mosquito a "maringouin." On Bois Blanc Island near Michilimackinac, the missionary heard a man praise a hunting dog thus: "ce chien avait le Manitou pour le perdrix." The dog's talent for locating partridges was attributed to—using an Algonkian word—a powerful spirit. Colonial metaphors expressed prejudices about the mission Indians' passion for alcohol: to drink a large glass of liquor was to "boire le coup Abenakais" (quaff an Abenaki's draft). Nautical and military expressions salted Canadian speech: a heavy snowfall or gale was a "broadside" (*bordée*) and a finely dressed woman was "all rigged up" (*gréé*). A fleeing deer had "uprooted the flag and decamped." The Canadian climate called forth new words, such as "poudrerie" for a light snowfall. The North American turkey was already a symbol for folly: "je n'en serai le dinde" (I would not be the turkey for that) was a refusal to play the dupe. Colonists were fond of metaphors: a clock was "the stomach's drum," since it called people to the table just as a drummer summoned soldiers to assembly. A sincere man had "no back door at all," and "to kick at the sun" was to get so drunk that one could not stand upright. The French description of an indiscreet babbler as "la trompette du quartier" (the neighborhood's trumpet) was modified in New France to "the fort's trumpet."[9]

Canadian speech was simple, direct French, free of the circumlocutions and affectations of literary *français*. The spoken language became standardized and fixed in New France more than a century before it achieved stability and general acceptance across France. Again, the colony had achieved a governmental goal well before the parent kingdom. Only on Ile Royale and Newfoundland did Euzkara, the Basque tongue, rival French as a means of communication between colonists. Breton Gaelic, the language of whalers and fishers off North America's Atlantic coast, had left few traces in the 1700s. This early stabilization of the language is a key to the distinctiveness of Canadian French, which is a fusion of seventeenth-century dialects, enriched by borrowed Amerindian and nautical terms. Later visitors were more critical of Canadian French because their standard for judgment, metropolitan French, had continued to evolve. In about 1807 John Lambert noted, "previous to the conquest of the country by the English, the inhabitants are said to have spoken as pure and correct French as in old France; since then they have adopted many anglicisms in their language, and have also several antiquated phrases, . . . For *froid* (cold) they pronounce *frête*. For *ici* (here) they pronounce *icite*. For *prêt* (ready) they pronounce *parré*; besides several other obsolete words which I do not at present recollect. Another corrupt practice is very common among them, of pronouncing the *final* letter of their words, which is contrary to the custom of European French."[10] What had been acceptable usages in the early 1700s had become archaic, "corrupt," and strange when encountered in nineteenth-century Canada.

In the seventeenth century, there is evidence that the newcomers' speech was as heterogeneous as their origins. At Trois-Rivières in 1658 Marie Armand, Mme. David, asked to be excused from giving verbal testimony, "inasmuch as she has difficulty speaking French." Her new husband was a Norman, but her origins were not identified. A witness in Quebec's Prévôté Court during the late 1660s said that he could not follow what had been said because the defendant was speaking to the plaintiff "in his patois."[11] Later immigrants were handicapped if they did not know the dominant language. Such was the case of Yves Phlem, a Breton farmer accused of practicing surgery without having been formally qualified in that art. In his sworn statement before a priest, Phlem said that when he was an adolescent,

> He was taught to bleed, to dress wounds and [learned] several remedies to cure different diseases. . . . the desire to travel, which comes naturally to Bretons, led him to indenture himself at St. Malo [in about 1720] to come to Canada on a ship. . . . It is impossible to say how difficult it was for him to survive in the beginning. The science that he had acquired and which was the only one that Providence had granted him was useless because he only understood Breton. However, since the Good Lord always provides the necessary means to those who live according to His precepts, his [Phlem's] ignorance of the French language was not an obstacle that prevented many persons with different ailments from consulting him.

In 1734 Phlem contracted to cure a facial tumor for five hundred livres, and he was as incapable as any licensed surgeon in arresting the cancer's spread. The patient, Jean Bilodeau, died in Phlem's house. The amateur surgeon attracted the royal officials' attention when he went to court to demand the balance of his fee. The magistrate ordered him not to act as a surgeon without official letters verifying his competence. With a casual indifference to authority, Phlem declined to be examined by the lieutenant of the king's surgeon or the royal physician in New France and he quietly resumed his curative work.[12] The migrants to French North America, even those from France, were never all French-speaking.

Sobriquets, or nicknames—so popular among soldiers—sometimes gave a clue to the bearer's geographic or cultural origins. The names *Gascon, Provençal, Lyonnais, Poitevin,* and *Langevin* identified the emigrant's home province or town within France. *Poitevin* indicated roots in Poitou Province or the city of Poitiers; an Angevin came from Anjou Province or Angers town; *Normand* and *Gascon* speak for themselves. The *Lallemand* and *Langlois* families are sometimes traceable to German and English ancestors.[13] They could also refer to the proverbial traits of those foreigners, whether having blond hair or a taste for beer. Jean Chasse *dit* (called) Bourguignon (the Burgundian) was also known as "la joue percée" (hole in the cheek). Since this forger of currency escaped hanging, he did not graduate to "le cou cassé" (broken neck). He was executed in effigy.[14] As picturesque as Chasse's appellations were the nicknames *Pret à boire* (ready to drink), *Brin d'Amour* (blade of love), *Bon appetit, la Déroute* (wrong turn), *Danse l'Ombre* (dances in shadows), *Vin d'Espagne* (Spanish wine), and *Frappe d'Abord* (strikes first). Some descriptive sobriquets, such as *Lafontaine* (fountain), *Bellehumeur* (good-natured), *Jolicoeur* (light heart), *Tranche-montagne* (mountain-slicer—that is, boaster), and *Sanschagrin* (no worries) replaced the original surname and became distinctively Canadian family names. The Acadians, having grown primarily from a small nucleus of settlers from Brittany, Normandy, and southwestern France, were distinguished by a few widely used surnames that did not appear in the St. Lawrence Valley before fugitives arrived there in the 1750s. The family names *Amirault, Aucoin, Belliveau, Comeau, Chiasson, d'Entremont, d'Eon, Doucette, Gallant,* and *Melanson* proclaim their owners' ancestral ties to *l'Acadie.*

By 1700 more than surnames set the Canadians and Acadians apart from other French-speaking Roman Catholics. "Les Canadiens" had their own traits, like the proverbial boastful Gascons or the litigious Normans. The differences were not sufficiently great to allow one to speak of a new nation. Writers spoke confidently of the Canadians' shared characteristics, such as excessive pride, vanity, and insubordination. The natives of the St. Lawrence Valley, in turn, labeled their neighbors to the east. They described someone as "entêté comme un Acadien," or as stubborn as an Acadian. J. C. B. observed, as well, the distinctions made among Canadians, while identifying their common characteristics.

> The residents of Montreal call those of Quebec *sheep* because the latter have a gentler character and are less bellicose. In reprisal, they [Quebeckers] call Montrealers *wolves,* a just description since only Montrealers visit Amerindians and the woods . . . In general, the *Canadiens* are forthright, kind, and hospitable . . . but they are poorly-educated.[15]

Outsiders were more disparaging about the intellectual and material life of the Acadians. At Port Royal De Dièreville wrote his poetic lament "Nothing before my eyes but streams and forests, huts of mud and cottages; . . . How one can live here I don't know. Oh, what a scene of poverty! Already I, with but a taste, have had enough of this new France, and here what penance for the Old I'll do."[16]

The Relationship of
Status and Wealth

The outsiders' claim that social order had broken down in New France should be taken with a large grain of salt. The "bon ordre" desired by French administrators was a clear hierarchy of social groups. Newly arrived officials were offended by the blurring of social distinctions in Canada, apparent in dress and behavior. Canadian tenant-farmers could hunt wild game and ride horses, and their daughters dressed in fine clothes more suitable for ladies of rank. The colonists' ostentation in clothing was noted by French and foreign travelers. In the matter of legal rights and functions, familiar distinctions were missing. Like the clergy and nobility of France, Canadians paid no direct taxes to the king; they were subject only to duties on imported goods. The crown itself had reduced the functional distinction between social orders. A March 1685 royal decree had permitted the colonial nobility and gentry to engage in all branches of commerce without a loss of rank and the notables used this right. In France a noble who dabbled in retail trade forfeited his privileged status. In the 1750s the Marquis de Montcalm saw this relaxation of metropolitan rules as the undoing of social distinctions: "everyone [in Canada] wants to engage in commerce; the Estates are in confusion."[17]

Another French aristocrat, Chevalier de la Pause, was more cautious. There were, he wrote, three social "orders" in New France, but they were not the legal estates of clergy, nobility, and commoners. He defined the "classes" in Canada as follows: "colonial military officers and members of the *Conseil souverain* are the first [estate]. Second are the merchants and Marine Department administrators [*les gens de plume*]; and the third [consists of] the *habitants* who live by their labor and on their land [*dans leur bien*]."[18] This threefold division of society overlooked the clergy, skilled craftsmen and other city residents, fishermen, or fur trade workers. It did, however, acknowledge the inequality of social ranks in *la Nouvelle France*.

Evidence of social inequality, especially in the towns, appeared in judicial records of assault cases. *Canadiens* might have saucy tongues, yet they dared not raise their fists against superiors, even in self-defense. A Quebec artisan boldly reproached a prominent merchant in public, saying, "do you realize that your manservant and I have something in common [as your creditors]; if you had paid your debts, you would not be carrying such a fine fur muff." The merchant rewarded this impertinence with the drubbing of his cane.[19] The colony's notables commonly chastised inferiors by hitting them with a walking stick or the flat side of a sword. At a Montreal funeral in 1699 the beadle bumped Sieur d'Argenteuil's son while filling in the grave. The gentleman called the beadle "a beggar, an unfortunate, and a wretch," and when the grave-digger tried to explain the accident, he was knocked down and beaten with a cane.[20] Sieur d'Argenteuil could do this with impunity because social inferiors dared not meet force with force; they endured such assaults with nothing more than a plaintive cry, such as "Why do you beat me without cause?" or "Sir, I beg your pardon . . . , I have done nothing to you."[21]

Social inferiors' passive submission to physical abuse by their "betters" acknowledged their low status and, since social rank affected court judgments, it was unwise for a man to strike his superiors. That response was deemed a challenge to the social order. Injuring a person of higher standing, especially one's legal master, was an act of rebellion. When a Trois-Rivières merchant was struck by his servant, the employer described the blow as "a crime deserving exemplary punishment to ensure the repose and security of this country's families."[22] If the roles were reversed, an injured subordinate could claim only medical expenses from the worthy assailant, but not damages, and a response in kind would erase that modest entitlement. Thus, it was not prudent to fight back against people of higher standing. In 1709 two soldiers who had assaulted a Montreal apothecary were sentenced to die for their crime. The assailants escaped from prison in women's dress—obviously with help—and the death sentence had to be carried out in effigy, upon a painted panel. The only person to suffer physical punishment was a painter, Jean Berger, who had witnessed the assault and composed a burlesque song mocking the apothecary's legal pursuit of the soldiers. Berger was exposed publicly in an iron collar attached to a post, fined court costs, ordered to pay twenty livres in damages to the druggist, and banished from Montreal. A painter was a craftsman who ought to have treated the learned apothecary and the court with more respect. He seems to have fled from the colony with his English-speaking wife.[23]

Assault cases are crude evidence of social inequality in New France; they do not permit one to delineate the gradations of rank within colonial society. To do that, one must consult other sources. Official rulings on *préséance,* or protocol, did define the top levels of the social pyramid and the prerogatives of each level. Royal officials, as we have seen, were troubled by the apparent blurring of ranks and by the colonists' pretensions to higher status. This tendency to self-elevation was another by-product of anonymity among the immigrants. Because each newcomer's ancestry and background were not generally known, it was possible to inflate one's own credentials. Colonists did not question the sanctity of the social order, they merely sought to raise their standing within it. Because noble status was the dream of people in the Third Estate, an aristocratic lineage usually was claimed by the charlatans. Detroit's founder, Antoine Laumet, the self-styled noble Sieur de Lamothe Cadillac, was not alone in claiming aristocratic origins that were not his birthright. In 1681 Quebec's Sovereign Council began an investigation into "usurpers of nobility in this land," and then referred the matter to the crown.[24] Upon the minister's order, Intendant Jacques de Meulles issued an ordinance in October 1684 forbidding anyone to use the noble title "esquire" (*écuyer*) in public or in legal acts without giving proof of his nobility.[25] In September 1721 Quebec's Superior Council registered the king's order restricting the right to wear a sword in public—an insignia of authority and noble rank—to military officers, ship's captains, and gentlemen.[26] Because members of the colony's military and administrative elite had taken advantage of the 1685 decree to invest in commerce, and associated with commoners in trade, these worthies were assertive in claiming the honors and prerogatives owed to them. The outward marks of social superiority acquired an exaggerated importance. The elite's attachment to visible symbols of lofty status was evident in the 1730s when colonial officers resisted the metropolitan rule that litigants appear in court disarmed. They wanted to wear their swords when appearing before the Superior Council at Quebec.[27] Their tenacious attachment to this mark of high standing was understandable, given the ambiguities of colonial society.

Since relative standing was acknowledged by placement in public ceremonies, colonists were deeply offended when located behind someone they regarded as a lesser being or when denied some special mark of respect to which they felt they were entitled. Unseemly brawls broke out over positioning in religious processions or the sequence for receiving Holy Communion in church. In 1694 Quebec's bishop-designate and Montreal's governor quarreled in the Franciscans' new chapel at Montreal over whose prayer stool should be closest to the altar. Monsignor Saint-Vallier ordered the removal of all prayer stools, and, when the local governor had his chair put back, the future bishop refused to consecrate the chapel and declared it closed to worshippers.[28] To avert such embarassing squabbles, the king's ruling of April 1716 outlined the protocol for royal officials in places of worship and public ceremonies. In order of precedence, the governor-general of New France came first as the king's representative, preceded by his personal guards, followed by the local governor or Quebec's *lieutenant du Roi*, then the intendant to the left-hand side, the members of the *Conseil supérieur*, the officers of inferior law courts, parish wardens and, finally, other congregants.[29] The king had to intervene on several occasions to resolve disputes over public honors and precedence.[30] These rulings provide an index to New France's social structure, but they were externally imposed standards and dealt with only the upper levels of colonial society.

Modern North Americans are impressed by material wealth, and today's historians, naturally, are attracted by accounts of property as the true measure of social standing. The notarial archives of the French Regime do contain estate inventories for everyone who died with an heir, so there are evaluations of each person's assets at death. The notary-recorder customarily was assisted in his appraisal by two expert assessors, and their estimates were close to real market value, as subsequent estate auctions testify.[31] Over a long life, men accumulated property until their forties and then gradually dissipated assets to support themselves in old age. In table 1, "Montreal and Quebec Region Estate Inventories," which summarizes seventy-five assessments made in 1684–1734, the successive appraisals for Jérôme Lonquetin, farmer, in 1704 (when his wife died) and in 1723 (when he died) show a gradual decline in the value of his moveable assets from 942 to 816 livres. The smallest estate belonged to a farmer's widow. When a craftsman or farmer died in his twenties or in extreme old age, his legacy would be small because the man was at the beginning or long past his earning stage. Debts could exceed the value of the assets; see, for example, Claude Chasle, Noël Levasseur, Louis Brassard, and Pierre Bazinet in table 1. Real estate, when listed, was rarely appraised because fixed assets, including land, acquired before marriage or inherited from kin, passed on to blood relations and not to one's surviving spouse. That conformed to the principle of the *Coutume de Paris* that family lands should remain in the hands of that lineage.

Moveable assets (*biens meubles*) were itemized and evaluated so that they could be precisely divided among a person's legitimate heirs. Unfortunately, the full value of an estate was masked by the incomplete recording of credits. By tacit understanding, widows were allowed to take the money and to pocket it without a declaration. Silverware—another form of accumulated wealth—was often treated in a similar way: listed without an appraisal. As for debts owed to the deceased, accounting among New France's semiliterate lower ranks was haphazard; it might depend on paper slips, wooden tally sticks (with one notch for each transaction), and memory alone. A baker's widow confessed complete ignorance of her late husband's accounts, and that was that.[32] The "net worth" of most people cannot be established because there was rarely a comprehensive and accurate listing of all assets, including real estate. When their worth can be computed, it should be treated with caution since some assets, invariably, were overlooked. Only the moveables, with allowance for omissions, allow a comparison between individual colonists of different occupations.

Although one's calling was a prime consideration in establishing social status, it is a challenge to determine a deceased person's principal occupation because it was commonplace in the colony for an individual to engage in a variety of activities. An officer in the garrison troops, for example, would also be a seigneur, and he was probably active in some commercial venture, such as the fur trade. His military commission was the key to his social standing and he would have been offended to be addressed as a merchant-investor. A stonemason could be a building contractor and might serve as an expert assessor for the law courts. Outside the towns, craftsmen usually combined skilled manufacturing with farming in order to survive. Once a person's principal occupation, as stated in the inventory, has been confirmed and individuals are ranged according to the total value of moveable goods possessed, the discrepancy between wealth and the hierarchy of occupations in Old

Regime France is apparent. One's position in the eyes of others seldom corresponded to the value of material goods owned; status, evidently, did not depend upon wealth.

People in Old Regime France had firm notions about what made some occupations honorable and what made other vocations base. Work that engaged the head, rather than the hands, was esteemed. Physicians, whose heads were crammed with questionable medical theories, but never wielded the knife, could look down upon surgeons as mere mechanics who had learned their trade by apprenticeship. The "nobility" of one's working materials as well as the standing of one's patrons placed silversmiths above locksmiths, who, in turn, sneered at farriers. Silversmiths fashioned ornaments and vessels from noble metals for the service of the church and for the gentry; farriers served farmers and carters by shaping iron shoes for horses' hooves. By virtue of being the king's servants, royal court officers preceded seigneurial magistrates. The ranking of skills could be affected by special connections; for example, carpenters benefited from their craft's association with St. Joseph, the earthly father of Jesus Christ. These were some of the considerations that determined one's placement in public ceremonies.

A Corpus Christi procession, commemorating Christ's Last Supper, held at Angers, France, in 1637 arranged all of the city's trades into eight categories according to these principles. Judicial and municipal officials—in the absence of royal officers—as well as the learned professions were placed at the apex of the "ancien ordre." Next came the cloth merchants, booksellers, apothecaries, surgeons, and goldsmiths. The ceremonial hierarchy provided for six more ranks and passed on down through food retailers, clothiers, iron workers, painters, building crafts, leather workers, butchers, and bakers. At the very bottom were street-porters and journeymen bakers. Leatherworkers appeared at two different levels, as did butchers and bakers, and it is obvious that the procession's organizers were uncertain about the dignity of certain trades.[33] Despite some difficulty in reconciling the cultural prejudices and social rules of the day, Anger's "ancient order" gives us the approximate ranking of occupations that immigrants brought with them from France to North America. The importance of ceremonial precedence among craftsmen was evident at Quebec in 1646, when the colony had no more than six hundred European settlers. At a discussion about the forthcoming Corpus Christi procession at Quebec, someone reminded the planners "that it was necessary to retain the honorable order of crafts."[34]

In table 1 there is no close connection between the traditional social ranks and recorded wealth. Canadian society had passed through the initial period of flux and was now firmly established. With that stabilization, there was a greater range in wealth in the 1700s. A bigger sample would yield similar results. Government officials and merchants tended to be near the top, but so, too, were a tannery owner, masonry builders, a butcher, and several other craftsmen, as well as a few farmers.

Montreal (M) and Quebec (Q) Region Estate Inventories, 1684–1734

Valuation in *livres of account* to the nearest *livre*. N/G = not given.

SOURCES: Archives du Quebec [AQ], Quebec, Greffes des notaires, L. Chambalon, F. de la Cetiere, J. E. Dubreuil, N. Duprac, F. Genaple, E. Jacob, J. C. Louet, P. Rivet; AQ, Montreal, Greffes . . . , A. Adhemar, J. B. Adhemar, G. Barette, B. Basset, J. David, M. Lepallieur, C. Maugue, M. Moreau, J. C. Raimbault, P. Raimbault, N. Senet, M. Tailhandier, cloture d'inventaire (10 dec. 1709).

ESTATE INVENTORY	OCCUPATION	MOVEABLES	IMMOVEABLES	CREDITS	DEBITS	NET WORTH
J. F. Martin de Lino 1722Q	Crown Attorney	11,457[a]	listed	8,848	2,895	17,410
C. de Monseignat 1718Q	Naval Comptroller	11,291	N/G	5455	N/G	
P. Gauvreau 1721Q	King's Gunsmith-Silversmith	8,542	listed	4,100	80	12,562
C. Demers 1717M	Baker	6,971	N/G	1,102	4,238	3,835
P. Perthuis 1716M	Fur Trade Outfitter/Retailer	5,391	N/G	5,639	N/G	11,030
M. R. C. de St.Romain 1717Q	Major's Widow	5,250	N/G	1,187+	N/G	
E. Charest 1699Q	Tannery Owner	5,081	17,900	923	8,140	15,762
M. Gagnon 1696Q	Farmer	4,931[b]	N/G	42	244	4,729
J. B. Neveu 1715M	Merchant	4,735+	listed	N/G	38+	4,697+
J. Tessier 1717M	Farmer	4,253	N/G	195	2,135	2,313
S. Dugue 1688M	Officer-Seigneur	3,879	N/G	1,966	721	5,124
L. Girard 1715M	Farmer	3,841	N/G	650	167	4,324
A. Adhémar 1714M	Royal Notary	3,309	N/G	1,119	2,202	2,226
C. J. de St.Denis 1704M	Lieutenant-General	3,108	N/G	11,995	12,701+	2,402
F. Lefèbvre 1718M	Farmer	2,784	listed	N/G	N/G	
J. Minet 1706Q	Merchant	2,687	listed	761	164	3,284
B. Bleigne 1731M	Stonemason	2,387	450 (house)	N/G	N/G	
C. G. P. de Langloiserie 1722M	King's Lieutenant-Seigneur	2,331	N/G	furnishings held by his children	2,956	−625
L. Brien 1718M	Tailor-Farmer	2,141	N/G	N/G	1,200	
D. Corbin 1724Q	Shipwright	1,886	listed	200	N/G	
U. Tessier 1690M	Masonry Builder	1,882	N/G	75	745	1,212
M. Cadet 1703Q	Butcher	1,720+livestock	N/G	3,660	898	4,482

			other bldgs. & land			
C. Chasle 1698Q	Retired Cooper	1,655	listed	24+	2,616	−937
C. D. de La Jemerais 1720M	Military Captain	1,588	230 (house)+	25,694	43,796	−16,284
J.B. Pitallier 1730M	Blacksmith	1,359	200 (house)	536	1,008	1,087
P. Prudhomme 1724M	Locksmith-Armourer	1,332	N/G	N/G	N/G	1,107
V. Lenoir 1703M	Joiner-Carpenter	1,285	listed	248	426	
R. G. de Varennes 1693M	Officer-Regional Governor	1,156+livestock	N/G	N/G	N/G[c]	
F. Gacien 1729M	Roofer	1,117	listed	N/G	1,624	833+
J. Fauconnet 1721Q	Barber-Wigmaker	1,115	none	31+	313	
J. Poupart 1734M	Farmer-Tailor	1,056	listed	N/G	120	
C. Baillif 1699Q	Builder-Architect	1,047	5,000	3,046	68	9,025
I. Hervieux 1700Q	Nailsmith	996	1,925	427	633	2,715
J. Lonquetin 1704M	Farmer	942	N/G	25	48	919
P. Rainville 1731Q	Farmer	919	listed	202	6	1,115
P. Perrault 1715M	Farmer	888	listed	41	256	673
J. Lonquetin 1723M	Farmer	816	400 (buildings)	N/G	300	916
J. Desrochers 1684M	Farmer	771	2,657	N/G	462	2,966
J. Dumay 1708M	Farmer	796	N/G	N/G	802	
P. Cuillerier 1716M	Retired Merchant	757+	listed	4,000	none	4,757+
Jos. Maillou 1703Q	Masony Builder	735	9,904	750	2,788	8,601
E. Prévost 1717M	Fur Trader, ex-Soldier	709	N/G	N/G	500	209
P. Thibièrge 1700M	King's Gunsmith	699	N/G	N/G	N/G	
P. Tabault 1714M	Farmer-Canoeman	644	listed	106	N/G	750
F. Bourassa 1710M	Sabotier-Farmer	627	listed	N/G	100	
J. L'Huisser 1713M	Farmer	626[d]	listed	4,322[e]	N/G	
J. Brunet 1732M	Butcher	573	N/G	N/G	167	
J. Poidras 1703Q	Farmer-Joiner	566	800	N/G	214	1,152
J. Filiau Dubois 1713Q	Joiner	506+	partial list	315	N/G	
P. Payement 1726Q	Blacksmith	488	listed	652+	166+	974
H. Danys 1690M	Farmer-Carpenter	475	N/G	N/G	15	
P. Evé 1713Q	Carter	465	listed	223	86	602
F. LeBer 1698M	Merchant	450	3,100	N/G	1,656	1,894

ESTATE INVENTORY	OCCUPATION	MOVEABLES	IMMOVEABLES	CREDITS	DEBITS	NET WORTH
P. Perras 1684M	Cooper	426	200	N/G	N/G	
N. Perthuis 1733M	Baker	374	N/G	N/G	N/G	
F. Constantin 1704Q	Voyageur	314	N/G	27	170	171
N. Levasseur (age 24) 1704Q	Joiner	302	listed	90	950	-558
F. Dolbec 1732Q	Farmer-Weaver	302	listed	59	437	-76
J. Brusseau 1700Q	Miller	297	1,250	N/G	559	988
J. Bourbon 1695M	Farmer	295	800	N/G	94	1,001
C. Chaboulié 1708M	Wood Sculptor	293	N/G	242	201	334
J. Milot 1700M	Retired Toolmaker	289	N/G	N/G	N/G	
L. Brassard 1718M	Retired Farmer	263	farm	N/G	760	-497
P. Moreau 1704M	Former Soldier	261	N/G	N/G	1,640	-1,379
E. Forestier 1700M	Baker	231	N/G	N/G	1,142	
J. Viger 1720M	Shipwright	225	listed	N/G	708	
J. Sedillot 1703Q	Farmer	211	800	N/G	214	797
P. Bardet 1730M	Baker	197	N/G	N/G	N/G	
J. B. Maillou 1690Q	Stonemason	187	750 (house)	40	N/G	977
B. Dumouchel 1733M	Shoemaker	187	N/G	N/G	216	
C. Faye 1709M	Farmer	183	listed	N/G	278	
P. Bazinet 1708	Farmer	175[f]	N/G	35	376	-166
J. Girard 1713Q	Navigateur	151	listed	in kind	1,459	
J. Mouchère 1706Q	Tanner	84	N/G	4,312	N/G	
C. Moitié 1688M	Farmer's Widow	39	1,200	N/G	368	871

a. Wife had a drapery shop whose stock accounted for 6,058 livres.

b. Included 2,650 livres in currency.

c. Before the notary had listed and evaluated all of the assets, the widow renounced her share of the community goods because of the debts.

d. Sale of the moveables realized 749 livres.

e. This included 4,321 livres in coins and card money.

f. The moveables evaluated at 108 livres sold for 97 livres. Unthreshed grain was not given a value and is not included in this figure.

Clothing workers and food tradesmen tended to be near the bottom of the scale, based on the moveables' value, yet the baker Charles Demers had more than eight thousand livres in assets. Not only were there these anomalies of wealth, but there is no consistency in the economic level of any one occupation: a farmer could have moveable possessions worth from 175 to 4,931 livres, even though most agriculturalists were clustered in the 600 to 950 livres range. Taking into account a farmer's high capital investment in buildings, livestock, and crops, many cultivators were better off, materially, than some gentlemen. The range of fortunes in the Montreal District, from 40 to 7,000 livres in portable assets, was surprisingly limited. Greater fortunes were to be found at Quebec, where a crown attorney and a naval comptroller, who was also secretary-councilor on the *Conseil supérieur,* had more than 11,000 livres in moveable possessions. The wealthiest residents of the colony were still small fry by the standards of La Rochelle, the port to which a few of Canada's most successful entrepreneurs repaired. The estate inventories of that French city's worthies filled small books. In general, the extremes of wealth and poverty known in Europe were absent from New France. The Canadian peasantry had a secure existence and landless beggars were a rare sight in the colony.

The regional differences in wealth and the anomalies within each occupational group were recognized in a 1754 proposal to impose a head tax upon the fifty-five thousand residents of the St. Lawrence Valley. Clergymen and nuns were to be lightly taxed while the governor-general, intendant, and bishop of Quebec were to contribute handsomely, from 600 to 1,200 livres. Their social prominence was thus conflated with actual wealth. Judicial officers were rated at 50 to 100 livres, and other officials were assessed on the basis of their income. Court clerks earned a great deal as copiers of legal deeds and were to be taxed twice as much as judges. The tax assessment recognized regional differences in wealth: residents of the poor Trois-Rivires District—apart from the ironworks' employees—would pay only the smallest amount. Most laymen there were to pay one livre each. Elsewhere, occupation and wealth guided the proposed levy upon town residents, who were divided into five classes. At Quebec there were deemed to be 1,200 lay heads-of-households in a population of 8,000. They were divided into:

- 1st—One hundred well-to-do merchants (*Négotiants des plus aisés*) at 30# [livres each],
- 2nd—One hundred Masters of Trades and others at 30#,
- 3rd—Four hundred [master craftsmen] less well off (*moins aisés*) at 10#,
- 4th—Six hundred carters and day-laborers at 3#,
- 5th—5,326 people, children of all ages and servants whom we believe should not count for more than 3,000, considering the children under seven years of age and the invalids, at 20 sols (1 livre).

Montreal's 4,000 residents were assumed to be more prosperous: all of its crafts-men were assessed thirty livres each, and the estimated 250 day-laborers were ex-pected to pay ten livres each. As for the countryfolk, they were divided into:

- 91 curates whose benefices could be appraised, one with another, at 75#,
- 1,500 well-off farmers (*habitans*) at 40#,
- 1,500 less well-to-do at 25#,
- 2,000 [poorly off?] at 15#,
- 4,200 women who are paying with their husbands (*femmes qui payent avec leurs Maris*),
- 2,000 [fur-trade] voyageurs, hired men, free bachelors (*volontaires*) at 6#,
- 29,909 whether heads of families, their wives, or children and servants, en-tered as 18,000 [taxable people], allowing for children below seven years of age, [each] at 20 sols.[35]

The variable impost for farmers, from one to forty livres, recognized the disparity in resources among them. The most prosperous agriculturalists were to be taxed as much as a member of Quebec Superior Council or Montreal's civil magistrate. The 1754 capitation tax list reinforces the impression given by estate inventories: per-sonal property seldom corresponded to the social rank of one's occupation.

STATUS AND CONSUMPTION PATTERNS

Although property records discredit the belief that society in New France was made up of economic classes, the inventories draw attention to expenditure, rather than property or income, as a material index to one's social standing. Military officers and public officials were distinguished by their large debts. With 1,600 in move-able goods and a wretched house, Captain François Christophe de La Jemerais of the Marine Troops owed 43,800 livres as well as debts unknown to his widow.[36] When the liabilities of Montreal's chief judge (*lieutenant-général*) approached 13,000 livres, his wife halted the inventory by renouncing her inheritance rights.[37] This act freed her of responsibility for paying the estate's debts, which would have left her desti-tute. The widow of Trois-Rivières' local governor, too, waived her claim on the estate, "believing it to be more burdensome than beneficial, for which reason she retains her dowry, dower, and the matrimonial rights contained in her marriage contract."[38] These debt-ridden legacies were not the result of reckless imprudence; they were the consequence of social expectations.

High social rank demanded an appropriate way of life, even if a person lacked an income sufficient to support that scale of living. Failure to conform to popular expectations brought disgrace and disapproval to the delinquent. According to a colonial gentleman, Governor-General Jean de Lauson's pious frugality in the 1650s had dishonored the governor. "He was," said the informant, "scarcely liked because of the little care he took to uphold his reputation (*caractère*), living like a servant, surviving on pork and peas like a craftsman or a yokel (*manant*)."[39] De Lauson should have conducted himself with the grandeur befitting his high office; he should have surrounded himself with servants, rather than living like one.

Given the insecurity of the colony's elite about its position and the high value placed on visible marks of rank, it is not surprising to find the fortunes of the notables depleted by outward display. "You see no rich people in this country," wrote Father Charlevoix about New France, "and it is really a great pity, because there they love to obtain honor with their goods and almost no one amuses himself with thrift." According to this observant priest, Canadians would scrimp on meals in order to be well dressed.[40] After all, clothes were for public display and meals usually were eaten in private. This sartorial show and other forms of conspicuous consumption demanded by one's social rank produced the large debts seen in the estate inventories. The colonial elite ran up debts while social inferiors, free of the same demands, could accumulate and hoard money. An eighty-four-year old farmer at Château Richer managed to amass 2,650 livres in currency, while another cultivator in Varennes had tucked away in "a little sack," 2,800 livres in card money, as well as 1,521 livres in gold, silver, and billon coins.[41] He had done this in wartime when specie was in short supply. A bachelor tanner at Quebec was found to possess only 84 livres in clothing and furnishings, but, when his private papers were examined, it was found that he held 4,312 livres in promissory notes from people to whom he had lent money.[42] Perhaps this tanner was a creditor of his pretentious betters. Could this man or the two farmers have put away so much money if their rank had demanded expenditure on visible display? All were in humble occupations, and miserly self-sufficiency was acceptable in a peasant.

For their social superiors, the situation was reversed: their way of life discouraged economy and this is evident in the estate inventories. Not only did they have to spend money freely to uphold their rank, but they were also hampered in their investments by a concern for their status. Some commercial activities were not proper for a gentleman. Military officers and senior administrators put their capital into land and assumed the costly obligations of seigneurs for the sake of prestige. Buying a landed estate was not a very profitable investment in a colony where land was plentiful and labor was dear. Although some officers were directly involved in the fur trade, because there was a stigma to retail trade, elite members preferred to act as passive, investor-partners in maritime and fur-trading ventures. Such investments entailed a risk, yet they also promised a quick return. There were exceptions. Angélique Chartier de Lotbinière, the high-born wife of the king's attorney at

Quebec, ran a drapery shop, and this may have been socially acceptable because she was a woman and because of the prestige enjoyed by Parisian drapers, who belonged to one of the "Six Grands Corps"—the city's premier guilds.[43]

In *la Nouvelle France* social rank dictated economic behavior; it was not wealth that determined one's place in the social order. Contrary to our notion that money can buy respect, the colony's social leaders were obliged to live in a manner suitable to their station, whether they could afford to or not. High status required a liberal expenditure of money in meeting sumptuary obligations, whether for fine clothing or for hosting lavish dinners. As a result, the worthies of New France left their heirs little more than a good name. In this way, economics submitted to a social imperative.

THE COLONISTS' SOCIAL HIERARCHY

When repudiating her husband's indebted legacy, the wife of Trois-Rivières' governor referred to her property rights, as stated in a marriage contract. Practically everyone who married in New France concluded a marriage agreement before the church wedding. The accord expressed the intention to wed and carefully defined the respective property rights of each partner. Thousands of these agreements survive in the notarial archives. The *contrats de mariage* are superior to the often-incomplete, postmortem *inventaires des biens* as a gauge of the social expectations and consumption patterns demanded by one's rank. French historians have used thousands of marriage contracts to estimate the wealth of different occupational groups at Paris in 1747–54. In particular, they have relied on the recorded contributions made by the partners to their future community of goods. These historians have assumed that one's material fortune was as important as a person's profession in the social hierarchy.[44] Even if one accepts their assumption that social standing in France had an economic basis, such a study could not be reproduced for New France because of the peculiarity of Canadian marriage accords.

Colonial prenuptial agreements rarely gave the value of a man's contribution, and a quarter do not mention the bride's dowry, if there was one. A dowry, or *dot,* was not required by law—it was a social custom—and, given the scarcity of European women in New France during the seventeenth century, it was not always demanded among the lower ranks. When humble folk presented a dowry with their daughter, it was often a practical contribution to the new household, such as food and livestock or free board in the parents' home for a few years. In 1744 the father of a betrothed girl promised her future husband, a blacksmith, "two steers, a cow, a horse, two sheep, a pig, [and] a feather bed with a Montpellier woolen coverlet."[45] At Louisbourg newlyweds were frequently offered a few years' free board in the home of the bride's family.[46] Dowries in kind were seldom given a monetary value. Despite this shortcoming, marriage contracts made in New France can be used to reconstruct the colony's social order with more precision than could be achieved with postmortem accounts of estates.

The two precisely stated items of information that invariably are provided in a premarital agreement are the value of the wife's dower (*le douaire préfix ou conventionnel*) and an amount called *le préciput* (the preferred portion). These were parts of a widow's inheritance rights. Under the *Coutume de Paris*, the body of civil laws prevailing in New France, married women were treated like minors. They were placed under the tutelage of their husbands, who could manage the couple's combined assets without the wife's consent or approval. Apart from nobles and wealthy merchants, it was rare for a couple to remain separate as to goods after marriage; most entered into a partnership which pooled all of their assets. The laws, however, provided safeguards for a wife's property rights and for her material security, should her spouse die or be proven unfit to govern their shared estate. Once again, the compassionate authoritarianism, so evident in government, was manifest in the colony's matrimonial law. Before marriage, a woman could be given a contractual choice between customary dower (*le douaire coutumier*) or a prefixed dower, as stated in the marriage accord drawn up by a notary. Customary dower allowed a widow to enjoy one half of her late husband's estate for life. The alternative, dower of a fixed value, was stipulated in the marriage agreement and was a precise sum that a widow could take in money or goods from the couple's estate, no matter what its debts were. This option freed the bereaved wife from financial obligations that would deprive her of a means of support, and it also relieved her of the administrative responsibilities attached to the enjoyment of her husband's real estate. Most agreements made in *la Nouvelle France* provided a prefixed dower of so many hundreds of livres, although the notables preferred an annual pension for life to a lump sum payment. The amount chosen reflected the groom's social position, and herein lies the contract's value for defining social strata.

Claude-Joseph de Ferrière, an Old Regime jurist, described matrimonial dower as "a benefit that a living wife takes from the goods of her predeceased husband, and which is granted to provide her with a decent existence (*une subsistance honnête*) according to the rank (*la condition*) of her spouse."[47] Prefixed dower, then, had to be commensurate with the standard of living expected by a person of that degree. Since a wife was a dependent, her rank was determined by her husband's position. Thus, *douaire préfix* expressed the consumption needs of a man of that social level. It provides, as a consequence, a numerical and comparable indicator of rank within colonial society.

The *préciput,* or preferred portion, was one of several, lesser benefits conferred upon the surviving spouse, whether male or female. By ancient custom, the survivor was entitled to withdraw personal effects from the mass of goods before the joint estate was legally divided. A wife took her clothes, her rings and jewelry, and a fully furnished bed or a roomful of furniture. In 1721, during an inventory, a gunsmith's widow at Quebec reserved for herself, as her *préciput,* all her clothes and linen underclothing, as well as "a cherrywood cot with turned legs, a straw mattress, a feather bed with ticking and its bolster, a wool-filled mattress, a [bed-]frame curtain (*tour de lit*) of green Rouen serge bordered with golden ribbon, with its iron rods, canopy, and 'bonne grace,' a Catalogne-style Normandy cover, with a sewn, printed cotton quilt."[48] Men of gentle birth could include a horse and martial arms among their personal effects.

Préciput seems to have begun as a monetary alternative for this ancient right; in time, it became an additional privilege, conferred by contract, and not a substitute for personal possessions. Like the prefixed dower, the preferred portion reflected the groom's status. Widows in the colony retained the right to *préciput,* even after renouncing the joint estate and the customary dower that went with it. It was possible for a married woman to repudiate a debt-burdened community of goods and to depart with her personal effects, the preferred portion, the value of her dowry, and all that she had contributed to the common estate, as well as taking her prefixed dower out of whatever had belonged to her late husband. The unfortunate creditors then scrambled for the leftovers. The civil law's overriding concern for a widow's welfare was another example of that protective concern for the weak that permeated institutions in this Roman Catholic colony.

A skeptic might object that, because contractual dower was not tied to actual wealth and because it was a form of self-evaluation, it represents personal aspirations rather than reality. In theory, a man could choose any amount he liked. After all, when the time for payment came, he would be safe in the grave. In fact, the choice of dower was subject to social approval, and this condition restrained wishful estimates of one's worth. A marriage contract was signed and approved by relatives, friends, and other witnesses in a public ceremony that was more than a token formality. Contracts state that the betrothal and accord were made, "by the consent, advice, and counsel of the persons hereafter named," or, "by the agreement and consent of their relatives and friends here assembled." Colonists had a good idea of what prefixed dower was appropriate for a groom of each occupation, and the amount was sometimes adjusted in the document if the original amount was judged to be inappropriate. This popular consensus was an effective control upon native-born colonists, who could not pretend to be more than they were. As a consequence, choices of dower within each occupational group were amazingly uniform.

Recent immigrants and foreigners were less inhibited, and they sometimes overstated their social value in selecting dower. This tendency is apparent for Timothy

Sullivan, Samuel Payne, and Andreas Spennert in table 2: The Social Hierarchy of New France as Revealed by Prefixed Dower in 124 Marriage Contracts. They may have done this out of ignorance or ambition, or because, as outsiders, they felt compelled to assert their worth in the eyes of the *Canadiens*. Timothy Sullivan, alias "Sylvain," was the son of a physician in Cork, Ireland, and had come to Canada from the British colonies. In addition to his inflated dower of 2,500 Canadian livres, he later produced a spurious document testifying to his lineage as "the son of Cornelius Daniel O'Sullivan, Count of Killarney . . . and Lieutenant General in the armies of King James II, of glorious memory, . . . descended from the most ancient and illustrious [noble] houses in Ireland," while affirming that Timothy was a former captain of dragoons.[49] A "son of Blarney" would have been closer to the truth. Eventually, Governor-General de Beauharnois and Gilles Hocquart concluded that Sullivan was not even the qualified physician that he claimed to be and was nothing but "a charlatan."[50]

A foreigner's social position in New France was so uncertain that it could be affected by his colonial bride-to-be. For example, when an Italian surgeon, Jean-Fernand Spagniolini, first married a commoner in 1737, the dower was 800 livres— a reasonable sum for a surgeon.[51] After his first wife's death, the surgeon took as his second bride a Boucher de Niverville, whose family belonged to the Canadian gentry of military officers and seigneurs. This wife's prefixed dower was a life annuity of 250 livres—a jump up in value and a change in its nature. Annuities were favored by the elite. Spagniolini was so intimidated by his lofty future in-laws that the *préciput,* here said to be the value of a furnished room, was raised in their presence from 500 to 1,000 livres.[52] Among themselves, Canadians judged a man's rank by his employment and, possibly, by his family, and they had a firm idea about the dower that was appropriate for each calling.

The *Canadiens'* sense of their own social ranking is apparent when the 124 marriage contracts made in 1689–1729 are arranged in descending order, according to the amount of the prefixed dower. I verified the groom's occupation, as stated in the matrimonial agreements, in censuses, like the 1716 listing for Quebec City.[53] If the groom's principal vocation could not be identified, the contract was discarded. When the *douaire préfix* was the same for several couples, the arrangement within that subgroup was guided by the amount of the preferred portion or by the contract's date. There were a few inconsistencies, like the deeds for foreigners, yet the result is a visible hierarchy that is astonishing in its regularity. Look at one vocation in the same place in a single year, say, the three farmers of the Côte de Beaupré in 1710. The terms of their marriage agreements were identical: 300 livres contractual dower and a *préciput* of 200 livres. Likewise, in 1712–13, three different tanners in Montreal and Quebec all elected a prefixed dower of one thousand livres, while in 1713–16 three Quebec *navigateurs* (master mariners) opted for 600 livres. Their family ori-

The Social Hierarchy of New France As Revealed by
Prefixed Dower in 124 Marriage Contracts, 1689–1729

SOURCES: Archives du Quebec [AQ], Greffes des notaires, J. Barbel, L. Chambalon, F. de la Cetiere, J. E. Dubreuil, J. R. Duprac, F. Genaple, E. Jacob, H. B. Lariviere, J. C. Louet, J.Pinguet, F. Rageot, P. Rivet; AQ, Montreal, Greffes . . . , A. Adhemar, J. B. Adhemar, M. LePallieur, M. Moreau, P. Raimbault, M. Tailhandier; AQ, Trois-Rivieres, Greffes . . . , J. B. Pottier, F. Trottain.

MARRIAGE CONTRACT	AMOUNT	GROOM'S OCCUPATION	PRECIPUT
A. Prefixed dower as an annuity in Canadian livres			
F. Gallifet de Caffin, 1697Q	600	Town Major	6,000
H. Hiché, 1713Q	500	Wholesale Merchant	3,000
C. Bermen de la Martiniere, 1710Q	500	Prevote & Admiralty senior judge	500
N. Bulteau, 1717Q	300	Intendant's Maitre d'Hotel	500
F. de Gannes de Falaise, 1713M	300	Army Captain	
C. de Monseignat, 1693Q	200	Governor's Secretary	1,000
J. F. Hazeur, 1708Q	200	Barrister of Paris Parlement	500
Jacques Page, 1715Q	150	Silversmith & Clockmaker	800
B. Single payment in Canadian livres			
P. Rigaud de Vaudreuil, 1690Q	12,000	Colonel/Commander of Troops in Canada	3,000
J. F. Martin de Lino, 1712Q	8,000	King's Attorney	1,000
C. Juchereau, 1692M	6,000	Army Lieutenant	1,500
C. de Bled, 1716Q	6,000	Wholesale Merchant	600
F. Chambellan, 1717Q	6,000	Silversmith	1,000
C. de Ramezay, 1690Q	5,000	Army Captain/Trois Rivieres' Governor	
F. Perrault, 1715Q	5,000	French Merchant	1,500
G. de Lorimier, 1695TR	4,000	Army Captain	2,000
C. L. St. Olive, 1716M	4,000	Apothecary	
G. Baudouin, 1714Q	3,000	Surgeon	1,000
N. Gaudin Lapoterie, 1723Q	3,000	Silversmith	1,000
J. Page, 1723Q	3,000	Silversmith	500
T. Sullivan, 1720M	2,500	Physician	1,250
P. Gaulthier de Varennes, 1707Q	2,000	Army Ensign	1,000
C. Hédouin, 1716Q	2,000	Ship's Captain	1,000
J. Maillou, 1720Q a.	2,000	Builder-Architect	500
J. A. de Fresnel, 1694TR	1,500	Army Ensign	2,000
C. Barolet, 1716Q	1,500	French Merchant & Clerk	400
S. Payne, 1725M	1,500	Silversmith	500
P. Tessier, 1728M	1,500	Masonry Builder	500
H. Belisle, 1690Q	1,500	Surgeon	300
P. Gauvreau, 1705Q b.	1,200	Gunsmith-Silversmith	500
D. Pauperet, 1710Q	1,200	Hatmaker	500
N. de Rainville, 1727Q	1,200	Masonry Builder	400
F. de la Joue, 1689Q	1,000	Masonry Builder	600
D. Janson, 1726M	1,000	Builder-Architect	300
J. Giffard, 1700Q	1,000	Rural Seigneur	500

MARRIAGE CONTRACT	AMOUNT	GROOM'S OCCUPATION	PRECIPUT
F. Rageot, 1711Q	1,000	Royal Notary & Court Usher	nil
P. Perthuis, 1713Q	1,000	Fur Trade Outfitter/Retailer	500
P. Perthuis, 1716Q	1,000	Fur Trade Outfitter/Retailer	500
J. Huppé, 1728Q	1,000	Hatmaker	500
P. Mestoyier, 1704Q	1,000	Soldier-Tailor	500
C. Renaut, 1714Q	1,000	Soldier-Tailor	500
J. Valeran, 1713Q	1,000	Painter	400
J. B. Parent, 1713M	1,000	Joiner	400
C. Cliche, 1728Q	1,000	Joiner	300
P. Robereau, 1712Q	1,000	Tanner	500
E. Gauvreau, 1712Q	1,000	Tanner-Currier	300
J. L. Plessy, 1713 M	1,000	Tanner	300
J. Loyseau, 1713Q	1,000	Tinsmith	300
G. Lefèbvre, 1712Q	1,000	Cooper	300
S. Thomas, 1724M	1,000	Miller	300
A. Spennert, 1690Q	1,000	Shoemaker	nil
L. Enouille, 1712Q	800	Army Corporal & Roofer	400
F. Dumontier, 1695TR	800	Army Sergeant	300
J. E. Comte, 1716Q	800	Barber-Wigmaker	300
J.B. Soullard, 1717Q	800	Gunsmith	200
C. Vivier, 1706Charlesbourg	800	Farmer	200
J. Ferron, 1692M	600	Shoemaker	400
E. Moreau, 1706M	600	Shoemaker	300
J. Payan, 1710Q	600	Shoemaker	200
J. B. Brunet, 1715Q	600	Toolmaker	300
R. Dolbecq, 1712Q	600	Butcher	300
J. Maillou, 1695Q	600	Stonemason	300
J. Valade, 1716M	600	Stonemason	300
R. Duprac, 1716Beauport	600	Stonecutter	300
A Louineau, 1713Q	600	Navigateur	300
P. Rosa, 1714Q	600	Navigateur	300
C. Chenust, 1716Q	600	Navigateur	200
C. Hedouin, 1704Q	600	Sailor	200
C. Ripoche, 1705Q	600	Voyageur	200
H. Cain, 1713Q	600	Tailor	200
J. B. Gadiou, 1715Q	600	Roofer	200
J. Renaudet, 1717Chambly	600	Soldier	200
M. Beriault, 1711Q	600	Joiner	150
J. Barodot, 1696TR	500	Military Surgeon	500
T. Dardenne, 1715M	500	Voyageur-Fur trader	500
A. Forestier, 1701M	500	Joiner	300
J. Filiau Dubois, 1713Q	500	Joiner	300
J. Bonneau, 1712Q	500	Journeyman-Baker	300
J. Métivier, 1717Q	500	Glazier	300
L. Jannot, 1718M	500	Farmer	300
P. Latour, 1712Q	500	Metal Founder	300
J. B. Pepin, 1729M	500	Blacksmith	250

MARRIAGE CONTRACT	AMOUNT	GROOM'S OCCUPATION	PRECIPUT
P. Chamare, 1712Q	500	Farrier	200
J. Amiot, 1707Q	500	Locksmith	150
E. Dubreuil, 1713Q	500	Notary & Court Usher	250
P. Boisonnière, 1715M	500	Army Corporal	300
J. Deliere, 1717M	500	Soldier-Tavern Keeper	300
J. Crenet Beauvais, 1713Q	500	Sergeant-Tavern Keeper	250
B. Couton, 1691Q	500	Soldier-Hatmaker	250
P. Richer, 1716M	500	Army Sergeant	200
P. Jourdain, 1705Q	500	Army Corporal	200
J. Prime, 1695TR	500	Private Soldier	200
J. Minet, 1693Q	500	Merchant	200
J. B. Dufresne, 1717M	500	Farmer	200
C. Rivet, 1717M	500	Farmer	200
J. Dasilva, 1722Q	500	Stonemason	200
J. Chesnier, 1713Q	500	Shipwright	200
J. J. Cheval, 1725M	450	Wigmaker	300
D. Corbin, 1707Q	400	Shipwright-Carpenter	200
J. P. Daveluy, 1712Q	400	Stonemason	150
H. Belisle, 1705TR	400	Surgeon	nil
J. Germain, 1698TR	300	Private Soldier	200
J. Chapeau, 1713Q	300	Private Soldier	150
P. Sleve, 1705Q	300	Private Soldier	clothes
J. Girard, 1715Q	300	Shoemaker	200
J. Bossu, 1705Q	300	Shoemaker	150
C. Aubert, 1710Beaupré	300	Farmer	200
A. Simard, 1710Beaupré	300	Farmer	200
J. Hains, 1710Beaupré	300	Farmer	200
P. Tabaux, 1714M	300	Farmer	200
N. Chaput, 1716M	300	Farmer	200
T. Hunault, 1717M	300	Farmer	200
J. Baribeau, 1697TR	300	Farmer	150
J. Barbot, 1705ND des Anges	300	Farmer	150
N. Chappelot, 1692M	300	Farmer	nil
N. Tessier, 1716M	300	Miller	nil
P. Leclerc, 1712Q	300	Carpenter	200
M. de Rome, 1705Q	300	Journeyman-Carpenter	100
A. Beaune, 1717M	300	Voyageur	100
D. Gagnon, 1727Q	300	Carter	100
P. Dassilva, 1713Q	200	Carter	150
P. Dupuy, 1712Q	200	Day Laborer	150
J. de la Fond, 1697TR	200	Farmer	100
J. Arcand, 1718Q	100	Farmer	100

a. Convertible to a 100 livres annuity

b. Convertible to 60 livres "De Rente ou pension viagere."

NOTE: the devaluation in Canadian card money in 1714 led many to define dower and preciput in French livres, especially in 1717–18.

gins and real wealth cannot have been identical, yet their social standing, evidently, was the same. The elite felt that it was demeaning to deal in anything but thousands of livres, if a life annuity were not chosen. For the rest of the population, the prefixed or contractual dower fell within the range of 200 to 1000 livres, making gradations of rank seem more subtle than they probably were. One farmer's bride was given 100 livres as her prefixed dower, but a sum under 200 livres would not insure a decent existence for anyone and that is why it was usually the bottom limit for contractual dower.

In summary, the hierarchy of New France in the St. Lawrence Valley, based on the ideas of its residents in 1689–1729 about social status and worth, as reflected in their choice of prefixed dower, could be stated as follows:

I. THE ELITE (3,000–12,000 livres)
   Senior commissioned military officers (major, colonel)
   Judicial officers
   Junior commissioned military officers (ensign, lieutenant, captain)
   Wholesale merchants
   Silversmiths

II. GOOD AND PROFITABLE OCCUPATIONS (1,000–2,000 livres)
   Ships' captains
   Masonry builders
   Tannery owners
   Surgeons/Wigmakers
   Hatmakers
   Coopers
   Armorers/Gunsmiths

III. RESPECTABLE TRADES (600–800 livres)
   Soldier-craftsmen
   Notaries
   Joiners
   Metalworkers
   Noncommissioned military officers
   Master mariners/Voyageurs
   Tailors

IV. MODEST OCCUPATIONS (300–500 livres)
   Shoemakers
   Food tradesmen
   Stonemasons/Stonecutters
   Retailers

Carpenters/Shipwrights
Private soldiers
Tenant farmers

V. BASE OCCUPATIONS (200 livres)
Journeymen craftsmen
Carters
Day laborers

This sequence was the commonly accepted ranking based on an occupation and its perceived dignity. It is an order that was defined by the people of the period, and it must have governed the colonists' behavior in other matters. By their selection of a certain sum as contractual dower, people revealed how they looked upon themselves and how they were regarded by others. That elusive reality in the minds of a bygone people, who were often illiterate, is brought to light by the marriage contracts. As a consequence, this scale is superior to any reconstruction of society in New France by latter-day historians applying their own standards for ranking people. Prenuptial accords did not cover the colony's full social spectrum because they were limited to the laity, who were free to marry. High ecclesiastics, as well as nuns, who came from the leading families, are not shown. They would have belonged to the first rank, as would the transient French administrators. To the fifth and lowest rank, one should add indentured servants and apprentices, who were not permitted to wed during their term of service. Slaves and Amerindians are also missing from this table of social strata. The voids are at the very top or at the very bottom of the hierarchy. Even with these omissions, marriage contracts are the most comprehensive and reliable source for identifying the different levels of colonial society. They embrace the bulk of the European-stock population.

Compared with the social pyramid in seventeenth-century France, Canadian society had its own peculiarities. The old, hereditary nobility was scarcely present in New France. Canadians saw few people from the ancient families of France's *noblesse d'épée,* apart from the governor-general and the bishop of Quebec. The other senior administrators tended to come from the judicial "nobility of the robe," which was recently ennobled, as were a few colonial military officers. Some of those who had received estates from the Company of One Hundred Associates had come from the minor nobility and gentry of France. These members of the lower range of the aristocracy, such as royal officials and military officers, as well as a number of wholesale merchants, acted as the colony's social elite. This group was, effectively, Canada's nobility, and, in keeping with metropolitan values, those of aristocratic lineage followed a distinctive pattern of life, without excluding newcomers.[54] In this elevated group, ownership of a seigneury was a common trait. In the French Regime a landed estate was an appurtenance of rank. It allowed a person to add the lustrous "Sieur de (lord of) ———— (the seigneury's name)" to his Christian name. "Pierre LeGardeur" was a fine name, and, for an officer, "Pierre LeGardeur, Sieur de Repentigny" was even better. Merchants and commoners bought estates from the heirs of the original, gentlemanly recipients to acquire this attribute of gentility.

Possession of a landed estate did not admit a seigneur to the ruling circle. Observe the relatively low dower of 1,000 livres assented to by Joseph Giffard, who was a rural landlord and nothing more. Most lay seigneurs had other vocations and lived in the towns. The learned professions were represented in Canada by a few judicial officers. Lawyers had been deliberately excluded from the colony and there was only one physician at Quebec. French contempt for commerce had softened in the colony, because wholesale merchants were close behind the king's agents, as were silversmiths, who were still the "aristocracy" of the crafts. Reverence for those who served the crown and for martial values allowed private soldiers, despite their low origins and frequent involvement in petty crime, to claim an ascendancy over honest tenant-farmers. Gunsmiths, too, may have gained prestige by repairing firearms and thereby serving the colony's defenders.

Although Canadians, as a rule, separated wealth from rank, there is evidence that their social prejudices could be bent by material considerations. Observe the surprising advance into respectability of tannery owners, whose enterprises were stinking places that treated the skins of dead animals, reasons enough to taint their money. Revulsion for tanning could be overcome. The high profits of this trade and Intendant Bégon's own tannery may explain the colonists' willingness to admit tannery owners into the second rank of society. Masonry construction, especially projects for the crown, seems to have been equally lucrative, and this material consideration, as well as builders' service to king, church, and the social elite, would explain the elevated standing of master builders in stone. Canadians, evidently, were willing to modify the social hierarchy of Old Regime France without abandoning the values upon which it was built.

In the 1750s a French officer of the metropolitan army (*troupes de terre*) was taken aback by the Canadians' exaggerated deference for those with royal commissions and honors: "those who had been awarded the Cross of St. Louis were as highly esteemed as lieutenant generals & *cordons bleus* [knights of the Order of the Holy Spirit] in France. Those who commanded armies [*sic*], of which the largest were 300 men, were respected in the colony like field marshals in France. A captain of the king's vessels who arrived in the colony was regarded as a divinity & habitually behaved with a great deal of arrogance."[55] The marriage contracts qualify this picture of military ascendancy by showing that the king's civil officials enjoyed a standing higher than that of the colonial garrison officers, who were recruited increasingly from New France's landed gentry. Most of the civil administrators had come from France, and this connection with the homeland seems to have enhanced their prestige.

Were the Canadians more rank-conscious than their European cousins? There is a hint of that in the letters of Mme. Elisabeth Bégon, a *Canadienne* living in France. She was offended by the lack of respect for rank in the mother country: in 1750 she wrote, "since we honor those who are first, I do not like the small difference between the social estates here and the little subordination I see."[56] Here was a pretty reversal of the French travelers' comments about her colonial home! It appears that the legendary insubordination of the Canadians was overstated by outsiders from France, and that the colonists' own acknowledgment of social differences was overlooked.

SOCIAL MOBILITY IN CANADA

The colonists' opportunities for rapid advancement diminished over the decades, as the colony's social structure hardened and because one's progression depended as much upon royal patronage as it did on ability. In the mid-seventeenth century, when New France was still taking form, a speedy ascent was possible for the talented few. Pierre Boucher (1622–1717), whose *Histoire Véritable* has been quoted, was a carpenter's son of extraordinary intelligence. He was educated in Canada by the Jesuit fathers and entered the governor-general's service as a soldier and interpreter in Iroquoian languages. The next governor-general made Boucher the town captain of Trois-Rivières, where his prudent conduct and the death of a foolhardy commandant revealed Boucher's ability as a military leader and diplomat. Pierre Boucher organized the settlers for self-protection, successfully defended the little French settlement at the river junction, and then negotiated a truce with the hostile Iroquois. Governor Dubois Davaugour chose this talented man to give an account of the New France's perilous state, in person, to King Louis XIV. That report was the origin of Boucher's book. The colonial emissary was ennobled and made governor of Trois-Rivières. In 1667 Pierre Boucher retired to develop his model seigneury of Boucherville, and he is remembered as the founder of an aristocratic colonial dynasty.[57] It was an impressive achievement to go from woodworker's son to noble in a lifetime.

Pierre Boucher's career was exceptional, and yet it illustrates a point about social mobility in *la Nouvelle France:* even men of outstanding ability depended on official recognition and their superiors' patronage in order to rise to a high social rank. Boucher's elevation was aided by sympathetic governors-general, and he was brought to the king's attention by others. Even after the colony had developed its own native-born elite, that group remained utterly dependent upon royal patronage and the recommendations of the governor-general and intendant. The local nobility and gentry were unable to control or to dominate the colonial administration, as did the elites in the British colonies. The Canadian gentlemen could never become an entrenched oligarchy.

By the 1700s the church and masonry construction were the few remaining avenues by which low-born colonists might ascend to a higher station in society. Through successive marriage contracts, we can trace the rise of Jean-Baptiste Maillou (1668–1753) of Quebec City. Maillou was the son of a wooden shoe maker, a low step in society. In 1685 Jean-Baptiste was apprenticed to Claude Baillif (c1635–99), a French builder and architect, for three years.[58] Maillou and his older brother Joseph worked as masons and stonecutters for Baillif, whose design books and clientele they inherited, and then went into partnership as independent contractors. For his first wife, Jean-Baptiste selected a tailor's daughter. Their 1695 marriage accord described him as "M[aître]. Masson," and the guest list at the signing of the deed left no doubt that this was a plebeian event. Apart from his immediate family, the stonemason's witnesses were a toolmaker, who was also his brother-in-law, with a cousin who styled himself "marchand" (merchant), and Baillif, "architect [and] his friend." It was customary for employers to witness their dependents' nuptial agreements. The groom chose a prefixed dower of just 600 livres.[59] After his first wife's death, Maillou remarried eight years later to a merchant seaman's daughter. He was still close to his low-ranking origins, but his star was rising.

Joseph's premature death left Jean-Baptiste in charge of their flourishing construction business, which was employed by the church, by Quebec's merchants and officials, and, most importantly, by the colonial government. Maillou's satisfactory execution of government contracts for fortifications at Quebec and Crown Point commended him to the administration and, in 1719, he was given the honorific title of *Architecte du Roi* (architect to the king). In the absence of architectural schools, an architect at this time was a builder who could draw up plans, elevations, and specifications and was conversant with the classical orders of decoration. An undated plan by his hand for a parish church has survived in the Quebec Seminary's archive. Maillou's work as a surveyor and expert estimator for the courts indicated that he had other valuable skills. The intendant's confidence in Jean-Baptiste's ability was shown in 1728, when Maillou was made deputy to the Overseer of Highways (*Grand Voyer*), responsible for the alignment of buildings along Quebec City's streets.

When the *Architecte du Roi* signed his third marriage contract in 1720, the bride-to-be, the prefixed dower, and the list of witnesses at the deed's signing proclaimed his new position as a minor officer of the crown. Maillou's wife was the daughter of a ship's captain—the social superior of her predecessors—and Maillou granted her a contractual dower of 2,000 livres, which was worthy of his official role. The guests were more numerous—numbers were often proportionate to standing—and the witnesses now comprised a cousin who was a royal notary, three members of Montreal's mercantile group, a government clerk (*écrivain du Roi*) who was a close friend, and Maillou's protector, the intendant of New France and his wife. "Sieur Jean Maillou, Architecte," as he was described, had his foot upon the threshold of the colonial elite.[60] He was a propertied and influential burgher of Quebec and, in 1736, he built himself a six-room stone dwelling on St. Louis Street, in the Upper Town, close to the governor-general's palace. As an indicator of Maillou's acquired prestige, he was buried in the crypt of Quebec's cathedral. One of his sons became a silversmith while a daughter entered a nunnery, and none of his children followed him in the construction trade. As in the case of Pierre Boucher, advancement was the result of a conjunction of natural ability, opportunity, and a high official's patronage. Maillou was the intendant's protégé.

Joseph-Michel Cadet (1719–81) was the son and grandson of butchers. His only connection with the colonial government was a stepfather who was a clerk in the Department of the Navy. This Quebec entrepreneur expanded his activities from butchering into provisioning ships and, then, into overseas trade, using his own vessels. Cadet had supplied the colony's troops and officials with meat in the 1740s. Access to bigger government contracts required influential patrons, and he was obliged to pay for them. The military adjutant at Quebec, Michel-Jean-Hugues Péan, presented Cadet's proposal to act as purveyor general (*Munitionnaire-général du Roi*) for the military forces in Canada to the colony's intendant, François Bigot. The supply contract was signed in October 1756 and, in a private agreement acknowledged later by Péan, Cadet gave the adjutant, the intendant, and the governor-general each a fifth share in the business and in its profits.

The efficient merchant-butcher made a fortune in the French and Indian War, supplying rations for the king's forces throughout New France. After the loss of Canada, the French government prosecuted Cadet for wartime profiteering. He was temporarily imprisoned and heavily fined, yet he still had enough money to buy estates in France, to see his two daughters married to minor nobles, and to have a son established as a French seigneur, as was Cadet senior. The enterprising Quebec butcher ended his life as a propertied gentleman in France.[61] Commercial profits were invested in land and in the social status an estate conferred upon its owner. Cadet had business acumen, yet he had to pay off royal officials to obtain lucrative government contracts. Without a great man's influence, progress upward was still possible, as in the case of Charles Hédouin, a farmer's son who became a master mariner and then rose to the rank of a ship's captain (see table 2), but it was a less spectacular ascent.

Matrimonial contracts reveal the possibilities of social mobility, but, more importantly, they bear witness in a number of ways to the Canadians' clear sense of rank and of their place within the social order—whatever French observers might write. The choice of a spouse was usually limited to a person of the same social level, as the next chapter will show. In the late eighteenth century a gentleman wrote, "Canadian parents do not wish to marry off their daughters according to their [the daughters'] inclinations, but according to a rigorous suitability (*une rigoureuse convenance*) and a rigid equality in fortune."[62] By European standards, the colony's social spectrum was compressed and simplified. Estate inventories and marriage contracts, when examined together, show that the colonists separated social value from material resources. Wealth was a secondary consideration when defining social position. Canadians ranked people primarily by their occupation, and they expected individuals to conform to the mores of that group. These mores included a scale of living deemed appropriate for that stratum. The emphasis on visible marks of status in *la Nouvelle France* magnified the importance of that obligation. It could not be shirked with impunity. In prefixed or contractual dower, people identified the scale of expenditure expected of a person in that position. From this amount, we can obtain an idea of each man's standing in the social hierarchy.

Rank was not entirely divorced from revenue. Income tended to increase, the higher one went up the social scale. In 1743 a captain in the marine troops was paid 90 livres a month; the ordinary soldiers under his command earned a tenth of that amount.[63] Admission to the colony's elite brought greater opportunities for profit from government appointments. Military officers hoped to command a post in the continent's interior in order to exploit the trade with Amerindians of that region. The crown's faithful servants were rewarded with royal pensions. These gains hardly kept pace with the expenditures demanded of a notable; officers were forever complaining about their "poverty." Wealth was a consideration for advancement, but it was not a reason for promotion. In 1707 the ennoblement of Joseph-François Hertel de la Fresnière was opposed on the grounds that he could not maintain himself in the manner befitting a noble.[64] Before the appointment of Henri Hiché as king's attorney at Quebec, the intendant had to assure the minister responsible for colonies that the candidate had enough income to "support him[self] honorably."[65] The French crown, through its senior officials in New France, controlled access to military commissions, public offices, and patents of nobility. The criteria for granting these appointments and honors were past service to the monarch, what was called "zeal for the [king's] service," ability, and family connections. Because public offices, military commissions, and ennoblement were not for sale in New France, money alone could not buy social advancement.

A C A D I A N   S O C I E T Y

The social order in Acadia cannot be reconstructed with the same certainty as that in the St. Lawrence Valley. Because most Acadians were illiterate and the few records of their daily lives, including notarial deeds, were destroyed or scattered during the mass expulsions in 1755–58, their world is largely beyond reconstitution. One has to rely on the superficial impressions of visitors and administrators, who, as we have seen, could be mistaken in their perceptions. The outsiders' observations on *les Acadiens* recall descriptions of the Canadians. In 1692 Antoine Laumet, otherwise known as Lamothe Cadillac, wrote, "with regard to the Creoles or [European colonists who are] natives of the land [Acadia], they are well-built, of good height, and they would be accepted without difficulty as soldiers in a guards' regiment. [They are] well-proportioned and their hair is usually blond. [They are] robust, and will endure great fatigue; [they] are fine subjects of the king, passionately loving the French of Europe." Acadians were a close-knit people bound by many ties created by intermarriage, which increased when British acquisition of Nova Scotia in 1713 cut off immigration from the French empire. The same commentator noted their "great affection among themselves, assisting each other with pleasure."[66] Auger de Subercase, the governor of Acadia, wrote in 1706 that the Acadians, "do not appear to be French at all, although well-built and handsome. They love only court cases and this colony will never be well established until a means is found to deprive them of this quibbling spirit." This love of litigation could not be turned to good account by making them assistant judges, because, the writer added, they would be "quite incapable, not knowing how to read or to write."[67] Only Port Royal had schools for children, and, with the British exclusion of Roman Catholic religious orders, apart from the secular clergy, the schools closed. Illiteracy became universal among the laity.[68]

Jean-Chrysostome Loppinot the elder, a notary and court clerk at Port Royal who aspired to be the king's attorney there, sent the minister of maritime affairs dramatic accounts of the anarchy among the Acadians, possibly to show himself to be a friend of public order. "Nothing is more necessary than the establishment of public order, whether for tavernkeepers or for the residents who sell by weight or by English bushels." The use of this English volume measure reflected the close commercial ties with New England, whose traders supplied the Acadians with ironware, fine cloth, rum, and salt. These "Englishmen" kept stores in Port Royal, the principal settlement. Trade with the British colonies was illegal, but the French colonial administration was unable to stop this commerce. Judicial officers were treated with contempt, and soldiers, instead of policing the settlement, were intimidating the colonists.[69] Acadians worked on Sundays and religious holidays, sold brandy to the Micmac Indians, "and the women there lead a quite scandalous life." If we believe Loppinot's letters, he would have corrected these abuses if Governor de Subercase had not obstructed his initiatives.[70] Knowing the willful Acadians, more would then have joined the northward march of families to get away from tighter government regulation of their lives.

These stories of insubordination in Acadia have a major difference from those emanating from the St. Lawrence Valley: the Acadians not only defied the tiny colonial administration at Port Royal, they continued to demand a say in the civil government, long after the Canadians had given up on their syndics, or elected spokesmen. In 1706 it was reported that "the colonists asked that the Syndic of the Country be changed every year by a plurality of voices," and, surprisingly, the king was willing to accede to this demand.[71] This willingness to tolerate democratic impulses is evidence of the monarch's indifference to Acadia during the years of royal government from 1670 to 1710. Louis XIV wanted the region to remain French without having to expend much money or attention on this peripheral settlement. The great monarch was even willing to countenance a small measure of representative government.

Acadia was more egalitarian than Canada, although it was not free from discord, envy, and crime, as Henry Wadsworth Longfellow's epic poem "Evangeline" (1847) would have us believe. Acadia also had its social distinctions. Villages were dominated by the oldest farmers and craftsmen with a hint of a superior class provided by some merchants, the occasional notary, and a priest. The seigneurial system was but a legal shadow in Acadia: the landlords sometimes collected dues, but exercised no other legal powers. Colonists migrated northward from Port Royal and settled where they pleased. The small French royal administration wandered from Port Royal to the Saint John Valley and around the Bay of Fundy, like a head in search of its body. When a friar undertook enumeration of Port Royal's residents in 1671, he found sixty-eight families, all headed by farmers or craftsmen. The two authentic gentlemen, who could have been social leaders, lived far from the settlement. Being Acadians, the villagers did not always treat the inquisitive friar with respect. Three would not answer his questions. Pierre Melanson, tailor, "refused to give his age and the number of his livestock or lands and his wife told me that I was such a fool to run through the streets [asking] for these things." Étienne Robichaud, plowman, "did not want to see me. He left his home."[72] Censuses of Ile Saint-Jean in 1728 and 1752 described a similar, yet more cooperative population of farmers, craftsmen, and fishermen, with a few merchants, officials, and soldiers. Thanks to the growing Acadian migration to the island, its residents acquired the social values of *Acadie*.

Only Ile Royale possessed a clearly stratified society like Canada, thanks to Louisbourg's dominant group of administrators, military officers, wholesale merchants, and fishing contractors. This fortified seaport was more an outpost of

Europe than a North American community, despite its lineage going back to Plaisance on Newfoundland. The yearly arrival and departure of hundreds of fishermen and traders from France constantly renewed Louisbourg's links with the Old World and with metropolitan culture. The islanders' short history within the French empire from 1713 to 1758 was not time enough to develop a distinctive character that would have set them apart from their kin in France.

THE EMERGENCE OF NEW PEOPLES

Those who emerged as definable and separate peoples—though not yet nations—were the mainland Acadians and the Canadians who had spread from the St. Lawrence Valley to the Illinois Country. Both peoples were Roman Catholic and French-speaking, as well as socially conservative. The Acadians clung to a thoroughly European diet of beef, wheat, and peas in a region ill-suited for those crops. Did not the Canadians regard these maritime neighbors as extremely bullheaded? In the absence of a strong, royal authority, French traditions of village self-rule revived in Acadia. In the St. Lawrence settlements, where the crown's power was visible and tangible, European patterns survived in modified form, and Canada had a clearly structured social order. These overseas French subjects had changed in spite of themselves, and the identities they had developed would survive for centuries to come. The vainglorious Canadians and the stubborn Acadians were no longer French people who just happened to live in North America; they were new provincial peoples.

The Canadians' distinctiveness was apparent in the way they constructed their rural, wooden homes. Here we have a tangible measure of the colonists' new, North-American identity. Starting with the half-timber construction techniques of northwestern France, the Canadians developed an entirely wood-filled frame called *pièces de bois sur pièces de bois* (pieces of wood upon pieces of wood), sometimes described as *poteaux en coulisse* (slotted posts). Squared timbers with tenons at each end were inserted, horizontally, into grooved uprights and formed insulated walls that could expand and contract with the severe temperature changes of the St. Lawrence Valley. Later in the eighteenth century, some timber structures had dovetailed corners, like the log dwellings of British North America. The American log house had Scandinavian antecedents, but the *pièces-sur-pièces* structures of the Canadians seem to have been an indigenous development. Like the people who built them, these timber dwellings had fully adapted to the new environment, a land of forests and brutally cold winters.[73]

CHAPTER 7

Group and Institutional Loyalties:
Social Rank, Occupation, and Parish

THE CHOICE OF MARRIAGE PARTNERS

Although the existence of social ranks in Canadian society has been demonstrated, and it is clear the people were ranked by occupation, one might ask if there was any solidarity among people of the same standing or trade. Here marriage contracts prove their value, because they identify all the guests present at the signing of the accord, in addition to the witnesses required by law—another notary or two strangers. The invited guests came from the couple's social circle, and contracts identified them as shared friends or as particular companions of the bride or of the groom. It was an honor for a person outside the family to be invited to sign the wedding accord. Louis Franquet, a military engineer, recalled that on the eve of his departure from Montreal in August 1752, "M. the Baron of Longueuil, who was about to marry his oldest daughter to M. de Maizières, a lieutenant in one the of the marine companies stationed at Louisbourg, begged me, in view of the bond that I had formed with his future son-in-law on the voyage we made together [from Ile Royale to Canada], to please attend his marriage, to sign the [prenuptial] contract, and to take the place of the nearest relative."[1] The lieutenant, evidently, had no kin in the colony. This was a flattering invitation that Franquet could not refuse.

Among the lower orders of colonial society, the lists of witnesses in marriage agreements underline the importance of the family as the basic social unit. Except for among immigrants, kin usually outnumbered friends among the invited witnesses. A voyageur who was about to marry at Quebec explained—almost apologetically—that his guests were a cousin and a friend, "for want of a larger number of relatives."[2] Recent arrivals in New France drew on whatever relatives they could find, in the absence of close family. Those without kin felt the loss keenly: a pregnant woman whose father-in-law would not pay for her lying-in at another's house mournfully described herself as "a poor woman who quit her father and her relations [in France] to come to this land, hoping to live here according to God and reason, which she cannot do because of their [her in-laws'] bad moods. . . . She has in this land no kin or friends nor the means to survive."[3] Bonds of blood entailed mutual aid and of this support she was bereft. By marriage, other immigrants reconstructed a sustaining network of family ties, similar to the one they had known in the homeland. After a few generations, the extended family satisfied most of the Canadians' and Acadians' social needs, and it provided business partners too.

For a colonial-born groom in a manual trade, the usual number of relations and friends at the signing of a matrimonial agreement fell between seven and twelve; on average, ten invited guests were present. Farmers had more witnesses, because established cultivators were usually native-born, and their many relatives lived nearby. Adult sons who did not inherit the parental farm, in whole or in part, preferred to settle on adjacent, vacant lands in order to maintain close contact with their parents and siblings.

Looking at the witnesses' occupations, when identified, one sees that shoemakers and metalworkers belonged to crafts with some sense of community, though the occupational bond was not a strong one. Take the case of Jean Loyseau, tinsmith from Rochefort, who was betrothed to a Quebec locksmith's daughter in 1713. His chosen witnesses to the notarized betrothal were three friends: a cooper, a shoemaker, and a blacksmith—the only fellow metalworker. On the bride's side were her parents, two brothers, an aunt and uncle, and, as friends, another locksmith (who was also her cousin) and a joiner-carpenter.[4] The affinity of metalworkers did not exclude friends in other trades. The artisans' social superiors formed an even more tightly knit group.

In elite wedding contracts, the guest list was very different, both in the number and in the nature of the witnesses. Those present to honor a high-ranking couple ranged from 2 to 128 people. The average number of invited guests, based on sixteen deeds, was 32—more than three times the usual number in attendance at a farm couple's gathering. Here one must distinguish between the witnesses due to patronage and those who were truly from the groom and bride's social group. Officers and employers often came to sign a former dependent's marriage accord. This was a paternalistic gesture expected of social superiors; it was a mark of good will. It also signified consent to the union, which a serving soldier or employee would need to have from his officer or master. Minor functionaries, like Jean-Baptiste Maillou, could count on the dazzling presence of a few senior officials. These worthies, however, stood out from the rest of the modest assembly and would not have been mistaken for intimates of the soon-to-be wed couple. Patron-and-dependent relationships inflated the guest list for contract signings and weddings, but they do not explain the large turnout at the betrothal of high-ranking couples drawn from officialdom, the military-seigneurial families, and the most successful merchants.

Among government administrators and commissioned garrison officers, social links extended well beyond one's immediate family. The solidarity of these allied elites was unmatched by other social strata in *la Nouvelle France,* except for the clergy. When *maître* Jean-François Hazeur (29), a Parisian lawyer and the son of a member of the *Conseil supérieur* at Quebec, agreed in 1708 to wed a Martin de Lino, another family entrenched in the civil government, 128 people appeared to put their signatures on the marriage contract. Most notaries satisfied themselves by noting the indisputable social lions first, along with close kin, such as the couple's parents. The rest of the assembled witnesses were usually listed in no particular order. In the 1708 Hazeur-de Lino agreement, notary Louis Chambalon began with the parents, brothers, sisters, uncles and aunts of the betrothed pair. Thereafter, he enumerated the guests in strict order of precedence: the governor-general and his wife, the intendant and his son, the first councilor of the Superior Council, followed by the oldest councilor, the vicar-general, the councilor-secretary, a councilor's widow, the senior judge (*lieutenant-général civil et criminel*) of Quebec's *Prévôté* and Admiralty courts, the subordinate magistrate (*lieutenant-particulier*), the king's attorney, the colonial *prévost des maréchaux de France,* the spriritual director of the *Hôpital-Général* nuns, the military commander's wife, garrison captains and their wives, one ensign, a treasurer of the naval department, a keeper of the king's stores, the governor and intendant's secretaries, a clerk of the lower court, a clerk-notary's widow, a notary's wife, the surgeon-major's widow, two seigneurs, a seigneur's widow, and sixteen "burgesses and merchants of this said town" with their respective wives.[5] This list of witnesses confirms the fact that a married woman's status was determined by her husband's standing, even if he were dead. It also reflected the current prejudices in France: those who served the king with pen and sword were placed well above merchants, however useful they were to the economy.

Compared with the rest of the population, the colony's noblemen were more likely to put off marriage until late in life, remain bachelors, or leave the colony because they could not find a suitable mate there.[6] Love, however, has a way of overcoming social prejudices. When a young officer of the old nobility married the daughter of a well-educated Quebec merchant in 1720, the governor-general complained that the bishop had performed the marriage without his permission as the officer's great uncle and as his commander. The match, said Governor-General Rigaud de Vaudreuil, was an unworthy one, because the bride was "a girl of base birth and without goods . . . whose mother he had seen serving in the tavern run by the bride's father."[7] This account misrepresented the father, Mathieu-François Martin de Lino, who was a member of the Superior Council and not a tavernkeeper. The governor-general posted his offending great-nephew to Ile Royale, which was still in a primitive stage of settlement.

That marriage was part of a dissolution of barriers between the worlds of the aristocracy, the civil administration, and commerce. In New France mercantile families were gradually admitted into the charmed circle. The fact that civil administrators and military officers participated in business ventures softened their prejudice against the materialism of commercial life. According to Intendant Duchesneau in 1679, "members of the Sovereign Council are obliged to enter commerce because their salaries are too small. Officers, gentlemen and seigneurs are poor; they hunt and trade. Their sons are traders."[8] In the next two decades, some of the prominent merchants who had signed the 1708 marriage accord (Martin Cheron, Guillaume Gaillard, and François Foucault) were appointed to Quebec's Superior Council, and one mercantile family, the Fleury de la Gorgendières, intermarried with the military elite.

Most alliances would not have been love matches because, when high status and extensive properties were involved, matrimony was too serious a matter to be left to the young couple. Parents expected to have a say in the choice of a child's mate. Legally, their consent was required for any child under the age of twenty-five. Lieutenant Séraphin Margane de La Valtrie was among the army troops sent out to protect the colony in 1665 and, agreeable to the king's offer of land for would-be settlers, he decided to remain in Canada and to wed. Lt. Margane was just short of his twenty-fifth birthday when he married in August 1668. His father in Paris reproached the young officer with "the fault of having let yourself be led by your eyes and marrying without my agreement (*mon adveu*) and without respect for the laws, and without deference to the advice of your near kin (*vos proches*)."[9] The family's honor and reputation were at stake and the bride was the child of a fishing and fur-trading entrepreneur. Parental approval, signified by a father's autograph on his child's marriage contract, was taken seriously. In the case of a minor, the father and mother's consent had to be recorded in the deed. This was evident when one father, whose daughter was about to be married, transferred his authority over her to his brother with these words: "you know what I said to you in our father's presence that I placed her in your hands to dispose of her as though she were your own, therefore you may do all that you will judge [suitable] for her good and for the family's satisfaction. . . . Not being able to attend [the signing of] the wedding contract, I ask you to stand in for me and to conclude all the [legal] acts that are necessary."[10]

We have one notable's assurance, albeit from the late 1700s, that among prominent Canadians, the parents selected husbands for their daughters with an eye to the man's social suitability and fortune.[11] A "good marriage" was one with someone of higher rank and, if possible, greater wealth too. Even humble folk responded to these considerations. In 1682 Pierre Charon, a Longueuil farmer, received a letter from his daughter Charlotte at Cap de la Madeleine, asking her parents to consent to her marriage because her suitor was "a good lad . . . who can read and write well and who has a fine piece of land (*une belle terre*)." Her father still sought confirmation of these facts from a trusted informant and, if the marriage seemed advantageous for his daughter, he and his wife were prepared to give their consent to the union.[12] Parents always acted for their daughters when the girls were under the age of twenty-five, as were most brides in New France.

Marriages at the highest level of society were negotiated by heads of families, and woe to the child who resisted their plans. Orphan Marie-Jeanne Renaud d'Avène Desmeloizes, aged sixteen, was pledged by her guardian to a gentleman she did not wish to marry. The arrangement had been negotiated by her grandfather, as her guardian, with another member of the Superior Council, whose son was to be the groom. Marie-Jeanne had been a former Ursuline novice, but the reason for her opposition to the match was never disclosed. In a May 1711 document postponing the wedding, it was stated that if there were no marriage by September the recalcitrant party would forfeit ten thousand livres. When she would not budge, her infuriated grandfather gave a townhouse from her inheritance to the rejected man. In 1716 her brother-in-law, as an adult man, took up Marie-Jeanne's cause and, in court, accused the grandfather of acting out of "feelings of vengeance," and unjustly disinheriting her. The parties settled the matter out of court in 1716. The girl never did marry.[13]

THE FORMATION OF A COLONIAL ELITE

During the eighteenth century, marriage ties developed between families entrenched in the civil administration of New France and the officers of the *Troupes de la Marine*. We can see the merger of these two occupational groups in the lists of guests present at the signing of marriage contracts. Putting aside relatives of the couple, who would have been at the signing no matter what their social position, we find recurrent surnames among the other guests at these notable marriages: Aubert, Bécart, Chartier, de la Colombière, Denys, Dupont, and Macard. Apart from the men of the Denys family, the heads of these families were administrators, with commercial interests. They were the social leaders to whom the officers attached themselves. In the 1702 marriage contract of Ensign Jacques Joybert de Soulanges and

Marie-Anne Bécart de Grandville, from a bureaucratic family, the Chartiers and Macards appeared as in-laws. Again, we find the signatures of members of the Denys and Dupont clans along with those of marine officers and a few who were not at the 1708 Hazeur-de Lino nuptials. At the 1702 signing, military families, such as the LeGardeurs, outnumbered the government notables. The highest officials also attended these functions, but they were really visitors from France, acting as guests-of-honor rather than as members of the colony's dominant social group.

The coalescence of senior officials, military officers, and merchant-entrepreneurs into a peer group during the early eighteenth century is evident in the 1733 marriage contract of Captain Pierre-François Rigaud de Vaudreuil (34) and Louise-Thérèse de Fleury de la Gorgendière (20). Her father was the general agent of the *Compagnie des Indes* in Canada and a seigneur, married to a Jolliet, and kin to the aristocratic Joyberts. Prominent among the guests were members of the Aubert, Chartier, Denys, LeGardeur, and Martin de Lino families. Others who had been signatories to the 1708 accord were also present. Of the seventy-four witnesses, twenty-nine belonged to known officers' families, nineteen were connected with the civil administration, and ten were engaged in commerce.[14] The linkage between these three occupational groups was now well established.

The ambitious Timothy Sullivan, self-styled physician, insinuated himself into this select group by eloping in January 1720 with Marie-Renée Gaulthier de Varennes, an older woman whose parents had been the governor of Trois-Rivières and a granddaughter of the famous Pierre Boucher, lord of Boucherville. She was the widow of the heavily indebted Captain François-Christophe Dufrost de La Jemerais and had six children to support. Elopement denied her relatives any say in her choice of a second husband. She had several male relatives who were marine officers. Contrary to custom, the couple's matrimonial agreement was concluded months *after* the wedding, yet her family was mollified when Sullivan paid off her considerable debts and saw to the education of his wife's children. As a pious Roman Catholic, Sullivan gained the clergy's confidence; the bishop had granted him a dispensation from the banns of marriage. The clergy, nuns, and military officers petitioned to have Sullivan accredited as a physician. Governor-General Rigaud de Vaudreuil and his wife took an interest in his welfare and helped obtain letters of naturalization and the appointment as king's physican on Montreal Island for him in 1724. Sullivan's extravagant vanity and fiery temper, however, alienated other people. He was thrice charged with assault and, when he savagely beat his wife in 1737, her brother and a nephew tried to rescue her from her enraged husband. Sullivan held them off with a poker and a sword, boxed his wife, and shouted at all three. Even in the presence of a priest, who tried to play the conciliator, Sullivan continued to threaten his wife. She obtained a legal decree of separation from the

Montreal court in 1738 and the offended husband protested that "God and the church had given him a wife, [and] there was no civil magistrate who might issue such a separation or an order against [his right of] visitation" with her. The turbulent Timothy wanted to have a church court judge his case.[15]

Sullivan's story provides an extraordinary example of family solidarity at the top of colonial society. Despite his devious marriage and offensive behavior, Timothy Sullivan's in-laws had organized the 1723 petition on his behalf and protected him as a kinsman. In 1742 he jabbed Montreal's chief magistrate, Guiton de Monrepos, in the chest with a cane during an argument over the judge's order that a tenant vacate one of Sullivan's rental houses because of its ruinous chimney. Court ushers were then ordered by the irate judge to arrest Sullivan. In the past, ushers who had had the temerity to deliver writs to the physician's home had been attacked and so these ones wisely sought military reinforcement before approaching the redoubtable "Thimothée Sylvain." The duty officer at the guardhouse that day was Sullivan's brother-in-law, Jacques-René Gaulthier de Varennes, and he refused to provide help. This delay allowed Sullivan to escape with his belongings from the infuriated magistrate's jurisdiction. It was an amazing display of family unity because the fugitive was an unwanted and unloved relative of the Gaulthiers. De Varennes was stripped of his command for misconduct. The colonial elite was outraged that one of their own was being threatened by Montreal's chief judge. According to the intendant, the magistrate's relentless pursuit of the runaway Irishman, "whose wife is related to the entire colony," had "antagonized many worthy people." "Sieur O'Sullivan," as he now called himself, prudently remained at Cap de Varennes, beyond Judge de Monrepos's reach.[16]

Colonial notables in public offices used their power to protect their own interests. Most were seigneurs, and when the 1711 Edicts of Marly dealing with seigneurial obligations were delivered to the Superior Council at Quebec, they were registered but not fully published. The edict enforcing tenants' duties was proclaimed; the act against landlords who had not granted tenancies and whose estates were undeveloped was withheld. Delinquent seigneurs were to forfeit their estates to the king, while the land of negligent tenant-farmers would revert to the lord of the manor. By selective publication of the 1711 edicts, the seigneurs on the council looked after themselves very neatly. This was not the first occasion when councilors used their authority for their own benefit. Their self-serving favoritism had been evident in the distribution of indentured workers sent out at the king's expense in the 1660s.

Although we can trace the development of a self-conscious and mutually supporting group of administrators, officers, and merchants which dominated European society in New France, this group did not fuse into a single monolithic and powerful class. It was divided into factions by the governor-general and the intendant. Real power lay with these high appointees from France and they each built up a following from members of different families. Their use of patronage weakened the colonial elite. The king's engineer, Jean-Nicolas Desandrouins, wrote in the 1750s, "be a relative or a friend of one of the members of high society and your fortune is made!"[17] That assertion was not completely true: associates of the colonial elite did not enjoy automatic preference in public appointments and in receiving government contracts. They had to petition the king and the minister of maritime affairs for consideration and for vacant positions.

Aristocratic families lobbied for favors in competition with one another, with each petitioner reciting his merits and past services, or those of his children. Seigneurs and ex-officers recommended their sons for an officer's commission in the marine troops. In 1748 Joseph Hertel de Saint-François wrote to the minister to report the heroic death of his fifteen-and-a-half-year-old son Joseph, an officer-cadet, on his *sixth* raid against the British colonies. Joseph's death proved the valor and devotion of the Hertels. "You see, Monsieur, that my hope now resides in the five [children] who remain to me. I [will] have the honor of recommending them to you as they become able to serve. I have every reason to be content with the care you have shown toward us until now. They [my other sons] are very promising." As for his oldest son's death, "his loss is sad, as it would be to many other fathers and mothers, and it might be of some use to those who follow him, if they march in his footsteps. It is this favor that I await from Monsieur the [Governor] General."[18] Without the endorsement of the governor-general and the intendant, pleas for preferment were futile. Lieutenant Margane de La Valtrie was reminded by his father that, by Heaven's grace, he had enjoyed "the aid, benevolence, and protection of Monsieur the Intendant," and that he should "cultivate well this assistance by a person of such great merit." A great man's protection, it was said, "could do everything in . . . Canada" for an officer in the king's service.[19] In 1714 Acadia's former governor, Daniel d'Auger de Subercase, advised his protégé Charles-Joseph d'Ailleboust on how to succeed as an army officer: "devote yourself to your profession and to your commanders. That is the way of becoming something and be assured that I will not be useless to you in this land [France] and that I will give all my care to your establishment and advancement." He authorized the young officer to draw thirty gold pistoles on de Subercase's credit to ensure a successful beginning to his career on Ile Royale.[20] The money would allow d'Ailleboust to outfit himself and to play the gracious host—happy man to have such a patron! A less fortunate man complained that his advancement was blocked by "a rival, who is well-supported by the governor-general (*bien épaulé du général*)."[21] Unsuccessful petitioners were forced to occupy themselves with running their manors, a task some other officers left to their wives.

The colonial elite's unity was weakened by the need to win influential patrons and by rivalry between families. This group was made up of three overlapping, yet distinct groups of varying status and differences between these groups surfaced in conflicts. In the social order of the day, military officers were considered to be superior to wholesale merchants, while inferior to civil administrators and royal magistrates. The supremacy of the king's officials is evident in the dower provisions of marriage contracts. Two other sources reveal the persistent social gap between the lofty administrative families and the more numerous military officers. The first piece of evidence is a list of the members of the *Conseil souverain,* later called the *Conseil supérieur,* at Quebec—the highest court in the colony.[22] The second is a survey of all holders of the Cross of St. Louis, a military honor accorded to senior officers in the marine troops who garrisoned the colony.[23]

When the high court, originally called the Sovereign Council, was established in 1663, some notable lineages sprang from the original lay members. The Damours, LeGardeur de Tilly, Rouer, and Ruette d'Auteuil families retained council seats for two generations. Two sons extended the Rouers' presence until 1744. A pair of councilors appointed in 1664 did equally well: the Denys family was represented by a father and a son until 1731 and, from 1664 to 1749, *three* generations of the Chartier de Lotbinière clan were councilors. Later appointees were unable to retain a presence for so long a period, though the Auberts de la Chesnaye, Hazeurs, Gaillards, Guillemins, and Cugnets produced father-and-son teams that sat on this body for thirty to forty years. This less-secure tenure was consistent with the new government policy of asserting control over its appointees. Although councilors drawn from the colony's elite used their powers to favor their interests as a group, they never monopolized the council seats, nor did they have mastery over this organ of government. Control seemed to be within the grasp of the leading families in the seventeenth century, when the monarch appeared to accept the automatic transmission of government positions to qualified sons *en survivance* (by inheritance). In 1695 Alexandre Peuvret was received as secretary-councilor "en survivance de . . . son père."[24]

In the early eighteenth century government ministers in France awakened to the potential loss of control over the councilors in Canada. Not only was the claim to survivorship rights rejected; subsequent appointees now served at the king's pleasure and not for life. The councilors could be dismissed at will. Moreover, the council lost much of its legislative and regulatory power in the eighteenth century and was reduced to its role as a high court of appeal. The king's intendant in New France now issued ordinances on public order and settled disputes that had formerly gone to the council for a decision. Within the towns royal magistrates took over the policing of crafts and markets from the high court. The council was also renamed *le Conseil supérieur* in 1703, banishing all notions of sovereignty that the members might entertain.

The barriers to the elite's control of the local administration were both formal and informal: professional qualifications had to be buttressed by a great man's support to obtain an office. The formal obstruction was disclosed in a 1749 dispatch that recommended one candidate for appointment to the Superior Council at Quebec as "a boy from a well-born family and one who has completed his studies and has been received as a lawyer [in France]."[25] Family connections were not enough to warrant appointment; legal training and proven administrative competence were also required. This was especially true for the attorney-general's position. Sons of colonial families already in the administration learned law and legal procedures as their father's deputies or they were sent to France for formal legal training. Some served an apprenticeship in lower courts, as did Jean-François Hazeur, whose claim to his father's council seat by right of succession was rejected. Even qualified colonists "de famille bien née" (of a well-born family) suffered from discrimination. The governor-general and intendant had to agree on nominees for the council and they used their patronage in favor of immigrants from France. The king's high officials nominated their secretaries, financial officers of the Department of the Navy, officials of the *Domaine du Roi* (the royal concessions), wholesale merchants, agents of fur-trading companies, and even a physician. Seventy percent of the forty-three councilors and attorneys-general who were appointed after 1700 were metropolitan Frenchmen from these occupations.

Apart from the physician, the appointees would have had some knowledge of commercial law to justify their selection. Those born in New France were handicapped by the limited education available to them. When Attorney-General Louis-Guillaume Verrier started giving classes in law at Quebec in 1733, his "school" became a cheap and convenient way to qualify for a government position. Nine subsequent appointees to the Superior Council were his former students, yet only four had been born in the colony. Even with legal training, Canadians lost out in competition with metropolitan candidates for appointments to the civil administration. The number of regular councilors increased from five to twelve in 1703, and, thereafter, lay appointees from France outnumbered native-born colonists by twenty-seven to ten. Three of the five men who were ecclesiastical councilors—because the bishop was entitled to a representative—were Canadians by birth. Looking at the entire body of royal law-court officials in 1712–40, including lowly clerks, only 40 percent of them were colonial-born.[26] In the 1730s, for every Canadian given a seat on the Superior Council there were six appointees from France. During the 1750s five new councilors were named, yet not one had been born in the colony. There was a clear preference for metropolitan candidates in the selection of councilors.[27]

Because the crown insisted that a royal office-holder be financially capable of maintaining himself in the dignity appropriate to his post, one might think that men from France were favored because they possessed the wealth and standing that colonists lacked. Some of the outsiders, in fact, came from a low level in society. Jacques de la Fontaine de Belcour was a court musician's son; Guillaume Gaillard had been the personal servant of Jean-François Hazeur (the lawyer married in 1708); Michel Bénard was the child of a royal soup cook, and seven other French appointees to the council had come to New France as merchants. The rise of Jacques Barbel (c.1670–1740) to the office of chief clerk of the Superior Council was the most dramatic ascent. Barbel appeared in New France in the 1680s as an army sergeant, and was appointed a royal notary in 1700. The benevolent protection of the governor-general and intendant was revealed when a charge against him for seducing and impregnating a widow was quashed. He rose steadily from legal attorney and notary to judge in two seigneurial courts, to clerk of Quebec's lower court, intendant's secretary, and then to chief clerk of the Superior Council in 1721. Some of the profits he made in maritime trade went into a subseigneury—a conventional purchase for the rising man. True to form, he died heavily indebted.[28]

The appointees' qualifications were more personal than professional. These men were the clients of the governor-general and intendant, who controlled access to public offices. The French councilors owed their position in the colony to their patrons and, as newcomers, they would have been more manageable than prominent colonists, whose prestige was already established. This strategic consideration may explain the discrimination against Canadians when appointing men to the Superior Council in the 1700s. For the favored clients, the weakness of this patronage system was that the regular change in governors-general and intendants could deprive the dependents of a beneficent patron.

While the proportion of native-born Canadians among the councilors diminished in the eighteenth century, their share of the marine officer corps expanded. When granting officers' commissions in the garrison troops, the French monarch gave preference to colonists. The colonial residents did not have to purchase their commissions, as was the case in France, and their share of these appointments increased over time. By 1700, 40 percent of the marine officers were natives of New France and most garrison officers in the eighteenth century were Canadians.[29] Looking at the families in which two or more generations received the Cross of St. Louis, a special award for long-serving officers, we find that the leading military families in the colony during the eighteenth century were:

D'Ailleboust	LeGardeur**
Aubert**	Le Moyne
Bellot	Le Neuf
Bermen de la Martinière**	Le Picard de Noray
Boucher*	Le Roy de la Potherie
Céloron de Blainville	Lienard de Beaujeu*
Chaussegros de Léry	Le Marchand de Lignery
Coulon de Villiers	Marin de la Malgue
Daneau de Muy	Noyelles
Dazemard de Lusignan	Péan
Denys de Bonaventure/de la Ronde**	Pécaudy de Contrecoeur**
Gallifet*	de Ramezay*
de Gannes	Rigaud de Vaudreuil**
Herbin	Rouer de Villeray**
Hertel**	Sabrevois
Jordy de Cabanac	Saint-Ours*
Juchereau*	Saint-Vincent
Lacorne	Testard de Montigny
Lefèbvre du Plessis	

Families that also occupied judicial and administrative positions are marked with a double asterisk; those who took brides from families in the civil bureaucracy bear a single asterisk.

The overlapping of the administrative elite and the military officers is slight: eight out of thirty-seven families. Army officers were more likely to marry the daughters of other commissioned officers or of families in commerce, who were close to their social level, than to wed bureaucrats' children. The royal officials were obviously superior in rank: more administrators married officers' daughters than officers married civil officials' daughters. This was a matter of status as well as of numbers: men could marry just below their social level without a loss of standing. Intelligent and attractive women from lesser families could marry upward because they were regarded as dependents who would assume the husband's rank. In a male-dominated society, like New France, women could rise socially through matrimony. "Inferior" men are usually denied access to women of superior standing. It is evident from marriage patterns that civil administrators of the crown and magistrates were at the apex of colonial society.

THE COLONIAL OFFICERS

An army career was the resort of junior branches of families in the civil administration, such as the Aubert de Gaspé line. It was second best to a government office. Canadians avidly sought officers' positions, not only out of military ardor, but also because their chance of getting a civil office was slender. The Canadian gentry eventually dominated the officer corps of the colonial garrison troops and was the most coherent and self-conscious part of the social elite. The marriage connections of the martial LeGardeur family (d'Ailleboust, Chaussegros de Léry, Juchereau de Maur, Le Neuf, Nicolet, Payen de Noyan, Robinau, Rocbert, Saint-Ours, Saint-Père), and of the Pécaudy de Contrecoeur clan (Denys, Gaulthier de Varennes, Lacorne, Péan, Saint-Ours) suggest a military caste in the making. Only five of the seventeen brides taken by men of these two families came from administrative families; eleven were the daughters of fellow officers and seigneurs.

The profession of arms was open to the colony's notables, and they regarded an officer's position as an honorable calling for people of their rank. There was a social cachet in being an officer in the king's troops; military service was the traditional function of the French nobility. The organization of the marine troops into independent companies, however, meant that a captaincy was the highest rank achieved by most colonial officers. For commanders of posts on the colony's western frontiers, where one could engage in private trade, the officer's role was an avenue to wealth. The governors-general, however, were more likely to retain the most lucrative posts for their own profit or to entrust them to their own dependents. Army officers did not ordinarily exercise formal power in colonial society, except when providing police support for the law courts. The appointment of a colonial-born military officer, Pierre Rigaud de Vaudreuil, as New France's governor-general in 1755 was a major exception. Ordinarily, Canadians were minor partners in their colony's government.

To become army officers, Canadians depended upon the goodwill of metropolitan officials. They besieged the minister of maritime affairs, the king, and colonial governors-general with petitions seeking admission of their sons to the officer corps. Each marine company had positions for a captain, three junior officers, and two officer-cadets. There was provision for two additional young gentlemen who would serve as ordinary soldiers with the expectation of filling the first officer-cadet's vacancy. As a rule, the marine troops did not recruit colonists as private soldiers, for fear of diverting manpower from agriculture. At the very least, the petitioners wanted an appointment as a supernumerary officer-cadet with an *expectative,* that is, the right to fill the next vacancy. "All the gentlemen and officers' sons," wrote a cynical official in the 1730s, "want to enter the [king's] service; which is praiseworthy in itself but, since most are poor, several join [the marine troops] to obtain a small income in the king's pay, more than from any other motives."[30] Military detachments on Ile Royale or Ile St. Jean, in Louisiana and the French West Indies opened up more positions for Canadian officers to fill.

Each death or departure of an officer from the troops put the colony's leading families in a state of excitement as they speculated about who would receive the vacant post or be promoted as a consequence. An officer's wife at Montreal informed her brother of the latest appointments of post commanders throughout the colony, concluding, "this movement given to the officers will cause some dreams, [but] only the favored ones will be able to celebrate. . . . The much-awaited promotions will not settle the discontented. It came out that Sabrevois has the major's position." The distribution of the profitable posts was also the subject of gossip: "Deschambeau said that Mr. de Rigaud had . . . obtained a post to re-establish himself [financially]."[31] In 1752 the king's lieutenant (the senior captain) at Louisbourg, Charles-Joseph d'Ailleboust, told his brother about the disruptive effect of Ile Royale's new governor upon the colony's promotion system: "M. le Comte de Raymond obtained a royal decree which gives precedence to the first commissions of all those gentlemen who came from France [with him] and, as a consequence, most of the officers here find themselves behind them. . . . There are no replacements to be made, not even for a major's position, which was vacant because of the death of poor de Gannes. He died at Comte de Raymond's residence, . . . he is still warm this morning. I believe that he will not be interred until tomorrow for fear of burying him alive."[32] The new governor wanted to educate colonial officers in mathematics, gunnery, and writing, which, to judge from the painfully awkward letters of some of them, was needed. After the count's departure, harmony was restored: in 1755 another officer at Louisbourg wrote, "the replacement of officers has been done to everyone's satisfaction. There was nothing that caused jealousy among us."[33] The strained relationship between colonial and metropolitan officers had not disappeared, and it was particularly evident during the French and Indian War, when battalions from the kingdom's regular army arrived in New France. Professional soldiers from France were contemptuous of the marine troops that garrisoned the colonies.

The warlike spirit shown by Canadians during the reign of Louis XIV had succumbed to material concerns in later years, if we can believe the testimony of observers from France. In the 1750s, newly arrived French officers, such as Louis-Antoine de Bougainville, Chevalier de la Pause, and Pierre Pouchot, described the colonial officers as deficient in military knowledge and skills and the marine troops as slovenly, undisciplined, and scattered about New France beyond their officers' control. As for the marine officers' mastery of guerrilla warfare, de la Pause noted that their corps

was much better in the past and degenerates daily. The comfortable example of the European troops, the number of French officers admitted to it; the small pay and few perquisites, and lack of opportunity for the individual have caused these officers to neglect preparation for raiding parties with the Indians or of accustoming themselves to stern hardship. Today, there are not more than a few Ensigns and two or three Lieutenants in the entire corps [who are] fit for that type of warfare; one group is busy with trade; the other intrigues to obtain some post or to go and exploit it [commercially] for someone else. Few concern themselves with war and military spirit.[34]

Nonetheless, marine officers, like those of the Hertel family, still led raiding parties of colonial militiamen and Amerindian allies against British frontier settlements.

Although military officers in *la Nouvelle France* speculated in commerce, some retained an aristocratic contempt for merchants and traders that emerged in a conflict. When Fort Niagara's commandant, Pierre-Joseph Céloron de Blainville, heard that his improvident brother had been served with a merchant's summons for unpaid debts, he inscribed a haughty note to the unfortunate creditor, M. Pierre Guy of Montreal, who had advanced goods on credit to him too. Captain de Blainville wrote that "I am taking measures so that, in future, my wife will not need to take anything from you. My credit is so well established that everyone will be happy to deal with me. I cannot tell you how conscious I am of the proceedings you have undertaken against my brother. However well established your fortune might be, you might still find yourself, at some time, in need of a friend. Experience teaches us that however wealthy one might be, a person is often obliged to have recourse to it [another's help]."[35] There was something menacing about this statement, and de Blainville assumed that a trader should be pleased to extend credit to a military officer, even if the gentleman defaulted on his debts. Despite his repeated protestations of solvency while demanding goods, de Blainville was a delinquent debtor just like his brother. Notwithstanding this, the long-suffering Pierre Guy continued to supply goods to the officer's family and to provide him with financial help from 1744 to 1747, suggesting that one had to extend financial credit to members of the military elite or face serious consequences.[36]

THE MERCHANTS

The wholesale merchants of Montreal, Quebec, and Louisbourg were much closer in rank to the officers than the latter would admit, and they were infinitely more literate, cosmopolitan, and well informed. Captain de Blainville wrote phonetically. In a way, the men of business hardly belonged to New France. The traders and importers were part of a transatlantic community. Some were agents of French commercial houses who were only temporarily resident in North America. All maintained an active correspondence with associates and suppliers in Europe. Because political and military affairs influenced overseas trade, letters to merchants in the colony contained printed news gazettes, snippets on current events, and local gossip, along with price quotations, accounts, and bills of lading. Success in commerce depended on accurate and timely information on anything affecting trade.[37] The world of trade had an information-gathering network rivaling that of any government. Delivery of letters between French suppliers and merchants in the colonies was ensured by making multiple copies of each one and dispatching them on different vessels. Even if a vessel were lost or captured at sea, the mail still reached its destination.

Typical of the commercial correspondence, which blended business matters with public news and private intelligence, is a 1757 letter sent to Léon Cabarrus, a Louisbourg merchant, by his brother Étienne at Bayonne. The missive gave a long account of their shared financial affairs, of cargoes sold or lost to foreign privateers, and it expressed Étienne's annoyance that a bulk shipment of shoes had been appropriated by royal officials who would only pay for the shoes' wholesale value, not allowing for the cost of freight and insurance. When officials were helping themselves to an unknown quantity of barrel staves in the brothers' Louisbourg warehouse, an additional fifty-six pairs of shoes were stolen. For this loss, Étienne blamed officers of the Marine Department and not the French crown. Reverence for the king shielded Louis XV from popular criticism. "You might have learned," wrote Étienne, "of the horrible attempt against our good Monarch['s life]. There is no Frenchman who did not tremble upon hearing of it. Yet the criminal is still being tortured to make him confess who might have brought him to this shameful act. We must never cease praying to and praising God that he might preserve for us the best of all Kings." Étienne asked Léon what news he had from "Canada." Rather than pay wartime insurance, which could equal half the value of the cargo, or risk all on a single vessel, the Cabarrus brothers were distributing their shipments between small, speedy schooners to lessen the chance of a total loss. Étienne considered following the example of others and equipping his schooners as privateers to recover from the enemy a part of what he had stolen. War was dreaded as the great disrupter of overseas trade, and merchants' letters contained many prayers for peace.[38]

The merchants in New France had varying degrees of attachment to the colony. *Marchands forains,* or *pacotilleurs,* were seasonal visitors from France who intended to sell all of their merchandise after arrival in midsummer and then go home, with the money and goods taken in exchange, before November. A few wintered over in the colony. These peddlers had the weakest bond to *la Nouvelle France,* and their activities irritated local traders and established retailers. In 1685, 1719, 1727, and 1741 the latter submitted petitions against the transient hawkers, who, having no overhead costs for a store, undersold established traders and acquired the foodstuffs and other products that the country folk might have taken to shops in town to exchange for manufactured goods.[39] The petitioners made much of their commitment to the colony's welfare, yet several of these were only loosely tied to New France.

At Quebec the resident factors representing major French trading companies delivered imported goods and liquor to local retailers and smaller distributors, such as Pierre Guy of Montreal. Because many of the company agents in the eighteenth century were Protestants, who could not marry or raise a family in this officially Roman Catholic colony, they, too, eventually returned to France. They had no prospects outside commerce.

The Protestant bachelors at Quebec were almost forced by their legal exclusion from other callings to put money back into their businesses; their Calvinist values may also have inhibited expenditures on luxuries. They were accepted socially, to a degree. A Quebec factor described Pierre Guy's Protestant suppliers, François Havy and Jean Lefèbvre, who represented a Rouen firm, as "gallant and likeable men," whose losses in King George's War (1744–48) "afflicted everyone equally," which would not have been the case "if they were not such loved and honest people (*aimés & honnetes gens*)."[40] Pierre Guy hosted the two company agents when they visited Montreal, and was invited to stay with them at Quebec. When Guy and other members of Montreal's militia came to Quebec in the summer of 1745, to defend the capital against an expected attack, he stayed with the two Protestants but preferred to dine elsewhere with fellow Roman Catholics ("avec messieurs ses confrères").[41] Mother de Sainte-Hélène of Quebec's hospital might entrust her letters and packages to Havy and Lefèbvre's ship *Centaure,* yet privately she hoped that the work of her brother, a Jesuit in Dieppe, "with Heaven's aid, will make [the city] as Catholic as it is now heretical and depraved."[42] One could use the services of Protestants without approving of them.

Government and militia appointments—even the occupations of midwife and notary—were closed to "those of the so-called reformed religion." Every nominee for a public office had to present a priest's certificate, attesting to his Catholicity, before admission to office. The road to ennoblement was open only to Roman Catholics, who, if they could afford it, sank their money into estates and acquired the other trappings of aristocratic life. They could invest in land and in the advancement of their children: a formal education for the sons and, perhaps, a nun's dowry for a daughter. One could say that many of the Roman Catholic merchants were in business in order to get out of it; that is to say, they were traders for as long as it took to accumulate enough capital to move into a higher vocation.

That social transformation could be accelerated by government patronage in the awarding of contracts or purchase orders and in the allocation of appointments. In 1705–27 the French government spent about six hundred thousand livres annually in Canada.[43] In the 1705 expenditures, 37 percent went to pay the garrison troops, their officers and staff officers, while another 3 percent was spent on fortifications. In wartime government expenditures were in the millions of livres and the profits to suppliers were proportionately greater. Government provisioner Joseph-Michel Cadet of Quebec sold the king goods worth eleven thousand livres in 1744, and during King George's War, his annual sales surpassed forty-one thousand livres.[44]

Colonists in the wholesale trade operated on a smaller scale, and they lost ground to the metropolitan merchants. The official explanation was that the local men lacked capital for large ventures. In 1732 the intendant reported that "Canada's merchants do not profit . . . from half the trade here. It is the La Rochelle merchants and those of Rouen who send their agents [like Havy & Lefèbvre] here loaded with a great quantity of goods [who dominated commerce]."[45] Three years later, it was said that the colonists controlled just one-third of the import-export trade.[46] If we accept the observations of the governor-general and intendant, that share dropped to a quarter in the 1750s. According to Governor-General Duquesne de Menneville and Intendant François Bigot, the Huguenot merchants, "represent fourteen firms conducting three-quarters of the country's trade, and if they were expelled, it would do a great injury to the colony, Canadian traders not being numerous enough nor rich enough to provide all that it needs."[47] The safe domain of the Canadians was in retail shopkeeping and in the fur trade out of Montreal, where their knowledge of local conditions and of native Indians gave them an advantage.

Quebec's nationalist historians of the 1950s and 1960s, Michel Brunet and Guy Frégault, claimed that New France had possessed its own indigenous commercial class that presided over colonial society, as was the case in some British North American colonies. The evidence, however, is that the wholesale merchants at Quebec had stronger ties with the mother country than with the colony. Few saw themselves as Canadians and, as we already know, they alone were not society's leaders. The ambitious French wholesaler, like the high government officials and senior officers from France, had his eyes fixed on a return to the homeland. He endured life in the colonies as a temporary period of suffering to entitle one to come home to a superior position, just as purgatory prepared souls for entry into paradise. In 1707 a military engineer bemoaned his extended exile at Quebec: "chief engineers of [fortified] places in France . . . enjoy a climate very different from that of Canada, a wretched place where I am spending the best years of my life imperceptibly [*Insensiblement*]."[48]

Like the indentured servants, soldiers, and public officials, the wholesale merchants' thoughts often turned to France for more than business. A study of seventy-six "merchants" active in Quebec City in 1717–45 found that 38.2 percent were factors or agents of French firms, 15.8 percent were really government functionaries who combined a public office with private trading, and 46.1 percent were colonial-born entrepreneurs. Five were women, usually the wives or widows of merchants who ran the business in their spouse's absence. An examination of furnishings listed in postmortem inventories reveals that the merchants adhered closely to current French fashions and tastes. Few of the merchant-factors and functionaries intermarried with Canadian families in trade. The bond with France went beyond their tastes and interests. Of the *twenty-three* merchants still alive at the time of the British Conquest, eleven had departed for France, or soon relocated to the mother country. Those aged fifty or older, being close to retirement, were inclined to stay in the conquered colony. Only two of the remaining families, the Fleury de la Gorgendières and the Perraults, prospered under British rule.[49]

Since May 1717, when a royal decree authorized merchants at Quebec and Montreal to assemble together and to discuss their common interests, the mercantile community had a corporate structure. Merchants were also allowed to elect a spokesman, or syndic, to speak "in the name of all" and to make "necessary representations for the good of their trade" to government officials.[50] This allowed the merchants to function as a group and to make their wants known to government, as they did in their petitions against the *marchands forains*. Although the governor-general and intendant did not exclude the seasonal traders from France, as the petitioners wished, the resident merchants were free to engage in collective action and to defend their economic interests. These rights were denied to urban craftsmen, who had a deeper commitment to New France.

CRAFTSMEN AND THE LICENSED PROFESSIONS

The feeble attempts of these artisans at self-organization in order to influence public policy were rebuffed by the royal government. The king's officials were hostile to unauthorized associations among the lower-ranking colonists, especially when these self-constituted groups had economic aims. The fragmented nature of the crafts in New France was not solely due to official disapproval for collective action by social inferiors. Cooperation with strangers, outside family ties, was hampered by the skilled workers' own craft particularism. They had no collective class consciousness, even if others grouped them together as "gens de métiers" (crafts people). In his *Lettres persanes* (1721), Baron de Montesquieu's imaginary Persian visitor to France observed that "even the humblest workers argue over the merits of the trade they have chosen; everyone believes himself to be above someone else of a different calling, proportionately to the idea he has formed of the superiority of his own."[51] This concern with the status of one's own trade had been evident at Quebec in 1646, when the annual Corpus Christi procession was being planned. The organizers were reminded "that it was necessary to preserve the honorable order of crafts." An ecclesiastic present belittled such worldly distinctions and the ceremonial precedence was relaxed to allow the two oldest artisans to come first, after some wag suggested that "the fathers should lead the children." Each craftsman in the procession carried a wax taper, and one of the patriarchs, a stonemason, proudly ornamented his candle with a shield bearing the "arms" of his trade: "mallet, dividers, and ruler."[52]

In addition to its insignia, each craft had its own patron saint, and that saint's feast day was an occasion for tradesmen to come together to affirm their identity as members of a distinctive and honorable occupation. It was customary to hold a dinner, supplemented with liquor, for members of the craft after the religious celebration. The disorderly celebrations of drunken smiths and charcoal-burners of the St. Maurice Ironworks after a high mass on their patrons' festive days brought a reprimand from the bishop of Quebec in 1755. "Under the pretext of honoring them [the saints] . . . several villagers indulged themselves in scandalous excesses. . . . We charge the missionary [there] to warn the parish residents that if, in the future, we learn of people committing the same disorders, we will forbid any special ceremony on these days."[53] Workers had other religious rituals for expressing their fellowship and craft pride. In 1645 Quebec's toolmakers agreed to sponsor the distribution of *pain-bénit,* or holy bread (not the Eucharist), at the Christmas eve mass. The bread was blessed and then distributed to the congregants, in order of rank, while the *Credo,* or confession of faith, was sung.

The expression of craft solidarity in *la Nouvelle France* was usually confined to pious observances and dinners because trade guilds did not exist in the colony. The exclusion of self-regulating craft associations began, accidentally, when the rank of master craftsman was opened to all comers by the 1627 charter of the Company of One Hundred Associates, which stated that, "to encourage more of His Majesty's subjects to transport themselves to the said places and to undertake all sorts of manufacturing there," a tradesman who practiced his craft in New France for six years would be reputed a master artisan in Paris and in other towns of France. The same privilege was restated in the 1664 charter of the *Compagnie des Indes occidentales.*[54] This concession was made to attract skilled workers to the colony, even for a sojourn of a few years. In France the regime of *métier libre*—the free and unregulated practice of manual trades—was used to draw journeymen-artisans into barren or depopulated regions. In most French cities trade corporations controlled access to the rank of master craftsmen and the associated right to have one's own workshop. The guilds supervised apprenticeships, tested the graduates' competence, and admitted qualified candidates to the rank of master. In theory, artisans returning to France, after living in the colony for the requisite number of years, were entitled to set up shop with their own journeymen and apprentices without having to seek the local guild's approval. At least one artisan from Canada, with ministerial support, attempted to claim this right in France.[55]

As a consequence of the 1627 and 1664 charter privileges, and in the absence of guilds, craftsmen remaining in New France were free to work independently at their trade, if they could afford to do so and if the colonial government did not impose any restrictions. The legal distinction between journeymen and master tradesmen had been dissolved in the colony and a worker could pass from employee to self-employed artisan if he had the money to establish his own workshop. The title "maître" was used to describe the self-employed craftsman; it did not signify possession of a legal privilege. The determination of a worker's competence was left up to his clients, who were sometimes forced to accept mediocre workmanship, provided the item was serviceable.[56] The courts might appoint someone to examine a disputed piece of handiwork. It was the French crown, not guilds, that licensed a select number of occupations, such as those of notary, surgeon, baker, and butcher. Sometimes an outstanding worker was honored with formal letters of mastery—a gesture akin to the modern ritual of giving someone the symbolic "key to the city," although there are no town walls or gates to be unlocked.[57] Since there was no private right to test candidates, to license workers in most trades, or to limit the number of artisans in a trade, craft guilds were superfluous. The social needs of colonial artisans were satisfied by a few small religious brotherhoods.

The king's officials in New France were not comfortable with the unregulated state of the crafts; they felt that some way of ensuring good quality, apart from the rule of *caveat emptor,* had to be imposed. During the governorship of Louis Buade de Frontenac, regulations were passed in 1673 and 1676 promising to create "sworn masters from each craft . . . elected and named by a plurality of votes by artisans in their trade" to inspect workmanship within the town of Quebec. The inspectors were to be confirmed in their office by the crown, making them agents of the government.[58] There is no evidence that these craft inspectors were ever elected or appointed, and the idea was probably swept aside by Frontenac's 1677 interdict, issued at the crown's behest, against elected spokesmen and unauthorized gatherings.

Proscription of workers' associations proceeded from the belief that they would restrain competition in commerce and force up the price of goods and services. There was also an official abhorrence for unsanctioned gatherings among the lower ranks. Private assemblies, wrote French jurist Edmé de Fréminville, "always savor of licentiousness and only have in mind evil ends as their goal."[59] In short, if a private gathering had not sought prior government authorization, then it must have something to hide. Open mastership in New France began as a provisional measure to encourage the establishment of artisans and to facilitate the diffusion of their skills, and then was maintained as government policy. Officials in the parent state were increasingly hostile toward craft guilds, which impeded government management of the economy. This hostility may have helped perpetuate the laissez-faire policy for manual trades in the colonies, although eighteenth-century intendants, such as Jacques Raudot, still spoke of a time when "it might please His Majesty to establish trade corporations."[60]

When a profession was officially organized for better regulation, members of that group—like the merchants—could collectively petition the government without fear of punishment. New France's administration tended to license only those trades affecting the health of the populace. Town bakers and butchers had to accept a fixed price schedule and court supervision and, in return, they were assured of an exclusive right to sell those foodstuffs with a profit sufficient for a decent living. When their livelihood was endangered, the licensed retailers were entitled to a hearing. Other tradesmen tried to petition on the basis of their economic survival, but the administration upheld the distinction between officially organized trades and self-constituted groups, which, if they involved the lower orders, were treated brusquely.

In May 1729 a representative of Quebec's master roofers, who were unlicensed, petitioned the Superior Council for a monopoly on roofing work. Other woodworkers installed board roofs and the roofers usually applied wooden shingles, which, in 1727, were outlawed within the towns as a fire hazard. The roofers' living was thus threatened. Shingles, they said, had been the customary roofing material in Canada, "from what could be called time immemorial," and now carpenters provided the cheapest lawful form of roofing. If slate or some other fireproof material were not required by law, said the roofers, or if they were not given a monopoly of roofing work, "they would only be able to support their families in the most modest circumstances." On the attorney-general's advice, the council rejected this petition of "the self-styled master roofers of this said town . . . since there is neither any mastership nor sworn trade nor even any exclusive right to practice any art or trade in this town." That categorical statement overlooked the government-licensed trades, which were given a monopoly. As a limited concession, wooden shingles were permitted on the angles and edges of roofs.[61] That concession was insufficient to assure the roofers a living; only one roofer was enumerated in the 1744 census of Quebec. When a roofer and toolmaker appeared before the council in 1758 as "spokesmen of the burgesses and citizens of Trois-Rivières town" to appeal a lower court decision, the two were dismissed without a hearing. Other courts and officials were forbidden to deal with these syndics, because "they have not proven by what right they hold the said title."[62] It was more than a matter of missing documentation; the councillors were hostile to popularly selected spokesmen, especially if they were common artisans.

Notaries and surgeons, who were in licensed occupations and were socially superior to most craftsmen, were more successful in defending their livelihood and even in extending their privileges. In 1668 Quebec's town notaries won their case against a seigneurial scrivener who had drawn up deeds within the town.[63] Quebec's surgeons petitioned in 1710 to prevent the surgeons of visiting ships from exercising their art in the colony, "because it is important for the public good that no one engage in surgery unless his capability be known . . . and to prevent the evil caused by the mania of many people for novelty." The local surgeons were as concerned with retaining their clientele as they were with upholding medical standards. By law, all surgical practitioners in New France were to be examined and licensed by royal agents: the *lieutenant du premier chirurgien du Roi* (deputy of the king's first surgeon) or the *Médecin du Roi* (king's physician) at Quebec. Since the interlopers were defying royal authority by treating patients without a license, the intendant responded to the 1710 petition by decreeing a stiff fine and other penalties against unregistered, nonresident surgeons who worked in the colony.[64]

Success emboldened Quebec's surgeons and, two years later, they asked the Superior Council to have the number of authorized practitioners within the town fixed at four, as well as for an order that all surgeons from abroad be forbidden to work or sell medications in the colony. The *lieutenant du premier chirurgien du Roi* himself presented the 1712 surgeons' petition to the Superior Council and, after verifying his credentials, it considered the matter. The request, nonetheless, was not granted.[65] The real issue in this case was the self-interest of the Quebeckers, who wanted to exclude other surgeons from their town. The colonial administration was still interested in upholding the standard of medical care and it repeated the interdict on unregistered newcomers then, and in 1716, 1737, and 1750. Quebec's surgeons did not get all that they wanted in 1712, yet they did receive a respectful hearing and they obtained some beneficial legislation. That was the advantage of being a licensed profession.

Because the government of New France was unreceptive to self-constituted groups from the lower orders of society, especially when they had economic goals, and the practice of most manual trades was open to all, the artisans' expression of trade solidarity was limited to craftsmen's religious confraternities. In France *confréries* were placed under clerical supervision and, legally, their property belonged to the Roman Catholic Church, which functioned as an arm of the state. Even with these safeguards, jurists were skeptical about the piety of the brother-members. Edmé de Fréminville wrote, "these associations all had religion in view and its more exact practice, but they eventually degenerated into begging, factionalism, and disorders while covering themselves with the pleasing veil of religion. . . . If one denied the craftsmen and others the suppers they hold, one would remove all of their devotion and [the confraternity's] justification."[66] The suspicion that getting inebriated at a banquet was the principal religious act of the brethren or that these groups might harbor secular ambitions led to a number of legal restrictions. In 1660 the Paris *Parlement* ruled that no one could establish "any associations, confraternities and congregations" without the king's approval in letters-patent. The diocesan bishop's consent was also required. In 1674 the kingdom's Council of State forbade brother-hoods to collect money from the public; they had to be paid for by their members. As a final blow to the confraternities' independence, a 1689 decree of the Parisian *Parlement* denied the groups the powers of discipline or compulsion over their mem-bers.[67] The objective of these laws was to reduce artisans' religious brotherhoods to tame adjuncts of the church. The same goals and suspicions were evident in the actions of New France's magistracy.

The consequences of being subordinated to the clergy are illustrated by the history of two craft brotherhoods in *la Nouvelle France*. By metropolitan standards, these colonial groups were anemic affairs and only three are known to have existed. The weakness of these artisan confraternities corresponds to the fading affinity of colonial workers for fellow tradesmen. Here was a collective craft activity that was not forbidden by the government, and yet, little was made of the opportunity to organize and work together. Although colonists retained a pride in their family's trade, with the passage of the generations, they lost any sense of community with strangers in the same occupation.

La Confrérie de Sainte-Anne was the product of the immigrant generation from France that had the knowledge, will, and ability to reconstitute some of the homeland's craft traditions. This brotherhood appeared when there were scarcely two thousand Europeans in the St. Lawrence Valley. The group was founded by Quebec's wood sculptors and joiners, who, since the early 1650s, had sponsored a high mass in honor of their patroness, St. Anne. In April 1657 seven workers peti-tioned the acting vicar-general—there being no bishop at the time—for a special place in Quebec's parish church so that they might have a permanent association. Earlier action had been prevented, "because of some difficulties that had arisen be-tween the said joiners."[68] This was an early instance of the internal strife that would also disrupt another group in Montreal. Approval was given and, in the May 1657 act of foundation, the cleric allowed members to use the existing side-chapel of St. Anne. The act called for a membership of good and faithful Roman Catholics, su-pervised by the parish curate, and it concluded with an exhortation to meet once a month "in their chapel" to recite the patron saint's litanies and to receive spiritual instruction, "as is done in well-regulated confraternities."[69]

Jean Levasseur called La Vigne, a joiner from Paris and a former member of that city's Confraternity of St. Anne, was the originator of the Quebec brotherhood. He served as dean and perpetual director of the colonial group in its first thirty years. Levasseur intended to reproduce the Paris confraternity in its entirety. So that the woodworkers would have their own pew, he rented a place in the chapel and promised to make a decorated bench like those of French brotherhoods. The confraternity at Paris provided an account of its history and customs. This text and Levasseur's memory probably were the guides for an ambitious constitution titled "Statuts De La Confrairie de Ste. Anne," which called for a twelve-man executive. Only five positions were ever filled and, as an epitaph, the words "very badly observed" were inscribed upon the document.[70]

Bishop François de Montmorency Laval approved a more modest constitution in 1678 and provided closer, priestly supervision over the brethren. There were to be only two *maîtres-confrères* elected for staggered, two-year terms of office. The senior of the two had nominal authority to manage the group's revenues and accounts. The chaplain, however, had the second key needed to open the strongbox and assisted in the accounting. All alms and dues received were to be used only for religious services and decoration of the chapel. This requirement precluded banquets or assistance for the poor, as anticipated in the first charter. Charity was restricted to funeral services and, funds permitting, requiem masses for deceased members. The 1678 constitution stated that the retiring director would submit his records to the curate or another ecclesiastic named by the bishop, "to direct the confraternity (*pour diriger La confrairie*)."[71] Thus were the ultimate authority and clerical author of the second charter disclosed.

Quebec's woodworkers also lost control of the membership. The earliest statutes did not exclude other artisans, and the brethren may have welcomed wives, children, and friends to their devotions. The new charter explicitly received all "honorable people of good morals" as regular members. Associate, nonvoting members of both sexes were also accepted, "provided they are not scandalous." The 1678 constitution, therefore, sanctioned the transformation of a craft brotherhood into a devotional group for all of Quebec's laity. The surviving membership roll, which began in 1683, recorded the influx of tradesmen of all sorts with their wives, as well as a few notables. Women outnumbered men.[72] Bishop Laval had authorized two other religious confraternities for the general public, but the popularity of St. Anne led more people to enroll in the woodworkers' association. As a consequence, the joiners and sculptors were soon in the minority and the brotherhood no longer belonged exclusively to their craft. The confraternity carried on, with one interruption, until its chapel was destroyed in the 1759 siege of Quebec. The association was well organized and successful, yet that success owed more to popular veneration for St. Anne than to the vitality of craft traditions in Canada.

Montreal's *Confrérie de Saint-Eloi* was founded in 1676 by five metalworkers; the group's history reveals the faltering sense of community among colonial artisans. The confraternity was notably deficient in brotherhood. The members, as magistrates suspected, were more interested in merriment than religion and the brawls accompanying their annual libations were the group's undoing. The association expressed the unusual fellowship of smiths, who often stood as godparents for a fellow worker's child or acted as witnesses to another's marriage contract during the seventeenth century. No other manual tradesmen showed this much kinship, yet the metalworkers' unity did not endure long. All the founder-members were French immigrants, although three had lived in New France for a score of years and two had arrived as adolescents. For most of them, ironworking was a family tradition. There were over a dozen metalworkers on Montreal Island at the time, but only the original five were identified as members. This was the only-known craft brotherhood in seventeenth-century Montreal and, if it were the best that could be done by a trade with an exceptional sense of craft loyalty, then it appears that the social fragmentation of colonial artisans was well under way in the immigrant generation.

Compared with the Confraternity of St. Anne, the St. Eloi (Eligius) Brotherhood was a rudimentary organization. Its charter was a one-paragraph document drawn up on 4 December 1676, in which the workers declared their intention "to mark the feast day of St. Eloi, to have a High Mass said, to distribute blessed bread [*pain bénit*], and to contribute one gold *pistole* [coin] each to treat ourselves [to a banquet] and to pay the one who has the mass said." A pistole was then worth eleven livres and was more than enough to cover the costs. Members then drew lots to establish the sequence in which each one would act as that year's organizer for the mass and dinner.[73] No officers were elected, although the oldest, Pierre Gadois, acted as *doyen,* or dean. A few days later, the smiths signed a "concordat" with the parish wardens of Notre-Dame de Montréal parish, confirming their intention to sponsor a high mass on the feast day of the metalworkers' patron saint. The mass was to be celebrated by priests in the presence of a deacon, subdeacons, and two chanters in the choir. The blessed bread was to be decorated with six candles, also provided by the sponsors.

A conflict between two members, René Fezeret and Simon Guillory, disrupted the confraternity. Fezeret was to have been the banquet host in 1677, but his wife's hostility to the event forced the brethren to relocate their meal to Gadois's home. During the supper, Guillory goaded Fezeret by calling him *"moraille"* (horse tongs) and by telling him that the gunsmiths present were doing Fezeret, a blacksmith and locksmith, a great favor by suffering his presence. Even in this little circle, there remained a divisive sense of occupational ranks. This particular dispute, however, did not go beyond an exchange of words.[74]

In 1678 Guillory was the last *confrère* to receive *pain-bénit* at the church service, and he suspected Fezeret of arranging this slight to his dignity—the other brethren later claimed that Fezeret admitted it. The others then mocked Fezeret when he lost in a card game after their supper. A fight erupted between Fezeret, Guillory, a third member, and their respective wives. It was a disorderly conclusion to a day for reaffirming the comradeship of all metalworkers. Three members, including Simon Guillory, blamed René Fezeret for all the troubles and, two days after the banquet, they added a postscript to their constitution stating, "we have banished Fezeret from our association as a troublemaker (*un séditieux*)."[75] This expulsion assumed that they had the power of self-government without clerical guidance. In the magistracy's eyes, this assumption was presumption indeed and, to the workers' misfortune, the matter came to the attention of the Montreal Baillif's Court in the winter of 1680–81.

During that winter two complaints were heard by Montreal's court against the metalworkers' confraternity of St. Eloi. Fezeret protested that he had been libeled as "a troublemaker" and demanded a public retraction of the insult with punitive damages against the authors of his expulsion, as well as nullification of that expulsion.[76] He had not heard of the ban until 1680 because there had been no celebration in 1679. The omission, Fezeret pointed out with righteous satisfaction, was due to Simon Guillory's negligence. This information brought the church wardens into court and they demanded that the brotherhood's "concordat" with them be enforced.[77] As acting dean, Pierre Gadois had tried to compel Guillory to do his duty, and he had endeavored to reconcile the two enemies. Gadois assured the judge that the remaining members would continue to sponsor the religious observance, as promised.[78] The magistrate was unsympathetic and he intended to chasten the unruly brethren.

The church wardens coveted the confraternity's annual dues, which, they felt, would be better spent on Montreal's church than on banquets. They blamed the disorders on the meals, which, they claimed, were "contrary to the ordinances forbidding culinary feasts [*régals*]." The wardens asked that the dues be applied exclusively to religious services and to the upkeep of the parish church.[79] The next day Fezeret seconded their wish for enforcement of the unidentified "ordinances prohibiting such assemblies." He accused the other *confrères* of holding an illegal gathering to expel "a very decent man (*un tres honneste homme*), as I claim to be, and without any reasons" in contempt of the king's orders and justice, behaving like "people without sovereigns or law."[80]

Judge Migeon de Branssat's verdict in February 1681 was a fatal blow to the metalworkers' brotherhood. He ordered the group to pay for the high masses on their patron saint's day and to expunge the ban on Fezeret. The three originators of the expulsion were fined six livres each. They were deprived of any authority over the membership and forbidden to hold any more "gatherings or banquets." The dues, it appeared, would go entirely to the parish. Celebrations in honor of St. Eloi were confined to the high mass with distribution of holy bread, and the church wardens could force the metalworkers to pay for the service.[81] Within five years of its foundation, the little confraternity had been reduced to a band of involuntary sponsors for a religious ceremony. Without secular functions, the association probably died with the original members because there are no later references to it.

Montreal was also the home of a third documented artisan confraternity, which appeared in the 1720s. There is no reference to a written charter, which, given past experience, may have been an advantage. In appearance, the cobblers' brotherhood was a loosely organized group with one yearly gathering, like the metalworkers' group. This later association, however, escaped clerical supervision and served its members' material interests, which is exactly what the civil authorities feared from workers' associations.

The first record of the Montreal shoemakers' *Confrérie de Saint-Crépin et Saint-Crépinien* dates from October 1728. Three representatives of the society, Jean Ridday *dit* Beauceron, Edmé Moreau, and Jacques Viger, presented a request to Montreal's royal law court to have a fellow shoemaker forced to provide the blessed bread at mass on St. Simon's Day since he had failed to do it on their patron saint's day "in the accustomed manner." The delinquent cobbler replied that he had "never refused to obey the ancient rule of the confraternity" and would comply even though he was not bound to do so by any written act, but that no one had contributed money for the mass. The magistrate ordered him "to furnish an honorable blessed loaf, as is customary" and advised the plaintiffs to have the entire membership share the cost of the yearly mass if they wanted their association to continue.[82]

Evidence that the Brotherhood of Saints Crispin and Crispian was more than a religious group came in the following year. In August 1729 the same three representatives of the confraternity delivered a petition to Montreal's magistrate. The petitioners pointed out that, contrary to Intendant Raudot's July 1706 ordinance, a local butcher named Joseph Guyon Després was engaged in tanning and shoemaking. Their appeal was endorsed by twenty-three shoemakers. It was an impressive showing; more remarkable was the fact that over two-thirds of the subscribers were colonial-born, even if French immigrants, some of them former soldiers, headed the list and had provided two of the three spokesmen. Guyon Després's integrated business was hurting the shoemakers.

In 1729 the shoemakers pointed out that the combination of three crafts in one enterprise did "a considerable injury to all the supplicants. Inasmuch as the said Després and his wife take skins from their butchery, and hides from their tannery, and by having [their own shoemakers] use the said hides, they can sell shoes at a much lower price than . . . all of the said petitioners." The butcher, they said, was peddling his cheap shoes in the rural areas as well as in town. This illegal activity left the self-employed shoemakers without work. The petitioners were, they said, "very unhappy that, after spending a part of their youth in learning the shoemaker's trade and having made an establishment to earn their living and to support their families, they now find it impossible to do so, having no work." This was the conventional plea of an endangered livelihood. A copy of the intendant's 1706 ordinance was attached to their petition.[83]

Montreal's *lieutenant-général* was in an awkward position: the intendant's ordinance was being violated and yet enforcement of the law would encourage a low-ranking pressure group—a dangerous concession. After hearing both sides and consulting with the crown attorney, the judge referred the matter to the current intendant at Quebec for a decision.[84] There is no surviving account of the shoemakers carrying their case to the colony's capital. On principle, the intendant could have refused to see this self-constituted group. Quebec's shoemakers had failed to prevent local tanners from employing journeymen-cobblers and the failure of Quebec's roofers in defending their craft in May 1729 justified pessimism. The object of the Montreal shoemakers' complaint was, moreover, a seigneur and, later, a government provisioner, and they had been snubbed in the past.

The Superior Council had rejected an earlier petition from Montreal's shoemakers. In 1712 they had asked for permission to have shoe leather delivered to their shops on Sundays and holy days, after mass. Tanneries were located outside the town and delivery would have allowed the artisans to begin work early on the next day. Productive labor was forbidden on religious holidays. The shoemakers said that the delivery of goods was permitted elsewhere and that, if their request were denied, they and their families faced imminent ruin. Once again, the welfare of the workers' families was invoked to win sympathy. Unmoved by this appeal, the council firmly refused their proposal.[85]

These three petitions set Montreal's shoemakers apart from the other unlicensed crafts. The cobblers were able to organize themselves more than once to defend their trade and had obtained a copy of a law that had been published in manuscript years before. Since the same three spokesmen of the Confraternity of Saints Crispin and Crispian also led petitioners in 1729, the brotherhood had brought the shoemakers together for more than religious observances. The same group could have been behind the 1712 petition. The impressive support mustered in 1729 might show that the master cobblers were united; it could also be a measure of their desperation. Apprenticeship indentures show that, until 1730, shoemaking had been the fastest-growing and most popular trade in the Montreal region. After this date, the number of apprentice joiners and metalworkers surpassed the apprentice shoe-makers, who, even for a reduced training period of two years or less, paid their instructors nothing. Service beyond two years was the usual method of paying for craft training. The waning popularity of shoemaking might well reflect the difficulty of competing with journeymen shoemakers employed by tanners and butchers, such as Després.

The rarity of workers' associations and the leadership provided by immigrants from France suggest that the artisans' corporate traditions were dying. Native-born Canadians seemed indifferent to trade associations. They were less likely than European newcomers to act in concert with others in the same trade. Quebec's royal shipyard was the scene of Canada's first recorded strike by skilled workers, but the strikers were not colonists. Both Canadians and metropolitan craftsmen were employed in the shipyard. In poor weather local workers, who were being paid by the day, were laid off; while the French contract workers were kept on the job. They downed tools in protest. An official dispatch in October 1741 is our only record of the strike. It reported that "the carpenters sent from Rochefort [in France] have done their duty well. In the beginning, however, M. Hocquart [the intendant] was obliged to punish them for their disobedience, once only, with imprisonment and iron manacles when they went so far as to refuse an order and would not work inside the king's sheds, although employed by the month, when the Canadians were released because of bad weather." Thanks to the intendant's firm action, it was said that the rebellious workers "have recognized their fault and are very docile."[86] The colonial shipwrights took no part in this protest.

The 1741 strike and the history of artisan confraternities in *la Nouvelle France* reveal two things. They expose the repressive instincts of an administration that equated "bon ordre" with the subordination of the lower ranks of society. The magistrates' concern with social discipline and their fear that private combinations would increase the cost of goods and labor made them intolerant of self-constituted workers' groups with secular goals. The second thing revealed by these episodes is that colonial workers were less likely than European immigrants to band together in trade organizations. Canadians were not only discouraged by official hostility to such groups; they found it difficult to cooperate with strangers.

The Canadians' preference for family independence and self-employment—a predisposition hindering cooperation—is also revealed by the business partnerships concluded before the colony's notaries. There were obvious advantages to a commercial partnership between two or more craftsmen. It was more economical to share one workshop and one set of tools instead of maintaining separate and competing establishments. A master tradesman was both the producer and retailer of his wares and it would be more efficient to share these functions with another.

Associates could draw on greater capital and credit than an individual and so increase their trade. Despite these obvious benefits, colonial artisans shunned business alliances. For instance, in running a workshop and in selling, colonists preferred to use dependents, such as a wife, children, or apprentices.

The number of surviving partnership contracts between craftsmen is small. No more than 150 appear to have been made in the history of New France. Like other artisans' associations, craft co-partnerships were in decline. Fewer contracts were made before notaries even as the colony's population grew. The file of a minor seventeenth-century Montreal notary, Claude Maugue (fl.1677–96) contains seven *actes de société* between craftsmen, and other deeds refer to six additional accords. In the same region in the following century, one has to ransack eight notaries' files to find an equivalent number of artisans' partnership contracts. At Quebec the same trend appears in three successive notarial files of equal size: twelve craft partnerships were passed by Louis Chambalon (fl.1692–1716); six were registered by Jean-Etienne Dubreuil (fl.1708–34), a former shoemaker with a clientele of artisans; and the records of Claude Barolet (fl.1728–60) contain only merchants' alliances, which remained vital. The decline in craftsmen's partnerships was absolute and, compared with the population's growth, dramatic. Canadian craftsmen were probably finding partners within their own family and because partnerships between relatives did not need the legal force of a notarized contract, they were mostly unregistered.

The nature of the few accords that were made is also revealing. Partnerships were concentrated in trades demanding substantial operating capital or great physical exertion. A blacksmith's forge was an expensive investment in hearth, tools, charcoal, and a stock of bar iron. It was also difficult for one person to hammer hot iron and simultaneously work the bellows that forced air into the forge's fire. A blacksmith needed a helper as well as a financial backer. The distribution of eighteen agreements made at Quebec in 1692–1740 is revealing: five in metalwork, four in butchering, three in baking, two in masonry construction, two in tanning, and one each in milling and pottery making.[87] The partnerships between two butchers and one between a former journeyman and a butcher's widow were expressly "to facilitate the said trade and to find more easily the credit that they might need."[88] The range of nine artisan co-partnerships made at Montreal in 1727–59 was more limited: four in metalworking, three in tanning, and one each in shoemaking and in wood-sculpture.[89] Tanning accounted for a quarter to a fifth of all craft partnerships and, like ironworking, it was a costly undertaking. Financial necessity, and the absence of a close relative who could help, had forced the signatories into association with an outsider.

Among these artisans' alliances, one rarely finds a partnership between craftsmen of equal standing who were capable of matching each other's contribution.

Such partnerships were usually confined to metalworking and masonry construction. In more than three-quarters of forty-five contracts, a single artisan was allied with a merchant-investor, a lesser speculator, an aged craftsman, or a tradesman's widow—people with material and financial resources but lacking the skill and strength to do the work. The partners' ages can be obtained from parish registers and they confirm that these were unequal alliances. There was, typically, a senior partner in his forties or older who provided the established tannery, forge, bakery, or brewery. The junior associate was invariably a skilled craftsman who was single and in his twenties. Such arrangements allowed the young artisan to work for himself before he could afford to set up in business alone. For the investor-owner, a partnership got around the problem of finding a journeymen—rare birds in the colony—and it gave the craftsman a profit-sharing incentive that made him more productive than a salaried employee. Elevating the worker to the rank of a partner made good business sense.

The terms of craft partnerships in *la Nouvelle France* make it clear that the junior partner was taking the place of an indentured worker. The artisan-partner was usually fed and housed at the company's expense and enjoined to work assiduously at his trade. Some accords, like the service indentures, inserted penalty clauses for absences or a premature departure. Sick leave might be limited to eight days in the year. The intention was to keep the skilled associate on the job, as one would wish of a journeyman. A third of the partnerships were for one year or less—the same duration as most journeymen's indentures. The investor-partner's duties were more loosely defined, if they were stated at all; he would occasionally help in buying materials and assist in selling the products. Most were passive and left the business in the craftsman's hands. The worker-partner was to give a regular accounting of their trade. This is what the *Code Marchand,* or royal ordinance of March 1673, called a *société en commandite.* It was different from customary partnership, or *société ordinaire,* which was an agreement "between two or several people, and in which the partners contribute their money and attention equally." Profits and losses were shared equally.[90]

In New France the partners' respective obligations followed the pattern for a limited partnership while the worker-partner came to enjoy the rewards of a co-partner. The investor-partner bore almost all the business expenses. At most, the craftsman shared the cost of raw materials and other operating costs, such as the expense of additional workers. Investors could demand repayment of their initial outlay before sharing the profits; most did not do this. They were content to retain title to the fixed assets. With few exceptions, the gains from manufacturing partnerships in the colony were divided equally. So strong was the conviction that an artisan-partner was entitled to parity that, despite preliminary arrangements favoring the investor-partner, agreements still gave the customary assurance that the fruits of the enterprise would be "divided between them equally by half." Half the profits were also given by trade concessionaires to their factors and by merchant-shopowners to their storekeepers; owners of small vessels sailing out of Quebec promised half of the voyage's profits to the principal navigator too.[91] That, evidently, was the price to be paid to overcome the Canadians' aversion for hired service in order to obtain skilled services.

The ability of craftsmen to command the partnership rights of a *société ordinaire* in what were really *sociétés en commandite* testifies to the difficulty of finding journeymen. This anomaly, the brevity of partnerships, their small number, and their provisions were the result of the colonists' preference for self-employment and family independence. These same ambitions hindered cooperation with fellow tradesmen in the same craft, whether in business or in manufacturing partnerships, or even in associations or protests. These values were the rock upon which the immigrant workers' corporate traditions foundered.

The Rural Population, Parishes, and Seigneuries

The craftsmen of New France were concentrated in the towns; outside the towns, society was more atomized and collaboration between different families more difficult. In the St. Lawrence Valley, during the eighteenth century, four-fifths or more of the European population lived on the land. Most of the immigrants from France had come to Canada with manual trades and from towns and cities, yet their future was to be in agriculture. The European settlement pattern of compact farming villages was, however, not reproduced in the St. Lawrence Valley. Rural families lived on isolated farms, rather than in hamlets, which accentuated their separateness. Apart from the three major towns in Canada, there were just six villages. Intendant Jean Talon had tried to concentrate the rural population in defensible, compact villages, but the Canadians resisted his wishes and chose to remain on their scattered farmsteads, despite their vulnerability to Iroquois attack.

Because farm dwellings were located close to the river banks, they were often part of a loose string of generously spaced homes known as a *côte* settlement. There is little evidence of interfamily collaboration apart from occasional protests or gatherings within the framework of a parish. The surviving intendants' ordinances show that these country folk had to be prodded and pushed to organize themselves and cooperate to build and repair roads, erect bridges, or construct church buildings.[92] Shared pastures existed, yet they required little management by the users. The Acadians had villages, although they would have seemed dispersed to European eyes, and labor on the construction and maintenance of dikes brought different families together. People in the villages of the Illinois Country also worked together voluntarily. The rural Canadians, who usually lived outside organized villages before the 1750s, had only the church to bring them together. The local parish, with the passage of time, became the focus of their collective existence.

In the countryside of continental New France, the church parish emerged as the one public institution that provided a framework for community activities beyond interaction with one's own relatives. The bishops of Quebec were slow to sanction these regional subunits of their diocese. When Quebec's future bishop, François de Montmorency Laval, arrived in Canada in 1659, there were three established parishes. He sanctioned fourteen more parishes in 1678, and his successor, Bishop Saint-Vallier, added more in 1692–1724. In September 1721 the royal and ecclesiastical authorities defined the boundaries of eighty-two parishes in New France, yet most were to be served by missionaries or by the priests from the nearest parish.[93] Coadjutor Bishop Pierre-Herman Dosquet wrote in 1730, "that among about a hundred parishes in the diocese of Quebec, there are now only about twenty with titular curés; all the others, many of which are not even erected as parishes, are ministered to by simple missionaries."[94] Parishioners served by itinerant missionary priests heard mass once a month. The foundation of a parish with a permanent place of worship and a resident curate required a concentrated population and adequate revenues, quite apart from the bishop's authorization.

With the yearly tithe payable to the church by farm families fixed at one-twenty-sixth of the grain harvest, there had to be more than fifty families in a parish to support a priest. The tithe was a curate's principal source of income from parishioners; supplementary revenue came from special religious services and pew rentals. These fees were inadequate for a priest's sustenance, and the king had to provide a supplementary stipend to each curate or pay for a Franciscan friar to serve the poorest communities as well as military garrisons. As the number of resident priests increased, attendance at services in the local chapel became a weekly event. On Sundays and holy days, people gathered and gossiped outside the church doors until a bell summoned worshippers inside. After the service, public announcements were made at the entrance and auctions were held in the same location. Religious festivals and public processions also brought the parishioners together. It was at special events and regular services that people met future marriage partners. Every year, the farmers would chose one of their own to serve on the three-man vestry board (*la fabrique*) for a three-year term. Each warden's term was staggered and the senior man in his last year of office was the "warden in charge," subordinate only to the curate. The wardens, or *marguilliers,* collected parish dues and managed the revenues and physical assets of their parish. If the chapel required a new roof or the cemetery fence needed to be replaced, they would make the necessary arrangements. In the St. Lawrence Valley the parochial vestry board was the only popularly elected body that did not require explicit government approval to exist. The parish was not an institution that the rural colonists created for themselves, nor one that they fully controlled, yet it would be the dominant social institution, after the family, in their lives.

The church became a social center for rural folk, and the parish acquired educational, military, and legal functions. A minority of energetic *curés* provided children with an elementary education as well as the mandatory catechism classes, if there were not a local school run by the sisters of the *Congrégation de Notre-Dame*. The king's government found parishes a convenient administrative unit for organizing the colonial militia, in which every man, aged sixteen to sixty, was obliged to serve. The farmer appointed as captain of the parish militia company served as the government's agent in the countryside. The captain, his ensign, and two militia sergeants had the prestige of being the king's servants. This administrative use of the parish strengthened its importance as a social institution. The priest's spiritual leadership was augmented by his power, in the absence of a notary, to draw up wills, marriage contracts, and other legal documents and by his informal role as an arbiter of disputes.

The land for the church was usually donated by the seigneur whose family was entitled to occupy the first pew to the right of the high altar. The militia captain and seigneurial judge—if there were one—sat behind the seigneur, and the church wardens had their own special pew beside or immediately behind the militia officer. The parochial hierarchy was also maintained in religious processions and by the sequence in which one received the priest's blessing, received the sacraments, or was sprinkled with holy water.[95] Very few seigneurs had the right of presenting their own candidate for appointment to the curacy. The right of presentation belonged to those who had built a church at their own expense, but Bishop Laval foiled lay benefactors by refusing to consecrate any privately constructed chapel that was not built of stone—an expense beyond the means of most seigneurs. Laval also refused to grant curacies for life; parish priests were subject to his will and were removable at his wish. He created a centralized autocracy within the colonial church that matched the secular order aspired to by King Louis XIV.

The seigneurial landholding system, with a lineage going back to 1623, was an older institution than the parish and it has been traditional, in Canadian historiography, to treat this system as a formative influence upon rural society in French Canada. Seigneurial tenure, like all matters dealing with landed property, generated a mass of documentation and legislation and, if the volume of records and rules were proportionate to social importance, then this institution would overshadow all others. In fact, the seigneuries did not require cooperation among tenant-farmers and, apart from the large Montreal Island seigneury of the Sulpician Fathers, manorial estates did not challenge the parochial structure as a framework for rural life. When Gedéon de Catalogne made an on-the-spot survey of seigneuries in Canada in 1712, he identified seventy-eight lords of the manor and identified their occupations. Of these, 61.5 percent were military officers, civil functionaries, merchants, and mariners who usually lived elsewhere until retirement. Add to the seigneuries of absentee landlords the eleven manors owned by religious institutions, and one can see that most tenants had a distant and impersonal relationship with their seigneur.[96]

This landholding system was really a convenient legal framework, borrowed from France, for allocating land to settlers. The lord had to grant vacant land to any sincere applicant and, because uncleared land was plentiful and settlers few, he could demand only modest annual dues from tenants. According to Richard Colebrook Harris, "in newly settled seigneuries the total payment for a single roture [tenancy] was just over twenty livres; in older seigneuries where more land was cleared and hence more grain taken to the [lord's] banal mill, it reached approximately thirty-three livres. Thirty-three livres would buy fifteen days of [unskilled] manual labor, [or] a small cow. . . ."[97] When the seigneur had a gristmill on the estate, the tenants were required to take their wheat to the mill to be ground into flour for a charge of one-fourteenth of its weight. A few landlords had a seigneurial court which facilitated the collection of dues, but, because "the administration of justice was an expense for the seigneur rather than a source of revenue which it was in France . . . almost all Canadian seigneurs allowed the administration of justice . . . to pass out of their hands."[98] In the 1600s these estates were underpopulated status symbols for the owner and, in the eighteenth century, when a denser population provided more revenue, big lay seigneuries were divided into *fiefs* or fractional estates, so that more people could have the prestige of being a seigneur.

The bond between tenant and landlord was contractual, not personal, and could be terminated by the farmer by selling or abandoning his land concession. Earlier historians, such as Francis Parkman and W. B. Munro, were deceived by the medieval terminology used in seigneurial documents into thinking that this was a feudal system. Others, who attributed the linear farms of the St. Lawrence Valley to this landholding system, assumed that seigneurialism left a similar imprint upon colonial society. Strip farms running back from the riverbank existed in the Mississippi Valley without a landholding system of lords and tenants. The land was conceded by the king's representatives. The pattern was determined by a practical need for access to water and transportation by river, with a variety of terrain afforded by a lot stretching backward inland.

When historical geographer R. C. Harris looked at how people distributed themselves over the land, he found that concentrations of dwellings—the *côtes*—straddled seigneurial boundaries. A parish might encompass more than one seigneury, or there could be several parishes within a large, well-populated estate. If houses clustered around any structure, it was the parish church and not the seigneur's manor house. The church became the nucleus for rural villages, as artisans and retired couples settled close to it. This magnetic role of the parish chapel is apparent in old French-Canadian villages, which have a church, often capped with silver spires, at their core. Physical evidence and other facts led to Harris's conclusion, "that the seigneurial system left an altogether insignificant impression on the geography of early Canada. Settlement expanded along the St. Lawrence and patterns of social and economic activity developed there in ways that rarely reflected a seigneurial framework. . . . The seigneurial system itself was largely irrelevant to the [human] geography of early Canada, and it is reasonable to conclude that it was equally irrelevant to the way of life that emerged there."[99]

Evidence that the parish, rather than the seigneury, was the geographic unit that commanded the allegiance of countryfolk was a 1714 protest by Côte Saint-Léonard's residents against being transferred from Pointe-aux-Trembles parish to the new parish of Rivière des Prairies. When the protesters made no headway with their bishop, they intercepted the man delivering communion bread to the newly designated parish church and, when he refused to take it to their old chapel, they seized the bread and took it to one protester's home. When a court baillif tried to retrieve it, he was driven off by a group armed with sticks and stones.[100]

CONCLUSION

Apart from the family, the parish was the nearest thing to a community for most Canadians. Townsfolk had no right to participate in municipal government; appointed royal officials took the place of elected civic magistrates. The king's officials also licensed and regulated urban bakers and butchers, surgeons, royal notaries, land surveyors, fur traders, and, eventually, Quebec's carters. These men were organized for better supervision by the crown, not by themselves. Other trades were free to operate to their customers' satisfaction. Without guilds or elected craft inspectors, artisans grouped together in a few religious confraternities. Until the 1720s such groups were confined to devotional activities under clerical supervision. The workers' social superiors, the merchants, were allowed to give some institutional form to their occupational solidarity, to elect spokesmen, and to submit collective petitions to the government—activities not permitted to manual workers.

As for occupational unity, that was most evident among military officers, who were allied to senior government officials and to the wholesale merchants, who were admitted into their charmed circle. The colonial elite's cohesion and its experience in lobbying government for favors and in giving voice to its interests served it well after the British conquest of New France. Other colonists lacked a comparable class or occupational unity. For all of colonial society, the one social institution that framed daily life was the family. This body received an allegiance unmatched by loyalty to any public institution or geographic location in *la Nouvelle France*. It was always present in the settlements, even where the influence of the government and church was weak.

CHAPTER 8

The Sovereign Family

IN THE ABSENCE OF GUILDS, MUNICIPAL CORPORATIONS, VILLAGE COMMUNES, AND other private institutions, apart from the church, which was already under the monarch's sway, the family assumed a dominant role in early French Canada. This social institution received the colonists' ultimate loyalty. Fidelity to one's kin was invoked to end family disputes. In February 1719, as parishioners gathered outside Bécancourl's chapel on the Feast of St. Mathias, a squabble occurred between in-laws. Two sisters accused Marie-Thérèse Carpentier, the second wife of their brother, Pierre Bourbeau *dit* Lacourse of Champlain, of trying to engineer a marriage between her twenty-two-year-old brother, Noël Carpentier, and their younger sister, Marie-Anne-Geneviève. They thought that the Carpentiers were beneath them, and one called Marie-Thérèse "a wretched and insolent creature who dared not look the world in the face, reproaching her with having made love to her husband [Pierre] Bourbeau four years before the death of his late wife." Marie-Thérèse had borne her first child by Bourbeau eight months after their marriage, and the two sisters may have suspected her of entrapping their brother into matrimony. The husband of one of them alleged that he knew just what sort of people the Carpentiers were, because, "he had read the letters of judgment (*lettres d'avis*) from Trois-Rivières [court] in which were her family's titles (*les tiltres de sa famille*)." Marie-Thérèse repeatedly asked them "if they were greater lords than she." The brother-in-law replied that "he had only the rank of a decent man (*la qualité d'honeste homme*)"—an allusion to her reputed immorality. Despite the apparent equality of farmers, they did believe that some agricultural families were better than others.

People watching this dispute pointed out the impropriety of arguing at the chapel door and said "that [such behavior] did not befit them, being all related to one another, as brother-in-law and as sisters-in-law." The speakers believed that a family should be united, at least in the presence of outsiders. Marie-Thérèse still complained to the Trois-Rivières court of being publicly defamed, but her complaint was dismissed and the disputants were fined ten livres each for their disrespectful conduct outside a church.[1] The magistrate may have thought it wise, as well, to keep this family conflict out of the court.

Colonists thought of themselves as family members first; individual freedom of choice without regard for family obligations was an alien concept. So, too, was the notion that a person could be offended without having the insult extend to his or her kin. The idea that a personal calumny was a collective insult was expressed by a Quebec merchant, Étienne Landeron, in 1681. Landeron complained to Montreal's court that a butcher, in a mutual exchange of epithets, had called him "a thief, a cheat and a rogue (*Le traittant de Voleur, frippon, Cocquin*)." Such calumny, protested the merchant, was "a manifest injury to the good name and reputation of the petitioner and of his family, who have always been reputed honest folk."[2] Landeron, as a good paterfamilias, spoke for all of his dependents as well as for himself. French civil law, let it be remembered, treated the family and not the single person as the basic unit of society. The law spoke of family obligations rather than of personal freedom. This led, naturally, to the modern French-Canadian tendency to think in terms of collective rights with a corresponding coolness toward the assertion of individual civil rights by members of Quebec's ethnic minorities. This focus on collective interests also reflects French-speakers' concern for their group's identity and status.

In the French Regime, nepotism, far from being a vice, was the moral duty of every good family man. A person who had achieved a position of power and influence was expected to use his connections and influence to obtain help for other family members. To withhold one's assistance from a needy relative would be immoral. That was the implicit assumption of the letters sent to emigrants from France. In May 1755 the widowed sister-in-law of Gaspard-Joseph Chaussegros de Léry, a military engineer in Canada, begged him to write to the colony's governor-general and the minister of the navy to obtain a position as clerk-in-training (*élève écrivain*) for her son, who was, she wrote, "still out on the street." De Léry complied and asked the minister "to grant me the favor of obtaining for my nephew, the son of my dead older brother, a captain in Vendôme, the post of junior clerk for the king at Toulon, where his property is located." At the same time, de Léry sought a lieutenancy at Louisbourg for his youngest son.[3] The administration accepted the propriety of such requests because, after all, the state endorsed family solidarity, and officials, like the intendants, owed their position to family connections.[4] Patronage ran through the government, from top to bottom.

The royal government encouraged family solidarity by compelling members to help one another. The mutual assistance that ensured a person's survival was to come, firstly, from one's kin. Royal officials pressed families to take responsibility for the care of orphans and indigent parents or siblings. After a father's death, the local court authorized an assembly of at least seven relatives or, failing that number, close friends, to select guardians for the children still in their minority. There would be a principal tutor and an assistant guardian—called a subrogate tutor—for the fatherless children. Because the principal guardian acted in the father's stead, the family would choose a close male relative: an adult brother of the children or an uncle. The mother, if she were still alive and had not remarried, could be the deputy or subrogate tutor.

In New France, the few testaments and wills that were made could not designate a guardian, which meant that custom, the courts, and family members decided who would be responsible for the children's welfare. Guardianship was an unpopular duty because a ward, upon reaching the age of majority, could challenge the tutor's management of the inheritance and even seek damages for any financial losses incurred. It was prudent, therefore, to draw the relations into a major decision involving the child's legacy. The guardians, once recognized by a magistrate, would call a gathering of relatives to decide the fate of the minor children and to determine how their inheritance would be managed. In February 1737 farmer Zacharie Bolduc, as guardian of his orphaned niece Louise, summoned the subrogate tutor and five other relatives and friends to Beaupré seigneury, "to discuss among themselves how to support the girl's attendance at school for this year, from the property which might belong" to her late mother. Bolduc obtained their recorded approval for sending Louise to a school of the Sisters of the *Congrégation de Notre-Dame* for one year, with the cost of her board and tuition to be deducted from her inheritance.[5] With the support and involvement of a large family, fatherless children were prepared for earning their living and aided in establishing themselves.

The orphaned children of immigrants and the infants of unwed mothers lacked a kinship network's support, and they obtained shelter on hard terms. A single mother with a small child had no bargaining power. In 1736 an abandoned wife described herself as "incapable of feeding and maintaining" her eight-year-old son, whom she bound to a merchant as "a domestic servant until . . . the full age of twenty years." At Louisbourg a widow likewise indentured her son to someone who would provide his upkeep, "not being in a situation to do it [herself] without help."[6]

The unfortunate children of the poor were hired out as unpaid servants until the age of eighteen or even twenty-one in order to have food, care, clothing, and shelter. One orphan girl was indentured in 1714 "until she might be provided for by marriage or otherwise."[7] A maidservant's mother was paid six livres "for her consent" to the girl's servitude and her acknowledgment "that she will not be able to take back her said daughter" before her daughter's term of service was completed.[8]

Poor and fatherless children provided couples, who could not afford an adult servant, with domestic helpers. It seems that indentured children provided up to two-thirds of the colony's household servants in the 1700s. This reliance on the involuntary labor of paupers and orphans tends to confirm Father Charlevoix's claim that adult Canadians spurned the role of a servant. The intercession of royal officials in the settlement of foundlings during the eighteenth century suggests that foster children were exploited and abused when they lacked a powerful advocate, such as a royal official, to defend them.[9] Adolescents had a chance of being apprenticed to a craftsman to learn a manual trade, but most artisans would not accept any child under the age of twelve, except as an unpaid servant.

Canadian mothers could be as protective of their children as any mother bear defending her cubs when placing an older son in apprenticeship. In 1731 Angélique Lafontaine directed Jean-Baptiste Dubord to apprentice her sixteen-year-old son Pierre to a carpenter. "I give you permission, in my absence," she wrote, "to indenture my little boy. Make a good agreement [*faite bien son marché*] because if he is mistreated, I will have him removed [from the master]." She demanded to know what upkeep her son was to receive, what payment would be made to the boy, and she told Dubord to ensure that the apprentice be given sufficient tools to be able to work at his new trade. The boy's appointed guardian drove a hard bargain and obtained the carpenter's promise that his apprentice would receive a new outfit of clothing and tools—all carefully listed—at the end of his five years of service.[10]

Another, equally demanding mother exasperated a tailor to whom she entrusted her son for training; the signing of the apprenticeship contract was put off until the boy's father returned. The tailor made a verbal promise before witnesses to give the boy a vest, suit, or hooded coat, to train him in eighteen months—half the usual time—and, at the mother's insistence, to excuse the apprentice from sifting flour and carrying water for the household. Two months later, with the father present, the agreement was to be put into writing. At this time, the mother insisted that her son's work be confined to tailoring, excluding all menial tasks, such as fetching firewood. Because the master was to receive no compensation for instructing the boy in his trade, apart from the apprentice's help in his shop and home, the tailor refused to take the apprentice "on such a basis [and said] he absolutely refused to be her servant (*valet*)." The Montreal court rejected the parents' demand that the crafts-man be ordered to instruct their son.[11]

Marguerite Prieur, at Quebec, investigated the reputation of the Montreal joiner to whom her eighteen-year-old son, Prisque-Barthélemi Verreau, wished to be apprenticed before sending her written consent in July 1727. She told her son that he should show himself worthy of such a noble master's gentleness by doing his duty, "as an honorable man and by pleasing those with whom you live. I advise you, especially, my poor son, not to forget God and the Holy Virgin to whom I recommend you every day, and your good patron St. Prisque. Always have a fear of God and never let yourself fall into licentiousness. . . . You would not wish to detract from or tarnish the reputation of our entire family. I hope that you will console your poor, dead father by making yourself loved and esteemed by everyone in Montreal, as he did when he was there." Duty to one's family, apparently, extended to its deceased members. She promised to send her son a pair of moccasins and assured him of her maternal affection; his stepfather, with masculine reserve, could express only his fear that the boy could slide into debauchery or fail to complete his term of service.[12] An open statement of love for one's stepchild or child was considered unmanly, and men left statements of affection to their wives.

Just as government ministers and administrators tended to enunciate categorical rules and then make exceptions or grant exemptions from them, so the patriarchal family, sanctified by law, was compromised in practice. In New France, the wives of craftsmen and farmers were economic partners and the spouses of merchants, artisans, and shopkeepers often represented their husbands in law courts or concluded notarized contracts on their behalf. The frequent absences of men for trade or warfare created an opportunity for women to manage the couple's joint property, even without a formal power of attorney or legal recognition as a *marchande publique,* entitled to administer property in her own name. Caring for large families was probably more effective than the law in curtailing the ambitions of married women to engage in commerce.

Canadiennes born in the colony had, on average, eleven live births in a lifetime. Women coming from Europe were less fertile, probably because of an inferior diet in their homeland. A high death rate among infants would leave the typical Canadian family with seven children.[13] At Port Royal (Annapolis Royal) in Acadia during the eighteenth century the fertility of women was the same, but more children survived because the settlement's isolation shielded it from many imported epidemics. Three-quarters of the children born there reached adulthood.[14] It was proverbial that children were the riches of the poor, and the young performed valuable work in craft shops and on farms. In the countryside youngsters began to help their parents by scaring birds away from the ripening crops, caring for smaller siblings, and tending livestock. As children grew, they assumed greater responsibilities in the household. The outnumbered parents, who depended upon this assistance, could not impose a rigid obedience to their will. Circumstances forced them to take their children's interests into account. Men still expected to play the stern paterfamilias, and that is evident from a father's letter to his son, who had sought his approval for an apprenticeship contract. Note the difference in sentiments from those expressed by the mothers quoted above.

Twenty-two-year-old René-Michel Levasseur had left his parents' home at Quebec after a disagreement and, in June 1745, he asked François Filliau Dubois, a Montreal carpenter-joiner, to train him. The young man had worked in the fields of an uncle's farm for three or four months, and this experience convinced him that a craftsman's life was preferable. His future master wrote to René-Michel's father, saying that he had taken his son in out of charity, "having seen him, a stranger to all in this town and without any shelter," dressed in ragged, dirty clothes, and knowing, "that he belongs to a good family." Because the young man evinced "a strong desire to stay with me to learn to work at joinery," Dubois was prepared accept him as an apprentice for a two-year term, if his father paid his son's clothing expenses, or for three years if the father declined to pay. He enclosed a crudely written note from René-Michel entreating his father to consent. His father found it hard to pardon his son's conduct because, after all, he was Noël Levasseur, sculptor and joiner, and he could have taught his son these woodworking skills. Nonetheless, he consented to a three-year apprenticeship.

Noël Levasseur wrote to the Montreal artisan about his son: "treat him and maintain him as a good father would do. . . . I trust that you will allow him a few moments for reading, writing and drawing, and that you will supervise his conduct as though he were your own son, so that he goes to church and receives the sacraments, and does not associate with drunkards and libertines. . . . Speak to him as a father, and make him aware of the right I had to punish him for the annoyances (*les déplaisirs*) he has caused me up to now, and do not let him forget it. . . . I would ask you to hide the affection (*les bontés*) that I still have for him and only let him know of my anger for his misconduct toward me."[15]

Curious documents called *sommations respectueuses* (respectful requests) prove that parents retained authority over their adult children. The law demanded that a father's consent be given for the marriage of a daughter under the age of twenty-five or for a son before his thirtieth birthday.[16] This requirement was upheld by Quebec's Superior Council in June 1741, when it declared that the wedding of a minor undertaken without parental approval was void. Minors intending to get married had to have the banns, announcing their intention, published in a church on three Sundays or holy days and their parents' or guardians' approval was to be recorded in the register of marriages.[17] The continuing subordination of an unmarried child, even as an adult, is evident in these respectful requisitions. Because matrimony entitled one to the aid and support of in-laws, parents expected to pass judgment on their child's choice of a marriage partner.[18] Marriage without parental consent was a justification for disinheriting the offending child. After the specified ages, the father's consent was not mandatory, but it was desirable. Grown-up children still hesitated to wed without that approval, possibly because they could still forfeit a dowry or a contribution to the newlywed couple's household, but also out of respect for their parents. Adults whose elders had refused to consent to their union registered three formal appeals begging their father or widowed mother to consent. Couples desiring to marry also sought the confirmation of other relatives, before a magistrate, that the desired partner was "a suitable and advantageous" match and that there was no formal impediment to the marriage.

Some of the respectful summonses came from underage children who, say, because of a premarital pregnancy, felt that marriage was imperative. What is surprising is that appeals also emanated from adults who should have been free to marry as they pleased. Take the case of Marie-Catherine Frontigny of Quebec, who told the judge of the Provost's Court in 1745 that "since her childhood, having no family goods (*aucun bien de patrimoine*) by which to survive, she had been obliged to learn the dressmaker's trade," yet she still had "great difficulty feeding and maintaining herself, having received no aid from her parents," not even from her stepfather, a notary. A farmer from Côte de Beaumont had offered to marry her. Her mother and stepfather opposed the match and threatened to disinherit her; the girl's late father had been a merchant and her stepfather's work as a notary placed her on a higher social plane, or so her parents thought. Marie-Catherine, "reduced to this sad situation," wanted to marry her suitor, whom she described as "an honest man and one who, by his work and savings, would enable her to live honorably." She claimed to be twenty-seven, but her real age was twenty-four—a point missed by her parents. Her stepfather responded to the first respectful summons by accusing Catherine of being "disobedient to their advice, who, far from following the precepts and education" provided by her parents, wanted to marry "out of caprice and an unparalleled stubbornness." He said that he and her mother would take Catherine back into their home and thereby "put her in a state to find a more suitable husband." If she persisted in her choice, they would look upon her as "a rebel" and, "following the example of refractory children (*enfants indociles*) who lack the respect owed to their mother and father," she would suffer "the penalties," and lose "the Lord's blessing that is only given to those who follow God's commandment about the respect due to parents." The parents avoided receiving the two subsequent petitions for consent personally by leaving their home. The judge then permitted the marriage to go ahead on 14 September 1745.[19]

Visitors from France felt that Canadian parents were too indulgent to their children and recommended the imposition of tighter discipline. Education, at this time, meant learning self-discipline as well as acquiring knowledge, and the colonists were reckoned to be poorly instructed in both areas. Colonial families, as we have seen from these and other letters, were not as relaxed as the visitors believed, and the relationship between generations could be stiff and formal. Father Charlevoix, a Jesuit scholar who liked the *Canadiens,* said that it was hard to excuse, "the little natural affection most of them show to their parents."[20] Baron de Lahonan, too, noted the colonists' evident lack of respect for their elders. One of the arguments advanced by Intendant Michel Bégon in 1720 for increasing the number of black slaves in Canada was that reliable servants were hard to find and that slaves would also free parents from dependence on their ungrateful offspring:

> Fathers and mothers who might have cleared extensive land and established their home, when rendered unfit for work through great age or infirmity, would be able to remain masters of their goods and be able to continue to exploit their property by means of their Negroes. They would no longer be reduced to depending upon their children nor be exposed to ill-treatment. Instead, their children always would have the respect and submission they owe to their parents, in the hope of having them take care to establish them [on their own farm]. Whereas, at present, because there is no one [else] to cultivate the land, elderly fathers and mothers are obliged to place themselves at the mercy of one of their sons and, to bind him to aid them in their old age, they make a gift to him of all their goods on condition that he feed, lodge and maintain them.

Such deeds of gift between parents and son, wrote Bégon, produced legal conflicts because the contracts' terms were not always carried out faithfully, because the parents later thought that they would be better off with another child as caregiver, or because other heirs, wanting their *légitime,* contested the favored child's right to the family farm after the parents had died. The most common complaint was about "the ingratitude of their children," who, once in possession of their parents' estate, came to regard their obligations as a burdensome act of charity. Slaves, the intendant thought, would prevent these family disputes.[21] In April 1721 Bégon revoked a maintenance accord because the ungrateful son had caused his parents so much distress.[22] A widow, who felt that her needs had been neglected by her daughters and their husbands, wanted to rescind a maintenance agreement with her sons-in-law in 1727.[23] There was some truth to the intendant's claim, although it emphasized the failures in such old-age maintenance agreements.

The system of *donations entrevifs* (deeds of gift between living persons) described by Intendant Bégon had come into existence in the early eighteenth century, after decades of experimentation with various arrangements for ensuring parents a secure and comfortable old age. Survival in that interval between a waning of one's ability to do hard work and death was a problem in an era without pensions or direct government assistance to the aged. Church-run hospices, such as Quebec's *Hôpital Général* (f. 1693), did offer a refuge for the destitute, the insane, and the aged. In the seventeenth century, when many men were without a wife or children, some bachelors entered into fraternal partnerships for mutual support. In 1674 Sergeant Jacques Berthet and Guillaume Richard agreed, "considering their long friendship . . . [and] since they are not bound by marriage, and have no children," to enter into a lifetime partnership that pooled all of their assets and labor. They would "regard themselves as full brothers (*freres germains*) and be bound to aid one another in all their needs and necessities while sick." The survivor would inherit their joint estate, to the exclusion of any other possible heirs. Unlike a matrimonial community of goods, there was a strict equality of the partners, and no payments could be made or debts incurred without their joint consent.[24]

The *donné* system, by which single men gave themselves as perpetual and unpaid servants to a religious order or institution, was a model for old bachelors and even for childless couples seeking a substitute for a family's care in their declining years.[25] Men retired to the hospice of the Charon Brethren (f. 1692) at Montreal and to the *Hôtel-Dieu* or hospital there, not simply out of devotion, but rather as servants for life in return for food and shelter. For example, Michel Hardy dit Jolicoeur, flaxspinner, had worked for the Montreal hospital for several years, and had "planned to retire to some [religious] community to spend the rest of his days there." In April 1709 the nuns of the hospital agreed to accept him as a permanent but unpaid employee, to feed and maintain him, and to have prayers said for him after his death, "as they are accustomed to do for the deceased nuns." Hardy could be expelled at any time, "for scandalous faults." A later amendment to the accord defined the faults in question as "drunkenness, theft, lewdness (*Jmpudicitté*), swearing, and blasphemy." It also guaranteed that Hardy would have his own room, which, he insisted, would be "separate from that of the servants." The nuns, for their part, specified that he could not admit any secular guest into his chamber and that he must never depart from the institution on workdays.[26] The notarial archives also contain lifetime maintenance agreements between bachelors and married couples, who accepted money or services in return for assuring him of a home and care.[27] Married couples without children sometimes made a reciprocal deed of gift (*don mutuel*) which deferred the division of assets upon the death of one partner, and gave the survivor the use of the dead spouse's *entire* share of the estate—not just a half of it—for the remaining partner's lifetime.[28] This arrangement secured the widow or widower against inheritance claims from any blood kin of the dead partner. These were the alternatives to a family's care that were forced upon childless colonists.

The sexes became evenly balanced in New France's population by 1698, and thereafter, most men were able to marry and look to their own children for support. Children were supposed to be insurance against destitution in the last years of one's existence. The parents decided when they wanted to retire and tried to set the terms for their care in old age. At first, there was no single pattern for ensuring this support. In 1711 a couple in their sixties appealed to Montreal's royal court to have their progeny summoned to make arrangements to preserve the family farm, which the parents could no longer work, and to provide them with 600 livres a year as a living allowance known as a *pension viagère*.[29] The law made it clear that all legitimate, inheriting children were to contribute to the support of their parents and parents-in-law. Article 334 of the *Coutume de Paris* decreed that heirs shared the burdens of a legacy in proportion to their entitlement, and one of those burdens was maintenance of a needy parent.[30] Pursuing each heir for a yearly contribution to the parents' living allowance was a nuisance. A more practical way of ensuring support, shelter, and care had to be found, especially in the countryside, which lacked public charitable institutions, like those in the towns. In the towns' hospices, nuns and religious brothers cared for paupers. Rural people were more willing than townsfolk to look after disabled family members, even when the relatives were insane; most of the inmates in the hospices came from the urban population.[31]

By 1720, the date of Intendant Bégon's dispatch about slaves, a pattern had developed in Canada for ensuring family care in retirement. Rural couples who no longer felt able to cope with the physical demands of a farm, or who had passed the age of sixty, or a parent who had lost a partner through death would give most of the farm to one son by deed of gift inter vivos, in return for that child's promise of lifelong support. In the towns, an aged craftsman might bestow his workshop and tools upon a son on the same terms.[32] A male relative sufficed as recipient, in the absence of a son, but daughters and sons-in-law were seldom so favored. The other children received gifts in kind, such as an advance on a daughter's inheritance at the time of her wedding. These were the country dowries of livestock, household goods, and, sometimes, a piece of land. Thus, the siblings who did not share the farmland received their *légitime* (half of an equal share) or a substantial benefit in cash or goods, and they could share in a further distribution of assets upon their parents' death. In their working lives, some farmers acquired vacant lands in the vicinity and helped other sons to establish their own farms as a way of keeping them in the neighborhood.[33] In these ways, the legal equality of all legitimate children as heirs was upheld and the parental farm was transmitted intact to one child.[34] Subdivision of the land would have reduced the concession farm's ability to support a family. These conditional transfers of property were known as *donations, démissions, cessions,* or *actes d'abandon.* Whatever the name, this arrangement fixed responsibility for support on one person. This was not the only possible disposition, but it became the dominant pattern among farmers for providing for one's old age. This solution emerged from a variety of experiments.

A precursor of the one-child-as-caregiver accord was the "life partnership" made with a son by Jacques Raté (sixty-four) and his wife Anne (forty-nine) of St. Pierre, Ile d'Orléans, in July 1694. "Considering their infirmity . . . for some time and the great age they have reached, not being capable of exploiting the few goods that God has been pleased to give them," they invited their twenty-six-year-old son, Jean-Baptiste, to live with them, work their land, and care for them in sickness and in health. When their son married, he would receive a cow and his family would be supported by the family farm. Jean-Baptiste was to be paid fifty livres a year, and when his parents died, he would receive a two-arpents-wide portion of the farm; the balance was to be divided among the other heirs.[35] Sometimes, parents rewarded one child's exceptional solicitude for them *after* that loving care had been demonstrated. In December 1715 Pierre Loiseau, a farmer near Lac St. Pierre on the St. Lawrence River, dictated the following deed of gift, with his parish priest as the recorder:

> I, the undersigned, Pierre Loeseau [*sic*] called Francoeur, habitant of Ile Dupas seigneury, in order to acknowledge the good services of my son Pierre Loeseau, also a resident of the said Ile Dupas, do give to him, in addition to the rights he might have as one of my children, 600 livres after my death . . . in recognition of the services he had rendered to me, both he and his wife, every day in my old age.[36]

The responsibility could devolve on one son after another arrangement failed. One sixty-four-year-old Montreal widow divided up her real estate and, in December 1743, had her five children or their representatives draw lots for each portion. They would then be collectively responsible for looking after her. It was impractical: two sons could not render aid because one was at Fort St. Frédéric on Lake Champlain and the other was in the Illinois Country. Therefore, the division of lands was voided in 1744 and responsibility for her care fell to the one son still in Montreal.[37] This was preferable to the fate of a widow whose lifetime maintenance agreement, made in 1686 with a farmer on Ile d'Orléans, fell apart after her husband's death. She and the caregiver were, "unable to agree together," and she became a charge of the Quebec City Poor Board in 1690.[38]

As can be seen, the choice of a son to be one's protector was not determined by primogeniture; convenience and compatibility were more important than being the first-born. When parents chose to retire from an active life, the best prospect as principal caregiver was a newly married son who had not yet established himself on his own land, and who would be glad to accept a cleared, stocked, and working farm in exchange for a promise to look after his father and mother. The parents could reserve a furnished room in the farmhouse and a portion of the kitchen garden for their own use while deeding over the rest of the farm and its buildings to the son who would look after them.[39] Although a third of the aged couples preferred to maintain a separate dwelling in retirement, a growing number did what was routine for a single widow or widower, and that was to become a part of the caregiver's household. By living in the same house and eating together, the dependent parents would share the same fare and comforts as enjoyed by their son's family.

The simple assurance of care, food, and shelter was not enough for later donors. Here we may detect a grudging attitude in the children who had taken on the parents with their property. By the 1730s the elders specified what they understood to be adequate maintenance, rather than leave the definition of their needs up to their progeny. The necessities of life, according to these agreements, were wheat, pork, beef, salt, firewood, candles, laundry services, and medical care when ill. Deeds then specified the exact amount of each commodity and of any cash allowance to be given to the parents every year. Nearly half of the deeds of gift, made upon retirement, included provision for a monetary allowance. In 1738 a Longue Pointe farmer and his wife insisted on a yearly allowance of "28 bushels (*minots*) of wheat, and 16 cords of firewood, . . . a milk cow that will not die, . . . a pig at least eighteen months old, . . . 8 *minots* of peas . . . in September." The parents retained six chickens and expected a yearly allowance, each October, of ninety livres in cash and forty livres in whatever goods they might require. When a parent died, there was to be a burial, "according to his/her estate and condition," a funeral mass, and ten requiem masses, "for the repose of his/her soul," in the following year.[40] In 1755 the Trois-Rivières court ordered each of Widow Gélinas's children, in-laws included, to give her two-and-a-half bushels of grain, twenty pounds of pork, three bottles of liquor, and four livres in money every year.[41] For her, brandy was a necessity of life; for others, it could be tobacco, which men, children, and women smoked in Canada.

When children failed to make provision for the support of a destitute parent, the intendant and the colony's magistrates forced the sons and daughters to do so.[42] By 1758 the quid pro quo of property for care was so well established that when a widow demanded a yearly pension of 150 livres from her children, Quebec's *Prévôté* court ordered her to give them all her real estate and furnishings, except for a bed and her clothes.[43] These orders, the hundreds of deeds of gift, and the increasing precision in the definition of a living allowance reinforce the impression that care in one's old age was not willingly provided by every child. That responsibility had to be incorporated into a legally enforceable contract, made before a notary, and a tenth of the donors later voided the agreement because a son was unable or unwilling to carry out the terms in full.[44] In a world of closely knit, extended families these legal precautions would not have been necessary. On the other hand, the low percentage of failed agreements and their widespread use indicates that family members, apart from the designated and favored caregiver, accepted these retirement accords and that family unity was not disrupted by them. Those children who did not honor and maintain their elders faced government sanctions and social disapproval.

Public censure was conveyed in a variety of ways. The colonists of *la Nouvelle France* did not undertake collective action to introduce innovations, yet they did act together to defend the status quo and orthodox morality. Colonists used gossip and tattling to chasten those whose conduct departed from approved patterns. The charivari, or mock serenade, for those who ignored the rules of propriety was transplanted from France and it survived in the colony. The serenaders punished deviants and, by their action, discouraged others from offending public sensibilities. The offenses were not against the church's canons or the state's laws, and this is why private sanctions were called into action. In the charivari youngsters and servants gave a cacophonic serenade with pots, kitchen utensils, and horns outside the homes of people whose conduct had outraged the serenaders' sense of propriety. The young might commit some other punitive mischief to register their disapproval, especially if they were not paid a bribe to desist. Their victims included old men whose brides were very young or widows who had remarried with unseemly haste.

The usual misdeed was premature remarriage after a spouse's death. Custom held that a widow should be in mourning for a year, out of respect for her late husband's memory. After a year of widowhood, she might remarry with decency.[45] In seventeenth-century New France, because of the shortage of eligible women and a bereaved woman's desire for support for herself and, possibly, for her children, the average first widowhood lasted twenty-seven months.[46] At Quebec, in June 1683, a twenty-five-year-old widow remarried three weeks after burying her first husband, and the newlyweds were treated to a week of noisy harassment by townspeople. Some of the mockery included a parody of Christian burial. Bishop de Montmorency Laval intervened in July and issued a pastoral letter stating that "for six days a great number of people of both sexes . . . [had] gathered together every night under the name of charivari," and had "committed very impious acts that are a complete derision of our [holy] mysteries and of the Christian religion's truths as well as of the church's most sacred ceremonies." The bishop told "the faithful" that such nightly gatherings were contrary "to religion, good morals, the public good, and the peace of every family." The disorder was continuing and the bishop intended to put a stop to it. He forbade the people of his diocese to participate in charivaris and instructed "fathers and mothers not to send or permit their children to go to them," and told employers to prevent their servants from attending charivaris, "under the threat of excommunication."[47]

Charivaris did not disappear, despite the bishop's condemnation. That may be a measure of their importance in upholding popular morality. In March 1728 Joseph Caron, a forty-two-year-old court usher of Quebec's Superior Council, married a twenty-five-year-old within four months of his first bride's death. He had committed a double infraction: a quick second marriage with someone who was much younger than he. The town's young people treated the couple to a nocturnal charivari and then the youngsters ran through the streets shouting, "Vive le Roi!" (long live the king!)[48] That cry showed the fundamental conservatism of the rioters: they were upholding morality and the social order, as they understood it.

Assertions of popular morality extended beyond matrimony to economic matters. The shortage of an essential commodity or a sharp price rise provoked collective demands for a return to earlier, less onerous circumstances. The colonists had a sense of "the just price," and sought to force merchants to adhere to the protesters' estimation of what was a proper and justifiable charge for a given commodity. Crop failures and enemy naval blockades created shortages that aroused public outrage. There was no understanding of the relationship of price with supply; price increases were attributed to human greed, not to a deficient supply. Consumers blamed a few, presumably greedy, traders who were alleged to have hoarded the essential goods in order to extort an inflated price.[49] That suspicion was sometimes well founded.

In 1704 a lack of salt led Montreal's merchants to buy up the available supplies in their district. Countryfolk marched on the town to demand that the price of salt be reduced to four livres a bushel and that the profiteers be punished. The protesters dispersed after being told that their gathering was illegal. War continued to disrupt the flow of goods from France, and in 1714, armed farmers advanced on Quebec and threatened to enter the town to compel the authorities to listen to their remonstrances about "the dearness of goods and . . . their misery." The power to put the world right was attributed to the civil authorities, and they were being asked to exercise that power and to force merchants to lower their prices. The demonstrators scattered when threatened by a military force and the protesters' three leaders were arrested.[50] At Louisbourg in 1720 the high price of wine and brandy sparked a demonstration before the governor's residence.[51]

Popular protests in *la Nouvelle France* were reactive and profoundly conservative. They originated from popular morality and not from any new political theory. In demanding that the authorities act to meet public needs, the demonstrators were acknowledging the royal government's supremacy and their own inability to solve social problems. The colonists' disunity and social conservatism made any collective intrusion into the colony's governance impossible. The only social groups that routinely influenced the administration were entrenched officials, the colonial gentry, and the great merchants, who had the occupational and status-group loyalty that enabled them to work collectively. These groups were also permitted to consult together and to frame communal petitions. In any struggle between rival families, these well-born and influential people were bound to prevail over their social inferiors.

If one needed more convincing evidence of the settlers' conservatism, it is in the food they ate in North America. They preferred familiar items to products of the New World. A. H. Clark found that Acadian farmers followed the pattern of mixed agriculture prevalent in the inland areas of western France, even though the damp, foggy, and cold climate of the Bay of Fundy was not suited to the cultivation of wheat and peas. The Acadians' diet was based on French staples: wheat, peas, cabbages, turnips, and apples. Maize, a native plant, was a secondary crop. Cattle, pigs, poultry, and fish provided meat.[52] In the St. Lawrence Valley in 1749, Peter Kalm found the same European crops and vegetables being cultivated, although apples were rarer and the presence of pumpkins, watermelons, and Indian corn showed a greater receptivity to New World products. "In this country they ate only wheat bread"; barley and oats were grown exclusively as fodder for cattle and horses.[53] That, too, seems to have been the destiny of potatoes, that most famous tuber of the Americas. When Kalm asked the Canadians why they did not plant potatoes for their own consumption, "they answer that they do not like them and laugh at the English who are so fond of them."[54] To emphasize the severity of the 1737 famine, Mother de Sainte-Hélène of Quebec's hospital wrote that "wheat was lacking, and the poor inhabitants (*habitants*) were reduced to eating tree buds, potatoes, and other things unsuited for the nourishment of mankind."[55] The age of *patates frites* and *patates pilées* lay beyond the horizon.

From the governmental and legal perspective, the ideal family was the patriarchal family and religion made marriage sacrosanct. In practice, the patriarchal ideal was often compromised without being displaced. Women bore the burden of preserving the union of husband and wife, and it could be a heavy yoke to bear. The clergy was loath to admit that a marriage had failed. Remember the priest who tried to mediate in the turbulent household of Timothy Sullivan. The sacrament of marriage was for life, yet the terms of that relationship could be changed when a woman's material welfare or her life was endangered. It was then that wives petitioned for a legal separation from their husbands. Divorce did not exist in the

Roman Catholic colony and ecclesiastical annulment of a marriage was beyond the reach of most colonists. The separation petitions usually came from women who had suffered for a long time: in Canada 83 percent of the petitioners had been married for six or more years.

There were two types of legal separation for an incompatible couple: division of property without a physical separation, or separation of bed and board as well as of all assets. The complete severing of the couple and of their community of goods was a drastic solution that was rarely undertaken. Four-fifths of the 149 petitions for separation recorded in the St. Lawrence Valley settlements were for a simple disso-lution of the matrimonial community of goods. This action restored personal prop-erty to the wife, along with her marital rights, such as *préciput*, and, possibly, a living allowance.[56] It did not mean that the couple would live apart. Parents from prominent families, when negotiating a marriage contract, often took the precau-tion of designating their daughter's dowry and personal effects as "biens propres," to be kept outside the jointly owned goods governed by the man. As a consequence, the petitioners for separation, as to property, tended to come from the lower ranks of society. They were the ones whose assets were held within a marital community of goods.

Petitioners seeking just a division of property usually claimed that the husband's profligacy and his mismanagement endangered his dependents' material welfare, depriving the wife of her patrimony and reducing the family to beggary. Desertion or a prolonged absence of the husband was occasionally cited in petitions. Misman-agement was frequently linked to bouts of drunkenness (*débauches*), on which the man squandered his earnings. Liquor was also the catalyst for domestic violence.

A separated wife's property could not be touched by her husband, and she could manage it in her own name, but she had to have enough resources to allow her to survive. When a Montreal carpenter's wife was granted a dissolution of their com-munity of goods in 1697 because of her husband's "bad treatment and continual debauchery . . . which consume the fruits of his labor and lead to the sale of their goods and livestock to pay for it," she was allowed to take her chest, a feather bed, clothes, a cow with fodder, two flatirons, a syringe, and all the tools she needed to earn a living by making mattresses.[57] A shoemaker's wife at Quebec, "burdened with three children whom she cannot feed because of the debauchery (*débauches*) of her husband," presented a copy of her marriage contract to justify a claim to her trousseau of a furnished bed, bedding, three hundred livres' worth of dinnerware and kitchen utensils, napkins and clothes, as well as a town lot she had received from her grandparents. Land from her blood lineage could not be taken from her. The court readily concurred with her request since her husband confessed to his "wicked conduct and vices (*sa meschante conduite et des débauches*)."[58] Despite his acknowledged faults, the couple expected to continue living together. One suspects that separations of property, especially among merchants, also were used as a way of limiting creditors' claims to the husband's portion, leaving the wife's assets inviolate.

Wives' petitions for separation of bed and board (*la séparation de corps et habitation*) were strongly resisted by the magistracy. Jurist Claude-Joseph de Ferrière advised judges that "instead of making these divorces [*sic*] easy, it is necessary to bring all the obstacles one can to oppose them." He claimed that willful wives saw physical separation as a way to escape from a man's natural authority over them.[59] If paternal and husbandly power were going to be sacrificed for a family's welfare, then the man's failings had to be monumental. Profligacy was usually mentioned, but it had to be augmented by some grievous sins, such as an attempt on the woman's life, repeated physical abuse, venereal infection, insanity, or a murderous hatred (*une haine capitale*) for her. Since wife beating was tolerated in this society, occasional physical abuse was not sufficient proof of a murderous hatred. Only a man could cite a spouse's adultery as a justification for a legal separation; it could not be invoked by a wife.[60] Since most petitions for separation came from women, they appealed to other considerations.

A woman seeking separation from bed and board in New France relied on accounts of repeated brutality, often with defamatory insults, witnessed by others, to make her case. She had to appeal to the judges' male prejudices and portray herself as a chaste and faithful companion—the model wife—who was the victim of undeserved abuse over several years. A young wife told Intendant Jacques Raudot that she had endured three years of harsh mistreatment, "sometimes at the risk of her life, and yet she never made a complaint" until it was apparent that her husband had an unshakable "aversion for her."[61] The welfare of one's children and the public scandal created by domestic violence could also be advanced in the arguments for separation. The 1731 petition of Jeanne Cromé or Crosnier to Louisbourg's Superior Council presented a compendium of reasons to justify a complete separation from her husband:

> In 1719 she wedded Jean[-Baptiste] Laumonier, master stone-cutter residing in this town and, that in the first eight or ten days of their marriage, her husband gave himself up to drunkenness and began to mistreat her without the slightest excuse. Since then he had continued his drunken bouts and has taken his abuse of her to such an extreme in beating the petitioner that she would be left [unconscious] on the spot. . . . The petitioner, who always had a true and exclusive attachment to her husband, has tried to endure patiently his ill humors and fury, by submitting to the blows he gave her, without wishing to complain to the courts, believing that he

would correct himself and that, in the end, they would live together in harmony. But far from that, he plunged more and more into debauchery by being drunk almost daily and, while in that condition, he created fantasies and vain delusions of jealous passion. . . . Everyone knows their cruel household, including the powerful people of this colony who have had the goodness to use their authority to put an end to the disorders of Laumonier and have compelled him to take back his wife, who had been forced to flee the house because of his bad treatment [of her]. However, since it is necessary for the petitioner to obtain a separation of dwellings, she will cite some of the effects of his maltreatment. She states that, in addition to the insults that her husband vomits against her, he deliberately shames her by leading her in front of his companions or other strange men in order to say every imaginable foolishness to his wife in their presence, . . . Then he threw himself on her, punching her in the face with his fist and kicking her in the stomach, without heed for the child with whom she was pregnant. From this treatment she suffered miscarriages. . . . Laumonier, being in his usual state of drunkenness, returns home at a late hour and has often brought his companions to the house, where his wife was sleeping, and he made her get up—naked but for the nightshirt (without considering the condition in which a woman might be), and . . . made her serve drinks to each friend in this state. He has even had the base effrontery to lift up her gown in front of these men, saying to them 'if you want to amuse yourself, here's my wife; isn't she a pretty whore?' He did more. Wishing to carry out his cruel intentions, he placed a hook under a beam in the house and prepared a rope, saying to his wife that he wanted to hang her. This he would have done if she had not escaped from him. The parish priest has done everything possible, several times, to encourage Laumonier to end his criminal transactions [*sic*] and to live in peace with his wife. He was unsuccessful in this because he [Laumonier] even abused her in the priest's presence. . . . She had been advised, for the peace of her conscience as well as for the security of her life, to present an appeal to the council for separation of body and goods from the said Laumonier. This being the sole means left to her to live contentedly and to avert the bad examples that her children receive from their father's disorders.

Jeanne Crosnier had appealed on behalf of her children as well as for herself. She had taken refuge in a nunnery, so there was no question of another man in her life. Jeanne had borne five children since their marriage, and three had died in the preceding four years, which made her tale of domestic violence believable. In Louisbourg the Laumonier family occupied a small house, on Rue de l'Étang, built of upright posts sheathed in boards. In it they ran a tavern, which explains why her husband expected her to serve drinks to his companions. Jeanne asked that she be given all the material benefits promised in her marriage contract, upon the dissolution of the couple's community of goods, so that she could live with her children apart from her husband.[62]

Judges sometimes responded to a woman's complaints with a lecture on wifely duties, concluding with an injunction to return to the marital home—a milder version of the admonition usually given to runaway servants and apprentices. A woman whose petition for separation was dismissed was told by the magistrate "to maintain the respect she owes to her husband," who, for his part, was ordered to stop maligning his wife.[63] This may have been what Jeanne received because, according the parish records, she bore two more children fathered by her brutish husband.[64] Her husband may have frustrated her appeal—there is no record of the hearing—and a poor woman could not afford the legal costs of a contested petition for physical separation.

Jeanne Crosnier's deliverance came, not from the courts, but from Laumonier's departure for the French West Indies sometime after 1734. He died there in 1741. Even before his death, Jeanne was calling herself "Widow Laumonier" and supporting herself and her children by running the small tavern and by taking in boarders. As soon as her first husband's death was confirmed, she married a carpenter called Jean Prévost. This match probably owed as much to her desire for material security as to mutual affection. Jeanne sold the Laumonier house within a year and she disappeared from Louisbourg, possibly with the evacuated French population after the fortified port was captured by New Englanders in 1745.[65]

In all her sufferings, Jeanne Crosnier must have appealed to God, the Virgin Mary, and her patron saint for deliverance from her ordeal. Colonists in distress resorted to the supernatural world for aid when their situation seemed beyond earthly help. The world of the divine gave many hope and the realm of magic promised power to humble folk without worldly influence.

———◆———

A protective formula addressed to the Virgin Mary to ensure the bearer's safety, 1740. From the Public Record Office (London), Series HCA 30.

CHAPTER 9

Magic and Religion in
the Colonists' World

IN MARCH 1757 FRANÇOISE BARRETE OF CIBOURE IN FRANCE WROTE TO HER husband, who was working as a shoemaker at Louisbourg. She folded the sheets of paper, sealed them shut—envelopes did not exist—and then wrote the address and inscribed the cover "Que Dieu Conduisse Le Porteur a Bon Port amen [may God guide the bearer to a safe haven, Amen]."[1] Other letter writers abbreviated the penned invocation to "Que Dieu conduisse" or "Q.D.C." Entrusting letters to a private carrier who braved storms, privateers and the possibility of a shipwreck was a hazardous way of communicating with others across the Atlantic Ocean. It was prudent to write this pious hope on the cover sheet to enlist Heaven's aid for the letter's safe arrival. The sender's prayer was not always gratified because many letters ended up in British hands with the captured ship's papers. On the other hand, that misfortune saved the correspondence for future generations, answering later historians' prayers for personal documents from the period.

The peoples of France and its colonies lived in a world ruled by supernatural forces which they tried to influence in various ways, both orthodox and irregular. God, the Virgin Mary, and St. Anne were implored to protect travelers. Voyagers might also carry a talisman to overcome the sea's dangers. These were not just holy medals and crucifixes. In the 1740s a priest was sent a slip of paper bearing a special prayer and his sister's instruction that he should carry it upon his person as shield against maritime dangers. The prayer read:

Que L'immaculée Conception de la tres Sacrée vierge marie mere de Dieu te Serve de passe port et te preserve de tout peril, tant sur mer que sur terre. Tota es pul[v]era [Maria] amica mea et macula originalis numquam fuit in te.	May the Immaculate Conception of the most holy Virgin Mary, the mother of God, serve as your passport and preserve you from all peril, whether on sea or on land. All is dust, Mary my friend, and the mark of original sin never was in you.[2]

Latin, the language of the Mass, enhanced the formula's magical power, as did a cross drawn at the top of the slip. A pilot copied a similar prayer into his memoranda book.[3]

These precautions were agreeable to church doctrines; other magic rituals were plainly superstitious and their purpose ignoble. For example, in 1699 at Trois-Rivières, two soldiers copied magic formulae on paper strips, as dictated by a third man in their marine company. One paper was described as "a note for magic" and the other written text was "to maintain an erection (*pour se rendre dur*)" for a certain time. The note-bearers caught the magistrate's attention by indulging in that soldierly vice of blaspheming "the holy name of God and [of uttering] other execrable curses." The two soldiers were sent to Quebec to face the Sovereign Council, which fined both of them for creating a public scandal. The originator of the magical texts seems to have had no faith in his own compositions because he tried to hang himself when he was told that he was to be separated from a girl for whom he had "an excessive passion of love." For the attempted suicide, rather than for his authorship of spells, he was publicly flogged and sent into exile.[4]

Latin prayers were believed to have an inherent magical power to protect and to assist the orator, even in profane matters. Peter Kalm, a Swedish-speaking Protestant, noted in 1749 how diligent the Canadians were in reciting their Latin prayers, without full comprehension of what they were saying. Journeys began with a morning recital of the Greek *Kyrie eleison* (Lord have mercy), followed by Latin prayers to the Virgin Mary. "It was both strange and amusing," Kalm wrote, "to see and hear how eagerly the women and soldiers said their prayers in Latin and did not themselves understand a word of what they said. . . . The people are very faithful in these observances, because everyone tries by these means to put God under some obligation and intends by it to make himself more deserving of some reward."[5] When Peter Kalm attended Mass in a church he observed that "most of the service was in Latin. It seemed as if the whole service was too much an external *opus operatum* (mechanical act). Most of it consisted in the reading of prayers with a rapidity that made it impossible to understand them, even for those who understood Latin. I could only get a word now and then and never a whole sentence, so that the common man could certainly get nothing of it nor derive any [instructive] benefit from it."[6]

1754 Ex-Voto painting, attributed to Paul Beaucourt, showing five young people who called upon St. Anne to save them after their canoe overturned in the St. Lawrence River at night. From the Shrine of St. Anne de Beaupré, Quebec.

Benefits certainly were expected from Latin prayers. When a Montreal gunsmith, Pierre Gadois, married Marie Pontonnier in 1657, he used a Latin invocation in a peculiar way to avert a rival's magic spell. Marie's rejected suitor, Corporal René Besnard, declared that the marriage would be forever sterile and he reputedly boasted to others that he knew how to render Pierre impotent by ligature (*nouement de l'aiguillette*). The ritual consisted of an incantation over a thrice-knotted string which represented Gadois's penis. The frightened groom took a friend's advice and recited the Latin psalm *Miserere mei, Deus* (God have mercy upon me) *backward* during the marriage ceremony to ward off the spell. This was a typical misuse of a Christian rite or text for private benefit. The action failed to protect the gunsmith: the couple remained childless, even after Bishop de Montmorency Laval had repeated the marriage blessing. The bishop waited for the passage of three years before annulling the marriage in August 1660, "because of permanent impotence caused by witchcraft."[7] Montreal's seigneurial court tried the suspected caster of spells and banished Besnard to Trois-Rivières. Gadois waited nearly five years before marrying again and, as evidence that the evil spell was broken, his second wife bore him fourteen children, with twins as the grand finale.[8] His "permanent impotence" was not so eternal, after all.

It was evident from the colonists' behavior that they feared misfortune would result from the omission of a religious act and were scrupulous in their Christian duties for fear of suffering God's retribution for their negligence. Kalm took note of the large, wooden wayside crosses along the roads of New France. The crosses were ornamented with the symbols of Christ's crucifixion: hammer, tongs, nails, a ladder, and a cock at the top of the central post, recalling St. Peter's false denial to the Romans that he knew Jesus. "Everyone who passes by [these landmarks] crosses himself, raises his hat or does some bit of reverence."[9] In the 1780s, after the conquest, two British officers in a post-carriage were increasingly irritated when their driver stopped at each roadside cross to kneel and recite a long prayer, as Canadians were accustomed to do. The officers sat, shivering, in the standing carriage. At the third halt, Captain Grattan seized the driver's long pigtail, or queue, "and declared, if he did not immediately drive on, he [Grattan] would instantly cut it off." The *Canadien* crossed himself, recited a brief prayer from the driver's seat, and then raced his horses to their destination, cursing the two heretical foreigners.[10]

Humans create gods in their own image, and the celestial kingdom mirrored the colonists' own society. Just as a relative in an influential position was expected to use his power to aid his kin, so a patron saint was the preferred intermediary for obtaining Heaven's favor. A direct appeal to almighty God might be too audacious. Individuals, as well as occupations, had their special saint, who acted as their mediator with God. A patron saint would be one's namesake or a saint whose feast day coincided with one's day of birth. The holy day of one's saint was the date to be remembered, not the actual birthday. When Bishop de Montmorency Laval suddenly relented in his refusal to permit Marie Morin to take her vows as a nun, as she wished, she attributed the bishop's change of heart to St. Joseph, because, "she had begun her noviciate on St. Joseph's day, [and] since she had been born on that day and she was of age on the same date." She thanked her patron saint and God for this evident miracle.[11] Devotion to the Virgin Mary meant that many girls in New France received "Marie" as one of their baptismal names. Canadians prudently enlisted the protection of several divine patrons by giving infants two or three saints' names. Marie-Madeleine Jarret de Verchères testified that, in 1692, when she was being pursued by Iroquois warriors, "I ran towards the fort, commending myself to the Blessed Virgin [for whom she was named], and saying to her from the bottom of my heart: 'Holy Virgin, mother of my God, you know I have ever honored and loved you as my dear mother; abandon me not in this hour of danger!'"[12]

Saints with a reputation for working wonders attracted devotees and became the subject of cults. When a saint or the Virgin Mary obliged with a desired favor, the benefit was publicly acknowledged by the successful supplicant. After the construction of the first chapel of St. Anne at Petit Cap, Côte de Beaupré, in 1658, this shrine to the mariners' patron, the Virgin Mary's mother, became a scene of miraculous cures. Mother Marie de l'Incarnation wrote in 1665 of these "great marvels . . . the paralyzed are seen to walk, the blind to recover their sight, and those sick with various maladies to recover their health."[13] In 1700 the curate of St. Anne's shrine recorded the experience of Jean Salois of St. Laurent, Ile d'Orléans, whose leg tendon had been cut by an axe, when he and his brother-in-law were felling a tree. Surgeons could not rejoin the severed tendon and Salois's leg muscles atrophied so that the limb could no longer bear his weight. At night the leg swelled up and caused him great pain. Salois promised to have ten Masses recited in St. Anne's honor if he could be relieved of his torment. The pain abated and he went to the nearby shrine to fulfill his vow. He also began a nine-day cycle of prayer. On the eighth day he found that he could walk without a stick or crutch. The restored leg was examined by the intendant, his wife, the king's physician, and other worthies who were "irreproachable witnesses to the miracle obtained for this man by the intercession of St. Anne." A thanksgiving mass was celebrated and, during it, the fortunate pilgrim took Communion and then climbed a ladder to hang his crutches on the chapel wall, "to serve as a monument to the benefit he had received."[14] His example was followed by hundreds of later pilgrims, who left crutches, leg braces, and plaques at the shrine to commemorate the cure they had received through St. Anne's intercession with God.

The present Shrine of Sainte-Anne-de-Beaupré also has a collection of colonial, votive paintings which attest, pictorially, to St. Anne's wondrous intervention to save or help people in distress, especially from shipwrecks. In their plight, the petitioners prayed to her and made a vow (*votum*) to acknowledge, in some tangible or visible way, the favor she had bestowed. Gratified petitioners who could afford a painting had one executed to show how the good St. Anne had heard their prayers and had won God's intervention to save the supplicants from death by drowning or some other disaster. The notation "ex voto [susceptum]" on the painting recalled that vow. Quebec City's chapel of Notre-Dame des Victoires commemorated the Virgin Mary's aid in repelling attacks by the British in 1690 and 1711. Disease and cold weather ended the 1690 siege and, in 1711, the invaders' fleet lost several ships and its fighting spirit off Egg Island near the St. Lawrence River's mouth. During the 1690 siege by New Englanders, the town's defenders attached a large painting of the Holy Family to the cathedral spire to call down Heaven's protection. What it brought down were cannonballs, as the besiegers wasted gunpowder and shot trying to smash the papist image. The Protestants' failure to hit the painting or to take the city seemed predestined to the Canadians because it was unthinkable that the Almighty would permit heretics to triumph over those of the true faith.

In 1743 caterpillars were the invaders and they devoured grain crops and meadows in the Montreal district. Bishop de Pontbriand issued an order for public prayers, saying that, just as the fortunate early start to cultivation should not be attributed to "purely natural causes, but rather to a special protection," so the blight of caterpillars was the flail "of divine justice" against sinful colonists, who must now show their "sorrow and repentance."[15] Rural parishioners were soon parading in religious processions and reciting prayers to drive away their creeping, plant-consuming enemies. Settlers in New France customarily responded to insect plagues with devout processions and public acts of contrition. In 1639, according to a Jesuit writer, when "the caterpillars, grasshoppers, and other vermin eating all that came out of the earth" appeared, "some processions and public prayers" followed. "Strange to say, the following day these little animals (*ces bestioles*) died and disappeared."[16] In his 1703 *Rituel du Diocèse de Québec,* Bishop Saint-Vallier provided Latin prayers and a "blessing of fields to expel grasshoppers, caterpillars, and all other creatures that harm the fruits of the earth." In 1743 the farm folk of Ile Dupas in La Visitation parish called upon the Virgin Mary for help against the caterpillars. Christ, they felt, would certainly respond to his mother's intercession. The farmers were probably saved by their insular location, but the credit for their protection went to the Blessed Virgin, to whom their prayers were addressed. In July 1743 the grateful residents of Ile Dupas had a notary draw up an acknowledgment of their gratitude for her aid, and it was registered with the local law court. In this document the settlers bound themselves to buy a priest's chasuble, suitable for services honoring the holy mother of Christ, as their thanksgiving for her aid against the insects.[17]

It is a challenge for anyone in the present, French- or English-speaking, to understand the mental and moral landscape of the people of *la Nouvelle France*. The colonists' view of nature and of their world was very different from our own perspective, which is based on secular and materialistic assumptions. In the scientific perspective, all causes are material and demonstrable; there is no room for a divine intervention that upsets the laws of nature. Nature, we believe, is orderly and knowable. Their world was a dangerous place ruled by a God whose wrath or mercy was unpredictable. War and sickness were regarded as Heaven-sent scourges to achieve some inscrutable, divine purpose. When people wrote "Dieu bénisse nos armes et nous donne la paix (may God bless our arms and give us peace)," it was more than a faint hope or a figure of speech; it was a sincere plea to God to exercise his sovereign power over human affairs in favor of the petitioner and his countrymen. The faithful could make themselves worthy of this benefit by submission, austere morality, and devotion.

No one doubted that the course of events followed some divine logic, beyond the understanding of mortals. The faithful, especially those in holy orders, were to submit to misfortune without complaint. In 1686 the chronicler of Quebec's Ursuline Sisters wrote, "it has pleased God to afflict this community for a second time with a universal conflagration which occurred on October 20th."[18] The possibility that the fire which destroyed the convent was the result of pure mischance was unthinkable; it must be celestial retribution for some misdeed or moral failing. Father Dollier de Casson's *Histoire de Montréal* (c. 1673) attributed all events to "the Providence of God"; no further explanation was required. The belief that divine providence ruled all things was shared by the laity, Roman Catholic *and* Protestant. In 1745 a writer at Sainte in France advised a colonist, "what must console one above all in different events is [the knowledge] that God has permitted them."[19] In the same year, amid war, the Protestant merchants François Havy and Jean Lefèbvre could write, "the master of the universe will restore order by giving us good times." Less philosophically, they prayed, "may God grant that this unfortunate war ends soon," and, "may God help us."[20] The colonists' universe was rational in the sense that every event had a cause and a justification, but the cause might be supernatural and the justification religious.

Being divinely ordained, disasters were heralded by natural signs, such as comets, lightning, or thunder. In 1661 the Quebec Ursulines' mother superior, Marie de l'Incarnation, told her son how Heaven had foretold Iroquois attacks upon the settlers that year:

> We had baleful portents of these misfortunes. After the departure of the vessels in 1660, signs appeared in the sky that terrified many people. A comet was seen, its rods pointed towards the earth. . . . In the air was seen a man of fire, enveloped in fire. A canoe of fire was also seen and, towards Montreal, a great crown likewise of fire. On the Island of Orleans a child was heard crying in its mother's womb. As well, confused voices of women and children were heard in the air giving lamentable cries. On another occasion a thunderous and horrible voice was heard.

According to Mother Marie, the great earthquake of 1663 and its aftershocks were preceded and accompanied by similar marvels: there were disembodied "howls and shrieking, . . . and . . . distinct and frightening voices. Some said, 'Alas!' Others said, 'Let us go!' and others, 'Let us stop up the rivers!' The sounds were heard sometimes of bells, sometimes of cannon, sometimes of thunder. We saw fires, torches, and flaming globes, which sometimes fell to the earth and sometimes dissolved in the air. A man of fire was seen with flames pouring from his mouth." The Jesuits also saw fiery portents in the sky. The clearest premonition of the earthquake was contained in a vision received by an Augustinian nun of exceptional virtue. She received "an infallible conviction—that God was ready to punish the country for the sins committed here, especially the contempt for ordinances of the Church." Amerindians educated by Christian missionaries blamed themselves for drinking brandy, while their pagan brethren said that the earthquake was caused by "the souls of their ancestors, who wished to return to their former dwelling."[21] This explanation for the heaving earth was dismissed by European Christians.

In believing in natural signs foretelling human misfortune and in supernatural causes for most events, the uneducated and the clergy were in agreement. The unin-structed countryfolk, however, gave greater weight to the devil and to black magic among the supernatural causes. These malignant forces were recognized in Bishop Saint-Vallier's 1703 *Rituel,* or book of ceremonies. His order of cermonies included the exorcism of demons, and he listed "the most assured marks of demonic posses-sion," such as speaking and understanding unknown languages—especially in giv-ing long, impromptu speeches, instinctive ability to find hidden or secret things, making known distant events, and performing "actions that exceed the natural force of the possessed person, in whatever condition or illness he might be."[22] Priests were warned not to mistake sick, "melancholic," or withdrawn people and lunatics for those in the devil's grip.

Even before the book's publication, the bishop's signs of satanic aid were part of colonial lore. In 1685, Jean Campagnard or Campagna, a forty-five-year-old plow-man at Beaubassin in Acadia, was tried for using sorcery to kill a father and daugh-ter with whom he had boarded. He was asked, "in 1678 did you not blow into the eyes of François Pellerin when he was working [with you] in the marsh?" Campagnard was not the only one to do this, apparently to remove some irritant in Pellerin's eyes. Pellerin was soon attacked by a hot fever and went to bed. When he was close to death, Campagnard reputedly said to him, "there, that will grind your barley well (*Voilà bien moudre pour de l'orge*)," which the plowman said was a jest from his homeland of Aunis. Campagnard added that many people had died in 1678, along with Pellerin and his daughter, and that he, too, was sick. Pellerin's widow testified that when she had struck Campagnard, "because of some impudence (*insolences*) he wanted to do to the girl, he told her that she would repent for it." Another girl was said to have been killed by touching a gift of butter from Campagnard. The plow-man seems to have been courting her as well as the daughter of Roger "Quessy" [Casey], an Irishman whose cattle fell ill and started to die. Casey said that Campagnard had come to his home with a bottle of liquor and, when rebuffed by Casey's daughter, he had threatened her with misfortune in eight days. In that pe-riod Casey's cattle sickened and the girl went to the priest to ask him to bless their fodder and drink so that they would not die. Sieur de la Vallière, Campagnard's former empoyer, threatened to run his sword through the suspected sorcerer if Casey's livestock continued to die. The animals recovered within a day of that threat.

Campagnard's neighbors claimed that he had threatened to bewitch them and were convinced that his extraordinary labor and good harvests were proof that he was being helped by Lucifer. Feats of superhuman strength were among Bishop Saint-Vallier's proofs of demonic possession. Luckily for Campagnard, Quebec's Sovereign Council heard the case on appeal and quashed the seigneurial court's sentence against him for witchcraft.[23]

The educated gentlemen who were sent out from France to be colonial administrators were increasingly skeptical about the reality of witchcraft and were reluctant to prosecute people for offenses against orthodox religion. Prosecutions for blasphemy nearly ended in eighteenth-century New France.[24] A magician's claim to be able to control natural forces at will no longer accorded with the view of educated people, shaped by scientists such as Isaac Newton, that nature was an orderly, self-regulating mechanism. The royal edict of July 1682 reduced the penalty for convicted fortune-tellers, conjurers, and charmers (*enchanteurs*) to banishment from the kingdom. However, this edict confirmed the death penalty for "self-styled diviners, magicians and enchanters" found guilty of concocting or using poisons or venoms, as well as for "persons evil enough to combine impiety and sacrilege with superstition." The sacrilege had to be more than the superstitious misuse of holy words taken from Scripture or prayers, although that, too, merited "exemplary punishment."[25] Later, the *Parlement* of Paris—a model for other jursidictions—prosecuted sorcerers only as frauds who deceived simple folk with their pretended powers. In the mid-eighteenth century, François Dareau, a jurist, wrote that "the light of [rationalist] philosophy has entirely dissipated the errors which formerly enthralled people, believing in sorcerers and in magicians, as some common people still do. Today the casting of spells is only a crime insofar as impiety and profanation [of holy objects] are mixed in with practices of those who claim to exercise magical powers."[26]

Article 4 of the July 1682 edict mentioned false denunciations for witchcraft, and colonial magistrates started to punish the accusers for malicious libel. As a result, in 1707 Jean Charpentier of Boucherville, who had been denounced for killing livestock with magic, received damages from his accusers. That outcome discouraged formal accusations of sorcery. The 1742 prosecution of a diviner in Canada was undertaken, not for his claim to be able to identify the thief who had stolen money from a shoemaker by magic, but for his sacrilegious use of a prayerbook and a crucifix in his ritual.[27] This was the last prosecution involving witchcraft in New France.

The refusal of eighteenth-century magistrates in *la Nouvelle France* to entertain charges against people for casting evil spells did not destroy popular belief in sorcery; it merely restricted the consequences for suspected sorcerers to private sanctions. Magic satisfied too many human needs to be discarded. Threatened by unseen and mysterious forces, colonists naturally attempted to control, or at least protect themselves from these forces. Magic rituals promised the practitioner some influence over the menacing forces. Witchcraft by others provided an explanation for sudden deaths, undeserved misfortunes, and crippling internal disorders, such as strokes, epilepsy, and sexual impotence. Magic also satisfied human desires that are still with us. Divination promised to unlock the secrets of the future, and who has not looked at a horoscope, now and then? One-sided affection—a familiar teenage experience—encouraged the suitor to consider potions, charms, and spells to convert the indifferent object of love into a responsive partner. The connection between magic and sexual attraction is evident in the terms still applied to alluring women: "enchanting, charming, glamorous," and—of course—"bewitching." All of these adjectives suggest that animal magnetism was being supplemented by something unnatural, something supernatural. In 1682 a seductive woman, whose Montreal tavern attracted young men, was accused by the parents of one of her lovers of having captivated him with a charm. Rumors spread that she had a book of magic to entice men.[28] The accusations against Jean Campagnard assumed that he was using evil spells to punish the young women who had rejected his sexual advances. Black magic (*maléfice*) enlisted supernatural forces to secretly harm those enemies or rivals whom the aggrieved person dared not threaten in public. In love and in conflicts, magic gave the powerless a way to shape events in their favor.

A witchcraft case that combined magic, heresy, and sexual desire occurred in New France during the winter of 1660–61. The suspected sorcerer was Daniel Will, a miller at Beauport. He had converted to Roman Catholicism after arriving in Canada. As a former Protestant, he would have excited distrust. Will wanted to marry Sieur Giffard's sixteen-year-old maidservant, Barbe Halé or Hallay. Our principal source is the knowledgeable Mother Marie de l'Incarnation, whose convent was visited by a parade of informants. In a letter of September 1661, she informed her son that

> It was discovered that there were sorcerers and magicians in this country. This became apparent in the person of a miller who came from France. . . . This man wished to marry a girl who had traveled with her father and mother in the same vessel [as he], saying that she had been promised to him, but, because he was a man of bad habits, no one would listen to him. After this refusal, he wished to obtain his ends by ruses of his diabolic art. He caused demons or goblins to appear in the girl's house, and with them specters that caused her a great deal of distress and fear. . . . Monseigneur [de Montmorency Laval] sent Fathers and went there himself to drive away the demons by the prayers of the Church. However, nothing improved and the

din became louder than ever. Phantoms appeared, drums and flutes were heard playing, stones were seen to detach from the wall and fly about, and always the magician['s apparition] was there with his companions to trouble the girl. Their design was to make her marry that wretch, who wished it also but wished to corrupt [fornicate with] her first. The place is far from Quebec and it was a great fatigue to the Fathers to go so far to work their exorcism. So, seeing that the devils were trying to exhaust them with this travail and weary them with their antics, Monseigneur ordered the miller and the girl brought to Quebec. The former was put into prison and the latter shut up in the house [convent] of the *Hospitalières* [hospital nuns].

A nun of the hospital, Marie-Catherine Simon de Longpré, Sister de Saint-Augustin, who watched over the girl at night, was also harassed by devils when the magician and "these hellish flies" arrived to torment the maiden. Sometimes they spoke through the girl's mouth. "Enraged because Mother de Saint-Augustin guarded the girl's purity with such care, the demons appeared to her in hideous forms and beat her outrageously. The wounds and bruises that marked her body were enough to show that they were realities and not illusions." The demons materialized as men, women, children, beasts, and phantoms; they tried to deceive the nun by appearing as bright angels. She and another nun, "were sometimes obliged to sew the girl up in a sack to hide her from the pressing importunities of the magician." God and the spirit of the Jesuit martyr Jean de Brébeuf, who was often seen by Sister de Saint-Augustin, sustained her determination to prevail. "Finally the demons and magicians withdrew, through the intercession of this holy man, who had spilled his blood for the upholding of the Faith in this country." As for the miller, he and "the other sorcerers have not been willing to confess. Nor is anything said to them, for it is not easy to convict persons in crimes of this nature."[29] This last sentence alluded to the lay magistrates' increasing reluctance to punish people for witchcraft.

The miller's later offenses were chronicled by Jesuit writers. Bishop Laval condemned Will as "a relapsed heretic, blasphemer, and profaner of the sacraments." Will was excommunicated for selling liquor to the Amerindians, yet briefly rehabilitated himself by an act of public penance. The bishop was not convinced that this former Protestant could be believed. At last, in October 1661, the civil authorities executed Will, "for having traded brandy with the Indians," or, according to another source, "for horrible blasphemies that he uttered and for having profaned with contempt the sacraments of the church, having done so by a simulated conversion when he abjured Protestantism."[30]

The clergy's belief in witchcraft was supported by Holy Scripture. The Old Testament tells of Saul speaking with a sprit through the Witch of En-Dor, and, in the New Testament (Luke 8:26–33), Jesus Christ transferred "unclean spirits" and devils out of a man and into a herd of swine. Following Christ's example, priests used exorcism rituals to drive away malignant spirits. The devil was assumed to be the master of these evil spirits and the principal source of the supernatural powers exercised by witches and sorcerers. In the *Summa Theologica,* St. Thomas Aquinas had linked sorcery with diabolism and heresy. In Exodus, 22:18, the Bible directed, "Thou shalt not suffer a witch to live," yet it was not until 1484 that Pope Innocent VIII authorized secular courts to prosecute those witches identified as such by the Divine Inquisition. An inquisitors' handbook written by two Dominican friars, the *Malleus Maleficarum* (1486), provided definitions of witchcraft and gave examples of cases from the authors' experience, principally in the German-speaking areas of the Rhine Valley and in Konstanz.

In the fifteenth century, church tribunals tried and convicted witches, who were then passed on to the civil authorities for punishment. Strangulation followed by a burning of the corpse was the fate of those condemned for witchcraft. Joan of Arc was tried by a church court and burned alive as a witch by secular authority in 1431. France's criminal courts assumed responsibility for the conviction and punishment of witches. The royal magistrates' cooperation with the clergy was necessary for a successful prosecution in New France. The growing intellectual distance between jurists and priests was matched by a social gulf that separated the well-educated judges from ordinary colonists, which allowed the magistrates to dismiss popular beliefs. The magistrates' independence prevented anything in Canada like the 1662 witch-hunt in Hartford, Connecticut, in which three died, or the notorious trials of 1692 at Salem, Massachusetts, that led to the execution of twenty people. New England's court officers were swept along by the belief in demonic possession held by ordinary folk and by Puritan divines.

Although the last court case in New France involving witchcraft was in 1742, folk magic persisted in French Canada into the twentieth century, despite clerical disapproval and the elite's scorn. We know this because, in the 1960s, Jean-Claude Dupont interviewed people in the Province of Quebec's Beauce County—most of them born in the previous century—about their supernatural beliefs and knowledge. The Beaucerons knew about using ligature to render a man impotent and they recalled sorcerers (*sorciers* and *jeteux de sort*) who could tell fortunes, cast spells, cure sicknesses, locate subterranean springs or hidden treasure, stop fires, cause droughts or epidemics, and perform superhuman feats of labor, just like Jean Campagnard of Beaubassin. Their popular lore blended Roman Catholicism with superstition. A Latin word from the Mass was inserted into an invocation to cure a toothache; a pack of cards hidden under the altar cloth acquired magical powers when the priest celebrated the Eucharist above it.[31] The continuity in oral traditions from New France was extraordinary. As in the French Regime, countryfolk used magic to supplement the beneficial tokens of orthodox religion, such as holy water, medals, or prayers, to enhance their effect. A herbal remedy administered with a Christian prayer or a superstitious incantation was sure to be more powerful. Magic and religion, for these people, were complementary approaches to the supernatural world; informants seldom saw them as being in conflict. Priests were regarded as men who exercised supernatural powers derived from God, just as the sorcerer drew his superhuman ability from Satan.

The stories collected by Jean-Claude Dupont and nineteenth-century folklorists show that, despite their continuity, oral traditions were given an increasingly Christian interpretation. Metamorphosis was the punishment of delinquent Christians. In Canada, the werewolf, or *loup-garou,* became a "hardened sinner," who did "not go to confession . . . [or] receive absolution," and failed "to take Easter communion for seven consecutive years."[32] The *feux-follets* (will o' the wisps) or glowing lights seen fluttering at night—possibly fire flies or luminescent marsh gas—were said to be the tormented souls of unbaptized infants, the damned, or the spirits of those who had not done penance in their lives. In New France, colonists, when making arrangements for their old age or dictating wills, sought to reduce the time their souls would spend in Purgatory, that intermediate place of suffering where unremitted sins were purged before the spirit could enter paradise. They asked for requiem masses after their death to shorten their souls' time in purgatory.

The devil is the dominant figure in French-Canadian folktales and sayings and this dominance suggests that countryfolk were obsessed with the demon and his powers. Tales, in which Satan represented the ever-present temptations faced by carnal and selfish humans, were Christian and didactic too. Stories told of opportunistic *Canadiens* who made bargains with the devil in return for some material benefit. In the tale of "la Chasse-Galérie" (the flying canoe) homesick woodcutters are magically transported from their isolated lumber camp to celebrate New Year's eve with their families at home. Satan demanded that they divest themselves of religious objects and not utter one holy word or touch a Christian symbol—removing all protection from his influence. A passenger of the flying canoe broke the spell by calling out God's name after dropping a paddle or by touching a steeple cross while flying over a church, and then all the woodsmen were spilled out and fell to the ground far below—a suitable punishment for having struck a bargain with the devil.

The story of Rose Latulipe, known throughout French Canada, is about a girl entranced by a handsome, dark stranger who arrived at a village dance, yet would not take off his gloves. His ruse was to keep Rose dancing past midnight and into Sunday, or from the last hours of Mardi Gras into Ash Wednesday, thereby profaning a holy day. The stranger also tries to remove the crucifix on a chain—her protection—from Rose's neck. The parish priest, with stole, holy water, and cross, arrives at the last minute to save Rose from her diabolic seducer. One sprinkle of holy water and "poof!" the intruder disappears in a cloud of sulphurous smoke. The lesson in this tale was that those who neglect their religious obligations for carnal pleasure can only be saved from themselves by a cleric's intervention. In other stories, Satan is not only defeated, he is tricked into doing a good deed, such as hauling stone for a church's construction. In another tale, a canny *habitant* offers his soul to the devil if the demon can fill his *tuque,* or stocking cap, with gold, knowing that the hat has a hole in it.

In French-Canadian folktales the devil offers great riches, sexual attractiveness, a fine home, relief from labor, or extraordinary powers to his targets; he is everywhere, sometimes in the form of a man, a bird, a horse, a toad, or a dog.[33] Belief that the evil tempter is omnipresent, ready to exploit human weaknesses, hints at the repressed desires of rural people. The moral of these stories is a very Christian message: God's power is greater than that of Satan. Legends also reinforced belief that divine protection emanated from religious talismans, such as Rose's crucifix, or from holy relics, symbols, and words. These things had an inherent, miraculous power. Sister de Sainte-Hélène was delighted when her order obtained martyrs' bone fragments from Rome, and four reliquaries were made to display them in the nuns' chapel. "We look upon them as protectors that God has sent to us," and, she assured a correspondent, "I have not failed to pray often to our holy martyrs to be your intercessors with God."[34] This is similar to the ancient Hurons' belief that every object was endowed with a spirit and that the spirit's power might be shared by the possessor or worshipper of that object.

The colonists' belief that the actions and objects of orthodox Christianity had a power that could serve profane ends was evident in Pierre Gadois's misuse of the psalm *Miserere.* It also appeared in a form of do-it-yourself marriage, called *mariage à la gaumine,* which was based on a very literal understanding of Roman Catholic doctrine. When a couple faced family opposition, faced clerical disapproval, or lacked official sanction to marry, they might stand up together during the Mass, with friends as witnesses, and declare themselves to be man and wife. They believed that they were united in the sight of God because they had made their declaration just after the priest had raised the wafer and recited, in Latin, Christ's words, "hoc est enim corpus meum (for this is my body)," which, by transubstantiation, changed the wafer into the body of Jesus, who was God on earth. This was the ritual that Protestants mocked as "hocus-pocus." To devout Roman Catholics, God was then truly and substantially present to witness the marriage. A couple might also make their declaration of intent just as the priest was blessing the congregation, so that his benediction fell upon their alliance as well.

When Paul de Montéleon, a thirty-year-old army officer newly arrived in Canada, wanted to marry a colonial officer's daughter, Vicar-General Glandelet forbade the publication of their banns of marriage because de Montéleon had not produced a certificate confirming his unmarried status, as was required of immigrants by the bishop's order in 1691. With the consent of the bride's family, the couple surprised the curate of Beauport parish, who was celebrating a wedding Mass in January 1711 for another pair. The priest reported that, "when I had arrived at that part of the Mass after the consecration [of the Host] and coming to the preface of the Pater [noster], I heard Sieur de Montéleon speaking and protesting loudly" about his right to marry Marie-Anne-Joseph de Lestringan. Over the priest's objections, these two declared themselves married and asked those present in the church to be witnesses to their act.[35]

Father Etienne Le Goff, a Franciscan friar, reported a similar experience in February 1737 when he was officiating in Louisbourg's St. Louis chapel: "after the blessing of the Mass, Jean Lelarget [*sic*], resident of this town, and [Marguerite-] Louise Sanson, approached the railing of the holy [altar] table" hand in hand and, after kneeling on the step, arose and declared, "in a loud voice that they were taking each other as man and wife." Another witness recalled Larget's statement that "he was taking *before God* Miss Sanson as his wife," and of how the friar quickly disappeared into the sacristy with the chalice, probably containing consecrated wine— the blood of Christ. None of the couple's invited witnesses had appeared and Larget had trouble persuading others to act as witnesses in their stead. When Larget told one spectator that he had just witnessed a marriage, the man replied, "if they were married, they need only go to bed together now." Jean Larget was a twenty-six-year-old master mariner and he had promised to marry his Acadian sweetheart two or more years before. His widowed mother, however, refused to consent to the match and, therefore, no priest would marry the couple. The two lovers were arrested, confined separately, "to prevent the accused from consummating their criminal plan," and then interrogated.

Members of Ile Royale's Superior Council heard Larget's startling testimony that *mariage à la gaumine* had been suggested to him by "Father Juvenal, a Récollet [Franciscan who] told him that M. de Gannes, a garrison officer, had done the same thing and that the curate had married them on the following day." Church rules and the kingdom's laws had been violated by this "profanation of the sanctity of the marriage sacrament," and the attorney-general recommended rigorous punishment, to preserve "the repose of families." The council was lenient: in its sentence of 11 April, it ordered Jean Larget to remain confined to the guardhouse for another fortnight, while his intended bride was to stay in a convent for the same period. Each was to pay three livres to the poor and perform an act of penance, and they were not to live together until properly married, which was accomplished five months later.[36] Sieur de Montléon had been fined twenty livres by Quebec's Superior Council, and the bride's parents paid one hundred livres for conniving to evade church rules. Another *mariage à la gaumine* occurred at Montreal in 1711 between a soldier and a woman whose husband was presumed dead. The intendant forbade them to live together, describing their conduct as a "sacrilege" and "an outrage against the church's authority."[37] In a 1717 pastoral letter, Bishop Saint-Vallier asserted that this unsanctioned form of marriage, which he described as a "crime, instead of diminishing, is becoming a custom." The bishop threatened anyone participating in a *mariage à la gaumine* with excommunication—denial of the sacraments.[38]

These improvised marriages were unusual; there were probably no more than fifteen in New France. The practice appears to have come from Europe because immigrants were involved in most of the reported cases. These acts, however infrequent, reveal how people understood the rituals of the Roman Catholic Church: God was present in the consecrated wafer to witness their deeds, and a priest's blessing could be intercepted to sanctify unholy behavior. These indications of popular belief are valuable because evidence about religious convictions among colonial society's lower ranks is rare.

It is hard to assess the quality of religious belief among the laity in *la Nouvelle France*. In the 1720s Father Charlevoix thought that the Canadians were pious and well instructed in their faith. Every child seems to have attended catechism classes, and the young were probably better informed than the children in Brittany, who, according to a French noblewoman, thought that the Virgin Mary had created heaven and earth.[39] Catechism classes had their comic moments: at Louisbourg, when a priest asked a girl to describe the Christian virtue of hope (*l'espérance*), she replied that "l'Espérance" was the sergeant who slept with her mother.[40] That was a very Christian *nom de guerre* for a soldier!

A researcher eager to assess the extent of religious devotion in the colony and who consults testaments and estate inventories in the notarial archives may be perplexed by the evidence. Wills made in anticipation of death followed the fixed formulae of notary's manuals. They invariably describe the testator as "sound in mind, spirit and understanding," with a knowledge that "nothing is more certain than death and nothing is more uncertain than the hour of its coming." Then, "as a Catholic Christian," the author recommends his or her soul to God and, perhaps, to the keeping of a patron saint. These sentiments were not original or spontaneous. More wills were made in the seventeenth century than in the next century, because there were proportionately more bachelors without natural heirs. French civil law predetermined the division of a legacy among children, which might be altered in maintenance accords, so wills were superfluous, unless the testator wanted to make

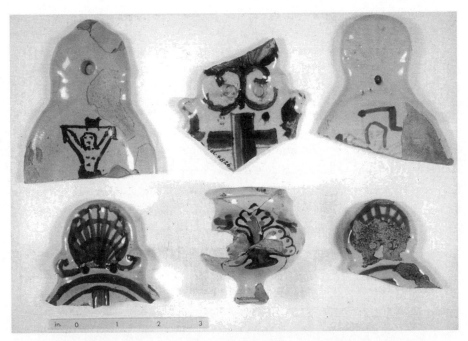

Fragments of French tin-glazed, earthenware holy water vessels for domestic use found at Louisbourg. From the Fortress of Louisbourg National Historic Park.

a special bequest to someone outside his family or to the church. Men and women made bequests to religious institutions to insure proper burial and requiem Masses for "the repose of his/her soul."[41] As a consequence, wills do not reveal much about personal beliefs, apart from a common concern for the welfare of one's soul after death.

Estate inventories, which are an excellent source of information about personal property, do not reflect the real extent of piety, especially in the 1600s. Valuable objects were more likely to be listed than religious tokens of small value. One inventory in five lists religious objects among the deceased person's effects. These items were devotional books, crucifixes, paintings of the Virgin Mary or a saint, and holy water vessels (*bénitiers*), which were placed inside the main door of a house for a blessing upon entry or departure. In the seventeenth century the owners were invariably government officials, military officers, or merchants. In the 1700s craftsmen at Quebec acquired these pious ornaments. It is exceptional to find such objects in a farmer's estate. Possession depended as much on personal wealth as on piety. In 1694 priests were to encourage householders to have "some good book" to be read aloud to one's family on holy days. In particular, Bishop Saint-Vallier recommended "the Life of Jesus Christ, St. Augustine's Confessions, the Lives of Saints, the Imitation of Jesus Christ, Grenade's Guide to Sinners, the Paedagogue of

Christian Families, St. François de Sale's Conduct at Confession and Communion, Busée's [César de Bus?] Meditations, the little book Think Well Upon It, another called Christian Thoughts, [and] Monsieur Abelly's Christian Institution."[42] These, indeed, were the sort of works found in the small libraries of the Quebec Superior Council's secretary-councilor, a merchant trained in the law, a Quebec master-builder, and a nailsmith. Other inventories list one or a half-dozen anonymous books, which must have included some devotional works. What is surprising is the presence of Bibles in three homes.[43] The Roman Catholic clergy disapproved of laymen reading Scripture by themselves, without priestly guidance. These lists are not exhaustive because items of small value were frequently omitted from postmortem inventories. An old, parchment-bound book was worth less than one livre.

The crucifixes that were listed tended to be costly, carved-ivory figures of Christ, mounted on a velvet background or enclosed in an ebony or gilded wood frame.[44] The Virgin Mary was a favorite subject for domestic paintings: both a king's attorney at Quebec and a Montreal builder had a costly crucifix and a painting of Christ's mother. When he died in 1717, Pierre Gauvreau, the king's gunsmith and armorer at Quebec, had "a painting representing the holy virgin in a black ebony frame," a painting of Louis XIV's coronation, "a big painting of St. Benedict with a gilt frame," and "another medium-sized painting in a gilt frame." These canvases were valued at twenty to sixty livres each.[45]

The clue that inventories were not exhaustive lists of devotional articles is the rarity of *bénitiers* among the items catalogued. Only five holy-water vessels were noted in ninety inventories, and the ones listed were made of silver, crystal, tin, or pewter. At Louisbourg fragments of tin-glazed, earthenware *bénitiers* show up in the ground if not in notarial *inventaires des biens après decès*. These vessels were worth only ten sols—a half livre. Absent, too, are the brass rings with Christian motifs, crosses, and religious medals which appear in profusion at sites occupied by the French in North America. These tokens of faith are recorded only in bulk quantities as part of a trader's stock; individually, their price was a trifle. Paul LeMoyne de Maricourt's estate included forty-five religious pendants called *agnus dei,* or lambs of God. Likewise, the rosaries used by all Roman Catholics are missing from the records unless we look at the merchants' stock lists. In the 1706 account of the stock of Jean Minet, a Quebec merchant-retailer, we find "23 common wooden rosaries," valued a two sols apiece.[46] Religious institutions also had boxes of medals and pendant crosses for distribution as gifts. Clearly, cheap religious items did not merit inclusion in estate listings, yet they existed and were commonplace possessions. Travelers noticed religious engravings on paper inside colonial homes, and these inexpensive prints are also missing from most inventories. Useful though the estate lists might be, they are not a good index to religious devotion among the colonists.

The clergy's zeal is better documented than lay piety, and both changed over time and varied from region to region. In the 1600s nuns and missionaries were animated by the crusading zeal and asceticism of the Roman Catholic Counter-Reformation. The Society of Jesus was founded in 1540 to reconquer souls lost to Protestantism and to win new worlds for Rome. When a Jesuit wrote about the men who were needed for the Canadian missions, he said that they must be "persons who are dead to themselves and to the world; men truly Apostolic, who seek God alone, and the salvation of souls, who love with real love the Cross [of suffering] and self-mortification; who do not spare themselves; . . . let them be men whose sole satisfaction is in God and to whom suffering is the greatest delight."[47] Other missionaries spoke of their "zeal for souls," and their willingness "to suffer for Jesus Christ."

To die for the faith in agony, like Jesus of Nazareth upon the cross, was a death to be envied. To surrender one's life was the ultimate act of self-denial. Seventeenth-century priests and nuns dreamed of winning "a martyr's crown." They likened the hostile Iroquois to the Muslim Turks assailing European Christendom's eastern frontiers. In 1640 Marie de l'Incarnation reported that a Jesuit priest had been taken by the Iroquois: "It is possible that we shall have a martyr in his person, which will cause great jealousy to the others, who sigh incessantly after this high grace. We have an agreement with the Reverend [Jesuit] Fathers that if this good fortune befalls them, we shall sing the [hymn of thanksgiving] *Te Deum* and, in return, they will grant us a share in the merit of their sacrifice."[48] In the 1640s six Jesuits and a lay assistant of the Huron and Iroquois missions were killed. One of the martyrs was Father Jean de Brébeuf, whose spirit helped Sister de Saint-Augustin to drive away the demons assailing Barbe Halé.

Fundamental to the Christianity of this period was a belief that humans had a conflicting duality of spirit and flesh. The two inclinations were irreconcilable; the triumph of one required the defeat of the other. The way to elevate one's mind and heart to the spiritual world and to achieve mental union with God, then called "perfection," was to subdue one's body and all concern for the material world. Total surrender of one's will to the divine will required contempt for the world and self-abnegation. Mother de Sainte-Hélène wrote in 1729, "I am not united to God as I ought to be, but according to the author of *The Imitation {of Jesus Christ}*, even after we have abandoned all, we have still not left ourselves."[49] Concern for self was the last barrier to be overcome in the quest for spiritual perfection.

For seventeenth-century ascetics, all pleasures of the senses were distractions that led humans astray. The devout practiced self-denial and mortification of the flesh. Even natural affection was distrusted: Sister Marie Morin attributed love for her parents and a desire to live with them to "the demon," while Mother Marie de l'Incarnation suspected that Satan was arousing maternal affection for her son to block her vocation for the convent. She tried to suppress her feelings for her son and abstained from wine, which might have afforded her some carnal pleasure. Likewise, Mother Marie added wormwood and gall to her food to render it distasteful and bitter so that she would not enjoy eating. Fasting, scourging one's back with a small whip, and wearing a hair shirt were the conventional means used by priests, nuns, and devout laity (*dévots*) to tame the flesh. Hair garments chafed the skin. Self-flagellation was practiced, for example, by Jeanne LeBer, a Montreal merchant's daughter who retired to a cell adjoining a chapel and who wore a haircloth shirt and corn-husk shoes. Being inured to pain and privation, the believer was freed from any concern for physical comfort and for self. Self-punishment was also a penance for sins of deed or thought and, by self-examination, the pious always found failings in their own conduct to be confessed and expiated.

One could take contempt for one's body and abasement of pride to extremes that shocked later generations. According to her contemporary, Father Paul Ragueneau, Sister Marie-Catherine de Saint-Augustin punished her body "with saintly cruelty by bloodied whips, belts bristling with [inward-facing] iron studs that penetrated the flesh, by continual fasts, . . . She often spent nights in prayer and slept on the cold, hard ground. She often experienced a repugnance and horror for various things. To conquer herself, she went beyond what she should have done in the ordinary course of things, She went as far as swallowing the stinking and putrid phlegm of poor people infected with very dangerous sicknesses for which she felt an aversion. She took up the phlegm in her handkerchief so that no one saw it, and . . . [ate it] wishing that she might [thereby] submit to [God's] grace."[50]

Given this professed contempt for self and for material comforts, the experience of hardship, isolation, and privation was welcomed. The Jesuits were resigned to all setbacks with an almost suicidal fatalism, even with gratitude. Misfortunes were embraced as tests of one's ardor, just as God had afflicted the patient Job to try his faith. This was the Christian fidelity in adversity that was incomprehensible to many Hurons. Confined to their convents, nuns could only sigh with envy as missionary priests went forth to risk death by drowning, starvation, or torture for their faith.

During the seventeenth century, Canada's laity shared in Counter-Reformation piety by dressing modestly, by eating frugally, by frequent confession and attendance at Communion, by reading pious books, and by avoiding worldly amusements. The bishops of Quebec sanctioned the confraternities of the Holy Family (f.1664), of the Holy Scapulary (f.1665), of St. Joseph (f.1693), and of the Sacred Heart of Mary (f.1722) to allow secular people the opportunity and incentive to pray together and engage in special devotions. The lay confraternities founded by craftsmen have already been mentioned. The pious were guided in their lives by the books of St. François de Sales. His *Introduction à la vie dévote* (1608) appeared in the year of Quebec's foundation and defined the path of godliness for zealous lay people, as well as giving them their name, *les dévots*. Quebec's founder, Samuel de Champlain, was a model of piety. His appeals for support from the king and the French Chamber of Commerce spoke of the honor and service to God, as well as of the material benefits, of colonizing North America. He credited his voyage of 1615 to "the intense love that I have always had for discoveries . . . with the intention of leading them [the native peoples] to a knowledge of God."[51] As proof of his sincerity, he brought four Franciscan friars as missionaries to Canada. Other exponents of lay devotion were Madame Chauvigny de la Peltrie, who paid for Quebec's Ursuline convent and aspired to teach native girls, and Jeanne Mance, who established Montreal's first hospital. They exemplified the practical and charitable spirit of the devotional movement.

In the early 1640s the Jesuits believed that they were witnessing the birth of a new Golden Age of Christian virtue among the settlers of New France. "Peace, love, and good understanding reign among our French people. . . . The principal inhabitants of this new world, desiring to preserve this blessing of Heaven, have ranged themselves under the banners of the holy Virgin, in whose honor they hear the holy Mass every Saturday, often frequent the Sacraments of life, [and] lend an ear to the sermons given to them. . . . This devotion has banished enmities and coldness; it has introduced good words instead of too licentious language; it has revived the custom in families of publicly praying to God, evening and morning." The colonists were said to be free of "wars, lawsuits, disputes, and quarrels." "This innocence," concluded the writer, "makes this a golden age for us."[52]

The foundation of Montreal in 1642 expressed that spirituality. This enterprise was undertaken for the conversion of Amerindians in what was then the remote hinterland of *la Nouvelle France*. The initiative came from a secret lay order of *dévots* called *la Compagnie du Saint-Sacrement*. The Company of the Holy Sacrament combated blasphemy, dueling, gaming, heresy, and lewdness as well as engaging in charitable work. Members of this association in France formed "la Société de Notre-Dame de Montréal pour la Conversion des Sauvages de la Nouvelle France (The Society of Our Lady of Montreal for the conversion of the Indians of New France)." They were inspired by a published Jesuit account of Montreal Island as the best place for such a mission. The island was at the confluence of the Ottawa and St. Lawrence Rivers, both of them routes for native traders coming east. One associate, Jérôme le Royer de la Dauversière, had such a precise vision of the place and its resources that it convinced his confessor that God desired this missionary enterprise. The Jesuits and wealthy *dévots* aided the settlement of pious clerics and lay people, along with seventy indentured workers, far inland from Quebec and on the

edge of Mohawk territory. The Mohawks attacked the French intruders and besieged "Ville Marie de Montréal"—the settlement's original name—killing unwary
settlers who ventured too far from the stockade's protection. Historian Edward R.
Adair claimed that Montreal was the only colonial city established in the Americas
for purely religious purposes.[53] The realization that Montreal Island was admirably
located for the fur trade came quickly to less-elevated minds and led to the undoing
of the founders' pious intentions. The holy city of the Virgin Mary became Abbé
Vachon de Belmont's "little Babylon"—a fur-trading center notorious for disorder
and drunkenness.

The military insecurity of seventeenth-century New France, the isolation, physical
hardship, and constant uncertainty of life helped to maintain an atmosphere of
intense devotion and strict morality until the 1660s. Death seemed imminent, and
that expectation focused minds on the hereafter. For some, the strain was unbear-
able. Sister Marie Morin, chronicler of Montreal's hospital, described the incessant
attacks of the Iroquois as "a kind of martyrdom." In 1659 three nuns from the
Province of Anjou arrived to help Jeanne Mance run the hospital. They had set out
with an "interior disposition of [self-]sacrifice and total abandonment to all that
God might wish to do with their persons." M. le Royer de la Dauversière advised
them to think only of "their immolation, by preparing themselves spiritually to
suffer martyrdom at the hands of the Iroquois." The relentless assaults upon the
Montrealers in the early 1660s, caring for victims of raids, and the prospect of a
slow death by torture worked on the nuns' minds. When attack alarms were sounded,
one sister was struck dumb and another paralyzed with fright. They would hide
either in the chapel or in their cells until the enemy had departed.[54] True, more
people died by drowning and other accidents than by Iroquois hands, but the tor-
ments inflicted upon captives, whose mutilated bodies were then cooked and eaten,
terrified settlers.

The worst year was 1689—twenty-four settlers at Lachine, near Montreal, were
killed and more than seventy taken prisoner. Bacqueville de la Potherie evoked
those perilous times when he drew a picture of "the plowman working his land,
though armed from head to toe, trembles at each step as his plow leads to the edge
of the woods because of his fear of being killed by these barbarians or, when he turns
his oxen to cut another furrow, [knows that] one might jump upon him to take his
scalp or to lead him, a prisoner, to their land to be burned alive."[55] This inescapable
menace caused many secular immigrants to flee the colony in the 1600s. Montrealers
took revenge on four Iroquois captives in April 1696. After baptism, the four warriors were burned alive in front of the Jesuit chapel by French settlers and their
aboriginal allies. Over six hours, wrote an observer, "they suffered the tortures which
they had invented."[56]

The zealous colonists described by the Jesuit writer were diluted by the thousands of crown-assisted immigrants in the 1660s. The carelessly recruited newcomers included, according to Marie de l'Incarnation, "many rascals of both sexes, whose conduct is often very shameful. It would have been of greater benefit to this new Church to have a few good Christians rather than many people who cause us so much disturbance."[57] One of these wretches was the Protestant miller, Daniel Will. The unlettered migrants were scarcely touched by the devotional movement, and their spiritual world was a blend of religious orthodoxy and superstition. Sister Morin blamed the troops sent out by the king in 1665 and in 1683 for ending the earnest piety of early Montreal: they had "ruined the Lord's vine and established vice and sin which is almost as common [here] now [in 1697] as it is in old France."[58] Garrison soldiers had all the faults of bachelors, with little pay and idle time. Mother de Sainte-Hélène at Quebec described herself in 1733 as living "in an age, in which people are so corrupt (*ou le monde est si corrompu*)." "We live," she wrote, "in a land that becomes more hard-hearted than ever (*plus dur que jamais*); we see nothing that might please us; people only speak of miseries, bad faith, of calumnies, or court trials, and divisions, . . . I believe that God is punishing this colony for the crimes that are committed here and the good people are suffering along with the wicked."[59] Granted, the nuns were predisposed to find fault with the world outside their cloister, but these comments do reflect the widening gap between the strict morality of the clergy and the colonists' daily behavior.

The increasing security of New France may have contributed to the relaxation in lay piety. A lasting truce was made with the Iroquois Confederacy in 1701 and thirty-one years of peace after 1713 removed the threat of attack. There was no rival faith to challenge Roman Catholicism in the colony, and thus, there was no spur to maintain a militant faith. Parishioners felt free to defy clerical standards of conduct. When Ile Royale and Louisiana were settled in the early eighteenth century, their clergy lacked the crusading zeal that had animated their predecessors in seventeenth-century Canada.

In the face of lay worldliness, the clergy in the St. Lawrence Valley tried to uphold the puritanical morality of the early 1600s. In 1682 Bishop de Montmorency Laval charged that Canadian women and girls, "forgetting their baptismal vows, appear dressed and ornamented with the displays of Satan which they have so solemnly renounced . . . and that, by wishing to please men's eyes, they make themselves the captives and instruments of the demon." Women not only appeared in public dressed in this wanton fashion, said the bishop, but they also entered "our churches, appearing in places consecrated to prayer and penitence with indecent clothes, revealing a scandalous nudity of arms, shoulders, and throats (*gorges*), satisfying themselves with covering them with transparent fabric, which often only serves to give more allure to these shameful nudities, the head uncovered or only covered with a transparent headdress, and hair curled in a manner unworthy of a Christian person." Women attired in this fashion were to be denied the sacraments and forbidden "to present holy bread, to come to the offertory, and to make collections in the churches."[60] Laval's successor as bishop of Quebec, Jean de Saint-Vallier, declaimed so often against the naked arms, throats, and bosoms of women that one suspects that he, too, was being distracted by these exposed body parts.

Bishop Saint-Vallier boldly set out guidelines for the conduct of the governor-general's family as "those who hold the first rank, their example serving ordinarily as the rule for others." The vice-regal couple was advised to avoid sumptuous meals, late suppers, balls, plays, and mixed dancing. Since the youth and vivacity of their daughter demanded active recreation, Saint-Vallier felt that she might be permitted "some decent and moderate dances, only with persons of her own sex, and in the presence of Madame, her mother."[61] Clerical hostility and the small potential audience killed the theater in New France. The unsupervised mingling of the sexes in the audience, as well as the impersonation of social superiors, troubled the bishop. An attempt in 1694 to perform Molière's satire of false piety, "Le Tartuffe," confirmed Saint-Vallier's dislike for plays. He warned the colonists about their inattention and gossip during Mass and "indecent and suggestive words," as well as about the vanity and immodesty of women's clothing. In directives to the priests and in pastoral letters to the faithful, Quebec's bishops castigated colonists for their drunkenness, absences from Mass, work on holy days, usury, slanderous gossip, blasphemy, letting children above the age of puberty share their beds, adultery, fornication, and failure to pay the parish tithe, and for leaving church during sermons.[62]

Departure from church during sermons, yet *after the Mass*, indicates that people had more reverence for the service in Latin than for preaching in French. Supernatural forces were active during the Mass, and its mysterious language commanded awe and respect. Episcopal injunctions, when coupled with the royal intendants' ordinances and rulings forcing parishioners to contribute the their church's maintenance, to help in the building of rectories or the fencing of cemeteries, to abstain from labor on religious holidays, to attend Mass rather than frequenting taverns, and to contribute candles and *pain-bénit* for services, and those forbidding them to race horses to and from the church or to sell goods at the church door give the impression of widespread defiance and irreverence after the 1690s.[63] The impression may be overstated, yet there were surprising instances of disrespect in colonial churches.

An intendant's ordinance of November 1706 reported the complaint of the priest of Côte de Beaupré chapel that "two of his residents, drunk with liquor, profaned this holy place, by quarreling and by threatening each other loudly," and that other parishioners left the church during his sermons, "to amuse themselves by smoking at the doorway or around it." Intendant Jacques Raudot blamed those who served alcoholic drinks on Sundays for these disorders.[64] Prosecutions for selling liquor to colonists and Amerindians were numerous enough to bear out the official claim that this was a widespread vice. Other claims about general problems are harder to confirm. The intendants' declarations responded to specific transgressions, which were then spoken of as universal vices. In an ordinance of 22 March 1710, Raudot stated that he had been "informed that the greatest disorder comes from some young men who . . . are not restrained by their fathers and mothers, [and] often cause all the scandal, pushing their impudence to the point of smoking near the church after leaving it to avoid the instructions that are meant for them, and going about neighboring houses threatening to molest those who might report their misbehavior."[65] The impetus for this new ordinance about disrespectful conduct in church may have come from one case in Montreal, earlier that month, when six people were convicted of fighting during divine service.[66]

The people of Côte de Beaupré witnessed even more extraordinary conduct in a place of worship: in June 1729 Charles Grenier tried to bring his dog into Notre-Dame de la Miséricorde church to share his pew. The senior church warden, Pierre Parent, tried to stop him, but Grenier insisted on bringing man's best friend with him and told the warden that even the king would not stop him. During the argument, two other men—one may have been Grenier's brother—supported the dog owner, and even struck Parent in the priest's presence.[67]

Religious celebrations were social events as well as solemn moments of devotion. The Canadians frequently came to blows over their position in church or in a procession. Montreal's governor and the bishop-designate set an example by quarreling over the proximity of their prayer stools to the altar, and judicial and military officers followed suit by demanding precedence over church wardens in the presentation of paschal palms, holy bread, or the pax, and in censing or asperging with holy water. Personal reputation became more important than the object of the ceremony.

There was a paradox: popular resistance to the clergy's material and moral demands occurred while observers testified to the Canadians' devout recitation of prayers. The colonists made a distinction between the faith, which they valued, and the church's human representatives, whom they sometimes defied. This distinction may be due, in part, to the shrinking social distance between priests and the general population. As the Quebec Seminary trained more colonial-born men for the priesthood, the faithful found themselves dealing with one of their own, a person whose background was known—possibly the son of another farmer. According to Cornelius Jaenen, "by 1760 . . . over 80 percent of the parishes and missions in the colony were ministered to by Canadian-born curates."[68] There was physical proximity as well as social affinity. The rarity of priests' residences forced many priests to board in private homes, exposing them to worldly ways. Most clerics behaved with propriety, but in the 1700s we encounter a few bawdy curates whose conduct would have been unimaginable in the previous century.

In 1730 Father Gervais Lefèbvre at Batiscan was accused by Madame de la Pérade, the seigneur's fifty-two-year-old wife, of scandalous conduct and of publicly reciting an obscene litany which defamed her. The accused, it was said, chanted the litany in the company of a priest from a neighboring parish when they were in a canoe with a witness present. Madame de la Pérade complained to the coadjutor bishop in March, and Father Lefèbvre responded with a civil suit against her for malicious defamation. In church a litany sought favors from God and the saints, usually deliverance from a list of sorrows. In this burlesque, the suggestive supplications were addressed to the *seigneuresse*, who is likened to a lecherous cow, willing to be mounted by a variety of males. The local notary recorded Lefèbvre's half-Latin litany as

> *Sancte la grande vache rouge, ora {pro nobis}*
> *Sancte Mme avec ses petites citrouilles, ora . . . ,*
> *Sancte Sacrebleu, iras-tu panser les vaches, ora*
> *Sancte Tourangeux foutu bougre ira tu voir si le moulin tourne, ora*
> *Sancte le bonnet a Boilleu soubs le chevet a Mde la Perade, ora . . .*

> *Holy big red cow, pray {for us},*
> *Holy Madame with her little pumpkins pray {for us} . . . ,*
> *Holy Heaven, will you go to rub down the cows?, pray {for us},*
> *Holy Tourangeux, the lecherous bugger will go to see you*
> *To see if the mill turns, pray {for us},*
> *Holy Boilleu's cap under the bolster of Madame de la Pérade's bed, Pray {for us} . . .*

"Tourangeux" could be "taure en jeu," or playful heifer—another unflattering allusion to the bovine lady. The grinding mill might be a double entendre for Madame de la Pérade's defective gristmill, which her tenants boycotted, and for a body's circular motion in copulation.

Witnesses summoned by both litigants contradicted one another, and their credentials were impugned in turn. Daniel Portail, sieur de Gevron, testifed that the priest was drinking wine with some of his parishioners in his residence when he told one that "if I had a little wife like yours, I would kiss her between the legs." Father Lefèbvre allegedly described the bishop of Quebec as "long tail," and boasted that he was "the great cod-piece (*la Grande Braguette*)" and hoisted up his cassock to substantiate his claim. In riposte, it was pointed out that Portail had been exiled to Canada under a *lettre de cachet* and, therefore, he was not a credible witness. Another who testified for Madame de la Pérade had fought with the priest when, two years before, the witness had attempted to marry *à la gaumine*. From the confusion of accusations and counterclaims, nothing seems certain save that Father Lefèbvre, although not the originator of the litany, had certainly behaved indiscreetly for a priest. The conflict was settled out of court in 1733 and Gervais Lefèbvre retained his curacy.[69] Bénin Le Dorz, the Récollet Franciscan superior at Louisbourg, was recalled to France in 1727 for habitual drunkenness and for neglecting canonical rules when performing marriages.[70]

The colonists' attachment to prayers, the sacraments, and religious rituals survived the loosening of ecclesiastical discipline in the eighteenth century. An extraordinary tale of devotion to Roman Catholicism is contained in the registers of Quebec's Hôtel-Dieu hospital. In August 1717 the registers noted the death of Georges Mabile, aged thirty-seven, born in St. Malo, France, and a resident of Plaisance, Newfoundland. He had stayed at Plaisance after French claims to Newfoundland were surrendered in 1713 and most French colonists had departed. Mabile came to regret the loss of a priest's ministrations and, though not trained as a carpenter, he built his own boat and sailed for Canada, leaving behind his unsold property. He arrived at Quebec six weeks later and was brought, in a weak state, to the hospital. There he died, as the chronicler noted, "very thankful for the great grace God had shown him in plucking him out of a heretical country and in granting him the succor of our mother, the Holy Church."[71]

Blasphemy cases before the courts can demonstrate both the power of orthodox religion and the weakness of ecclesiastical authority. On the one hand, the profane use of the names of holy objects or persons violates God's seventh commandment and is a sin against the church. On the other hand, the oath would not be powerful if it did not violate religious taboos. The swearer acknowledges the magical power of sacred things when he names them in a moment of strong emotion. Blasphemy was made a criminal offense by the king's ordinance of July 1666, which set fines and corporal punishments for offenders. Article 36 of the public order regulations issued by Quebec's Sovereign Council and the intendant on 11 May 1676 prescribed penalties for those who misused "the holy name of God" or spoke disrespectfully of "the most sacred Virgin, his mother, or of the saints."[72] In the court records, we rarely get the exact words used: the recording clerk usually noted the crime as "blasphemies and oaths against the holy name and honor of God."[73]

The ambivalence of blasphemers is evident in the 1679 case of Charles Catignon, keeper of the king's storehouse at Quebec. He was charged with "having said that

'God is not God.'" In fact, Catignon was reproaching the Almighty for his financial losses and then, upon reflection, he begged God's pardon for his intemperate words.[74] Clearly, he was not denying the existence of God, he was just questioning the divinity's wisdom and mercy toward him. Judicial indifference to blasphemy in the eighteenth century, unless it were combined with another crime against a person or property, reflected the secularization of values at the top of society. Among the lower ranks there remained a fearful reverence for holy objects. The French-Canadian armory of popular expletives is still dominated by references to sacred things: *calice* (chalice), *saint-ciboire* (holy pyx), *tabernacle, hostie* (blessed wafer), and so on. That vocabulary expresses the population's former awe for the articles of the Mass. Naming them broke the taboos of a devoutly Roman Catholic people, whereas English-speakers, when cursing, seem preoccupied with illicit sexual acts and excrement.

The evolution in the religious climate of *la Nouvelle France* is summed up in three successive portraits of nuns. The first is Father Hugues Pommier's postmortem painting of the ascetic *hospitalière* Marie-Catherine de Saint-Augustin. This portrait was painted in 1668, with her corpse as the artist's model, because she refused to sit for a portrait while she lived. A picture of one's physical self was held to be a vanity and it showed a concern for the material world, which Marie-Catherine had renounced. Those who knew and revered her, however, wanted a representation of her face. The artist and later restorers did their best to enliven their dead subject by opening her eyes and by rouging the greenish palor of her lifeless cheeks. The painters were not to blame if the picture is a wooden likeness of a stereotypical saintly woman, embracing a crucifix and gazing heavenward. In this portrait,

Left to right: The portraits of Sister Marie-Catherine de St. Augustin (1668), Mother Juchereau de St. Ignace (c. 1684), and Mother Thérèse-Geneviève Coutlée (c. 1805) sum up the evolution of French Canada's religious climate.

Father Pommier captured the puritanical zeal of New France's clergy and nuns in the first half of the seventeenth century, as well as depicting a self-abasing visionary.

The portrait of a later, Canadian-born *hospitalière,* Mother Jeanne-Françoise Juchereau de Saint-Ignace (1650–1723), was painted in about 1684 and is attributed to the artist-priest Jean Guyon. It shows the changed intellectual and moral climate of the colony in the late 1600s. She was the daughter of a merchant, seigneur, and member of the Sovereign Council.[75] Her face is that of a charitable and practical Christian. Mother de Saint-Ignace was not an otherworldly mystic who refused to permit a representation of her physical appearance. With her cooperation, the artist recorded her compassionate nature with the hint of a smile. The subject's eyes are not fixed on Heaven; they look out to the human world. She, it is said, was primarily concerned with the care of the sick and with the prudent administration of her hospital.[76]

The last of these three portraits probably comes from the 1790s, after the British conquest of New France. The Roman Catholic Church in Canada then was dependent upon the goodwill of the British governors-general, and its authority among the French-Canadian laity had weakened. Louis Dulongpré, the artist, has shown this member of Montreal's Grey Nuns, Sisters of Charity, engaged in the homely task of embroidering a priest's stole, not clutching a crucifix or some other symbol of her religious vocation. Mother Thérèse-Geneviève Coutlée (1742–1821) appears to be an amiable, earthy woman. Her jowls indicate that denial of the flesh was not one of her virtues. This picture is a measure of how far French Canada's religious climate had evolved from the self-sacrificing asceticism of the mid-seventeenth century. That age of rigorous piety, however, remained an example to which Roman

Catholic preachers and teachers could point as a model for later generations of French-speaking Canadians.

The religious faith of the colonists and their conviction that God would not abandon his people in New France helped sustain them in the French and Indian War (1754–60)—the conflict that shattered the French colony. In June 1757 Monsieur Meynardie at Quebec wrote to a business associate in Montreal, "all the news assure us that Louisbourg must be besieged, but God will always be for us and, I hope, will cause our enemy's plans to fail."[77] The author then escaped to France with others. French victories revived hope that divine intervention might yet save France's empire. How could Heaven permit the Protestant heretics to triumph? Anxiety was not stilled: "if God does not lend a hand promptly, I do not know what shall become of us."[78]

With Louisbourg's capture—for a second time—in 1758, recriminations began and hope fled. It was said that the French government had been too parsimonious, that the navy was too weak, or that treachery had given victory to the enemy. From the safety of La Rochelle, François Havy wrote to his former associates in endangered Canada, "for want of good regulation (*police*) and by continual changes that were made in the navy [ministry] , money—that great animator and essential nerve (*nerf*) of war and of things was lacking. May God give you better days and preserve you and all of poor Canada and, especially, its brave and poor (*pauvre*) people."[79] In August 1760 Louis Perrault told his brother of the military retreat from Trois-Rivières, as British forces pressed in toward Montreal, the last town in French hands: "thus you see that we will soon be English . . . it is not our fault."[80] When Montreal capitulated in 1760, there was consternation and incredulity. Mother Marie-Marguerite d'Youville, of that town's hospice, wrote, with puzzled resignation, "we had flattered ourselves that France would not abandon us, but we were wrong in our expectation. God permitted it so. May his holy name be praised."[81]

"The Apples Do Not Fall Far from the Tree": The Legacy of New France in Modern Canada

IT MAY SEEM LIKE A LONG STRETCH TO LINK THE MODERN FRENCH-SPEAKING Canadians with a colony that was absorbed by the British Empire in the 1760s. There are, however, traces of *la Nouvelle France* that have endured into the twentieth century, and their survival attests to the social conservatism of the European emigrants who settled in French North America. Most white newcomers before 1760 were single men who did not intend to make a home in the New World. Their sojourn overseas as soldiers or contract workers was a temporary exile to escape unemployment and hunger at home; it was not meant to be the prelude to permanent settlement abroad. The men, even the soldiers, were mostly urban craftsmen who knew little about their destination, and they embarked, trembling at the hazards, real and imagined, that awaited them. New France had a terrible reputation. One intendant wrote in the 1680s that "Canada has always been regarded as a country at the end of the world, and as a [place of] exile that might almost pass for a sentence of civil death, and also as a refuge sought only by numerous wretches until now to escape from [the consequences of] their crimes."[1]

Most migrants, both men and women, came as dependents whose passage across the Atlantic Ocean was paid by others. Religious dissenters and political rebels were to be screened out. The educated wastrels who were transported to the colony at their families' request did not remain in it for long. In New France, the newcomers were quartered in colonists' homes for three or more years, which helped them adjust to their new setting. After the 1670s, the minority who stayed married women from established families, which completed their absorption into the new society. The fusion of people from France's western provinces, from the Paris region, and from foreign countries and colonies was rapid. By 1700, Acadians and Canadians were well-defined colonial types with distinctive traits. The very mixed origins of the original settlers were forgotten and nineteenth-century *Canadiens* would boast of the purity of their French ancestry in contrast to the mongrel races that surrounded them.[2] Later immigrants to Quebec were expected to assimilate into the established culture and to adopt the same religious faith, if they were not already Roman Catholics. That assumption, minus the religious requirement, is implicit in the Province of Quebec's requirement that children of foreign immigrants must enroll in French-language schools.

Latecomers had a modest impact upon the Franco-Canadian identity, although, thanks to nineteenth-century Irish immigrants, there are strong Celtic elements in French-Canadian folklore. The jig and reel were generally accepted as the *gigue* and *rille*, which are now "traditional" French-Canadian country dances. By contrast, other areas of Canada depended on a never-ending and increasingly diverse flow of immigrants for growth. These newer settlements always included a high proportion of newcomers, who came with families and formed ethnic subcommunities that remained culturally distinct. Multiculturalism, even before it received the Canadian federal government's blessing in the 1970s, has long been a fact of life in the provinces west of Quebec.

Many Italian and Irish immigrants to Quebec after 1760 met the expectation that they would assimilate to the majority's culture. Amerindian converts to Christianity during the French Regime were supposed to do the same, and the Hurons of Lorette took this route. Descendants of the Iroquois converts who settled in the St. Lawrence Valley were resented because, despite being Roman Catholics, they became English-speakers. That choice was encouraged by their work as steel-frame construction workers in the adjacent state of New York. Franco-Quebeckers' frustration with their Iroquois neighbors exploded in 1990, after a native blockade of the Mercier Bridge to support another band's claim. White Quebeckers stoned cars carrying aboriginal families out of the Kahnawaké reserve at the bridge's south end.

The religious and ideological conformity of New France had various consequences. Unity of faith and the settlers' conservatism produced a coherent society in which fidelity to the dominant belief system was a social virtue. That cohesion was reinforced by later historical experiences. Defensiveness, aroused by restrictions on publicly funded French-language education outside Quebec in 1870–1920, demanded a unified response to meet the challenge. Deviants, such as the abstract artist Paul-Emile Borduas, who had rejected the conservative Catholic nationalism of the 1940s, went into exile.

Historians know that cultural continuity is maintained by transference or substitution and that what appears to be a break with the past is usually the displacement of one creed by a similar belief system. In Quebec ethnic nationalism has taken the place of religion. In "the Quiet Revolution" of the 1960s, Quebec's government assumed the Roman Catholic Church's role as guardian and promoter of French-speaking culture. For politicians of the only province with a French-speaking majority, this seemed to be a natural role. Because French Canada extended beyond the frontiers of Quebec, the provincial government could not claim to be the national government of all French Canadians. The Acadians of the Atlantic provinces would not accept such an assertion of power by Quebec's government. The pan-Canadian identity of French-speakers was an impediment to the assertion of Quebec's special status. In the late 1960s the Québécois nation was "discovered," which justified the Quebec government's claim to the rank of a "national"—not provincial—government within Canada.[3] Since then, Quebec has been redefined by its politicians as a nation-state, and the provincial legislature has become a "national assembly."

With the secularization of social values and the disappearance of visible distinctions that set French Canadians apart from other North Americans, language has become the key distinguishing characteristic and the focus of nationalist concern. Solidarity is still enjoined, not out of religious fidelity, but out of loyalty to a language group that feels it is besieged by an English-speaking world. It is a cliché of Quebec nationalists to describe their province as a French-speaking island in an Anglo-Saxon sea. They, however, enjoy swimming in that sea. The American entertainment industry and fashions from the United States have made inroads into Quebec, as they have elsewhere in the world. Quebeckers surpass other Canadians as consumers of "Big Mac" hamburgers—translated as "Gros Mac"—at McDonald's restaurants.

The customary French-Canadian emphasis on group solidarity and collective rights has been attributed to a defensive mentality awakened by assimilationist pressures; it is, however, a natural development from the religious, governmental, and legal heritage of New France, which placed family obligations above personal interests. Individualism in the colony meant family autonomy rather than personal individualism. The strong familial ethos is evident in the apartments built in Quebec's cities in 1890–1930; these buildings are really single-family dwellings stacked one on top of another—up to three floors, each with its own exterior staircase to the street below, its own entranceway, and a separate verandah. Despite the advantages for heat conservation and economy, a shared, internal stairwell and a common entrance for all of the resident families did not appeal to French-speakers. The interior distribution of space, as well, left little scope for the personal privacy that British-Canadians prized. As in the houses of New France, there might be a small entrance vestibule, but to get to the back of the residence, one passed through several rooms.[4] These buildings are a visible statement of French-Canadian social values in the early twentieth century.

Family solidarity has been an outstanding trait of French-Canadians: in 1954–55, when Philippe Garigue interviewed fifty-two Montrealers, he found that, on average, each informant knew of 215 relatives and could trace the family's lineage beyond three generations. "While awareness of descent and pride in the history of the family name is shown by the majority of informants, frequency of contact is highest between members of the same generation" with the same social status. One man saw 40 to 45 relatives every month, and kin were preferred by all when seeking professional services or personal advice, buying goods, hiring an employee, or finding a business partner.[5] The same preference for relatives and for functioning within a kinship network was evident in eighteenth-century New France.

French-speakers have long regarded insistence on individual freedom of action and independent self-expression as an Anglo-Saxon peculiarity. During the 1745 siege of Louisbourg, a town resident marveled at the lack of coordination between the two enemy commanders and commented, "only the English are capable of such oddities, which nevertheless form a part of that precious liberty of which they show themselves so jealous."[6] Among French colonists, family interests took precedence over individual rights and the *père de famille* defined those interests. The patriarchal family, which was blessed by the Roman Catholic Church and upheld by Quebec's civil law until the 1960s, meant that, even after the establishment of an elected, legislative assembly for Lower Canada (part of the Old Province of Quebec) in 1792, French-speaking voters were still drawn to authoritarian father figures who promised to protect and rule their people as a good father would do. Maurice Duplessis, a Quebec provincial premier who died in 1959, embodied the patriarchal tradition in Quebec politics. The Quebec Civil Code described the father and husband as the "chef de famille," and Duplessis was nicknamed "le chef."

The way in which elected, representative government came to French Canadians explains the historic deference to one man's leadership, despite democratic political structures. The division of the Old Province of Quebec in 1791 and the introduction of an elective assembly had come about because newly arrived American Loyalist refugees and British merchants in the province had insisted on representative government as the birthright of every British subject; it was not done in deference to the French-speaking population. Most educated *Canadiens* at the time distrusted elected legislatures as instruments of taxation and opposed the creation of a house of assembly.[7] Representative government was imposed on the French Canadians, despite their opposition to it.

Authoritarianism was always tempered by compassion, even two centuries after the end of the French Regime. The humane aspect of paternalism was evident in the attitudes of French-Canadian entrepreneurs interviewed by Norman W. Taylor in the 1950s. They valued long-serving employees and were reluctant to fire an inefficient worker whose family depended upon his earnings. One manufacturer said, "my manager is inept, but he has been with us for a long time; he was hired by my father. So what can I do?" The *patron,* or boss, had an obligation to old employees that overrode an objective appreciation of their value to the business.

Taylor's French-Canadian entrepreneurs displayed the same preoccupation with family independence and security shown by craftsmen and by Roman Catholic merchants in New France. These twentieth-century businessmen refused equity capital from outsiders because it meant a loss of control over their enterprise, and they were unwilling to borrow money from banks for expansion. In most cases, they had no desire to expand their enterprise if it meant bringing non-family members into the company's management and losing a personal relationship with the workers or direct supervision over all operations. "I don't like to owe money, I wouldn't consider a partnership or anything like that, I want to run my business myself," said a furniture manufacturer. These attitudes in the 1950s limited the size of French-Canadian firms; if the business were providing family members with jobs and a good living, that was enough. Expansion of the family business or a new line of goods carried risks. Compared with English-speaking businessmen, French-speakers were more concerned with enjoying life than with getting rich. Extra profits were put into government bonds and into real estate—the safest investments possible.[8] Family autarky and material security were then as important as they had been for farmers and artisans in *la Nouvelle France.*

During "the Quiet Revolution" of the 1960s the Quebec provincial government took over education and social welfare from the Roman Catholic Church. The creation of a provincial department of education in 1964 was the first step in taking French-language instruction out of the clergy's hands. Hospitals and asylums—traditionally an ecclesiastical domain—became the responsibility of Quebec's government. A Ministry of Cultural Affairs was also established. While assuming many of the church's functions, the state acquired some of the attitudes of an ecclesiastical establishment. The church was an authoritarian institution whose leaders expected to provide intellectual and moral guidance for the population. Populism—belief that political representatives should be guided by their constituents and faith in the wisdom of the common man—is not a part of French Canada's political tradition. The educated elite knows what is necessary for the public good, without having to consult the people. The old aristocracy of seigneurs and military officers has long since been displaced by elected politicians, of humbler origins, trained in the law. Commercial and technical expertise is now valued in the government bureaucracy, yet there remains a paternal condescension toward the general population. In the late 1960s I saw provincial civil servants being given a bulletin called *Mieux Dire,* which, with text and diagrams, showed them how to *properly* enunciate French words. I could not imagine a provincial or state government elsewhere trying to regulate how its employees pronounced words.

The population, then and sometimes now, was not organized to effectively challenge paternalistic leadership and its respect for authority is strong.[9] The French colonial government's hostility to self-constituted groups among the lowest social ranks, and the colonists' pursuit of family independence and material self-sufficiency, hindered voluntary cooperation with strangers. Family networks provided the associates one needed. France's communal traditions were not transplanted to the St. Lawrence Valley. Only in Acadia was there a form of village self-government provided by elders, and that exception was due to the French government's indifference to what happened in Acadia. The collective building of dikes to reclaim tidal marshes for cultivation and the maintenance of the embankments also encouraged interfamily cooperation among the Acadians. In nineteenth-century Ontario, friends and neighbors came together in "bees" to erect the massive, timber framework of a neighbor's barn or for some other major task. The helpers were rewarded with food and drinks and the beneficiary of one "bee" was expected to render the same service to others. Baptists, Presbyterians, and other Protestants organized and administered their own congregations; they hired and dismissed their ministers. If a school were needed, the local people would create one. Such spontaneous, self-organized cooperation with other families was rare in French Canada, apart from community dances.[10] In small, French-speaking settlements throughout Canada, the priest provided social leadership and the parish provided the institutional framework for community life. It was not a framework that the people created for themselves and it was always subject to external authority. The genesis of this pattern could be seen in eighteenth-century New France.

The unique cohesion of the estate-owning gentry of *la Nouvelle France* gave this group an advantage in the postconquest era. About 1,600 people left New France as a result of the defeat. The civil administrators, many wholesale merchants, and serving military officers departed with the French troops in the 1760s. Their fortunes were tied to the French empire, and the British empire's administration offered no employment to Roman Catholics, just as Protestants and Jews had been excluded from all public offices during the French Regime. The remainder of the elite, which had stayed in Canada, banded together to win the patronage of King

George III, their new sovereign. The state church, however, was now the Protestant Church of England, and British oaths of office required the candidate to disavow the Roman Catholic faith and to swear fidelity to the Protestant monarchs of the royal House of Hanover. The oaths' intent was to detect and exclude Roman Catholics who might support the Stuart pretenders to Great Britain's throne. Without government appointments and military commissions, Canada's gentry were reduced to the role of seigneurs, formerly an incidental role for the privileged leaders of society. For a group accustomed to enjoying the benefits of royal patronage, this was a distressing situation.

The British crown accepted collective petitions from all ranks of society. Just as they had made individual appeals to the French monarch on behalf of family members, the remaining Canadian gentlemen were quick to present addresses to the throne seeking readmission to government positions, financial rewards, and other concessions. In 1767 the Montreal region's seigneurs begged, "that all the subjects in this province [of Quebec], without any Distinction of Religion, may be admitted to any Office, the only basis of selection being that of capacity and personal merit. To be excluded by the State from participating in it, is not to be a member of the state."[11] This was not a plea for popular participation in government; it was a request for patronage appointments.

A 1770 petition to George III from "the Canadians of your Province of Quebec," both seigneurs and educated townsmen, repeated the appeal for admitting Roman Catholics to public offices and for a restoration of French laws and regulations, "the Basis and Foundation of their possessions, and . . . the rule of their families." They noted "how humiliating it had been to them to be excluded from the offices which they might fill in this Province, for the Service of Your Majesty, and the Comfort of Your Canadian People. . . . Could the religion we profess, Sire, . . . be a reason . . . for excluding a number of Your submissive and faithful Children from participation in the favors of the best of Kings, of the tenderest of fathers?"[12] The obsequiousness, the appeal to a paternal monarch, and the piteous wish for positions of profit and honor came naturally to a class nurtured on royal patronage under the Bourbons.

This address was entrusted to Sir Guy Carleton, the governor-general of Quebec, when he returned to England to make the case before a parliamentary committee for adapting the government and laws of the province to the traditions of the *Canadiens*. Like other British newcomers, Carleton mistook the seigneurs for a landed aristocracy—people of his own class—and called them "the Noblesse of Canada." British officers, such as Carleton, also admired the Canadians' martial valor and treated them as social equals. Naturally, the Canadian seigneurs were not going to correct the British officials' belief that the landlords were the aristocracy of the colony. Language was not an issue, and educated Europeans, like the British officers, conversed easily in French, then regarded as the language of high culture and intellectual discourse. There was no government plan to impose English on the conquered population before the 1790s. Language was not a political issue, strange as it might seem to the current generation of Canadians. One's religious faith, however, was another matter.

Religion was an impediment to public appointments because it had been the key to political loyalties in Europe since the sixteenth century. Just as the French army defending New France had contained English-speaking Roman Catholics, like James Johnstone, the British forces of occupation included Protestant French-speakers, both Huguenot and Swiss, such as Frederick Haldimand, a future governor-general of Quebec. Nonetheless, the British permitted Monsignor Jean-Olivier Briand to go to France in 1766 to be consecrated bishop of Quebec by French Roman Catholic archbishops. Briand provided a head for the Canadian church, which had been without a bishop for six years, and, with episcopal power to ordain priests, he ensured the continuation of the church. Thus did a major institution of the French regime, with educational and charitable functions, survive the change of rulers. By reassuring the Roman Catholic clergy and by conciliating the seigneurs, Sir Guy Carleton hoped to win the fidelity of the entire population of Canada. He assumed that the gentlemen-landowners commanded the obedience of their tenant-farmers and that the priests could also determine the Canadians' political allegiance.[13]

With the formal transfer of New France to Great Britain in 1763, the disappearance of French legal traditions seemed certain. British government policy assumed that a British territory ought to have English legal and political institutions, like those in the other British North American colonies. The Royal Proclamation of 7 October 1763 authorized the introduction of "the Laws of our Realm of England" by courts "hearing and determining all Causes, as well Criminal as civil."[14] Soon, that policy was compromised and then abandoned in favor of perpetuating the *Coutume de Paris,* which was familiar to the French-Canadian majority in Quebec. In 1767 Sir Guy Carleton complained to his superiors about the confusion and "chicanery" that had resulted from the mixture of French and English legal practices. His solution was to revoke the 1763 proclamation, "and for the present leave the Canadian laws almost entire," or to prepare an amended version of these laws "as a Canadian Code."[15] At Carleton's request, François-Joseph Cugnet compiled *An Abstract of Those Parts of the Custom of the Viscounty and provostship of Paris, which were received and practised . . . in the time of French Government,* which, after further revision, was published in London in 1772. The seigneurs' property rights and prerogatives were embodied in that legal code; without it, they could not exist as a privileged class.

The British government had been moving toward the compromise of retaining

English criminal justice while sanctioning continuation of French civil law in those areas most dear to the Canadians: property ownership, inheritance, matrimonial rights, and paternal authority. In 1766 the Rockingham government accepted this compromise in principle, and Solicitor-General Alexander Wedderburn's 1773 report provided the outline for the 1774 Quebec Act. Recent research has found no evidence to support the American revolutionaries' claim that the Quebec Act was passed to refashion the northern province into a model for ruling the rest of British North America and to make Quebec into a base for punishing mutinous colonists in the other territories.[16]

The 1774 Quebec Act, as passed by the British parliament, provided a new oath of office, inoffensive to Roman Catholics, and recognized the validity of French civil law, seigneurial land tenure, and the tithe collected by the Roman Catholic Church. Given the strong religious prejudices of the day, these provisions and the reaffirmation of the Canadians' right to freedom of worship, were remarkably liberal. Catholic emancipation from legal disabilities occurred in Canada fifty-five years before it was granted in Great Britain. The 1774 act stated that "in all Matters of Controversy, relative to Property and Civil Rights, Resort shall be had to the Laws of Canada, as the Rule for the Decision of the same."[17] Sir Guy Carleton, who imagined that the customary laws of Paris had "established subordination, from the first to the lowest, which preserved the internal harmony they [the Canadians] enjoyed until our arrival," took this concession as a license to restore the entire body of French civil usages, including those affecting commerce—an area where English law was to have been admitted. In this way, the British government's humane pragmatism combined with one governor's naïve enthusiasm for the French Regime to bring about a continuation of French civil law in the Old Province of Quebec and in its successor, the modern Province of Quebec.

Half of the twenty men appointed in January 1775 to the Governor's Council—an advisory *and legislative* body in the absence of an assembly—were French-speakers. Eight came from the old military-administrative elite of landowners.[18] When rebellious American colonists invaded Quebec in 1775, Carleton distributed military officers' commissions to the seigneurs, on the mistaken assumption that leadership of their tenants in war was one of their customary functions. The Canadian seigneurs gladly accepted this role because being an officer was the traditional role of a French noble. Despite the bishop of Quebec's call to enroll in the militia to defend the colony, most rural folk resisted military service and rejected their landlords' military leadership. Some handed their seigneurs over to the invading Continental Army. Carleton and other British administrators were astounded by this conduct; they had expected loyal gratitude for the Quebec Act. The presumed social leaders of French Canada were shown to have little influence over the rest of population, and, once a legislative assembly was established in the 1790s, elections allowed political leadership to pass to men of humbler origins. Although discredited as the natural leaders of French Canada, the seigneurial families continued to be favored in governmental and judicial appointments. They reciprocated with active loyalty to the British crown in war and during the *Patriote* rebellions of 1837–38 in Lower Canada.

The British government's willingness to compromise on the principle that a British colony should have English Common Law assisted the survival of French-Canadian culture, yet that very flexibility perpetuated the divergent intellectual traditions of the two language groups and increased the chances for later, mutual incomprehension. Educated *Canadiens* retained the bias for deductive reasoning that would distinguish them from the English-speaking newcomers. The 1791 severance of the Old Province of Quebec into Lower Canada, based on the St. Lawrence Valley, where most French-speakers resided, and Upper Canada, the principal destination for immigrants from outside the colony, created a political unit that was and would remain the home of a Roman Catholic, French-speaking majority. The division of the old province had been undertaken to appease the American Loyalists concentrated in the western region, who wanted freehold land tenure, Common Law, and representative government. Once that fast-growing area had been severed from the eastern portion, called Lower Canada, it was possible to maintain the legacy of the Quebec Act. The seigneurial system, embodied in the civil laws, survived in Lower Canada until 1854, far longer than the same landholding system in France. Despite reorganization and amplification in 1866, the civil law of the new Province of Quebec (created in 1867) retained principles and values from the French regime: contracts could not offend "good morals," articles 173–84 and 242–45 upheld the patriarchal family, and divorce was not recognized. In domestic matters, in its social conservatism and in its support for Roman Catholic morality, the Civil Code perpetuated the legacy of *la Nouvelle France.*

In the years after 1774, the civil code and church-run schools perpetuated a cultural preference for argument from abstract principles and, by corollary, a distrust of pragmatism. Louis-Joseph Papineau, as speaker of the Lower Canadian House of Assembly, became leader of the majority party in the early nineteenth century. He was a rigid man of principle who scorned all compromise. Historian Fernand Ouellet treated Papineau's inflexibility as a temperamental peculiarity.[19] This disposition, however, would have been reinforced by his training in a church-run college at Montreal and at the Quebec Seminary, as well as by his apprenticeship in French civil law. Law offices and Roman Catholic classical colleges have, for generations, been the training ground for French-Canadian politicians, from Papineau to Premier Lucien Bouchard of Quebec.

The course of the liberal-democratic rebellions against British imperial authority in Lower Canada during the 1830s revealed another legacy of New France. The inexperience of the *Canadiens* with voluntary self-organization resulted in confusion, indecisiveness, and a reliance on outsiders for military leadership.[20] French-speaking *Patriotes* preached democracy, republicanism, and cultural nationalism in fiery speeches. Having led their followers to the threshold of insurrection with verbal fireworks and a strategy of unyielding confrontation, the political leaders faltered. The principal *chef,* Louis-Joseph Papineau, who had served during the War of 1812, fled to the United States when the fighting began. Rank-and-file *Patriotes* fought under the leadership of a Swiss, an Irishman, and British and American immigrants. Only three commanders, Bonaventure Viger, Dr. Cyrille Côté, and Dr. Olivier Chenier, were French Canadians. The *Canadiens* produced few dynamic military leaders and were inclined to remain passively on the defensive rather than seize the initiative in combat—a fatal strategy. Their strongholds were reduced one by one by British troops and the loyal militia.

Their dependence on outsiders for leadership is surprising in what was, reputedly, a French-Canadian nationalist uprising, unless we consider French Canada's past. Some of the timidity and disorder can be blamed on the rebels' unfamiliarity with warfare and their inferior weapons, yet to these factors one must add the loss of a tradition of self-organization, resulting from the decline of popularly constituted organizations and communal traditions in New France. Rural *Patriotes* tried to take control of existing, local institutions created by outside authority, such as the parish or the militia companies, rather than create alternative institutions.[21] In the later development of Quebec's secular trade unions, Irish immigrants and English-speakers were often the principal initiators of workers' organizations. The French-speaking clergy organized tame Catholic workers' associations to counteract the appeal of the international unions.

The defeat of the anticlerical *Patriotes* and the rarity of voluntary associations among French-speakers explains the ease with which the Roman Catholic clergy assumed the social leadership of French Canada after the rebellions. Priests were free to define French-Canadian identity, and politicians deferred to their cultural leadership. The clergy's conservative, Roman Catholic version of nationalism dominated in French-speaking Canada until the 1950s. In school texts New France was recast as a missionary colony whose saintly colonists were models for the current generation. The young were told that they belonged to a heroic and apostolic race, whose duty was to remain faithful to the traditions of their devout ancestors. The life of a farmer, after a religious vocation, was held to be the most moral of occupations and one suited to the spiritual nature of the French Canadians. When the surplus rural population started to migrate to cities and even to New England in search of industrial work, the church and province created colonization programs to resettle these people on the land within Quebec. Clerical belief in the agrarian vocation of the French Canadians meant that church-run schools provided very little preparation for careers in commerce and the sciences.

The puritanical Catholicism of the seventeenth century was also extolled. The successful revival of Counter-Reformation asceticism may be measured by the absence of the naked human body in paintings exhibited by French-Canadian artists before Joseph Franchère's *Sylphide* (c.1916). A voluptuous nude, such as *A Venetian Bather,* painted by Paul Peel of London, Ontario, and acquired by the National Gallery of Canada in 1895, would have shocked French-Canadian viewers. There was not much of the legendary Gallic joie de vivre in French Canada from 1840 to 1945. Rather, the religious atmosphere was one of repression, guilt, and shame.

The providential view of human affairs held by the faithful did not offer much optimism. In a divinely regulated universe, human action counted for little. The fatalism of the lower classes was summed up in the French-Canadian proverb "celui qui est né pour un petit pain, n'en aura un gros (whoever is born for a small loaf of bread, will never have a big one)." The socially conservative ideology propagated by the clergy was not seriously challenged. In Canadian provinces outside Quebec, the dominance of parish institutions, including schools and credit unions, in French-speaking communities ensured their survival, at a price. The church, however, was more concerned with preserving Roman Catholics than with maintaining the French language, and when insistence on French instruction imperiled public funding of parochial schools then language might be sacrificed. With the secularization of social values, there was an urgent need to find lay leaders to take over the priests' role as community spokesmen and to establish cultural institutions and schools outside the parish framework. For a population inexperienced with self-constituted, secular associations, that was a challenge. The evidence that spontaneous self-organization still does not come easily to many French-speakers is that peculiarly Québécois institution: the *animateur sociale*. An appointed social initiator is required to coordinate and activate social groups. Among English-speakers, an "animator" is someone who makes live-action cartoons.

The patriarchy upheld by French Canada's legal and religious traditions has had a long history. Even the republican *Patriotes* could not conceive of an active political role for women. What helped to discredit the British monarchy in their eyes was the 1837 accession of Victoria as monarch of Great Britain. It was considered unnatural for a young woman to exercise political authority.[22] That bias was consistent with the law: the married man exercised paternal authority (*la puissance paternelle*) over his dependents. Article 174 of Quebec's 1866 Civil Code stated, "a husband owes protection to his wife; a wife obedience to her husband." The words may have been borrowed from France's *Code Napoléon* (1804), but the sentiment was identical in the *Coutume de Paris,* which made husbands the sole lords and governors of a couple's joint property and deprived wives of financial independence. Not until 1931 were married women in Quebec given legal control of their pay and of any purchases made with those earnings. Wives were not granted complete legal equality until 1964. Quebec's women had obtained the right to vote in provincial elections in 1940—being the last women in Canada to receive the provincial suffrage. The word "receive" is used advisedly. Female suffrage had been achieved nationally in 1918, largely at the instigation of English-speaking feminists. Most French-speaking women were indifferent to the cause of female suffrage, and the Roman Catholic clergy was hostile to the movement. The senior clergy in Quebec resisted the legal and political emancipation of daughters and married women because, according to Monsignor Louis-Adolphe Paquet, it would destroy masculine authority and repudiate the natural inequality of the sexes.[23] Since the 1960s the tendency of French-Canadian men to mistake virility for virtue has faded.

The masculine bias of the civil law and church doctrine was counterbalanced by a compassion for the weak. Roman Catholic teachings about the need for forgiveness and for charity gave a humane aspect to French-Canadian culture. New France was ahead of the British colonies in providing assistance and shelter to the unfortunate, and, starting with the foundation of Quebec's hospital in 1639, religious orders provided these services. In the nineteenth and twentieth centuries a separate, parallel system of schools and hospitals developed in Quebec for Protestants and Jews. After the 1950s social welfare provided by church-run institutions, organized on a diocesan basis, was replaced by a province-wide, government-run system of health care and social assistance. Just as the provincial government took over the church's role in running schools, it has inherited the ecclesiastical responsibility for the needy, the sick, and the aged. The result is a highly integrated and centralized system of welfare and medical services. The range of social services provided by the Quebec government exceeds that supplied by other provinces: it comprises day-care for children, income supplements, automobile insurance, consumer protection, and generous family allowances.[24]

A cynical explanation for the "unique nationalist and social-democratic political culture" in Quebec is that the self-interest of the French-speaking "technocratic elite" is served by an expanding, interventionist state because of the jobs it generates and the power it accords to this social group.[25] This argument of bureaucratic self-interest overlooks the heritage of government paternalism from New France and the Roman Catholic Church's doctrine of good works. Quebec's so-called "social democratic ethos" is a new label for a very long established outlook. Roman Catholic social teachings are probably more influential than socialist theory in ensuring general acceptance of the provincial government's welfare state.

Both aspects of church and state in New France, compassion and authoritarianism, are present in the policies of Quebec's provincial government. Quebec's parliamentarians, like lawmakers of the French Regime, believe that there is a legislative solution to every social problem, and they are attracted by categorical rules. As in *la Nouvelle France,* the legislative reach is extensive. The interest of the Franco-Québécois nation provides the ideological rationale for intervention formerly supplied by royal absolutism. Place names can be changed, whatever residents may wish, and there is a preference for French nomenclature. When a province redefines itself as the nation-state of one language group, it necessarily reduces all other language groups to subordinate status. Ethnic nationalists are uncomfortable with the visible evidence of cultural diversity. Thus, St. Andrew's East, founded by the Scots, was renamed Saint-André d'Argenteuil and the Payne River is now Rivière d'Arnaud. The personal names of the newborn must pass official scrutiny before registration in Quebec. Immigrants who have not been educated in English within Canada are obliged to send their children to French-language schools. Quebec's draconian regulations on the language of public signs are the best-known examples of intrusive authority in action.[26] The explanation is that the preeminence of the French language must always be visible and that the use of any other language, especially English, threatens the survival of French.

In the late twentieth century, the patriarchal and Roman Catholic values in Quebec's civil code have been replaced by egalitarian and secular standards shared by the rest of North America, such as the legal equality of women. Alteration of content has not meant an abandonment of deductive logic, which is characteristic of French legal reasoning and still affects intellectual debate in the Province of Quebec. The 1989 program of the *Parti Québécois* (PQ)—a separatist party established in 1968—is a modern example of the idealism and deductive reasoning inherent in the province's legal tradition. The principles that are the basis for political arguments come from nineteenth-century European cultural nationalism and are presented in a declaratory fashion as self-evident truths. Language is treated as the defining trait of nations: "Without the French language, the Québécois nation would no longer exist." Within Quebec people are classified by language as *francophones* (French-speakers), *anglophones* (English-speakers), or *allophones* (those whose mother tongue is neither French nor English). The political platform uses the terms *peuple* (people) and *nation* interchangeably. Nations are spoken of as organic beings with a single mind and "a national will (*une volonté nationale*)"; they are objective realities. The French-speaking residents of Quebec are assumed to be so distinctive as to be a nation apart from French-speaking Canadians residing elsewhere. That distinctiveness is asserted rather than defined.

Parti Québécois speakers, when addressing outsiders, often begin by insisting that the listeners must acknowledge that "Quebec is a nation; it is a people." What is the point of this demand? This insistence has as its objective the establishment of a basic premise from which logical deductions—in the rhetoric of European nationalism—may be drawn. Each nation, it is said, has its own national homeland, and, for the Franco-Québécois, that homeland is the province of Quebec. To be *"un peuple normal,"* in the PQ argument, a people must have its own sovereign nation-state. "Normal" does not mean according to a statistical norm, but rather how things ought to be in a perfect world. The everyday expressions "ça, c'est normal (that's normal)" or "c'est naturel" are an assertion of what is right and proper and not, as English-speakers might imagine, what is generally done by people. Every "nation" has the right of self-determination, and, in the best of all possible worlds, each nation should have its own politically independent state. This is the idealism in the PQ argument. Multinational states may outnumber nation-states, but the latter represent the right way. The coexistence of aboriginal nations within Quebec is acknowledged, but their territories necessarily have a subordinate status in the Québécois homeland.

Canada, it is said, cannot be the homeland of the Franco-Québécois because it is not a "true" federation of autonomous states and because Canada, according the late PQ leader René Lévesque, contains "two nations in the same land." The other nation, the PQ postulates, is a monolithic and homogeneous "English Canada."[27] That bigger "nation" is said to control the federal government, which, reputedly, uses its power to impose English Canada's will upon the smaller Québécois nation. *Péquistes,* as PQ supporters are called, see Canadian history as the story of an eternal antagonism between two nations, which makes their continued coexistence impossible: "this incompatibility is unconquerable (*irréductible*), irreversable." "Quebec," states the tract, "must be master of its own house," and "is on the march to becoming a complete and normal society." If one accepts the initial and the following premises of this argument, then it proceeds with relentless logic: the Franco-Québécois are a nation; all nations have the right of self-determination; and self-determination means a politically independent state of Quebec.

To this sequential deduction from abstract principles are added some pragmatic arguments, such as a promise of financial savings by eliminating one level of government or the assertion that only an independent Quebec can guarantee the survival of the French language, "threatened, if not excluded, everywhere else on the North American continent." *Péquistes* believe that, historically, French-speakers in North America have been a victimized people. This can be sustained by a selective reading of the past. Dislike of compromise is evident in the statement that "it is no longer acceptable that the future of the Quebec people be constantly subjected to the complicated arbitration" of federalism. There is even an echo of past values in the assertion that "the family constitutes the [basic] unit, par excellence, of our societies and the source of their dynamism."[28] It is appropriate that the platform of Quebec's most nationalist, political party, by reasoning deductively from unquestioned axioms, is faithful to the intellectual tradition of New France.

Given the different patterns of reasoning favored by French- and English-speaking Canadians, it is not surprising that they often misunderstand each other or resent the other language group's resistance to arguments that seem utterly convincing to one's own group. Arguments of principle collide with appeals to pragmatism, to what is achievable. The pragmatic approach follows English Common Law practice of appealing to precedents: previous court decisions in similar cases. Case law invokes what has been done in the past as a guide for the future. This is the pattern of legal argument in every Canadian province but Quebec and in every American state except Louisiana. To someone reared in the intellectual traditions of French Canada, such an approach to problems seems like unprincipled expediency and, indeed, English-speaking Canadians have been indifferent to federal government initiatives that have encroached upon the provinces' jurisdiction over education and social welfare. The original constitutional division of powers between the federal and provincial governments, made in deference to Quebec's distinct institutional heritage, is forgotten in the pursuit of national standards for health care and postsecondary education. It is usually politicians from Quebec who, fortified by their belief in provincial autonomy, must point out that the constitutional division of authority, a principle of federalism, has been violated.

The *Parti Québécois* argument is most persuasive to someone whose intellectual tradition is rooted in French civil law and has been shaped by Roman Catholic doctrines, whose truths are defined by those in authority. Cultural nationalism appeals to the heart as well as to the mind, and so one cannot treat it as a cerebral exercise in persuasive logic. Yet, it seems that these two intellectual traditions, rooted in law and experience, which foster different approaches to problem solving, help to distinguish Canada's two major language groups, one from another. When the August 1992 Charlottetown Accord of Canadian provincial premiers and the country's prime minister stated that "Quebec constitutes within Canada a distinct society, which includes a French-speaking majority, a unique culture and a civil law tradition," it was acknowledging a historical truth. Moreover, those distinguishing traits of language, culture, and civil law are traceable to the French colony of *la Nouvelle France.*

Much has changed in Quebec, Acadia, and the other parts of French Canada in recent decades: religious practice has declined, family bonds have been loosened, technology and urban society have been embraced. In 1984 Quebeckers had the lowest birth rate in Canada: 1.45 children born to every woman of child-bearing age, as opposed to a national average of 1.7. This result of artificial birth control, a practice condemned by the Roman Catholic Church, reveals the collapse of clerical authority. In the 1990s, 40 percent of the children born in Quebec were born out of wedlock—an indication of the changed relationship between the sexes and the weakening of matrimonial conventions. As elsewhere in North America, there has been a sizable Asian, Caribbean, African, and Latin-American migration into the French-speaking regions of Canada. This makes the definition of Canada, even of French-speaking Canada, difficult. The pre-1945 stereotype of the French-Canadian "Habitant farmer," contained in the poems of William Henry Drummond and immortalized in the drawings of Edmond Massicotte, as deeply religious, conservative, blessed with numerous children, and living in a small, culturally homogeneous parish, has nothing to do with the lives of most French-speakers in Canada today.

There still remains a perceptible legacy from New France that sets French-speaking Canadians, especially those in Quebec, apart from their diverse compatriots. It is a legacy that goes beyond language. There are still elements of compassionate authoritarianism, of Christian humanity, of family solidarity, and of dogmatic idealism that are traceable to *la Nouvelle France*. How much of that legacy, now altered by the passage of time, will survive into the twenty-first century I cannot say. Historians usually face backward, and this makes them unreliable prophets of the future. Twentieth-century French Canadians were the heirs of New France and, in some respects, the apples had not fallen far from the tree.

Endnotes

INTRODUCTION

1. Archives nationales de France, Archives des Colonies, série G2, vol.198, dossier 176: Requête en plainte de Joseph Felix Chenay, 8 September 1743.

2. Guy Frégault, *Canadian Society in the French Regime* (Ottawa: Canadian Historical Association, 1962), 16.

CHAPTER I

1. The 1671 census of the settlement enumerated just 73 permanent residents, of whom 29 were adolescents and children. See C. de la Morandière, *Histoire de la Pêche française de la morue dans l'Amérique septentrionale (des origines à 1789),* 2 vols. (Paris: Maisonneuve et Larose, 1962), 2:1009–10. In 1691 the resident French population of Plaisance was 155, and in 1698, 188. See Dominion Bureau of Statistics (Demography Branch), *Chronological List of Canadian Censuses* (Ottawa: Ministry of Trade and Commerce, c1931), 4–5.

2. Archives nationales de France (ANF), Archives des Colonies (AC), série C11C, vol. 7, ff.101–101vo: Durand de la Garenne to the minister, 18 October 1711.

3. John Humphreys, *Plaisance* (Ottawa: National Museums of Canada, 1970).

4. Gustave Lanctot, ed., *The Oakes Collection: New Documents by Lahontan Concerning Canada and Newfoundland* (Ottawa: Public Archives of Canada, 1940), 55–57.

5. Naomi E. S. Griffiths, ed., *The Acadian Deportation: Deliberate Perfidy or Cruel Necessity?* (Toronto: Copp Clark, 1969), 30.

6. ANF, AC, série C11B, vol. 33 (1753), f.495: Isle Royale, Etat des Batiments venus en Peche Et traitte.

7. George Juan [Jorge Juan y Santacilla] and Antonio de Ulloa, *A Voyage to South America,* 2 vols. (London: L. Davis and G. Reymers, 1760), 2:363–74.

8. Geneviève Massignon, *Les parlers français d'Acadie: Enquête linguistique,* 2 vols. (Paris: Klinksieck, 1962).

9. Sieur de Dièreville, *Relation of the Voyage to Port Royal in Acadia or New France* (Toronto: Champlain Society, 1933), 92–93.

10. Metropolitan Toronto Library, Central Branch, Baldwin Room, *Lettres canadiens,* 2 ms. vols., vol. 1, 71: A son frère en Italie . . . il luy fait une description de la ville de Québec.

11. C. de Rochemonteix, ed., *Relation par Lettres de l'Amérique Septentrionale* (Paris: Letouzey et Ané, 1904), 34–35.

12. Carl J. Ekberg, *French Roots in the Illinois Country: The Mississippi Frontier in Colonial Times* (Urbana and Chicago: University of Illinois Press, 1998).

13. National Archives of Canada, Manuscript Group 24, L3, vol. 1, 435–38: 6 October 1729 letter of Jean-Baptiste Beauvais to his mother.

14. ANF, AC, série B, vol. 53, f.476, quoted in K. A. MacKirdy, J. S. Moir, and Y. F. Zoltvany, eds., *Changing Perspectives in Canadian History: Selected Problems,* rev. ed. (Don Mills, Ontario: Dent, 1971), 7.

15. S. Putnam, trans. and ed., *The Portable Rabelais* (New York: Viking, 1946), 619–20

16. ANF, AC, série F3 (Collection Moreau St-Méry), vol. 2–1, f.198: Memorial of Intendant de Meulles to the Minister, c.1684.

17. Pierre Boucher, *Histoire Véritable et Naturelle de Moeurs et Productions du Pays de la Nouvelle France* (Paris: Lambert, 1664), 149–50.

CHAPTER 2

1. Chrestien Le Clercq, *New Relation of Gaspesia, With the Customs and Religion of the Gaspesian Indians,* ed. and trans. William F. Ganong (Toronto: Champlain Society, 1910), 336 [my translation]. Olive Dickason's *The Myth of the Savage and the Beginnings of French Colonialism in the Americas* (Edmonton: University of Alberta Press, 1984) describes the varying preconceptions of Europeans about wild people. In the 1950s the screen inside Haarlem's Sint Bavo Cathedral and the sign of Soest's inn Im Wilden Mann introduced me to representations of Northern Europe's mythical wild folk. In British Columbia I found that a similar being, known as the "Sasquatch," was alleged to inhabit the coastal wilderness, which suggests that hairy forest men are a universal human invention to populate those areas where ordinary mortals fear to go.

2. Joseph-François Lafitau, *Customs of the American Indians Compared with the Customs of Primitive Times.* 2 vols., ed. and trans. William N. Fenton and Elizabeth L. Moore (Toronto: Champlain Society, 1974), 1:88.

3. Denis Diderot and Jean d'Alembert, eds., *Encyclopédie ou Dictionnaire raisonné des Sciences, des Arts et des Métiers,* 36 vols. (Lausanne: Société Typographique, 1778–1783), 9:59–60: CANADIENS, Philosophie des [my translation]. This is a later, probably pirated, edition. The author of the encyclopedia article seems to have been guided by Joseph-François Lafitau's *Moeurs des Sauvages amériquains* (1724) and, possibly, by Claude Lebeau's *Avantures* (Amsterdam: Uytwerf, 1738), which paraphrases Lafitau on pp. 308–10. Plagiarism is common among writers of the seventeenth and eighteenth centuries, making it difficult to identify the originator of an idea or argument. Gordon M. *Sayre's Les Sauvages Américains: Representations of Native Americans in French and English Colonial Literature* (Chapel Hill: University of North Carolina Press, 1997) deals with the literary conventions and European interests that shaped published accounts of the native Indians before 1800.

4. Claude-Charles Le Roy, Sieur de Bacqueville et de La Potherie, *Histoire de l'Amérique septentrionale* (1722), did differentiate between the Iroquois, Hurons, and other aboriginal peoples.

5. Marc Lescarbot, *The History of New France,* 3 vols., trans. W. L. Grant (Toronto: Champlain Society, 1907–14), 1:32–33.

6. Reuben Gold Thwaites, ed., *The Jesuit Relations and Allied Documents: Travels and Explorations . . . 1610–1791,* 73 vols. (Cleveland: Burrows Brothers, 1896–1901), 29:283.

7. See, for example, Lafitau, *Customs of the American Indians,* 90: "These good qualities are undoubtedly combined with a number of faults, for they are light-minded and changeable, inexpressibly lazy, exces-

sively ungrateful, suspicious, treacherous, vindictive, and so much the more dangerous in that they know how to and do conceal their resentment longer. They are cruel to their enemies, brutal in their pleasures, vicious through ignorance and malice, but their rusticity and lack of almost everything give them the advantage over us, in that they are ignorant of all the refinements of vice which luxury and abundance have introduced."

8. According to Claude-Charles de Bacqueville de La Potherie, an Iroquois Christian called Auriouaé, when told that the Jews had crucified Jesus Christ, responded, "if only I could have been there, . . . I would have avenged his death and I would have scalped them." See La Potherie, *Histoire de l'Amérique septentrionale,* 4 vols. (Paris: Nion and Didot, 1722), 1:338.

9. Thwaites, *Jesuit Relations,* 2:75.

10. Lescarbot, *History of New France,* 3:137–38.

11. See, for example, Father Julien Perrault's statement in 1635 in Thwaites, *Jesuit Relations,* 8:159: "Their skin is naturally white, for the little children show it thus; but the heat of the Sun, and the rubbing with Seal oil and Moose fat, make them very swarthy." Samuel de Champlain, Marc Lescarbot, Gabriel Sagard, Paul Le Jeune, and Joseph-François Lafitau said the same thing.

12. *Rapport de l'Archiviste de la Province de Québec* (RAPQ), 1930–31, 72: Colbert to Talon, 5 April 1667. In 1679 Colbert added the stipulation that French colonists should outnumber their aboriginal neighbors to ensure the dominance of European culture. See RAPQ, 1926–27, 100.

13. H. Provost, ed., *Le Séminaire de Québec: Documents et Biographies* (Quebec: La Revue de l'Université Laval, 1964), 36 (my translation).

14. Thwaites, *Jesuit Relations,* 5:23–27; 6:229. Father Jérôme Lalemant said as much about native intelligence in Ibid., 28:63.

15. Cornelius J. Jaenen, *Friend and Foe: Aspects of French-Amerindian Cultural Contact in the Sixteenth and Seventeenth Centuries* (Toronto: McClelland and Stewart, 1976), 17–19.

16. H. Biggar, ed., *The Voyages of Jacques Cartier* (Ottawa: Public Archives of Canada, 1924), 49–56.

17. Nicolas Denys, *Description and Natural History of the Coasts of North America,* trans. W. F. Ganong (Toronto: Champlain Society, 1908), 441.

18. Gabriel Sagard-Théodat, *The Long Journey to the Country of the Hurons,* trans. H. H. Langton (Toronto: Champlain Society, 1939), 183.

19. Thwaites, *Jesuit Relations,* 6:297–99.

20. Ibid., 8:111–13.

21. Biggar, *Voyages of Jacques Cartier,* 132.

22. Thwaites, *Jesuit Relations,* 1:173.

23. Sagard, *Long Journey,* 137. Compare this with Father Lafitau's account (*Customs of the American Indians,* 89): "their amazement at the first sight of Europeans was unbelievable. The long beards, cultivated by the latter at that time, made them appear incredibly ugly to the Indians." For more on the native aversion for beards, see Thwaites, *Jesuit Relations,* 44:287.

24. Thwaites, *Jesuit Relations,* 7:63.

25. Le Clercq, *New Relation,* 311. Sagard, *Long Journey,* 140, made a similar observation.

26. Sagard, *Long Journey,* 138.

27. Thwaites, *Jesuit Relations,* 4:197.

28. Ibid., 1:173–75. The assertions of Baron de Lahontan's imaginary Huron Adario (see below) echoed this statement.

29. Le Clercq, *New Relation,* 243, 253; Thwaites, *Jesuit Relations,* 44:295–97 [my translation]. Grace O'Malley, the legendary pirate queen from Connacht, Ireland, reacted in a similar way in 1593 when she received a lace handkerchief from Queen Elizabeth I of England. After using this costly handkerchief to wipe her nose, Grace threw it into the fire. When she was reproached for treating the queen's gift with such disdain and told that the English kept such things in their pockets, Grace rejected the idea and replied that the Irish were civilized people.

30. Le Clercq, *New Relation,* 346 (my translation). This seems to be Le Clercq's reconstruction of the speech from his memory and its portrayal of the Amerindian as knowledgeable critic of French society antici- pates the words of the mythical Huron Adario. Genuine native criticisms of French practices encouraged writers of the eighteenth-century Enlightenment to use imaginary foreign visitors to voice the writers' own criticisms of Old Regime France, thereby evading government press censorship.

31. Thwaites, *Jesuit Relations,* 15:234–35. The statue of Saint Christopher was destroyed in the French Revo- lution, so one can only speculate on its appearance to the Huron visitor. G. L. Le Rouge ["M.L.R."], in *Curiosités de Paris, de Versailles . . . et ses environs,* 2 vols. (Paris: Les Libraires associés, 1778), 1:28, wrote, "Remarquez au premier pilier de la droite, en entrant dans l'Eglise [by the main door], la statue de saint Christophe faite en 1413, par le Chambellan de Charles VI, nommé des Essarts, qui y est répresenté." The first edition of this illustrated guidebook was published in 1716.

32. Thwaites, *Jesuit Relations,* 68:212–15.

33. Le Clercq, *New Relation,* 106, 347.

34. Sagard, *Long Journey,* 134–37. Hurons told the Neutrals that French women had one breast and gave birth to several children at a time, and this may have been a retelling of what they had heard from secular Frenchmen. Marc Lescarbot, too, wrote that "some of our men made them [the Micmacs] believe that French women have beards on their chins." See his *History of New France,* 3:140–41.

35. Thwaites, *Jesuit Relations,* 21:292–307, has a discussion of the *donnés'* status and gives two examples of contracts made for the Huron mission in 1639 and 1642.

36. Ibid., 8:119, 145–47; 11:9. Another missionary who reproved a Huron for his un-Christian explanation for a disease was answered, "in the usual fashion of the Savages, 'You have your ways of doing [things] and we have ours, Oniondechanonkhron,' that is to say, 'our countries are different.'" See ibid., 8:119. Similar native comments about the relativity of religion appear in other volumes; see 3:123; 10:19; and 13:171.

37. Ibid., 25:247–49; see also 10:63.

38. Ibid., 11:250–51.

39. Ibid., 2:89.

40. François du Creux, *The History of Canada or New France,* 2 vols. (Toronto: Champlain Society, 1951–52), 1:200.

41. Ibid., 1:216.

42. Stone disks, four to five centimeters in diameter, made by Hurons, including two engraved with crosses which are clearly of European derivation, are to be seen in the Huronia Museum at Midland, Ontario. These resemble circular, native gaming counters, which were also carved from stone. The Hurons made pendants from fragments of copper pots obtained from the French, presumably after the pots had become unusable.

43. Thwaites, *Jesuit Relations,* 19:233. Father François Le Mercier, in ibid., 15:97, described the "perplexity" of a Huron at "our assertion that God was accustomed to try his most faithful servants through sufferings and tribulations."

44. Ibid., 17:139.

45. Ibid., 21:219; 25:35–36. See, as well, the complaint of a Christian Huron in 1648: "God has no pity on us because disease, poverty, misfortune and death assail us as readily as the Infidels" (ibid., 33:139). In the absence of contemporary aboriginal records, this account of Huron reactions to the Christian mis- sionaries is based on the published accounts of the missionaries. A concordance of European observations about the Hurons is provided by Elizabeth Tooker, *An Ethnography of the Huron Indians, 1615–1649* (Midland: Huronia Historical Development Council, 1967). Bruce Trigger's *The Children of Aataentsic: A History of the Huron People to 1660,* 2 vols. (Montreal: McGill-Queen's University Press, 1976) provides a detailed, sympathetic reconstruction of Huron history. The interaction of the Eastern Woodlands peoples with the French has been the subject of books by Alfred G. Bailey, Olive Dickason, Cornelius J. Jaenen, J. H. Kennedy, and Leslie F. Upton. I was helped in my preliminary research into the Kahnawaké Iroquois by Father Henri Béchard S. J. and by Gerald A. Rogers, former president of the Châteauguay Historical Society and a member of the Caughnawaga (Kahnawaké) Historical Society.

46. Thwaites, *Jesuit Relations,* 3:104–5. The contrast between the fatal impact of measles or smallpox among the Montagnais, who traded with the French, and its milder effect upon the Europeans is described in ibid., 8:87–89.

47. Joyce Marshall, ed. and trans., *Word from New France: The Selected Letters of Marie de L'Incarnation* (Toronto: Oxford University Press, 1967), 82–83. This story accords with accounts of speeches against the Jesuits in the 1639 *Relation.* See Thwaites, *Jesuit Relations,* 17:114–17, 120–23.

48. Thwaites, *Jesuit Relations,* 21:219; 26:302–3 (my translation).

49. Ibid., 18:25. A Montagnais chief made the same accusation in 1637; see ibid., 11:239.

50. Ibid., 17:117–19.

51. Ibid., 21:76–77 (my translation).

52. Ibid., 11:89. Father Le Jeune described the use of these pictures to instruct the natives and complained that the engravings on paper sent from France were too complicated to be understood. Like Garnier, he wanted simple and direct illustrations of four or five devils tormenting one soul "with different kinds of tortures," because, "fear is the forerunner of faith in these barbarous minds." A theatrical representation of Hell was presented at Quebec in 1640 for an Algonkian audience, with the desired effect of stimulating conversions. See ibid., 18:85–87.

53. RAPQ, 1929–1930, 36–37 (my translation). In the 1630s the Jesuits at Quebec were already using pictures to teach potential converts about Heaven and Hell.

54. Thwaites, *Jesuit Relations,* 9:99. Natives acknowledged this motive themselves; see ibid., 8:139 ("I am afraid of those horrible fires of Hell"); 10:15, 29; 11:87 ("Instruct me, for I do not wish to go into the fires") and 119; and 25:251 ("I never see a fire without thinking of that of Hell").

55. Ibid., 1:183.

56. Ibid., 33:145–47.

57. Ibid., 44:297; see also 1:378; 2:116; and 33:145. Lay writers, such as Michel de Montaigne and Marc Lescarbot, had already come to a relativist view of European aesthetics and social practices.

58. Ibid., 6:251–53; Le Clercq, *New Relation,* 254; F. Vachon de Belmont, "Histoire de l'Eau-de-Vie en Canada," in the Literary and Historical Society of Quebec, *Collection de Mémoires et de Relations sur l'Histoire ancienne du Canada* (Quebec: Cowan and Son, 1840) ; and Pierre Boucher, *Histoire Véritable et Naturelle ... de la Nouvelle France* (Paris: Lambert, 1664), 94.

59. D. Brymner, *Report on Canadian Archives 1885* (Ottawa: Maclean, Roger and Co., 1886), ciii.

60. Belmont, "Histoire de l'Eau-de-Vie en Canada," 2–6.

61. Sagard, *Long Journey,* 202.

62. Camille de Rochemonteix, ed., *Relation par Lettres de l'Amérique septentrionale* (Paris: Letouzey et Ané, 1904), 66. These letters were originally ascribed to Father Antoine Silvy, but later scholars attribute them to Canada's co-intendant Antoine-Denis Raudot.

63. Thwaites, *Jesuit Relations,* 5:50–51, 230–31. Boucher, *Histoire,* 94, repeated the claim that natives became drunk in order to commit crimes with impunity. The Amerindian perception of intoxication is explored in André Vachon, "L'Eau-de-vie dans la société indienne," Canadian Historical Association, Historical Papers, 1960, 22–32.

64. Thwaites, *Jesuit Relations,* 62:175–77, 183. This was in 1682; by the eighteenth century life on the mission had assumed a more settled state, even though liquor remained a problem. Self-punishing Huron converts were noted by Father Paul Ragueneau in 1646; see ibid., 30:39–41. One was a young Christian, troubled by "all the demons of impurity," who rolled naked in the snow. "More than one" applied hot "coals and burning brands" to their bodies to stifle their carnal desires. Similar penitential excesses occurred among the native Christians at Tadoussac. One can speculate about the sublimation of sexuality in these masochistic acts, but amateur psychoanalysis from such a distance in time and space seems presumptuous. Karen Anderson's *Chain Her by One Foot: The Subjugation of Native Women in Seventeenth-Century New France* (New York: Routledge, 1991) deals with the missionaries' imposition of a patriarchal view of marriage upon Amerindian Christians. The Jesuits adhered to the Pauline ideal of the Christian

wife as submissive helpmate to her husband and they did not see this model as a cultural prejudice, separable from the Christian faith. This ideal conflicted with the autonomy enjoyed by married women in some aboriginal groups. Ms. Anderson believes (but does not prove) that before the Europeans' arrival, relations between the sexes among the Eastern Woodlands peoples were based on equality, "complementarity," and female independence.

65. National Archives of Canada (NAC), C11A Series transcript, 38:210–12; Archives nationales de France (ANF), Archives des Colonies (AC), série C11A, vol. 41, ff.259vo–261vo, and vol. 43, f.147. The complainant was Maître Jean-François Martin de Lino. The Conseil de Marine considered the matter in 1719 but referred the issue to intendant Michel Bégon, who outlawed the transfer of French children to natives in 1720. The first adoption of a foundling arranged by a court prosecutor that I have located was dated 1726, the last year of Bégon's intendancy. Court-arranged adoptions were numerous in the Montreal District during the 1730s; all involved a gratuity paid to the adoptive parents by the Domaine du Roi (the king's revenue-producing concessions). Financial arrangements may have delayed implementation of de Lino's recommendation, which conformed with usages in France, under the Royal Edict of November 1706. These arrangements, nonetheless, were evaded. Witness the case of an illegitimate child secretly given to an Abenaki of Bécancourt in 1727, noted in Cyprien Tanguay, *A Travers les Registres: Notes recueillies* (Montreal: Librairie St-Joseph, 1886), 123.

66. Adolph B. Benson, ed., *The America of 1750: Peter Kalm's Travels in North America,* 2 vols. (New York: Dover Publications, 1966), 2:456–57. James Axtell, *The Invasion Within: The Contest of Cultures in Colonial North America* (New York: Oxford University Press, 1985), chap. 13, describes the ease with which British-American captives were assimilated into aboriginal tribes. Other prisoners were ransomed by their own families or by *Canadiens,* who undertook their conversion to Roman Catholicism.

67. Jack A. Frisch, "TARBELL (Tharbell), JOHN," in *the Dictionary of Canadian Biography,* vol. 3 (Toronto: University of Toronto Press, 1974), 615. RAPQ, 1930–31, 95–96. The king's wish for complete assimilation was restated in April 1668, in NAC, B Series transcript, vol. 1, ff.89–90.

69. ANF, AC, série C11A, vol. 7, ff.90vo–106vo: Rémy de Courcelle to the minister, 15 May 1669.

70. De Rochemonteix, ed., *Relation par Lettres,* 61–62.

71. The 1688 census gave the total number of mission Indians as 1,210, with 400 men. See ANF, AC, série G1, 461:2.

72. NAC, MG24, L3 (Bâby Papers transcript), 2:1006: Dubois Berthelot at Montreal to LaValtrie, 21 May 1747.

73. *Arrêts et Règlements du Conseil supérieur de Québec* (Quebec: Fréchette, 1855) (Also known *as Edits, Ordonnances royaux,* vol. 2), 16–17, 70.

74. Belmont, "Histoire de l'Eau-de-Vie en Canada," 13, 16.

75. This is the finding of Professor Jan Grabowski of the University of Ottawa, who presented a summary of his research in "French Criminal Justice and Indians in Montreal, 1670–1760," a paper presented during the "Canada's Legal History" conference at the University of Manitoba, 2–4 October 1997. See also his published paper "Searching for the Common Ground: Natives and French in Montreal, 1700–1730," in James Pritchard, ed., *Proceedings of the Eighteenth Meeting of the French Colonial Historical Society* (Cleveland: F.C.H.S., 1993), 59–73. Helen Stone and Patricia Kennedy, in their paper "Private Party Matters: Quebec Mission Indians and the Politics of Administering Justice in the British Regime," presented at the May 1996 Canadian Historical Association convention, found that the special legal status of the mission Indians and their right to resolve disputes among themselves continued after the conquest of New France.

76. Archives du Québec (AQ), Montréal, Juridiction royale de Montréal, pièces détachées, 23–25 February 1719: "Enquête Judiciaire Le Roy Vs. Jacques Detailly par Bouat."

77. NAC, MG24, L3, 2:659–60: Havy and Lefèbvre at Quebec to M. Guy, 28 July 1745. Mother de Sainte-Hélène of the Quebec hospital was equally disillusioned with the mission Indians in 1740, when she described them as "filthy (crasseux)," arrogant, and "nasty people (ce sont des vilaines M.srs) even though there are some fervent Christians among them." "Lettres de Mère Marie-Andrée Duplessis de Sainte Hélène," *Nova Francia* 3 (1927–28): 285.

78. RAPQ, 1947–48, 244: The king's memorial to Vaudreuil and Bégon, 19 March 1714.

79. ANF, AC, série C11A, vol. 43, ff.129–130: Vaudreuil to the Minister, 7 November 1720.

80. RAPQ, 1926–27, 126: Frontenac to the king, 2 November 1681.

81. Jean Lunn, "The Illegal Fur Trade out of New France, 1713–1760," in Canadian Historical Review, 20:1 (March 1939), 61–76.

82. NAC, C11A Series transcript, 7:46: de Denonville to the Minister, 13 November 1685.

83. Gabriel Sagard, *Long Journey*, 171–72, recorded that his interpreter, probably Etienne Brulé, followed the practice of native travelers in making an offering of tobacco to a man-shaped rock along a river. In Thwaites, *Jesuit Relations*, 10:165–67, Father Le Jeune describes this rock and the beliefs attached to it. Characteristically, he calls the rock's spirit a "demon." In 1667 Bishop de Montmorency-Laval deplored the participation of French traders in the Ottawas' pagan festivals. See H. O. Têtu and C. O. Gagnon, eds., *Mandements, lettres pastorales et circulaires des Evêques de Québec*, 6 vols. (Quebec: A. Coté, 1887–90), 1:68. The significance of aboriginal tattoos on the skin of Frenchmen is discussed in Sayre, *Les Sauvages Amériquains*, 165–79.

84. NAC, C11G Series transcript, 4:13, 31–32: King's memorial to Vaudreuil and Raudot, 6 July 1709; reply of Vaudreuil and Raudot, no date.

85. A. Lachance, ed., *Les Marginaux, les Exclus et l'Autre au Canada aux 17e et 18e siècles* (Montreal: Fides, 1996), 119–93. These were the Christian marriages performed by priests. Thirty-five marriages between European women and aboriginal men were recorded. Intercultural marriages may have faced social disapproval; see P. G. Roy, *Inventaire des ordonnances des intendants de la Nouvelle-France,* 4 vols. (Beauceville: l'Éclaireur, 1919), 1:44. A 1707 ordinance forbidding a settler, aged twenty-four, to marry a native woman of the St. François mission without his mother's consent.

86. Thwaites, *Jesuit Relations*, 1:93, from *La Conversion des Sauvages* (1610).

87. Ibid., 31:223–25; 47:169. See also 37:189: "the innocence of their mode of life while engaged in hunting amid those vast forests,—which were never made the haunts of the monsters of pride and ambition that ravage and set on fire the whole of Europe,—in a word, their goodness and sincerity, are their Father's joy and glory."

88. Ibid., 44:307; see also 8:127–29 and, especially, 283: "It seems as if innocence . . . had withdrawn into these great forests . . . Their nature has something . . . of the goodness of the Terrestrial Paradise before sin had entered it. Their practices manifest none of the luxury, the ambition, the avarice, or the pleasures that corrupt our cities." Brother Gabriel Sagard already had noted the admirable traits of the Hurons in *Long Journey*, 58, 88–89, 112, 140. Father F. X de Charlevoix was the Jesuit who went farthest in praising native virtues in his *Journal historique d'un Voyage* (1744), and yet he, too, was ambivalent about Amerindians: "We perceive in them a mixture of ferocity and gentleness, the passions and appetites of beasts of prey, joined to a virtue which does honor to human nature."

   This European ambivalence toward the aboriginal peoples, as well as all that has been noted above, reveals the inapplicability of the theory of "the Other," popularized by Edward Said's book *Orientalism* (1978), to French-Amerindian relations in the seventeenth century. According to this theory, Europeans used foreign peoples as a foil for defining themselves by attributing antithetical qualities, usually derogatory ones, to non-Europeans. These descriptions were also a political act because they justified European domination of "the Other." North America's aboriginal peoples were never important to the Europeans' sense of who they were, nor were French observers in New France consistently unfavorable in their impressions of Amerindians. Naturally, they emphasized what was most admirable or most repugnant to them. The eighteenth-century *philosophes* tended to select the laudatory observations and to build upon them in a way that was flattering to Canada's aboriginal peoples, who were presented as models to be imitated, not as inferior beings to be subjugated.

89. The distortion of native reality to serve outsiders' interests continues: late-twentieth-century North Americans and Europeans recast Amerindians into the original ecologists and they gave a monotheistic interpretation to native spirituality. "The Great Spirit" of pan-Indian religion, it is said, enjoins humans

to respect "Mother Earth." The historic Algonkians and Iroquoians did not see themselves as part of a beneficent system of nature. Except for the beaver, which was killed at a rate faster than it could reproduce, natives seldom took more from the environment than they needed, and this helped to conserve the stock of game. Human dependence upon the creatures of the earth was acknowledged in gestures of respect for their spirits, who were thought to consent to being caught. The bones of fish and animals that had been eaten could not be thrown to the dogs because that would offend the spirits of the prey, who thereafter would refuse to be taken. Self-interest enjoined a consideration for other creatures' souls. For Eastern Woodlands peoples, a multiplicity of spirits inhabited living things and inanimate objects. Christian missionaries ridiculed the idea of animals having immortal, reasonable souls and identified the many spirits venerated by aborigines with the devil. The romantic picture of the North American Indian as protoecologist, however, is so attractive that it has been incorporated into the aboriginal peoples' own present-day definition of themselves.

90. Louis-Armand de Lom d'Arce, Baron de Lahontan, *New Voyages to North America,* 2 vols., ed. R. G. Thwaites (Chicago: A. C. McClurg and Co., 1905), 2:535–38, 553–54.

91. Réal Ouellet, ed., *Sur Lahontan: Comptes rendus et critiques (1702–1711)* (Quebec: Éditions l'Hetrière, 1983), 99, 102.

CHAPTER 3

1. Charles Loyseau, *Cinq Livres du Droict des Offices* (Paris: la veufve L'Angelier, 1613), 756. Loyseau wrote the equally influential *Traité des Ordres et Simples Dignitez* about social ranks.

2. Albert Babeau, *La Ville sous l'Ancien Régime,* 2 vols. (Paris: Didier, 1884), 1:71–78.

3. Chevalier d'Arcq, *Mes Loisirs* (Paris: Desaint et al. , 1755), 75–76.

4. *Rapport de l'Archiviste de la Province de Québec* (RAPQ), 1930–31, 17: Mémoire du Roi pour servir d'instruction à Talon, 27 March 1665.

5. RAPQ, 1939–40, Inventaire des Documents concernant l'Église du Canada, 221: Testimony about the Easter sermon of Abbé de Fénélon, 25 March 1674.

6. RAPQ, 1926–27, 4: Mémoire du Roi pour servir d'instruction au sieur Comte de Frontenac, 7 April 1672.

7. *Jugements et déliberations du Conseil souverain de la Nouvelle-France* (JDCS), 6 vols. (Quebec: Côté and Dussault, 1885–91), 6:796.

8. Ibid., 3:219–23: Règlement pour les Pauvres, 8 April 1688. These local boards operated under religious auspices, with a priest as chairman and funds for their work being collected in church poor boxes or by voluntary donations solicited by collectors who were, "not to be too insistent, leaving each person complete freedom to practice charity according to his [religious] devotion (de faire sa charité selon sa devotion)." A copy of the minutes of the Montreal board from 1698–1700 is in the National Archives of Canada (NAC), MG 8, C5, 6:514–39. The Sulpician Father Superior and, when available, the bishop sat on this board, which consigned some of the unfortunates to church-run refuges, such as the Charon Hospice or Quebec's Hôpital-Général. These boards were not examples of royal paternalism, and there is no evidence that they survived beyond the first decade of the eighteenth century.

9. Mgr. De Saint-Vallier, *Catechisme du Diocèse de Québec* (Paris: Coustelier, 1702), 320–24: Leçon V. Des Bonnes oeuvres.

10. H. Têtu and C. O. Gagnon, eds., *Mandements, lettres pastorales et circulaires des évêques de Québec,* 6 vols. (Quebec: Côté, 1887–90), 1:419.

11. *Édits, ordonnances royaux, déclarations et arrêts du Conseil d'État du Roi concernant le Canada* (EOR), 3 vols. (Quebec: Fréchette, 1854–55), 1:7.

12. JDCS, 2:72.

13. 1677 memorandum of Father Dudouyt to Bishop Laval, in D. Brymner, ed., *Report on Canadian Archives { . . . } 1885* (Ottawa: Maclean Roger, 1886), civ–cv (my translation).

14. Marc-André Bédard, *Les Protestants en Nouvelle-France* (Quebec: la Société historique de Québec, 1978), 82–83, provides a brief outline of the Petits' history. Gédéon's flight to "the English" is mentioned in the Quebec Prévôté records, in NAC, MG 8, B1, 3:108–9: 1689 claims against the estate of Alexandre Petit. The grant of residency rights in 1677 is in JDCS, 2:174. The conclusion of the story was provided by the abstract of Gédéon Petit's will in the New York Historical Society Collections, 26 (1892–93):151. He still had 2,327 livres in Canadian card money when he died.

15. Archives nationales de France (ANF), Archives des Colonies (AC), série G1, vol. 406 (Louisbourg church register), 25 June and 24 July 1736; vol. 407, 11 April 1741, 12 November 1741, and passim.

16. Bédard, *Les Protestants en Nouvelle-France*, 46.

17. E. B. O'Callaghan, ed., *Documents relative to the Colonial History of the State of New York*, 15 vols. (Albany: Weed, Parsons and Co., 1853–87), 8:1019–21.

18. Moogk, "LYDIUS, John Hendricks," in the *Dictionary of Canadian Biography* (DCB), vol. 4 (Toronto: University of Toronto Press, 1979), 488–90.

19. "Lettres de Mère Marie-Andrée Duplessis de Sainte-Hélène," *Nova Francia* 2 (1926–27): 234.

20. Gaston Tisdel, "BRANDEAU, Esther," in DCB, vol. 2 (Toronto: University of Toronto Press, 1969), 95–96.

21. Irving Abella, *Coat of Many Colours: Two Centuries of Jewish Life in Canada* (Toronto: Lester and Orpen Dennys, 1990), 2. Other immigrants, such as "Jean-Baptiste Baruc," a captive from New York who was baptized at Montreal in 1693, might have been Jewish, but, in the absence of more evidence, this can be only speculation.

22. F. J. Cugnet and others, *An Abstract of Those Parts of the Custom of the Viscounty and Provostship of Paris, which was received and practised in the Province of Quebec, in the time of the French Government* (London: Eyre and Strahan, 1772), i–ii.

23. Pierre Lemaistre, *La Coutume de la Prevosté et Vicomté de Paris* (Paris: Cavelier, 1700), 560.

24. Syvie Savoie, "Les couples en difficulté aux XVIIe et XVIIIe siècles: Les Demandes en séparation en Nouvelle-France" (master's thesis, Université de Sherbrooke, 1986), 114. This corresponds with my own observations from a modest sample of sixteen petitions for separation. In France separation from bed and board was a matter for the church courts and this might seem to explain the rarity of petitions for physical separation in New France. In the colony there was an ecclesiastical court called the officialité, which resolved disputes involving people in holy orders. It does not appear to have judged disputes between members of the laity.

25. *Journal des Campagnes du Chevalier de Lévis* (Montreal: Demers et frère, 1889), 117–19. In 1704 men of the Montreal District met to protest the price being charged by local merchants for salt. This demonstration was taken more seriously, although the protesters dispersed quickly when told that such gatherings were forbidden. An ordinance passed by Governor-General Rigaud de Vaudreuil on 12 December 1704 declared that future assemblies of this sort would be punished as seditious and treasonable. See National Archives of Canada (NAC), MG 1, C11A series transcript, 24:36: Vaudreuil to the minister, 4 November 1706. The 1704 ordinance is reprinted in G. Roy, ed., *Ordonnances, Commissions, etc., etc., des Gouverneurs et intendants de la Nouvelle-France, 1639–1706*, 2 vols. (Beauceville: l'Éclaireur, 1924), 2:326–27. The minister responsible for colonies still criticized Vaudreuil for his "softness" in dealing with the 1704 rioters and said that he ought to have made "some examples of severity" of "the most mutinous ones" on the spot to deter future protests. See RAPQ, 1938–39, 118.

26. The grounds for losing inheritance rights are discussed in Claude de Ferrière, *Nouveau Commentaire sur la Coutume de la Prevôté et Vicomté de Paris*, 2 vols. (Paris: les Libraires Associés, 1770), 2:360, in connection with article 318. See also Claude-Joseph de Ferrière's article on "exhérédition" in *Dictionnaire de Droit et de Pratique*, 2 vols. (Toulouse: Dupleix, 1779), 1:575–77.

27. F. A. Pluquet, *Mémoires pour servir a l'histoire des Égaremens de l'Esprit humain par rapport a la religion chrétienne, ou Dictionnaire des Hérésies, Erreurs et des Schismes*, 2 vols. (Paris: Nyon, Barrois and Didot, 1762), 2:207; see also 1:5–16, 265–72. Pluquet also blames Christian heresies on human indocility, vanity, self-

interest, and blind fanaticism, which lead men to reject the Roman church's authority and its doctrines.

28. G. Roy, *Toutes petites choses du régime français* (Quebec: Garneau, 1944), 268–69.

29. Archives du Québec (AQ), Greffes des notaires du régime français, F. Genaple, 20 August 1699: inventaire des biens du feu Claude Baillif. Fournerie de Vezon's library is listed in Aegidius Fauteux, *Les Bibliothèques canadiennes: Étude historique* (Montreal: Arbour and Dupont, 1916), 17–20. Cameron Nish, *François-Etienne Cugnet: entrepreneur et entreprises en Nouvelle-France* (Montreal: Fides, 1975), 149–50, describes the numerous legal works in the library of this administrator and merchant-entrepreneur.

30. Pouchot, *Memoirs on the Late War in North America,* trans. M. Cardy (Youngstown: Old Fort Niagara Association, 1994), 210.

31. The maps and views are in the Archives du Génie (Paris), Article 14, Louisbourg, tablette 1, nos. 22, 23, 30, 53 bis; Article 15, nos.1–19; ANF, AC, série C11A, vol. 126, ff.226, 230, 233, 267; Dépôt des Fortifications et des Colonies, vol. 4, ff.180, 186, 198, 219, 225, 226; Bibliothèque nationale de France, Cabinet des Estampes, série 5, Topographie, Subdivision Vd, vol. 20a, nos. 40, 51. The maps come from the period 1731–58. Étienne Verrier drew up a plan for a parish chapel in 1737 and may have had an interest in reminding his superiors of this design. His son omitted the church on one of his plans, while other draftsmen followed Verrier père's example.

32. JDCS, 6:45. The 1749 Prévôté decision is in AQ, série NF 19, vol. 95, f.8.

33. In March 1667 the Quebec syndic was elected by ten men after Sunday mass; residents of Ile d'Orléans submitted their nomination in writing. There was a complaint that the beadle did not ring the church bell to announce the assembly, so a larger turnout may have been more common. See NAC, MG 8, B1 (Prévôté de Québec), 1:139–46.

34. Allana G. Reid, "Representative Assemblies in New France," in *Canadian Historical Review* 27, no. 1 (March 1946): 19–26, dispatches Francis Parkman's suggestion that this assembly might have been the dawn of democracy in Canada.

35. RAPQ, 1926–1927, 25: Minister to Frontenac, 13 June 1673.

36. AQ, Montréal, Greffes des notaires, B. Basset, 20 October 1675: Acte d'assemblée des habitans de Montréal.

37. RAPQ, 1927–1928, facsimile of 23 March 1677 ordinance opposite xvi.

38. NAC, MG 8, C5 (Juridiction royale de Montréal), 5:297–98: 10 October 1693 report against Sieur Martinet de Fonblanche.

39. The one exception is the case of Charles de Monseignat, comptroller for the navy in New France, who was informed in May 1702 that he must buy one of the new offices of Commissaires de la Marine et des Galères for thirty thousand livres in order to retain his position in Canada. ANF, AC, série B, vol. 23, f.104vo.

40. ANF, AC, série B, vol. 36, ff.407–8: Minister to Monseignat, 24 May 1714.

41. Edouard Z. Massicotte, *Répertoire des arrêts, édits, mandements, ordonnances et règlements conservées dans les Archives du Palais de Justice de Montréal 1640–1760* (Montreal: G. Ducharme, 1919), 126, and *Bulletin des Recherches historiques* (BRH) 34 (1928): 526.

42. John A. Dickinson, *Justice et Justiciables: la procédure civile a la Prévôté de Québec, 1667–1759* (Quebec: les Presses de l'Université Laval, 1982), 77–98. Despite the small benefit of excluding lawyers from the colonies, the exclusion was applied to Ile Royale in 1735. See ANF, AC, série B, vol. 17, f.110.

43. JDCS, 6:114. According to Steven L. Kaplan, *Bread, Politics and Political Economy in the Reign of Louis XV,* 2 vols. (The Hague: Martinus Nijhoff, 1976), French administrators were obsessed with the provisioning trades because they felt that their ability to govern—and the entire social order—depended on an abundant and reliable supply of food for the populace.

44. JDCS, 6:796, 834; RAPQ, 1947–48, 277.

45. Terence Crowley, "'Thunder Gusts': Popular Disturbances in Early French Canada," in Canadian Historical Association, *Historical Papers 1979* (Ottawa: C.H.A., 1980), 11–31. Colonial officials took protests against forced labor on public works more seriously because the crown's authority was being challenged, but no participant was executed for this act of sedition.

46. JDCS, 2:63–73; 3:870–71; 5:239–40; 6:270. Louise Dechêne, in *Le Partage des Subsistances au Canada sous le Régime français* (Ville St-Laurent: Boréal, 1994), believes that royal government was primarily concerned with grain supplies, and regulated the wheat market as well as commercial bakers. Its intervention was spasmodic and it was unable to prevent food shortages, which fell hardest upon the urban poor. My study is more concerned with government intentions than with the consequences.

47. Richard Burn, *The Justice of the Peace and Parish Officer,* 4 vols. (London: A. Strahan, 1797), 1:21–67, 276–312; 2:44–58; John Comyns, *Digest of the Laws of England,* 6 vols. (London: A. Strahan and Woodfall, 1792), 4:548–53, 652–53, 655–58. These books served as manuals for justices of the peace in the British North American colonies that became provinces of Canada.

48. This is based on bone fragment analysis of archaeological finds to identify food sources. See, for example, François Miville-Deschênes, *The Soldier Off Duty* (Ottawa: National Historic Parks and Sites, 1987), 50, which describes the shift from wild game to domesticated animals in the remains found at the Fort Chambly site in Quebec.

49. Richard Colebrook Harris, *The Seigneurial System in Early Canada* (Madison: University of Wisconsin Press, 1966), 72–75.

50. JDCS, 2:71; 3:328, 377, 383; 6:1056.

51. Ibid., 3:424–25.

52. AQ, Montréal, Greffes des notaires, Cyr de Monmerqué, 26 January 1733, describes a properly equipped mill at Champlain with a weighing arm and lead weights of ten, twenty-five, fifty, and eighty-five pounds.

53. The aune, or linear measure, used in New France was three pieds, eight pouces long, whereas the aune de Paris was shorter: three pieds, seven pouces, eight lignes. Otherwise, colonial measures seem to have followed Parisian standards. French inches and feet of the Old Regime are not identical to those used in English-speaking countries.

54. NAC, C11A Series transcript, 85:56–58.

55. EOR, 2:116–18; JDCS, 3:110, 205–6, 328, 377, 383; 4:163; Massicotte, *Répertoire des arrêts,* 94; Harold A. Innis, ed., *Select Documents in Canadian Economic History, 1497–1783* (Toronto: University of Toronto Press, 1929), 407.

56. Quoted in Louise Dechêne, *Habitants et Marchands de Montréal au xviie siècle* (Montreal: Plon, 1974), 25, footnote 22.

57. ANF, AC, série C11A, vol. 7, ff.90vo–91: Governor de Denonville to the Minister, 13 November 1685.

58. EOR, 1:38.

59. JDCS, 1:884.

60. Ibid., 3:604–5.

61. AQ, Quebec, Greffes des notaires, F. Genaple, 12–14 November 1699: Estate inventory of Étienne Charest senior; Joseph-Noël Fauteux, *Essai sur l'Industrie au Canada sous le Régime français,* 2 vols. (Quebec: Proulx, 1927), 2:435. Likewise, the estate of another Quebec region tanner, François Bissot, contained a functioning shoe shop. See AQ, Quebec, Greffes des notaires, R. Becquet, 27 April 1676.

62. EOR, 2:265–66.

63. Pierre-Georges Roy, ed., *Inventaire des ordonnances des intendants de la Nouvelle-France . . . (1705–59)* (IDI), 4 vols. (Beauceville: L'Éclaireur, 1919), 1:25–26, 48, 96.

64. IDI, 1:25; full text in ANF, AC, Collection Moreau de St-Méry, vol. 7F, fo.42.

65. AQ, Ordonnances des intendants (OI), vol. 1, ff.55vo-56.

66. JDCS, 6:351–52.

67. AQ, Montréal, Juridiction royale de Montréal, registres des audiences, vol. 11 (1726–29), f.456. See also Peter Moogk, "In the Darkness of a Basement: Craftsmen's Associations in Early French Canada," *Canadian Historical Review* 57, no.4 (December 1976): 399–439.

68. "Un lettre inédite du marquis de Denonville (20 août 1685)," in BRH 22 (1916): 85.

69. O. M. Lapalice, "Le cout de la vie à Montréal, au 17ème siècle," *Canadian Antiquarian and Numismatic Journal,* series 3, 13 (1916): 10–11.

70. AQ, IO, vol. 5, ff.48vo-49.

71. A. B. Benson, ed., *The America of 1750: Peter Kalm's Travels in North America,* 2 vols. (New York, Dover, 1966), 2:504.

72. RAPQ, 1927–1928, 90.

73. Nicolas de La Mare, *Traité de la Police, où l'on trouvera l'histoire de son Etablissement,* 4 vols. (Paris: Cot, 1705–38), 2:1240. This legal work was quoted by the intendant of New France in 1727; see ANF, AC, Collection Moreau de St-Méry, vol. 9, fo.17.

74. RAPQ, 1938–39, 31–32.

75. ANF, AC, série B, vol. 79, ff.66vo–71vo: De Ponchartrain to Raudot père, 30 June 1707.

76. Fauteux, *Essai sur l'industrie,* 2:485–92.

77. NAC, C11A Series transcript, vol. 37, 381–82. Lionel Groulx, "Note sur la chapellerie au Canada sous le régime française, *in Revue d'Histoire de l'Amérique française* 3 (1949–50): 383–401, argues that the *Compagnie des Indes,* rather than the royal administration, initiated the suppression of colonial hat making. This dramatic act was inconsistent with previous colonial economic policy.

78. RAPQ, 1930–31, 9. See also 43, which speaks of royal financial help, "to establish manufactures there."

79. Fauteux, *Essai sur l'Industrie,* 1:56–124; Dale Miquelon, *New France 1701–44* (Toronto: McClelland and Stewart, 1987), 213–16.

80. Jean Hamelin, *Économie et Société en Nouvelle-France* (Quebec: Les Presses universitaires de Laval, 1960), 33. These figures are probably limited to the St. Lawrence Valley settlements and do not include Ile Royale. Louisbourg was New France's most active port, and the island's fishery generated millions of livres, exceeding the value of Canada's exports.

81. Jacques Mathieu, *La Construction navale royale à Québec* (Quebec: la Société historique de Québec, 1971), mentions these factors as well as improper demands from the French navy, inappropriate lumbering, and poor curing of wood as the causes for the royal shipyard's failure to produce durable vessels.

82. NAC, B Series transcript, vol. 50, part 1, 129–30; vol. 52, part 1, 123.

83. RAPQ, 1927–28, 10, for example, noted that in 1689 the French crown was sending out tilers, brickmakers, and potters and asked the governor-general to ensure that they establish themselves in New France, to satisfy "the colony's needs" and to instruct residents in their trades.

CHAPTER 4

1. A. F. Prévost, *Manon Lescaut* (Amsterdam: Didot, 1753), 51.

2. Reuben Gold Thwaites, ed., *The Jesuit Relations and Allied Documents: Travels and Explorations . . . 1610–1791,* 73 vols. (Cleveland: Burrows Brothers, 1896–1901), 21:108–9 (my translation).

3. C. L. Livet, ed., *Oeuvres complètes de Saint-Amant,* 2 vols. (Paris: Jannet, 1855), 1:227.

4. Pierre Boucher, *Histoire Véritable et Naturelle . . . de la Nouvelle France* (Paris: Lambert, 1664), 155.

5. "Journal of a Captive, 1745–1748," in Isabel M. Calder, *Colonial Captivities, Marches and Journeys* (New York: Macmillan, 1935), 55.

6. Thwaites, *Jesuit Relations,* 10:187.

7. J. Nadal and E. Giralt, *La population catalane de 1553 à 1717: L'immigration française et les autres facteurs de son développement* (Paris: S.E.V.E.N., 1960).

8. Jean-Pierre Bardet's summary of Poussou's findings in "L'Immigration bordelaise, 1737–1791," *Annales de Démographie historique* (ADH), 1979, 445–55.

9. Jeffry Kaplow, ed., *Le Tableau de Paris* (Paris: Maspero, 1979), 144.

10. Here I have benefited from the observations of A. J. H. Richardson, architectural historian of Ottawa, about building tradesmen in seventeenth-century Quebec City, conveyed in a letter of 28 April 1978. Leslie Choquette, "French Emigration to Canada in the 17th and 18th Centuries" (Ph.D. diss., Harvard, 1988) has appended maps on the geographic origins of specific types of craftsmen (numbered 9–16) at the end of her thesis. These must be compared to her Map 1: Emigrant producing regions by order of

importance, to identify the differences from the overall pattern, which are subtle. These maps are absent in the published version of her thesis, *Frenchmen into Peasants: Modernity and Tradition in the Peopling of French Canada* (Cambridge, Mass.: Harvard University Press, 1997).

11. For a mechanical, neo-Marxist explanation of why the French peasantry did not migrate overseas in large numbers, see Roberta Hamilton, *Feudal Society and Colonization: The Historiography of New France* (Ganonoque: Langdale Press, 1988). The author posits that tenant farmers in "feudal" France had a more secure tenure on their land than copyholders or leaseholders in Britain, where the commercialization of agriculture produced surplus people in displaced cultivators who emigrated en masse to British North America, and generated surplus capital for investment in colonial development. The difference between feudal France and capitalist Britain, she believes, explains the contrastingly modest migration from France to New France. Apart from the fact that the author did no primary research on the topic and relied on secondary works of variable quality, this simple explanation ignores regional variations in land tenure in France, the distribution of occupations among immigrants, the effect of emigration propaganda and recruiters, the attitude of shipowners to the traffic in indentured servants, the cultural values of potential emigrants, and other considerations mentioned in this chapter.

12. Peter Moogk, "Reluctant Exiles: Emigrants from France in Canada before 1760," *William and Mary Quarterly* 46, no.2 (July 1989): 463–505, deals with this and other features of migration in greater detail, as does "Manon's Fellow Exiles: Emigration from France to North America before 1763," in Nicholas Canny, ed., *Europeans on the Move: Studies on European Migration* (Oxford: Clarendon Press, 1994), 236–60.

13. L. C. Wroth and G. L. Annan, *Acts of French Royal Administration concerning Canada, Guiana, the West Indies and Louisiana, prior to 1791* (New York: N.Y. Public Library, 1930), 53–54: Decree of 8 January 1710 authorizing the dispatch of "les condamnés aux Galères, les Bannis, les Vagabons and les Gens sans aveu" to the colonies as indentured servants.

14. R. C. Harris, "The French Background of Immigrants to Canada before 1700," *Cahiers de Géographie du Québec* 16 (1972): 312–24.

15. This is also the conclusion of L. Choquette, *Frenchmen into Peasants*. This can be accepted as an approximate observation because her data on sixteen thousand emigrants comes from flawed sources, most of it coming from published calendars of indentures and passenger lists from the seventeenth century, as well as genealogical dictionaries. Clerks and notaries recorded unfamiliar place names phonetically, and much depends on the modern transcriber's skill in decoding the names and connecting them with a modern location. Remote and small home communities pose a problem. One needs to test the published summaries against the manuscript records to establish the transcriptions' accuracy. The falsification of servants' indentures and false declarations in embarkation lists are a problem with eighteenth-century records, and these defects are discussed later in this chapter.

16. Archives du Port de Rochefort (APR), série IR, item 19: "Soldats engagés . . . jusqu'au 14 janvier 1749."

17. Gabriel Debien, "Les Engagés pour les Antilles," *Revue d'Histoire des Colonies* 38 (1951): introduction.

18. Christian Huetz de Lemps, "Les engagés du Bazadais au XVIIe siècle," *Les Cahiers du Bazadais* 10 (May 1966): 26–38; "Les Départs de Passagers Pyrénéens par Bordeaux au 18e siècle," *Bulletin de la Société des Sciences, Lettres et Arts de Pau* 3 (1968). The actual number of departures after 1720 would have been lower because of the merchants' and ship captains' evasion of maritime regulations calling for the transportation of contract workers.

19. The geographic origins are depicted graphically in R. C. Harris, ed., *Historical Atlas of Canada,* vol. 1 (Toronto: University of Toronto Press, 1987), plate 45.

20. Silvio Dumas, *Les Filles du Roi en Nouvelle-France: Etude historique avec répertoire historique* (Quebec: Société historique de Québec, 1972), 35–60. Yves Landry's more systematic demographic study, *Orphelines en France, Pionnières au Canada: Les Filles du Roi au XVIIe siècle* (Montreal: Lemeac, 1992) makes subtle corrections to Dumas's group portrait of the emigrant women.

21. Gabriel Debien, "Engagés pour le Canada au XVIIe siècle vus de La Rochelle," *Revue d'Histoire de l'Amérique française* (RHAF) 6 (1952–53): 221–33, 374–79.

22. Stanislas A. Lortie, "De l'origine des Canadiens-français," in *L'Origine de le Parler des Canadiens-français: Etudes* (Paris: Honoré Champion, 1903), 5–12, provided the statistics on provincial origins for recorded emigrants in Laurentian Canada in 1608–1700. Compare this with Archange Godbout's summary of the origins of 10,126 emigrants to the St. Lawrence Valley from France in 1600–1763: Ile-de-France—10.1 percent; Normandy—9.9 percent; Poitou—6 percent; Aunis—5.6 percent; Brittany—4.6 percent; Saintonge—4.1 percent; Guyenne—3.2 percent; and other provinces—56.5 percent. These figures from Godbout's *Origine des Familles canadiennes-françaises* (1979) are reprinted in Marcel Fournier, *Les Européens au Canada des Origines à 1765 {Hors France}* (Montreal: Editions du Fleuve, 1989), 24. The geographic distribution is shown visually, without percentages, in the *Historical Atlas of Canada,* vol. 1 (Toronto: University of Toronto Press, 1987), plate 45. The Université de Montréal's Programme de recherche en démographie historique, under the leadership of Dr. Hubert Charbonneau, with a sample of 8,527 settler-emigrants, placed the same seven French provinces at the top of the list of contributing regions, though the exact percentages varied from those of Lortie and Godbout.

23. Alfred Cambray, *Robert Giffard, premier Seigneur de Beauport* (Cap de la Madeleine: privately printed, 1932), 34–39, 73–77. The transcription of the 1634 contract is faulty and ought to be compared to the facsimile on the opposite pages. The stonemason, Jean Guyon, waited twenty years before selling his home in France.

24. Mme. Pierre Montagne, *Tourouvre et les Juchereau: Un chapitre de l'émigration percheronne au Canada* (Quebec: S.G.C.F., 1965), 31–86.

25. The notarized contracts were calendared by Maria Mondoux in "Les Hommes de Montréal," RHAF 2 (1948–49): 59–80.

26. Ralph Flenley, ed, and trans., *A History of Montreal, 1640–1672, from the French of Dollier de Casson* (London and Toronto: Dent and Sons, 1928), 244–47.

27. Of 224 men hired at La Rochelle for Canada in 1641–65, 38.8 percent were listed as agricultural workers or domestic servants and 20.8 percent were craftsmen in the building trades. Metalworkers and food preparers accounted for less than 6 percent each. Clothing trades, at 2.2 percent, were not favored. The 526 workers whose occupations are noted in the 1663 census of New France show a similar distribution: 30.3 percent in agriculture and domestic service, 23.7 percent in building trades, 7.4 percent in food trades or metalworking, and 6.8 percent in clothing crafts, such as tailoring and shoemaking.

28. Archives de la Bibliothèque de La Rochelle (ABL), Greffe de Pierre Moreau, Ms.1845, passim.

29. ABL, Greffe de Pierre Moreau, Ms. 1845, f.95. Observe that the notary did not bother to list the men's ages or their occupations—an indication of the impersonal nature of recruitment. In 1663 at Quebec Jean Chauveau or Chauvaux (b.1635) married Marie Albert, who came from his home parish, and they stayed in the colony. Jouin, evidently, returned to France.

30. *Rapport de l'Archiviste de la Province de Québec* (RAPQ), 1930–31, 103: Talon's observations, 1669.

31. RAPQ, 1930–31, 36, 41, 43: correspondence between Talon and Colbert, 1665–66.

32. A comparison of the lists of the king's *engagés* sent out in 1664–65 with the 1667 and 1668 censuses revealed the council's bias in distributing the workers to councilors, seigneurs, merchants, crown and company officials, and to religious orders. Of 114 men delivered by *Le Noir* in 1664 and *Le Cat* (this Dutch ship was probably called *De Kat*) in 1665, 57 could be found in the censuses. Most (38) had not gone beyond Quebec and its environs. The masters were notables and wealthy colonists (23), tenant farmers (16), religious orders (10), and craftsmen (4). The passenger rolls of the two ships, from the Archives de la Charente-maritime, Amirauté series, were published in RHAF 6 (1952–53): 392–93, 394–96.

33. *Jugements et Déliberations du Conseil souverain de la Nouvelle-France* (JDCS), 6 vols. (Quebec: Côté and Dussault, 1885–91), 1:29, 202.

34. RAPQ, 1930–31, 81: Talon to Colbert, 27 October 1667.

35. RAPQ, 1930–31, 87: Talon to Colbert, 29 October 1667.

36. National Archives of Canada (NAC), MG 1, C11A Series transcript, vol. 6, 116–17: De Meulles to Colbert, 12 November 1682.

37. Archives nationales de France (ANF), Archives des Colonies (AC), série C11A, vol. 6, f.399: De Meulles to Colbert, 12 November 1684.

38. J. Le Ber and G. Debien, "La propagande et le recrutement pour les Colonies d'Amérique au XVIIe siècle," Conjonction, No.48 (1953), 60–90.

39. Archives de la Charente-Maritime, Greffe de Beauchamps, 8 June 1692: Engagement Dupin-Baudouin. The journeyman-surgeon Dupin did not remain in Canada.

40. Archives du Séminaire de Québec (ASQ), Lettres, Carton N, No.121: Abbé Tremblay to François de Laval, Bishop of Quebec, 15 June 1703. Officials at La Rochelle encountered the same resistance in 1687 when seeking the craftsmen requested by Governor-General Denonville: "there is scarcely anyone who would wish to quit his establishment to go to a country like Canada, without some certainty of earning his living more richly than in France." See NAC, B Series transcript, vol. 13, 172–73.

41. RHAF 13 (1959–60): 412, 553–55. D. C. Harvey's *The French Regime in Prince Edward Island* (New Haven, Conn.: Yale University Press, 1926) provides a background history for these events. The colonizing work on the island of a 1731 concessionaire, Jean-Pierre Roma, is not as well documented.

42. This dependence is evident from contracts drawn up by La Rochelle notary Pierre Moreau that described the workers' destination as "the land of Canada in the said [Caribbean] islands" or those eighteenth-century accords, listed in RHAF 13 (1959–60) and 14 (1960–61), that provided for a salary payable in sugar and invoked the West Indies' standard for the indentured workers' maintenance.

43. NAC, MG 1, C11A Series transcript, vol. 17, 108: Intendant Bochart de Champigny to the minister, 1699; RAPQ, 1942–43, 415–416: Mme Vaudreuil to the minister; W. B. Munro, ed., *Documents Relating to the Seigniorial Tenure in Canada, 1598–1854* (Toronto: Champlain Society, 1908), 145, 149.

44. ANF, AC, série B, vol. 36, ff.336vo–337vo: Ordonnance qui oblige les V[aisse]aux. Marchands qui iront a l'avenir en la Nouvelle france d'y porter 4 Engagés Et 8. Soldats de Recrue, [donné] A Versailles le 20 mars 1714. The Compagnie des Cent Associés had a quota of one man for so many tons of cargo; in August 1664 Quebec's Sovereign Council inserted a similar stipulation in its proposed landing permits for ships coming to the colony. The proposal seems to have come to nothing because the crown was sending enough contract workers. See Jugement et Déliberations du Conseil Souverain de la Nouvelle-France (JDCS), 1:269–70. François Ruette d'Auteuil, in his 1715 memorial reprinted in RAPQ, 1922–23, 62–63, attributed this projected regulation that shipowners deliver one man for every ten tons of cargo destined for Canada to "le Conseil établi ensuite à Québec." Paul Emile Renaud's *Les Origines économiques du Canada* (Mamers: Enault, 1928), 237, gave a faulty paraphrase of this rule, which was issued, he wrote, by "le Conseil qui fut alors institué à Québec (1647)." Gabriel Debien took this as a reference to a 1647 regulation and Leslie Choquette has repeated the error. The Quebec council's idea was probably unknown to the French government and did not serve as a guiding precedent.

45. ANF, Archives de la Marine, série A2, Art. 23, ff. 634–43: Reglement au Sujet des Engagés et fusils a porter aux colonies des jsles françoises de l'Amérique et de la Nouvelle France [16 November 1716].

46. ANF, AC, série B, vol. 44, ff.56vo–57, 191–191vo, 196vo–197. In June 1721 printed copies of this offer were sent to Calais, Dieppe, Le Havre, Rouen, Honfleur, St-Malo, Morlaix, Brest, Nantes, La Rochelle, Bordeaux, Bayonne and Marseille. These ports and Certe were the only ones authorized in 1717 to trade with the French colonies.

47. ANF, AC, série B, vol. 44, f.197. The resistance of La Rochelle's merchants was acknowledged in August and the council decided that acceptance of prisoners would be voluntary and not compulsory.

48. APR, série IE, vol. 94, 381–82: Maritime Council to the Intendant at Rochefort, 9 April 1722.

49. ANF, Archives de la Marine, série AI, art. 62, pièce 11.

50. ANF, AC, série C11B, vol. 24, ff.103–103vo: François Bigot to the minister, 29 September 1742.

51. RAPQ, 1938–40, 3–103.

52. NAC, MG 1, C11A Series transcript, vol. 93, 327. François Bigot had just arrived from Louisbourg, where he, as *commissaire-ordonnateur,* had taken the enforcement of these trade regulations more seriously than had the previous intendant of New France.

53. ANF, AC, série C11B, vol. 31, ff.50vo–51: Jean-Louis, Comte de Raymond, to the minister, 4 November 1751.

54. ANF, Archives de la Marine, série F5B, art. 30: Classes: Bayonne, passagers pour les colonies 1749–77, f.72. Other voyages by the same schooner are noted on ff.53–54, 58, and 75.

55. Public Record Office, High Court of Admiralty, Series 30 (Hereafter PRO, HCA 30), Box 264, #186: B. Duvergé at Bayonne to M. Imbert at Louisbourg, 10 March 1757.

56. PRO, HCA 32 (papers of prize vessels with captors' reports) provided the opportunity to make this comparison. The crew rolls and indentures among the ships' papers frequently listed indentured workers who were not on board at the time of capture. Most prizes were taken on the outward voyage from France. For example, *La Fleur de Jour* of La Rochelle, 102 tons, and destined for Quebec, was taken in 1747. An extra sailor, in addition to the crew of twelve noted on the roll, was found, but the three indentured workers, declared upon departure and for whom contracts were made, were missing. See Box 112–1. Other examples are: 1744—*Le Saint Marc* of Olonne, destined for Canada via Bordeaux, crew of fifteen, no contract workers on board [Box 130–1]; 1745—*La Gracieuse* of Bayonne, 122 tons, destined for Quebec, with a listed crew of twenty-two and three *engagés* (aged twenty-two, twenty-nine, and thirty-two). When captured this ship had twenty-three mariners and four "boys" on board [Box 113–1]. Seventeen hundred forty-seven—*Le Fortuné* of Bordeaux, 200 tons, destined for Quebec with a crew of twenty-eight and one indentured shoemaker on board in place of the required four workers, by special permission; the English captors reported finding only twenty-six live crewmen and two dead bodies on the ship [Box 112–2]. Seventeen hundred fifty-seven—*L'Acadie* of Bordeaux, 160 tons, destined for Quebec and the West Indies, crew of twenty-two with three *engagés*. The British report reads "there was Twenty Two Mariners officers included on board" [Box 161–1]. Seventeen hundred fifty-seven—*L'Aigle* of Bordeaux, 200 tons, destined for the West Indies, crew of thirty-three with two contract workers (in place of three); this ship had thirty-six people on board when captured! [Box 161–1]. There were notarial contracts with the ship's papers for *La Fleur du Jour* and *L'Acadie,* but none on *L'Aigle,* which shows that false indentures were being made to satisfy port authorities.

57. RAPQ, 1926–27, 87: the king to Frontenac, 15 April 1676.

58. ANF, AC, série C11A, vol. 3, f.61: Acting Intendant Patoulet to Colbert, 11 November 1669.

59. This is the documented argument of Jacques Mathieu and Lina Gouger, in "Transferts de population," *Annales de Bretagne et des Pays de l'Ouest* 95, no. 4 (1988): 337–45.

60. RAPQ, 1930–31, 87, 125.

61. RAPQ, 1930–31, 69.

62. Landry, *Orphélines en France,* 188–202, 212–15.

63. Marcel Trudel, *Histoire de la Nouvelle-France, vol. 3: La Seigneurie des Cent-Associés, 1627–1663, Part 2: La Société* (Montreal: Fides, 1983), 72.

64. JDCS, 1:29.

65. RAPQ, 1930–31, 164: Talon to Colbert, 11 November 1671.

66. RAPQ, 1930–31, 152: Memorial from Talon to Colbert, 2 November 1671.

67. Ibid., 150: Talon to Colbert, 31 October 1671—"If my obedience in leaving Europe for America, in exposing my life to the various perils of the sea, and the sickness I have endured for seven years, and my work in a land as rough as this one was in its beginnings have merited some favors of the king, I would encompass them all in the permission, that I beg for, to return to France."

68. RAPQ, 1926–27, 8: The king to Frontenac, 5 June 1672.

69. RAPQ, 1930–31, 169: Colbert to Talon, 4 June 1672.

70. RAPQ, 1926–27, 80: The king to Frontenac, 22 April 1675. A later dispatch from the king suggested that the crown was as concerned about the colonists wasting their fortunes in such voyages. See ibid., 87.

71. E. B. O'Callaghan, ed., *Documents Relative to the Colonial History of the State of New York,* 15 vols. (Albany: Weed, Parsons and Co., 1853–87), 9:221: Colbert to François Charon de La Barre, 10 April 1684. By this time, the adjoining British colony of New York had become the goal of fugitives, and a royal ordinance was passed in 1684 against anyone removing to the English or Dutch settlements. See ibid., 224–25.

72. M. Fournier, *Les Européens au Canada: des origines à 1765 {hors France}* (Montreal: Editions du Fleuve, 1989), 30. Direct French migration effectively ended in 1710 with the British capture of Port Royal; thereafter peninsular Acadia was the British colony of Nova Scotia.

73. B. Bailyn, *Voyagers to the West: A Passage in the Peopling of America* (New York: Knopf, 1986); D. W. Galenson, *White Servitude in Colonial America* (Cambridge: CambridgeUniversity Press , 1981); R. O. Heavner, *Economic Aspects of Indentured Servitude in Colonial Pennsylvania* (New York: Arno, 1978); A. E. Smith, *Colonists in Bondage* (Chapel Hill: University of North Carolina Press, 1947); W. B. Smith, *White Servitude in Colonial South Carolina* (Columbia: University of South Carolina Press, 1961).

74. Boucher, *Histoire Véritable,* 136–38.

75. See the twenty-three indentures made in 1684 by René-Robert Cavelier de la Salle for "Louisiana" before La Rochelle notary Pierre Soullard in the Archives de la Charente-Maritime, Série E, Greffe d'Henri Rivière et Pierre Soullard, Registre 1673–84, 7 June–6 July 1684. Not only were the artisans' salaries 20 to 40 percent higher, but half of the men were obliged to serve for only two years and all were promised a prepaid return passage. These terms were far better than those offered for workers going to the St. Lawrence Valley. Premium salaries were also paid to men hired by the Compagnie de l'Acadie, indicating that Acadia, like Louisiana, was a less desirable destination than Canada.

76. Quoted by Christian Huetz de Lemps, "Indentured Servants Bound for the French Antilles in the Seventeenth and Eighteenth Centuries," in Ida Altman and James Horn, eds., *"To Make America": European Emigration in the Early Modern Period* (Berkeley and Los Angeles: University of California Press, 1991), 189.

77. ANF, AC, série G1, vol. 406, reg. IV, f.63; vol. 407, reg.1, f.14; vol. 409, reg.1, f.77vo and reg.2, f.25vo; série G2, vol. 212, dossier 552, pi èce 22 (c.1756 lease of house from Sieur Paris). The lives of this and other slaves at Louisbourg are described in Kenneth Donovan, "Slaves and Their Owners in Ile Royale, 1713–1760," *Acadiensis* 25, no. 1 (autumn 1995): 3–32.

78. ANF, AC, série C11A, vol. 43, ff.80–81.

79. Marcel Trudel, *L'Esclavage au Canada français, histoire et conditions de l'esclavage* (Quebec: Université Laval, 1960).

80. The Maritime Council withdrew two men, aged fifty-five and fifty-seven, as "too old," an imbecile, and two women from the 1721 shipment of prisoners and reminded port officials in France that "only people who can be useful by their labor" should be sent to the colonies, otherwise they would remain a burden on the crown and no colonists would want to take charge of them. See ANF, AC, série B, vol. 44, ff.241–241vo. The selection process failed to weed out worthless men in 1730, but the intendant and governor-general expressed their satisfaction with the 1731 shipment.

81. Peter W. Coldham, *Emigrants in Chains: A Social History of Forced Emigration to the Americas, 1607–1776* (Far Thrupp: Alan Sutton, 1992), chap. 5.

82. NAC, MG 1, C11A Series transcript, vol. 63, 26–27, 89–93.

83. ANF, AC, série C11B, vol. 24, ff.22–22vo: Duquesnel and Bigot to the minister, 14 October 1742. Their predecessors had expressed enthusiasm for the *faux-sauniers* in 1737–41 and had desired more of them.

84. ANF, AC, série B, vol. 77, ff.5–6: Minister to Duquesnel and Bigot, 12 June 1743.

85. ANF, AC, série C11B, vol. 25, ff.16–18: Duquesnel and Bigot to the minister, 25 October 1743.

86. ANF, AC, série B, vol. 44, ff.243–244: Maritime Board to M. De Silly at Le Havre, 3 and 28 September 1721. Supporting documents are attached to this correspondence, without revealing the nature of the boys' crime.

87. ANF, AC, série G2 (Conseil supérieur de Louisbourg), vol. 178, ff. 831–35: Interrogation of Jean Legouel in prison, 20 September 1725.

88. NAC, MG 1, C11A transcript, vol. 47, 265: The bishop of Quebec to the minister, 4 October 1725.

89. C. Le Beau, *Avantures du Sieur C. Le Beau,* 2 vols. (Amsterdam: Uytwerf, 1738), 1:67.

90. G. Malchelossse, "Faux sauniers, prisonniers et fils de famille en Nouvelle-France au XVIIIe siècle," *Cahiers des Dix* 9 (1944): 161–97. See also his "Les Fils de famille en Nouvelle-France, 1720–1750," in

ibid., 11 (1946) 261–311, in which he says that only ten of sixty-eigh exiled *fils de famille* became permanent settlers.

91. Pierre-Georges Roy, "Les Lettres de Naturalité sous le régime français," *Bulletin des Recherches historiques* 30 (1924): 225–32. The 126 letters are listed in G. Roy, ed., *Inventaire des insinuations du Conseil souverain de la Nouvelle-France* (Beauceville: l'Éclaireur, 1921), 119–21. The converts to Roman Catholicism are discussed at length in the official correspondence between France and Canada in 1705–7. After 1722, letters of naturalization cost one hundred livres (while also requiring a certificate of Catholicity) and this financial charge may have slowed the registration of foreign-born residents.

92. Because the *Historical Atlas of Canada,* vol. 1 (Toronto: University of Toronto, 1987), plate 45: "The French Origins of the Canadian Population, 1608–1759," gives more precise figures for the migration from France, one may wonder why estimates in round figures are necessary. The numbers given in the atlas are a computer-assisted reconstruction of the migration, primarily done by Mario Boleda, based on certain assumptions. This is not acknowledged. The plate's text understates the number of foreign, European settlers as "about 350." This atlas is a handsome production, but it occasionally fails the evidentiary basis for the plates and does not use cautionary words such as "probable" or "estimated," leading the reader to assume that the illustrations, tables, and maps are all of equal authority. This is not so. For example, given the vagueness of many building contracts and the lack of documentation for most rural dwellings, plate 56 on the proportion of colonial buildings according to construction technique (which has no "unknown" category) should be regarded as conjectural.

93. Jack Verney, *The Good Regiment: The Carignan-Salières Regiment in Canada, 1665–1668* (Montreal and Kingston: McGill-Queen's University Press, 1991), 147–85, lists each one of the military settlers and describes that man's fate.

94. ANF, AC, série B, vol. 27 (Canada, 1706), ff.89vo–90: Ordinance of 21 May 1698. The law's text did not reach New France until 1706 and war delayed its implementation. In 1726 the officials at Louisbourg asserted that a soldier's life ruined a man for the arduous existence of a farmer while Governor-General Duquesne claimed in 1753 that the men married sluts and wine-sops to get a discharge and were more likely to become tavern keepers than farmers. See ANF, AC, série C11A, vol.94, fo.98vo and série C11B, vol. 8, ff.16vo–17. These are obvious exaggerations because many former soldiers became productive craftsmen.

95. RAPQ, 1951–53, 9, 13 (Les témoignages de liberté au mariage).

96. The history of most residents of the colony can be traced in genealogical reference works such as the *Dictionnaire national des Canadiens français*, 3 vols. (Montreal: Institut généalogique Drouin, 1965) and Cyprien Tanguay's seven-volume *Dictionnaire généalogique des familles canadiennes* (Montreal: Sénécal, 1870–80).

97. G. Roy, ed., *Inventaire des papiers de Léry conservés aux Archives de la Province de Québec*, 3 vols. (Quebec: APQ, 1939–40), 1:62–63, as an example.

98. ANF, AC, série C11B, vol. 33, f.89: Governor Raymond of Ile Royale to the minister, 1753.

99. These points are made by T. A. Crowley, in "Forgotten Soldiers of New France: the Louisbourg Example," in the French Colonial Historical *Society's Proceedings of the Third Annual Meeting* (Athens, GA: F.C.H.S., 1978), 52–69, and by Allan Greer, "Mutiny at Louisbourg, December 1744," in *Histoire sociale/Social History* 10, no. 20 (1977): 305–36. Looking at a list of 585 recruits for the marine troops on Ile de Ré, an assembly point for reinforcements, in 1753, I found that 29 percent were below the required minimum height and were "Sans Esperence de croistre." See Archives du Port de Rochefort, série IR, no.20: Review of recruits . . . , Feb. 1753. Undersized recruits were acceptable if they had useful skills. See ANF, AC, série B, vol. 60, ff.61vo–62: Maurepas to Roston, 20 July 1734. There is fragmentary evidence that many were teenagers when they enlisted. The officers' and governors' opinions on the moral and physical qualities of the recruits sent to New France varied, but most were unfavorable. Governors-General Duquesne and de Beauharnois described the men as cowards, deserters, and thieves.

100. ANF, AC, série C11B, vol. 29, ff.213–213vo: Protest of Jean Hiriard (22) of Bayonne. This recalls the

trick of British military recruiters, who put "the king's shilling" in a drink which then was offered to an unsuspecting man. Acceptance of the drink and the concealed coin was taken to be voluntary enlistment in the monarch's armed forces.

101. Intendant Bochart de Champigny, 14 October 1698, quoted in Louise Dechêne, *Habitants et Marchands de Montréal au XVIIe siècle* (Paris: Plon, 1974), 87.

102. RAPQ, 1922–23, 64: Ruette d'Auteuil, 1715.

103. Y. Landry, "Mortalité, nuptialité et canadienisation des troupes françaises de la guerre de Sept Ans," *Histoire sociale/Social History* 12 (1979): 298–315.

104. Camille de Rochemonteix, ed., *Relation par Lettres de l'Amérique Septentrionale* (Paris: Letouzey et Ané, 1904), 4.

105. Archives de la Charente-Maritime, série E supplément, Registre 668: Mariages et inhumations de la paroisse Saint-Nicolas de La Rochelle, 7 January 1657 (marriage of Jacques Chaigneau and Louise Forrestier).

106. François Dupont in a land sale contract made on 24 August 1661 before notary Guillaume Audouart, quoted in Marcel Trudel, *Histoire de la Nouvelle-France,* vol. 3, part 2, 72. In 1667 the seigneuresse of Chavigny testified that she and her tenants had been forced to abandon the estate temporarily, "because of the incursions and frequent raids by the said Iroquois." See Archives du Québec, Actes de Foi et hommage, cahier 1, fo.181. Father Jérôme Lalemant admitted in the 1659–60 Relation that "the prospects of our French colonies would be admirable if fear of the Iroquois did not render a stay there dangerous." See Thwaites, *Jesuit Relations,* 45:190–91 (my translation).

107. Thwaites, *Jesuit Relations,* 9:187. Other examples of Le Jeune's efforts as an immigration promoter for Canada are in ibid., 7:238–45; 8:8–15, and 45:189–95.

108. Merrill Jensen, ed., *English Historical Documents: American Colonial Documents to 1776* (New York: Eyre and Spottiswood, 1955), 469–76. By contrast, I have found only one private letter from a colonist in New France recommending Canada as a place for resettlement. It was written in 1651 by a gentleman at Quebec to his brother-in-law at Tours. See Lucien Campeau, "Un Témoignage de 1651 sur la Nouvelle-France," RHAF 23, no.4 (March 1970): 601–12. The writer, Simon Denys, acknowledged the prejudices in his homeland: "when you hear people speaking of Canada in France, you imagine [it to be] an uncultivated desert full of horror." Characteristically, he and his wife still hoped to revisit France, despite their satisfaction with Canada.

109. Thwaites, *Jesuit Relations,* 7:243.

110. R. Mandrou, "Vers les Antilles et le Canada au XVIIe siècle," *Annales, Économies, Sociétés, et Civilisations* 14 (1959): 667–75.

CHAPTER 5

1. Etienne-Michel Faillon, ed., *Mémoires particuliers pour servir à l'Histoire de l'Eglise de l'Amérique du Nord . . . ,* 4 vols. (Paris: Poussielgue-Rusand, 1853–54), 1:65. The eyewitness was Marguerite Bourgeoys.

2. Of those presumed to be alive in 1663, 70.8 percent (sixty-eight out of ninety-six) became permanent residents. This information was extracted from A. Godbout, *Les Passagers du Saint-André* (Montreal: S.G.C.F., 1964), 11, 13–48; E. Z. Massicotte, "Les Colons de Montréal de 1642 à 1667," *Memoirs of the Royal Society of Canada,* vol. 7 (1913), Section 1, 16–22; and E. Z. Massicotte, "Une Recrue de Colons pour Montréal en 1659," *Canadian Antiquarian and Numismatic Journal,* 3d series, 10 (1913): 171–91.

3. The story of d'Agrain's recruiting expedition is in the Archives nationales de France (ANF), Archives des Colonies (AC), série B, vol. 42–1, ff.58–58vo, 201vo–202; vol. 47, ff.468–69, 485vo; and from the Archives du Port de Rochefort (APR), série 1E, vol. 94, 501–3, 621–25; vol. 95, 11–15, 57–58; vol. 100, 61.

4. APR, série 1E, vol. 96, 69–70: Maritime Council to the Intendant at Rochefort, 22 January 1721.

5. Henri-Raymond Casgrain, ed., *Voyage au Canada, dans le Nord de l'Amérique septentrionale fait depuis l'an*

1751 à 1761 par J. C. B. (Quebec: Brousseau, 1887), 16–17. The inconsistencies that raise suspicion about the author's self-portrait as a voluntary passenger are his claim that he originally left Paris, "to join my uncle who was captain of the posts at La Rochelle," and his misidentification of the *Chariot Royal*'s captain. J. C. B. wrote that when he arrived at the port in late March 1751 he learned that his uncle "had been buried a week before." There is no contemporary record of a capitaine des postes dying at that time. The author said that the ship, "was commanded by a naval captain named Salabery." ANF, AC, série B, vol. 94, ff.37vo–38, reported that this vessel sailed from Rochefort in June 1751 under the command of the Chevalier de la Filière, Lieutenant de Vaisseau. Moving from the impossible to the improbable, the author claimed that he was given a free passage to Quebec—an uncommon courtesy to a casual traveler without high rank. No one fitting his description appears on the "Liste des personnes auxquelles il a esté accordé passage sur la flutte du Roy Le Chariot Royal destinée pour Canada." Only a "Ch[evali]er de Billy Cadet a L'aiguillette" had the same initial letter in his surname. Finally, this well-educated voyager would have us believe that he freely enlisted as a private soldier in the colonial troops, who were notoriously underpaid, ill-clothed, and poorly quartered. My guess is that J. C. B. was a *fils de famille,* exiled to the colonies and forcibly enrolled in the garrison troops.

6. Reuben Gold Thwaites, ed., *The Jesuit Relations and Allied Documents: Travels and Explorations . . . 1610–1791,* 73 vols. (Cleveland: Burrows Brothers, 1896–1901), 68:226–31: Father Nau's letter to Father Richard, 20 October 1734 (my translation). This was supplemented by an English translation of Father Aulneau's letters: Arthur E. Jones, ed., *The Aulneau Collection, 1734–45* (Montreal: Archives of St. Mary's College, 1893), 7–24.

7. Rapport de l'Archiviste de la Province de Québec (RAPQ), 1947–48, 24.

8. Casgrain, *Voyage au Canada,* 18–20.

9. Louis-Antoine de Bougainville, *Adventure in the Wilderness* (Norman: University of Oklahoma Press, 1964), 307.

10. Thwaites, *Jesuit Relations,* 68:230–31 (my translation).

11. Casgrain, *Voyage au Canada,* 21–22. Fur trade voyageurs performed a similar initiation ceremony on those men making their first canoe trip into the Upper Great Lakes.

12. H. O. Têtu and C. O. Gagnon, eds., *Mandements, lettres pastorales et circulaires des Evêques de Québec,* 6 vols. (Quebec: A. Coté, 1887), 1:347–50.

13. A. Greer, *The Soldiers of Isle Royale, 1729–1745* (Ottawa: National Historic Parks and Sites, 1979), 36–58.

14. Casgrain, *Voyage au Canada,* 37–40.

15. *Diary of M. de Surlaville,* 3–18 Aug. 1751, from the Archives du Calvados, reprinted in R. M. Hutchinson, C. H. Moore, G. R. Proulx, and B. M. Schmeisser, *An Ordinary Soldier (Un Simple Soldat)* (unpublished manuscript report for the Fortress of Louisbourg staff, 1975), 12.

16. Pierre Pouchot, *Memoirs on The Late War in North America between France and England,* trans. Michael Cardy (Youngstown, New York: Old Fort Niagara Association, 1994), 76–77. Another French officer, Jean Plantavit de Margon, Chevalier de la Pause, made the same observation. See RAPQ, 1933–34, 208.

17. "Mémoire sur les postes du Canada adressé à M. de Surlaville, en 1754," RAPQ, 1927–28, 328, 334–35.

18. Thwaites, *Jesuit Relations,* 65:194–99 (my translation).

19. Casgrain, *Voyage au Canada,* 63, 149, 162–66, 179.

20. Archives du Québec [AQ], Greffes des notaires, Louis Chambalon, 12 August 1715, to which is appended a copy of the 6 May 1715 contract made at La Rochelle before the notaries Hirvoix and Grenot. Notarized records of the sale of immigrants' indentures in New France are very rare, as are those for the sale of transported prisoners' services, like that cited in footnote 21. Such transactions were usually undocumented. "Viton" did not remain in the colony. A recorded sale of an indentured worker's contract at Louisbourg is that of Jean-Marie Maison (28), journeyman-shoemaker from Dunkirk, to Charles Vallé, shoemaker, by Captain Joseph Brisson in July 1752. See ANF, série G3, carton 2041—suite (Greffe Morin), no.5.

21. AQ, Greffes de notaires, Claude Barolet, 9 August 1739. Any costs incurred or time lost as a consequence of fleeing their master would have to be made up by the two men. Laborde married a *Canadienne* in 1711; Larchet left the colony.

22. Archives du Séminaire de Québec (ASQ), MS C2, Grand Livre: 1674–1687, 250–51, and passim.

23. RAPQ, 1926–27, 123: Note on Frontenac's memorial about illicit fur traders, 1681.

24. JDCS, 1:30.

25. National Archives of Canada (NAC), MG 8, D1 (Trois-Rivières: Archives judiciaires, 1651–89), Cahier 2 (1654), 269: 3 March 1654. In 1636 the weekly diet for each of the Jesuits' indentured workers was "two loaves of bread, of about six or seven pounds, . . . two pounds of pork, two ounces of butter, a little measure of oil and of vinegar; a little dried codfish, . . . about a pound; a bowl-full of peas, . . . As to their drinks, they are given a chopine [pint] of cider per day, or a quart of beer, and occasionally a drink of wine, as on great feast-days. In the winter they are given a drop of brandy in the morning, if one has any." See Thwaites, *Jesuit Relations,* 9:156–57 (my translation).

26. Thwaites, *Jesuit Relations,* 6:47–49.

27. Kenneth Donovan, "Tattered Clothes and Powdered Wigs: Case Studies of the Poor and Well-To-Do in Eighteenth Century Louisbourg," in K. Donovan, ed., *Cape Breton at 200: Historical Essays in Honour of the Island's Bicentennial, 1785–1985* (Sydney: College of Cape Breton, 1985), 7.

28. ASQ, Séminaire 95, no.31: Regles Communes. The authors were identified by Noël Baillargeon, in *Le Séminaire de Québec sous l'Episcopat de Mgr. de Laval* (Quebec: Presses de l'université Laval, 1972), 132.

29. ASQ, Séminaire 95, no.32: ordre iournalier pour les Domestiques.

30. Thwaites, *Jesuit Relations,* 6:71.

31. ASQ, Ms. C2, Grand Livre: 1674–1687, 41–412.

32. ASQ, Ms. C2, 47.

33. ASQ, Lettres, Carton 'N,' no.61: M. Dudouyt at Paris to Bishop Laval at Quebec, 9 March 1682, 10.

34. RAPQ, 1939–40, 263–65: Bishop Laval at Paris to the gentlemen of the Quebec Seminary, May 1685. An anonymous writer at the seminary proposed in about 1695 that the seminary economize by keeping only those servants who were absolutely necessary and by appointing someone, "to oversee the room of the [indentured] people to . . . prevent the wastage of food, especially of bread." See ASQ, Séminaire 5, no.19: Ce que le Séminaire doit faire avec les engagés.

35. Guy Oury, ed., *Marie de l'Incarnation, Ursuline (1599–1672): Correspondance* (Solesmes: Abbaye Saint Pierre, 1971), 863. See also Joyce Marshall, trans. and ed., *Word from New France: The Selected Letters of Marie de l'Incarnation* (Toronto: Oxford, 1967), 343.

36. NAC, MG 1, C11A series transcript, vol. 6, 290–91: Jacques De Meulles to the minister, 4 November 1683.

37. RAPQ, 1939–40, 279: Mgr. de Laval to the seminary's directors, 9 June 1687.

38. JDCS, 1:548: Michel Riffault vs. Magdelaine and Claude Deschalais, 11 March 1669.

39. A. J. B. Johnston, *The Summer of 1744: A Portrait of Life in Eighteenth-Century Louisbourg* (Ottawa: Minister of the Environment, 1983), 59–61.

40. NAC, MG 8, C5, vol. 3, 19–29: Hubert and wife vs. de Lugerat dit Desmoulins, 29 October 1672.

41. AQ, NF 23, vol. 8, 4 March 1720.

42. J. F. Perrault, *Extraits ou Précédents tirés des Régistres de la Prévosté de Québec* (Quebec: Cary, 1824), 55.

43. Peter Moogk, "Thieving Buggers and Stupid Sluts: Insults and Popular Culture in New France," *William and Mary Quarterly* (WMQ), 3d series, 36 (October 1979): 524–47.

44. Roland J. Auger, *La Grande Recrue de 1653* (Montreal: S.G.C.F., 1955), 103–4. In 1966–67 M. Auger kindly introduced me to the genealogical sources that facilitated the reconstruction of each colonist's personal history.

45. Public Record Office (PRO), High Court of Admiralty Series 30 (HCA 30), box 264, letter 194: J. Barrère the younger at Bayonne to M. Laborde at Louisbourg, 23 October 1756. The surviving letters taken from French prizes of war correspond to the scale of commerce with each overseas possession and

there are very few private missives in this collection addressed to emigrants in Louisiana and the St. Lawrence Valley. The extensive trade with Ile Royale and the French West Indies means that most of the captured correspondence was with people on these French islands.

46. Archives du Québec, Montréal, Bailliages, pièces detachées (1681), M. T. Sallé at Paris to Claude Raimbault at Montreal, 15 March 1681. The family's fate was traced in Cyprien Tanguay's *Dictionnaire généalogique des Familles Canadiennes,* 7 vols. (Montreal: Sénécal, 1870–80), 1:507–8; 6:500; and by E. Z. Massicotte, in *Bulletin des Recherches historiques* 21 (1915): 78–81; and in "RAIMBAULT, Pierre" by Robert Lahaise, in the *Dictionary of Canadian Biography,* vol. 2 (Toronto: University of Toronto, 1969), 541–42. There is a thumbnail sketch of the wife as Madeleine-Thérèse "Salé," in Yves Landry, *Orphélines en France, Pionniéres au Canada: Lès Filles du roi* (Montreal: Lemeac, 1992), 369.

47. PRO, HCA 30, box 264, letter 122: Father Behola at St. Pée to St. Martin Duronea at Louisbourg, 14 February 1757.

48. Ibid., letter 130: Mariya Delapits at St. Jean de Luz to Pierre Laborde at Louisbourg, 2 April 1757.

49. Ibid., letter 95: St. Jean Mornigust at Ciboure to St. Martin Duronea at Louisbourg, 17 March 1757.

50. Ibid., letter 104: Marie Martin Duronea to St. Martin Duronea at Louisbourg, 12 February 1757.

51. R. C. Harris, *The Seigneurial System in Early Canada* (Madison: University of Wisconsin Press, 1966), 141–44.

52. Lina Gouger, "Montréal et le peuplement de Détroit, 1701–1765," in *Proceedings of the Eighteenth Meeting of the French Colonial Historical Society, Montreal, May 1992* (Cleveland: F.C.H.S., 1993), 46–58.

53. Moogk, "Thieving Buggers and Stupid Sluts," 524–47. The best summary of French jurisprudence on libel and of cases in France is François Dareau, *Traité des Injures dans l'Ordre judiciaire,* 2 vols. (Paris: Prault père, 1785).

54. C. M. Barbeau, *Folk Songs of Old Quebec {National Museums Buletin No.75}* (Ottawa: Queen's Printer, 1964), 2.

55. Pierre Boucher, *Histoire Véritable et Naturelle . . . de la Nouvelle France* (Paris: Lambert, 1664), 161–62. Father Paul Le Jeune, in 1659–60, claimed that many a diligent farmer with a family had achieved self-sufficiency, "in less than five or six years." See Thwaites, *Jesuit Relations,* 45:191–93. Marie de l'Incarnation opined that, "when a family commences to make a habitation, it needs two or three years before it has enough to feed itself, not to speak of clothing, furniture, . . ." See Marshall, *Word from New France,* 315.

56. JDCS, 1:201, 204.

57. RAPQ, 1922–23, 63: Ruette d'Auteuil.

58. JDCS, 1:303.

59. JDCS, 1:30.

60. E. L. Coleman, *New England Captives carried to Canada, 1677–1760* (Portland: Southworth Press, 1925), 91, 125, 290–92; *Dictionnaire national des Canadiens-français,* 3 vols. (Montreal: Institut Génealogique Drouin, 1965), 3:1807–8.

61. Esther Wheelwright's story is told in James Axtell, *The Invasion Within: The Contest of Cultures in Colonial North America* (New York: Oxford University Press, 1985), 297–300, and by G. M. Kelly, "WHEEL-WRIGHT, Esther," in the *Dictionary of Canadian Biography,* vol. 4 (Toronto: University of Toronto Press, 1979), 764–66. .

C H A P T E R   6

1. Archives nationales de France (ANF), Archives des Colonies (AC), série C11A, vol. 67, ff.97–99: Mémoire: Canada. Identical observations were made by Governor de Denonville in 1685, in ibid., vol. 57, f.94vo. Intendant Bigot in 1748 also noted the Canadians' versatility in manual skills, mainly for their own needs, in ibid., vol. 92, f.106.

2. National Archives of Canada (NAC), C11A Series transcript, vol. 54, 91–96; vol. 56, 68–79.

3. *Rapport de l'Archiviste de la Province de Québec* (RAPQ), 1930–1931, 18: Mémoire du Roi, 27 March 1665.

4. H. O. Têtu and C. O. Gagnon, eds., *Mandements, lettres pastorales et circulaires des Evêques de Québec,* 6 vols. (Quebec: Côté, 1887–90), 1:394–95.

5. J. H. Stewart Reid, Kenneth McNaught, Harry S. Crowe, eds., *A Source-Book of Canadian History* (Toronto: Longman, 1976), 34.

6. NAC, C11A Series transcript, vol. 26, 28–30: Raudot to the minister of the navy, 10 November 1707.

7. Ibid., vol. 27, 38: Memorials of de Louvigny and LeVasseur de Neré (1707).

8. F. X. de Charlevoix, *Histoire de description générale de la Nouvelle France,* 6 vols. (Paris: Nyon fils, 1744), 5:117. The same flattering comments were made by Chrestien LeClercq in 1691, by Abbé Olivet in 1736, by Peter Kalm in 1749, by Louis Franquet in 1752, by Bacqueville de la Potherie in 1753, and by General de Montcalm in 1756. Louis-Antoine de Bougainville, in a 1757 memorial, however, chided the Canadians for using "coarse expressions [*phrases vicieuses*] borrowed from the Indians' language [*sic*] and from maritime terms."

9. Pierre-Philippe Potier, "Façons de parler proverbiales, triviales, figurées, etc. des Canadiens au XVIIIe siècle," reprinted in *Bulletin du Parler français au Canada* 3 (1904–5): 213–20, 252–55, 291–93; 4 (1905–6): 29–30, 63–65, 102–4, 146–49, 224–26, 264–67. Mark M. Orkin, *Speaking Canadian French: An Informal Account of the French Language in Canada* (Toronto: General Publishing, 1971) provides an entertaining introduction to the subject. See also footnote 8 above for other sources.

10. J. Lambert, *Travels through lower Canada, and the United States . . . in the Years 1806, 1807, and 1808,* 2 vols. (London: Baldwin, Craddock and Joy, 1816), 1:176.

11. NAC, MG 8, D1 (Archives judiciaires de Trois-Rivières, feuillets séparés), 28: 8 May 1658; the 1660s case is cited in Adjutor Rivard, *Etudes sur les Parlers de France au Canada* (Quebec: Garneau, 1914), 20.

12. M. J. and G. Ahern, *Notes pour servir à l'Histoire de la Médecine dans le Bas-Canada depuis la fondation de Québec* (Quebec: privately published, 1923), 435–41. Phlem's 1734 contract to cure Jean Bilodeau is in Archives du Québec (AQ), Trois-Rivières, Greffe des notaires, A. B. Pollet, 16 September 1734 (registered 25 March 1736).

13. See, for example, AQ, Greffes des notaires, E. Jacob, 7 March 1707: marriage contract of Jean Langlois, "Anglois [Anglais] de Nation," with Anne Ratté, widow of Jacques Trépagny.

14. ANF, AC, Collection Moreau de St-Méry, vol. 11, f.55: judgment of Quebec's Conseil supérieur, 17 March 1742.

15. H. R. Casgrain, ed., *Voyage au Canada, dans le Nord de l'Amérique septentrionale* (Quebec: Bousseau, 1887), 49.

16. Sieur de Dièreville, *Relation of a Voyage to Port Royal in Acadia* (Toronto: Champlain Society, 1933), 82.

17. H. R. Casgrain, ed., *Journal du Marquis de Montcalm durant ses campagnes en Canada de 1756 à 1759* (Quebec: Demers et frère, 1895), 461.

18. RAPQ, 1931–1932, 10: Mémoire du Chevalier de la Pause, 1755.

19. NAC, MG 8, B1 (Prévôté de Québec), vol. 20–3: Jacques Dangueil Lallemand vs. François Perrault, 18 November 1729.

20. NAC, MG 8, C5 (Juridiction de Montréal: documents divers), vol. 6, 626–29: Pierre Chautreau dit Tourangeau vs. Sieur d'Argenteuil, 2 October 1699.

21. Other cases of this nature are cited in Peter Moogk, "Notables, Rank and Patronage: The Social Order of Early Eighteenth Century Canada," in Philip Boucher, ed., *Proceedings of the Thirteenth and Fourteenth Meetings of the French Colonial Historical Society* (Lanham, MD: University Press of America, 1990), 58–85.

22. *Jugements et Déliberations du Conseil souverain de la Nouvelle-France* (JDCS), 6 vols. (Quebec: Côté et Dussault, 1885–91), 2:377.

23. E. Z. Masssicotte, *Faits Curieux de l'Histoire de Montréal* (Montreal: Beauchemin, 1924), 38–44. It is not stated that this painter was the one who drew the execution in effigy. Berger's song described the assailants as making the druggist, Claude St. Olive, "dance in spite of himself," and of how the injured apothecary, "quickly sought the men of justice, giving out money freely, so that they [the soldiers] might be punished." This suggestion of judicial bribery and Berger's description of how all of the court officials

had profited from the affair, while laughing at the plaintiff over drinks afterward, would have been offensive to the same officials who later punished Berger. He is identified as a witness to the crime in AQ, NF 21, vol. 15, 4 April and 7 June 1709 (no pagination).

24. JDCS, 2:483–84.

25. University of British Columbia Library, Special Collections Division, Michaud Collection, copy of 10 October 1684 ordinance of de Meulles with the 15 April 1684 royal order.

26. G. Roy, *Inventaire des insinuations du Conseil souverain de la Nouvelle-France* (Beauceville: l'Éclaireur, 1921), 138.

27. Ibid., 193. The minister responsible for colonies granted gentlemen and officers in Canada a provisional exemption from this rule in April 1732.

28. G. Roy, "Les Chicanes de préséance sous le régime français," *Cahiers des Dix* 6 (1941): 67–81.

29. *Édits, Ordonnances royaux, déclarations et Arrêts du Conseil d'État du Roi concernant le Canada* (EOR), 3 vols. (Quebec: Fréchette, 1854–56), 1:352–55.

30. NAC, MG 1, B Series transcript, vol. 38–2, 454–55; EOR, 1:65; E. Richard, *Supplement to Dr. Brymner's Report on Canadian Archives . . . 1899* (Ottawa: Queen's Printer, 1901), 83, 102, 118, 136, 142, 157; G. Roy, *Inventaire des Insinuations,* 134.

31. Archives du Québec (AQ), Montreal, Greffes des notaires, A. Adhémar, 16–18 March 1713 (estimated at 626 livres; sold for 749); N. Senet, 29 October–4 November 1708 (estimated at 108 livres; sold for 97); AQ, Québec, Greffes des notaires, R. Duprac, 15–19 February 1731 (estimated at 917 livres; sold for 833). With only one case, Fernand Ouellet, "La mentalité et l'outillage économique de l'habitant canadien," *Bulletin des Recherches historiques* 62 (1956): 131–39, argued that estate auctions realized more than market value because bidding became a competition for prestige. I have found one instance where this might be the case: AQ, Quebec, Greffes des notaires, C. Barolet, 26 and 31 July 1752 (moveables of Noël de Rainville, estimated at 114 livres and sold at auction for 268 livres).

32. AQ, Montreal, Greffe des notaires, J. B. Adhémar, 30 October 1730: Estate of Pierre Bardet.

33. Meschinet de Richemond, *Inventaire sommaire des Archives départementales antérieures à 1790: . . . Charente-Inférieure, Série E supplément* (Paris: Dupont, 1892), 508.

34. C. Laverdière and H. R. Casgrain, eds., *Le Journal des Jésuites {1645–1668}* (Montreal: Valois, 1892), 48–49. It was decided to adjust the order to recognize the seniority by age of certain artisans.

35. ANF, AC, série C11A, vol. 99, ff.529–533vo: "Canada, 1754, Capitation." This head tax was never levied upon the colonial population, possibly because war intervened or because it was feared that the Canadians, who had never experienced such an imposition, might revolt.

36. AQ, Montreal, Greffes des notaires, M. Tailhandier, 27 March 1720.

37. Ibid., A. Adhémar, 2 September 1704.

38. Ibid., 1 July 1693.

39. ANF, AC, série F3, vol. 2, f.4vo: "Mémoire de Canada, 1697, M. de la Chesnaye."

40. De Charlevoix, *Histoire et description générale de la Nouvelle France,* 5:117.

41. AQ, Quebec, Greffes des notaires, E. Jacob, 24 January 1696; AQ, Montreal, Greffes des notaires, A. Adhémar, 16 March 1713. Billon is a copper-silver alloy, mainly composed of copper, and was used for coins of one and two sols in value.

42. Ibid. AQ, Quebec, Greffes . . . , F. Genaple, 27 March 1706: Estate of Jean Mouchère. Another Quebec region tanner left 5,365 livres in moveable property and about 12,000 livres in land and buildings. See the same notarial file, 12–14 November 1699: Estate of Etienne Charest.

43. In 1688 it was reported that Governor-General de Denonville's wife was running a shop in a room of his palace and had held a lottery to dispose of the unsold goods. Officers' wives were also reputed to have run liquor canteens and dry goods stores at their husband's posts. These accusations from unfriendly sources, which appear in the official correspondence, may have been a form of defamation: to connect a person of noble birth with the degrading role of retailer.

44. Adeline Daumard and François Furet, *Structures et relations sociales à Paris au milieu du XVIIIe siècle* (Paris: Colin, 1961).

45. AQ, Montreal, Greffes des notaires, F. Comparet, 8 August 1744.

46. K. Donovan, "Communities and Families: Family Life and Living Conditions in Eighteenth-Century Louisbourg," in E. Krause, C. Corbin, and W. O'Shea, eds., *Aspects of Louisbourg* (Sydney: University College of Cape Breton, 1995), 129–31.

47. C. J. de Ferrière, *Dictionnaire de Droit et de Pratique,* 2 vols. (Toulouse: Dupleix, 1779), 2:487–88. In C. J. De Ferrière and F. B. de Visme's *La Science parfaite des Notaires, ou Le Parfait Notaire,* 2 vols. (Paris: Mouchet, 1758), 1:201, the writers add that dower is to assure the widow of having food and "to recompense her for the cares and pains that she took for his household, to raise the children, and for the preservation of their shared goods."

48. AQ, Quebec, Greffes des notaires, J. C. Louet, 16 December 1721. An equally detailed account of a widow's "chambre garnie [qui] fait partie du préciput" is in ibid., J. C. Louet, 16 December 1743: Estate inventory of the late Nicolas Gaudin or Godin, at the request of his wife, Marie-Madeleine Gilbert.

49. A. Fauteux, "Un médecin irlandais à Montréal avant la Cession," *Bulletin des Recherches historiques* (BRH), 23 (1917): 304–7, exposed the inconsistencies and errors in this patent of nobility.

50. BRH, 23 (1917): 336, and Peter Moogk, "SULLIVAN, Timothy," in *Dictionary of Canadian Biography* (DCB), vol. 3 (Toronto: University of Toronto Press, 1974), 602–4.

51. AQ, Montreal, Greffes des notaires, A. Loiseau, 3 January 1737.

52. Ibid., 10 January 1745.

53. L. Beaudet, ed., *Recensement de la ville de Québec pour 1716* (Quebec: Côté, 1887).

54. Lorraine Gadoury, *La Noblesse de Nouvelle-France: Familles et Alliances* (Montreal: Hurtubise, 1992).

55. Pierre Pouchot, *Memoirs on the Late War in North America,* trans. Michael Cardy (Youngstown, NY: Old Fort Niagara Association, 1994), 76. See also the variant translation by Franklin B. Hough, *Memoir upon the Late War in North America { . . . }, 1755–60,* 2 vols. (Roxbury, VT: Woodward, 1866), 1:36. I was unable to locate a copy of the French original. W. J. Eccles, in "The Social, Economic and Political Significance of the Military Establishment in New France," *Canadian Historical Review* 52 (March 1971): 1–22, makes the case for the dominance of martial values, the officer class, and military priorities in the colony's life.

56. RAPQ, 1934–35, 72.

57. R. Douville, "BOUCHER, Pierre," in the DCB, vol. 2 (Toronto: University of Toronto Press, 1969), 82–87.

58. AQ, Quebec, Greffes des notaires, G. Rageot, 15 January 1685.

59. Ibid., L. Chambalon, 30 January 1695.

60. Ibid., J. C. Louet, 30 October 1720. More on Maillou's career can be found in Peter Moogk, "MAILLOU (Mailloux), dit Desmoulins, Jean-Baptiste," in DCB, vol. 3 (Toronto: University of Toronto Press, 1974), 419–21; and in Marc Grignon, *Loing du Soleil: Architectural Practice in Quebec City during the French Regime* (New York: Lang, 1997).

61. J. F. Bosher, "CADET, Joseph-Michel," in DCB, vol. 4 (Toronto: University of Toronto Press, 1979), 123–28. John Bosher argues that Cadet was made a scapegoat for the French defeat and "might have been acclaimed as a hero and a public benefactor," if the war's outcome had been different.

62. NAC, MG 24, L3, Undated letters A-L, 83–84: J. F. Cugnet to M. de Lavaltrie. The writer appears to be Jacques-François Cugnet (1757–97), the son of François-Joseph.

63. NAC, C11A Series, transcript, vol. 115–1, 111–12: "Canada, dépenses générales, 1741–1746."

64. R. Douville, "HERTEL de la Fresnière, Joseph-François" in DCB, vol. 2 (Toronto: University of Toronto Press, 1969), 282–84.

65. André Lachance, "HICHÉ, Henri," in DCB, vol. 3 (Toronto: University of Toronto Press, 1974), 291.

66. ANF, AC, série C11D, vol. 10, (no pagination): Mémoires de L'acadie . . . par le sr. De Cadillac, (1692). There is another copy of this memorial in vol. 2, ff.193–97.

67. Ibid., vol. 5, ff.259vo–274vo: Extrait des Lettres de l'Acadie de l'Année 1706—M. de Subercase, 22 and 25 October 1706.

68. Gisa Hynes, "Some Aspects of the Demography of Port Royal, 1650–1755," *Acadiensis* 3, no.1 (autumn 1973): 3–17. Port Royal was one Acadian community whose parish registers have survived.

69. ANF, AC, Série CIID, vol. 4, ff.297–99: Mémoire de plusieurs Choses qui regardent la justice de Lacadie . . . presenté par Loppinot Notaire Et greffier de Lacadie, 1703. Loppinot was the father of the officer of the same name at Louisbourg, mentioned in chapter 4. Ibid., vol. 4, ff.191–207, contains M. de Goutins's account, as commissaire and magistrate, of the disorders in Acadia in 1703, which he blamed on the governor, the soldiery, and their officer, Sieur de Bonaventure.

70. Ibid., vol. 6, ff.215–317vo: Loppinot au Ministre, 27 December 1707.

71. Ibid., vol. 5, f.222: Extrait du mémoire de M. de Subercase, 22 May1706.

72. *Report Concerning Canadian Archives for the year 1905,* 2 vols. (Ottawa: King's Printer, 1906), 2: Appendix A, 1–6.

73. The story of this building technique's evolution is partially told in Peter Moogk, *Building a House in New France: An Account of the Perplexities of Client and Craftsmen in Early Canada* (Toronto: McClelland and Stewart, 1977), chap. 2. The possibility that the maison en pièces-sur-pièces originated in Scandinavia was banished when I was able to examine structures from Denmark and Sweden at the Danish Frilandsmuseet, an open-air, architectural museum whose collection was drawn from the territories that once had been subject to Denmark's monarchs. Farmhouses from southern Sweden came closest to the Canadian technique: they had squared, fir timbers or heavy oak boards laid horizontally between oak or fir uprights. The difference was in the cornering. Swedish carpenters connected the timber infill to the corner posts with half-lap joints rather than by tenons fitted into a vertical slot, which ran the length of the corner post. French-speakers preferred pegged, mortise-and-tenon construction, even in furniture making. Some rural Danish outbuildings used oak boards mortised into uprights. As in Canada, the ample supply of timber in Sweden encouraged entirely wood construction, rather than half-timbering. The later use of dovetailed corners may have been an alternative to weakening the corner post with two deep vertical grooves. French fishermen on the Atlantic coasts of North America built short-lived structures whose walls were made of vertical posts driven into the ground. On Ile Royale this technique evolved into vertical posts set within a squared timber framework which, to arrest decay, was seated on a stone foundation.

C H A P T E R 7

1. L. Franquet, *Voyages et mémoires sur le Canada* (Quebec: A. Côté, 1889), 55–56.

2. Archives du Québec (AQ), Greffes des notaires, F. de la Cetière, 8 February 1705: Charles Ripoche and Louise Morel.

3. *Jugements et Delibérations du Conseil souverain de la Nouvelle-France* (JDCS), 6 vols. (Quebec: Côté and Dussault, 1885–1891), 1:556–57. The plaintiff was Marie Bourgeois of Dieppe, who had arrived at Quebec in 1667 with the girls sent by the king to marry colonists. She obtained a legal separation from her husband, Jacques Anet, in 1671.

4. AQ, Greffes, J. E. Dubreuil, 19 November 1713: Jean Loyseau and Marguerite Mercier.

5. AQ, Greffes, L. Chambalon, 4 March 1708, reprinted in G. Roy, ed., *Inventaire des contrats de mariage du régime français conservés aux Archives judiciaires de Québec,* 6 vols. (Quebec: Archives de la Province, 1938), 6:254–66.

6. L. Gadoury, *La noblesse de Nouvelle France: familles et alliances* (Ville La Salle: Éditions Hurtubise, 1992), 86.

7. Archives nationales de France (ANF), Archives des Colonies (AC), série C11A, vol. 43, ff.32–34: Vaudreuil to the minister, 20 October 1720. The governor-general had advised his great-nephew against this match and complained about the bishop's willingness to marry soldiers and officers after receiving thirty or forty pistoles for a dispensation from the banns of marriage.

8. ANF, AC, série C11A, vol. 5, ff.40–84.

9. National Archives of Canada (NAC), MG 24, L3 (Bâby Collection), Dated letters, vol. 1, 350–51: M. Margane to Margane de la Valterie, 8 June 1665 [*sic*].

10. NAC, MG 24, L3, Dated letters, vol. 1, 365: Maurice Rivet to his brother, 4 December 1683.

11. Ibid., Undated letters A-L, 83–84.

12. Ibid., Dated letters, vol. 1, 263–364: Charon to Mme. Bransollé, 22 November 1682. Charlotte Charon could not be identified in the 1681 census reprinted in B. Sulte, *Histoire des Canadiens-français, 1608–1880,* 6 vols. (Montreal: Wilson, 1882), 5:chap. 4, or be found in C. Tanguay's *Dictionnaire généalogique des familles canadiennes,* 7 vols. (Montreal: Sénécal, 1871–80).

13. AQ, NF 25, *Collection de pièces judiciaires et notariales* (CPJN), no.551 3/4: 23 July 1716. The deferral of the marriage agreement is in AQ, Greffes, Louis Chambalon, 4 May 1711, while the act identifying her as the resistant party is in AQ, Greffes, Jacques Barbel, 8 May 1711. The story of this mismatch was first told by G. Roy, *La Famille Martin de Lino* (Lévis: n.p., 1935), 38–39.

14. AQ, Greffes, H. Hiché, 30 April 1733, reprinted in Roy, *Inventaire des contrats de mariage,* 6:269–77.

15. AQ, Montreal, Greffes, C. J. Porlier, 3 March 1738: "Copie d'une Requeste du Sr. Silvain."

16. A. Fauteux, "Un médecin irlandais à Montréal avant la Cession," *Bulletin des Recherches historiques* (BRH), 23 (1917): 303–11, 333–38, 356–72; and Peter Moogk, "SULLIVAN, Timothy," in *Dictionary of Canadian Biography,* vol. 3 (Toronto: University of Toronto Press, 1974), 602–4.

17. Quotation from Gabriel, *Le Maréchal de Camp Desandrouins 1729–1792* (Verdun, 1887), reproduced in G. Frégault, *La Guerre de la Conquête* (Montreal: Fides, 1955), 57.

18. ANF, AC, série C11A, vol. 91, ff.246–47.

19. NAC, MG 24, L3, Dated letters, vol. 1, 350–51: 8 June 1665 [*sic*].

20. Ibid., Dated letters, vol. 1, 382: Subercase to M. Dailleboust, 24 March 1714. D'Ailleboust had earned Subercase's patronage by serving under him in Acadia as a junior officer. D'Ailleboust was unhappy on Ile Royale and, in 1719, he begged his mother, "try dear mother to have me returned to Canada at whatever price, whether by a patron or by money. It [my new rank] might only be as a[n ensign] expectative for a lieutenancy because I am dying of affliction and boredom when I am away from you." See ibid., vol. 1, 393–94.

21. Ibid., Dated letters, vol. 1, 460–61: Chartier de Laronde [*sic*] at Quebec to Chevalier d'Argenteuil, 7 May 1736. See also 471, where Governor-General de Beauharnois congratulated one of his protégés in 1739 upon receiving favors from the French royal court.

22. Using Pierre-Georges Roy's list in "Les conseillers au Conseil souverain de la Nouvelle-France," *Transactions of the Royal Society of Canada,* series 3, 9 (1915): 173–87, I sought each name in DCB, vols. 1–4, and then had recourse to Cyprien Tanguay's *Dictionnaire généalogique* for those not contained in the DCB. Nothing was found on Jacques Cailhaut de la Teysserie, councilor from 1664 to 1673. Clerks of the council, being minor functionaries, were ignored, as were the ex officio members: the governor-general, intendant, and bishop of Quebec. Two attorneys-general who never occupied their seats on the council were also subtracted from the lay appointees.

23. A guide to the leading military families is Aegidius Fauteux, *Les Chevaliers de Saint-Louis en Canada* (Montreal: Cahiers des Dix, 1940). Because the military order of St. Louis was instituted in 1693, it does not completely cover the seventeenth-century officers in New France. The Cross of St. Louis was a distinction coveted by all military officers, and the possessors were the most senior colonial officers. The recipients were again traced in the *Dictionary of Canadian Biography.* For French Canadians, a minor award is still compared to this honor: "ce n'est pas une croix de Saint-Louis" is another way of saying, as we might put it in colloquial North American English, "it's no big deal."

24. JDCS, 3:988–89.

25. Governor-General De la Jonquière and Intendant Bigot to the minister, 4 October 1749, quoted in Roy, "Les Conseillers," 181.

26. A. Lachance, *La Justice criminelle du roi au Canada au XVIIIe siècle* (Quebec: les Presses de l'Université Laval, 1978), 42.

27. There is a parallel with colonial Spanish America, where the European-born *peninsulares* were favored over the *criollos* of the colonies.

28. A. Vachon, "BARBEL, Jacques," in DCB, vol. 2 (Toronto: University of Toronto Press, 1969), 42–43.

29. W. J. Eccles, "The Social, Economic, and Political Significance of the Military Establishment in New France," in Eccles, *Essays on New France* (Toronto: Oxford University Press, 1987), 115.

30. ANF, AC, série C11A, vol. 67, ff.97–99.

31. NAC, MG 24, L3, Dated letters, vol. 3, 1,226–33: Mme. De Lavaltrie (whose husband was Fort Niagara's commander) to her brother, 29 August 1751. The writer's phonetic prose presents some problems in interpretation. The original passage reads "Le mouvement que lon done os offisie doit faire revé il ni ora que les favori qui pouront etenire [s'en tenir: get drunk] les promosion ce font bien atendre pour faire a lordiner bien des méconten ille tranpire que sabrevois a la majoritéz."

32. NAC, MG 24, L3, Dated letters, vol. 3, 1340.

33. Ibid., vol. 3, 1422: M. Destimauville to his uncle, 22 August 1755. The writer had just received the Cross of St. Louis, which may have made him more gracious than usual.

34. RAPQ, 1933–34, 208: Les "Papiers" La Pause: Dissertation sur le gouvernement.

35. NAC, MG 24, L3, Dated letters, vol. 1, 534–35.

36. Ibid., vol. 1, 511, 516–19, 528–29; vol. 2, 556–57 (when de Blainville warns Guy not to touch his salary), 624–27, 654–55, 666–69, 719–21, 727–29 ("you know how delicate I am about the payment of my debts"), 780–81, 814–15, 848.

37. Newspapers trace their origins to Renaissance merchants' bulletins that reported commodity prices in foreign markets. The "prix courants" (current prices) or, for Italians, "coranto," gave early newspapers their names; the Dutch still refer to a newspaper as a "Krant." Because the god Mercury was the patron of commerce, printed French newsletters were also called "Mercures."

38. Public Record Office (PRO), High Court of Admiralty, Series 30 (HCA 30), Box 264, letter 85: E. Cabarrus to L. Cabarrus, February/March 1757. The letters of François Havy and Jean Lefèbvre, merchants at Quebec, in the Bâby Collection (NAC, MG24, L3), are full of prayers for peace and one from 4 November 1743 (vol. 1, 500–1) describes how their ship, the *Centaure,* was stripped of its crew and forced to winter at Quebec because the French navy needed seamen to man its vessels. Government requisitions from merchants' stocks were a hazard of doing business in the colony. Another merchant even had his new weights and scales appropriated by the government (vol. 1, 512–14). The story of Havy and Lefèbvre is told in Dale Miquelon, *Dugard of Rouen: French Trade to Canada and the West Indies, 1729– 1770* (Montreal: McGill-Queen's Press, 1978). John F. Bosher, *The Canada Merchants, 1713–1763* (Oxford: Oxford University Press, 1987) presents a comprehensive picture of the different groups engaged in colonial trade.

39. NAC, C11A Series transcript, vol. 40, 221–27; vol. 49, 183–92; vol. 75, 3–25. There were twelve signatories to the c.1727 petition: Perthuis, de la Gorgendière, Dupont, Ignace Gamelin, Monière, Malhiot, Francheville, another Perthuis, C. N. Lamarque, Fornel, J. B. Demuy, Riverin, and Denoix. Seven of these are identifiable Canadians, showing who was suffering most from the peddlers' activities. The first Canadian merchants' petition against the itinerant traders was in June 1685. See AQ, NF 21, vol. 3, ff.19vo–22. The same conflict occurred at Louisbourg; witness the order of the governor and commissaire-ordonnateur in 1739 restricting transactions by *marchands forains* to ships and forbidding them to buy or sell on land, contained in ANF, AC, série C11B, vol. 21, f.105: Extrait des Reglemens de Police. An earlier royal decree of June 1722 forbade the itinerant traders to buy food at Louisbourg. See ANF, AC, série G2, vol. 178, ff.766–67.

40. NAC, MG 24, L3, Dated letters, vol. 2, 643–44: M. de Lamaletie at Quebec to M. Guy, 5 July 1745.

41. Ibid., vol. 2, 664–65: Havy and Lefèbvre to Mme. Guy, 3 August 1745.

42. "Lettres de Mère Marie-Andrée Duplessis de Sainte-Hélène," *Nova Francia* 5 (1929–30): 376: Letter to M. Feret, Dieppe apothecary, 4 November 1743.

43. This expenditure included some one hundred thousand livres raised within the colony by import duties,

by taxes on furs, and from the royal concessions of the Domaine du Roi.

44. G. Frégault, *Le XVIIIe Siècle canadien: Etudes* (Montreal: Editions HMH, 1968), 373–75, 382.

45. NAC, C11A Series transcript, vol. 58, 71–72: Hocquart to the minister, 27 October 1732.

46. Ibid., vol. 64, 51: Hocquart to the minister, 15 October 1735.

47. NAC, B Series transcript, vol. 101, 106: Royal memorandum to de Vaudreuil and Bigot, 15 July 1755. Duquesne's dispatch cannot be found in the C11A series, outgoing letters from Canada, and Bigot's letter on this subject, dated 3 October 1749, was located in the C11C series (for Ile Royale and Acadia), vol. 9, ff.139–41.

48. NAC, C11A Series transcript, vol. 27, 41: Levasseur de Neré to the minister, 12 November 1707. While it was routine for senior functionaries to return to France, native Canadians such as Pierre Le Moyne d'Iberville or Montreal letter-writer Marie-Elisabeth Rocbert, Mme. Bégon, retired to France, as did the merchants Denis Goguet, Pierre Desauniers, Nicolas Aigron Lamothe, and Antoine Pascaud—before the British conquest compelled others to do so. At La Rochelle there are several references to these and other expatriate Canadians in the St. Barthélemy and Saint-Jean du Perrot parish records. The analogy between life in a colony and purgatory is fully drawn by a M. Gérard on St. Domingue: "suis je Venu icy pour me divertir? Ny suis je pas au Contraire venu faire mon purgatoire? Puissent-il me servir d'introduction a un paradis terrestre. C'est La [en France] ou je vous attends Mes chers Amis." See PRO, HCA 30, box 255: Letter of 21 June 1755 to M. Tournez at Bayonne.

49. Kathryn A. Young, *Kin, Commerce, Community: Merchants in the Port of Quebec, 1717–1745* (New York, Peter Lang, 1995). Some of the conclusions and the percentages I have drawn from her data do not accord with her own views, which are that the merchants were "rooted colonials," that they were a cohesive community, and that their outlook was thoroughly mercantile. She challenges John F. Bosher's claim that Protestant and Roman Catholic merchants operated within separate trading networks. The writer argues more persuasively that inherited wealth and social position were essential to the success of a third of the Canadian-born merchants and that the merchant-functionaries benefited from the intendant's partisan distribution of supply and freighting contracts. The author's wide range of information is impressive.

50. *Édits, Ordonnances royaux, Déclarations et Arrêts du Conseil d'Etat du Roi concernant le Canada* (EOR), 3 vols. (Quebec: Fréchette, 1854–55), 1:369–70. 2:554–55, has the minutes of a 1740 election for syndic attended by seventeen Quebec merchants, including the Protestant François Havy.

51. C. L. de Secondat de Montesquieu, *Persian Letters,* trans. C. J. Betts (Harmondsworth: Penguin Books, 1973), 98.

52. C. H. Laverdière and H. R. Casgrain, eds., *Le Journal des Jésuites {1645–68}* (Montreal: Valois, 1892), 48. Twelve crafts were represented in the 1648 procession at Quebec. See ibid., 110

53. B. Sulte, *Les Forges de Saint-Maurice* (Montreal: Ducharme, 1920), 123–24.

54. EOR, 1:9. The privilege was accorded to colonial craftsmen after ten years of residence by article 34 of the *Compagnie des Indes occidentales'* 1664 charter. See ibid., 46.

55. Jacques Pagé dit Carcy, a colonial silversmith, claimed this right in Paris in 1713. See "Un Orfèvre canadien à Paris au dix-huitième siècle," in BRH, 32 (1926): 347. Pagé reconsidered his plan and remained at Quebec until 1729, before going to the West Indies, where he died. The *Parlement* of Paris disputed this right of colonial artisans when it registered the 1627 charter of the Company of One Hundred Associates. See ANF, AC, série C11A, vol. 1, ff.91–105vo.

56. See AQ, NF 21, vol. 3, f.41: complaint of client in August 1685 about twelve chairs and two stools made by a self-taught joiner who said "that he had made the chairs as best he could." NAC, MG 8, B1, vol. 3, 180–81, has a case in June 1689 about six chairs and two side tables of which a customer complained. JCDS, 3:339–40, notes a 1689 dispute over a wig that was not repaired to the owner's satisfaction.

57. AQ, Montreal, Juridiction royale de Montréal, feuillets séparés, 7 July 1729: recommendation for honorific letters of mastery.

58. G. Roy, ed., *Ordonnances, commissions, etc., etc., des gouverneurs et intendants de la Nouvelle-France, 1636–1706,* 2 vols. (Beauceville: l'Eclaireur, 1924), 1:135; also JDCS, 2:67.

59. E. de la Poix de Fréminville, *Dictionnaire ou Traité de la Police générale des villes, bourgs, paroisses et seigneuries de la campagne* (Paris, Gissey, 1758), 10.

60. EOR, 2:265–66. In 1666 Minister Jean-Baptiste Colbert saw the unregulated state of the manual crafts as expedient in "a colony, like Canada, that is still being born." See RAPQ, 1930–31, 44. In 1741 the governor-general and intendant, in their observations on a memorandum presented by the Quebec merchants' syndic asking that peddlers and rural traders be outlawed, declined to act until that undefined date, "when it is time to establish masterships, [trade] communities, and sworn guild inspectors (*jurandes*)." See H. A. Innis, ed., *Select Documents in Canadian Economic History 1497–1783* (Toronto: University of Toronto, 1929), 410. Because the crown drew revenues from trades corporations in France, there was no enmity in Louis XIV's government toward them.

61. AQ, Registres du Conseil supérieur de la Nouvelle-France, vol. 35, f.129vo.

62. G. Roy, *Inventaire des jugements et délibérations du Conseil supérieur de la Nouvelle France de 1717 à 1760*, 7 vols. (Beauceville: l'Eclaireur, 1932–35), 6:127.

63. NAC, MG 8, B1 (Prévôté de Québec), vol. 2, part 1, 96–97, 303–305.

64. AQ, Ordonnances des Intendants, vol. 4, f.68. A marginal note states that several copies were made of this ruling for distribution.

65. JDCS, 6:385–86, 429–30.

66. De Fréminville, *Dictionnaire ou Traité de Police,* 184.

67. Archives de la Charente-Maritime, Série E, registre 1326 (1660–1670), 13 December 1660; E. Coornaert, *Les Corporations en France avant 1789* (Paris: Gallimard, 1941), 234–36; C. J. de Ferrière, *Dictionnaire de Droit et de Pratique*, 2 vols. (Toulouse: Dupleix, 1779), 1:116; De Fréminville, *Dictionnaire ou Traité de Police,* 184–86.

68. Archives du Séminaire de Québec (ASQ), Polygraphie 29, no.1 (8 April 1657), reprinted in C. M. Barbeau, "La Confrérie de Sainte-Anne," in *Memoirs of the Royal Society of Canada,* Section 1, Series 3, 39 (1945): 1–8. A variant of this article appeared in *Les Archives de Folklore* 1 (1946): 72–86. David Levack, *La Confrérie de Sainte-Anne à Québec: Tricentenaire* (Ste. Anne de Beaupré: n.p. , 1956) provides a reverent and inspirational history of the confraternity.

69. ASQ, Polygraphie 29, nos.1a and 1b (1 May 1657).

70. ASQ, Documents Faribault, no.99 (1 May and 28 July 1657); Polygraphie 29, no.1c (28 July 1657), no.5: Statuts de la Confrérie de Ste-Anne (n.d.).

71. ASQ, Polygraphie 29, no.4a: Règles et statuts de la confrairie de Ste-Anne. This document was reprinted in H. Têtu and C. O. Gagnon, *Mandements, lettres pastorales et circulaires des évêques de Québec,* 4 vols. (Quebec: Côté, 1887–90), 1:101–3, and may have been a model for the first Catholic Trade Unions of the Province of Quebec. In 1714 the brotherhood adopted a three-person directorate, like that of a parish vestry board, to work with the curate. The group's ledger (Polygraphie 29, no.16) shows that there were about ten voters at each directors' election.

72. ASQ, Polygraphie 29, no.16: Cahier de la Confrérie.

73. AQ, Montreal, Bailliage: Pièces judiciaires, 15 December 1680: Copy of the confraternity's charter.

74. Ibid., 8 January 1681: Explanation by Gadois and Guillory for Fezeret's expulsion.

75. Ibid., 15 December 1680 copy of the charter with notation, 23 December 1680; Court register "Bailliage, 1665–1682," f.373. In the court hearing the authors of the expulsion emphasized the episode of the blessed bread, whereas Fezeret, the plaintiff, dwelt on what had happened during the card game. He said that they had been playing for sugarplums, which were then presented to their wives, and when he lost all of his, he offered to buy some from Jean Bousquet. Bousquet took his money, without giving up any candies, and the others made fun of Fezeret. The plaintiff said that when he was leaving, Bousquet gave him a parting push at the doorway and then a fight erupted. According to the others, Fezeret fell upon Guillory, shouting, "It's you that I want, and I've owed it to you for ten years." This reference to a long-standing feud is borne out by a December 1679 dispute in court between these two over borrowed goods and services owed. See the court register, f.293vo.

76. Ibid., pièces judiciaires, 14 and 18 December 1680: Petitions of Fezeret to the judge. The petitioner described himself as an armorer (a maker and mender of weapons) and not as a blacksmith.

77. Ibid., pièces judiciaires, 25 December 1680: Petition of Antoine Forestier and Abraham Bouat, church wardens.

78. In December 1679 Gadois had asked the court to compel Guillory to carry out his duties as that year's organizer. See AQ, Montreal, Court register "Bailliage, 1665–1682," f.292. Fezeret admitted that Gadois had often and pressingly invited him to come to his home and to eat a meal with the others. See ibid., pièces judiciaires, 8 January 1681: Fezeret's "Reponces." Sharing a meal or drinking together was regarded in law as evidence of reconciliation and could invalidate a claim for libel. Gadois's assurance that the remaining brethren would continue their sponsorship is contained in a document, dated 21 January 1681, in the same series. He blamed Fezeret for the disturbances in the two previous years. Olivier Quesnel, an armorer who was not involved in the fights, also affirmed tht he would do his duty as sponsor-organizer when his turn came. See the court register, f.382vo.

79. Ibid., pièces judiciaires, 7 January 1681: The church wardens' petition.

80. Ibid., 8 January 1681: Fezeret's supplementary petition.

81. AQ, Montreal, Court register "Bailliage, 1665–1682," f.383. A preliminary sentence on 23 January by the substitut du procureur fiscal had already upheld the charter and had nullified the expulsion.

82. AQ, Montreal, Juridiction royale, Registre des audiences, vol. 11 (1726–29), ff.317–317vo: 26 October 1728. A fairly accurate transcription of the court minutes was published by E. Z. Massicotte, in "La communauté des cordonniers à Montréal," BRH, 24 (1918): 126–27. Given the suspicions of earlier judges, this magistrate's easy acceptance of the group's request is surprising.

83. AQ, Montreal, Juridiction royale, pièces judiciaires, 19 August 1729: Petition of the master shoemakers of Montreal.

84. Ibid., Juridiction royale, Registre des audiences, vol. 11 (1726–29), f.456: 19 August 1729.

85. JDCS, 6:376–77.

86. NAC, C11A Series transcript, vol. 85, 356.

87. AQ, Greffes des notaires, L. Chambalon, 20 May 1694, 7 March 1695, 1 September 1698, 3 November 1699, 9 June 1700, 17 April 1701, 10 August 1701, 8 February 1702, 14 April 1704, 26 April 1707, 31 December 1708, 5 January 1709; J. E. Dubreuil, 27 August 1715, 24 February 1720, 15 December 1721, 11 November 1725, 14 March 1726, 18 April 1728.

88. AQ, Greffes, L. Chambalon, 31 December 1708, 5 January 1709.

89. AQ, Montreal, Greffes des notaires, R. Chorel de Saint-Romain, 12 April 1731; J. C. Raimbault, 17 August 1727; F. Simonnet, 7 November 1738, 4 February 1743, 21 December 1743, 7 November 1745, 17 June 1749, 10 January 1753, 6 September 1756.

90. C. de Ferrière, *Corps et compilation de tous les Commentateurs anciens et modernes sur la Coutume de Paris,* 4 vols. (Paris: Carpentier, 1714), 3:262; Jousse, *Nouveau Commentaire sur les Ordonnances des mois d'août 1669 and mars 1673* (Paris: Debure, 1775), 234–37.

91. AQ, Greffes des notaires, C. Barolet, 5 April 1734, 3 October 1736, 12 October 1740, 17 May 1747, 5 October 1752, 12 September 1753, 3 May 1755 (a junior partner received a third of the profits in this case), and passim.

92. G. Roy, *Inventaire des Ordonnances des Intendants de la Nouvelle-France,* 4 vols. (Beauceville: l'Éclaireur, 1919), passim.

93. EOR, 1:443–62.

94. J. C. Falardeau, "The Seventeenth-Century Parish in French Canada," in M. Rioux and Y. Martin, eds., *French-Canadian Society: Volume 1* (Toronto: McClelland and Stewart, 1964), 19–32, esp. 25.

95. The honors due to seigneurs in church and in religious ceremonies are described in the 8 July 1709 ruling of Quebec's Superior Council, reprinted in EOR, 2:154–57.

96. W. B. Munro, ed., *Documents relating to the Seigniorial Tenure in Canada* (Toronto: Champlain Society, 1908), 94–151.

97. R. C. Harris, *The Seigneurial System in Early Canada: A Geographical Study* (Madison: University of Wisconsin Press, 1966), 81.

98. Ibid., 190–91.

99. Ibid.,, 7–8. This verdict appears to be supported by Louise Dechêne, *Habitants et Marchands de Montréal au XVIIe siècle* (Paris: PLON, 1973). I have found no evidence that seigneuries provided a framework for rural society in New France during the eighteenth century.

100. AQ, Montreal, Juridiction royale, pièces judiciaires, 5, 11, 14 October 1715, cited by T. Crowley, "Thunder Gusts: Popular Disturbances in Early French Canada," in Canadian Historical Association, *Historical Papers for 1979,* 11–31, esp. 22.

Chapter 8

1. Archives du Québec (AQ), NF 23 (Juridiction de Trois-Rivières), vol. 9, 13 March 1719 (no page number). Identification of the litigants was assisted by René Jetté, *Dictionnaire généalogique des familles de Québec* (Montreal: les Presses de l'Université de Montréal, 1983), 147–48, 202, 671–72, 898.

2. AQ, Montréal, Juridiction royale de Montréal, Bailliages, 1681, feuillets séparés, Reply of E. Landeron to the 13 August 1681 petition of Michel Le Court.

3. Author's collection, 13 May 1755 letter of Irène Chaussegros in France to "Monsieur de lery chaussegros, ingenieur en chef du Canada, a quebeq," bought from Bernard Amtmann, Montreal bookseller. De Léry's 11 November 1755 letter to the minister is reprinted in G. Roy, ed., *Inventaire des Papiers de Léry conservés aux Archives de la Province de Québec,* 3 vols. (Quebec: APQ, 1939), 2:131–33.

4. J. C. Dubé, *Les Intendants de la Nouvelle-France* (Montreal: Fides, 1984), chap. 1.

5. AQ, Greffes des notaires, J. Jacob, 15 February 1737. In ibid., L. Chambalon, 4 April 1703, the guardians of a late nailsmith's offspring leased out his forge and properties to support the minor children. The limitation of formal schooling to one year was not unusual for the children of low-ranking parents. The guardianship of minors resident in the colonies whose inheritance might include property in France was addressed in the king's declarations of 15 December 1721 and 1 October 1741, reprinted in *Édits, Ordonnances royaux, Declarations et Arrêts du Conseil d'état du Rol,* 3 vols. (Quebec: Fréchette, 1854–56), vol. 1, 438–41, 557–59.

6. AQ, Greffes, J. Barbel, 30 March 1736; Archives nationales de France (ANF), Archives des Colonies (AC), série G3, vol. 2058, pièce 22: 11 April 1725—the second reference was provided by Kenneth Donovan of Fortress Louisbourg National Historic Park. Some children's contracts of servitude made at Montreal are listed in E. Z. Massicotte, "Le travail des enfants, à Montréal, au XVIIe siècle," in *Bulletin des Recherches historiques* (BRH), 22 (1916): 57–59, and more are to be found in the notarial archives of other districts. In AQ, Montreal, Greffes, A. Adhémar file, Massicotte found eleven infants' indentures made in 1688–1713. They usually bound the children until their sixteenth or seventeenth year,the preferred age for starting a craft apprenticeship.

7. AQ, Greffes, J. E. Dubreuil, 19 June 1714.

8. AQ, Montreal, Greffes, A. Adhémar, 1 December 1698: registration of a holograph contract. This may have been an attempt to forestall a mother's attempt to retrieve a foster child, as happened in 1712, when a laundress with many children asked for the return of a son, who had been bound out, because he was poorly fed and badly clothed by the foster parents. Her request was rejected. See AQ, Montreal, Juridiction royale de Montréal, registre des audiences, vol. 7, ff.787–787vo, 790–790vo.

9. The short-lived Poor Boards hired out foundlings, see AQ, Greffes, L. Chambalon, 9 August 1700, and then the king's attorneys of the local courts took on this function. See ibid., J. E. Dubreuil, 3 March 1718 and passim, H. Hiché, 28 November 1729, 20 September 1735 (the five-year-old son of a New Yorker who was expelled from the colony); AQ, Montreal, Greffes, J. C. Raimbault, 12 and 20 May 1730, 1 June 1730, 1, 19, and 30 July 1730, 2, 4, 8, and 26 August 1730, 19 September 1730, and passim. E. Z. Massicotte undertook a pioneer study of this subject in "Comment on disposait des Enfants du Roi," in

BRH, 37 (1931): 49–54. Private indenturing of older foster children continued at the same time.

10. AQ, Greffes, J. E. Dubreuil, 4 May 1731, indenture with attached letter. Girls were apprenticed only to dressmakers, and their apprenticeship indentures are very rare.

11. AQ, NF 21, Documents de la Juridiction de Montréal, vol. 4, ff.117–18, 127vo–128; vol. 8, ff.6–7vo. (Joseph DeSevres vs. Pierre Perras).

12. National Archives of Canada (NAC), MG 24, L3, Dated letters, vol. 1, 432–34: Marguerite Prieur to M. Verreau, 30 July 1727.

13. H. Charbonneau, Bertrand Desjardins, André Guillemette, Yves Landry, Jacques Lésaré, and François Nault, *The First French Canadians: Pioneers in the St. Lawrence Valley* (Newark: University of Delaware Press, 1993), 121, 191–92.

14. G. Hynes, "Some Aspects of the Demography of Port Royal, 1650–1755," *Acadiensis* 3, no.1 (autumn 1973), 10–11.

15. AQ, Greffes, F. Simonnet, 8 September 1745 indenture with appended letters of 29 June and 15 July 1745. The father's reply and the subsequent apprenticeship contract were published by E. Z. Massicotte, "Le Sculpteur Levasseur et sa famille," in BRH, 37 (1931): 496–99.

16. C. J. de Ferrière, *Dictionnaire de Droit et de Pratique,* 2 vols. (Toulouse: Dupleix, 1779), 1:575–77; 2:642–43.

17. EOR, 2:204–9. Marriage freed a minor from the legal disabilities of being a minor, which may have encouraged clandestine marriages before this date.

18. The key role of the parents in arranging some marriages, even among commoners, is suggested by an 8 February 1709 case before Quebec's Provost's Court when a merchant demanded that the parents deliver their daughter in marriage, as agreed, or pay him damages and costs.

19. "Les 'Sommations respectueuses' autrefois," *in Rapport de l'Archiviste de la Province de Québec* (RAPQ), 1921–22, 59–78. Marie-Catherine Frontigny's case appears on 66–70. She was not pregnant at the time, to judge from the surviving church registers. These legal summonses are rare, which may indicate that most children married with parental approval.

20. F. X. de Charlevoix, *Journal of a Voyage to North America,* 2 vols. (London: Dodsley, 1761), 1:267.

21. ANF, AC, série C11A, vol. 43, ff.80–80vo. This passage is quoted, in part, in Marcel Trudel's *L'Esclavage au Canada français* (Quebec: Les presses universitaires Laval, 1960), 31–32.

22. EOR, 2:457–60.

23. AQ, Montreal, Juridiction royale, Registre des audiences, vol. 11, ff.15vo–16vo: 10 January 1727.

24. AQ, Montreal, Greffes, B. Basset, 20 August 1674; for other fraternal partnerships, see ibid., A. Adhémar, 7 May 1702; B. Basset, 4 December 1674; T. Frérot, 31 April 1672; C. Maugue, 29 August 1690. The idea survived into the eighteenth century and in AQ, Trois-Rivières, Greffes, J. Caron, 6 December 1745, there is a lifetime partnership of two spinsters.

25. N. Baillargeon, *Le Séminaire de Québec sous l'Épiscopat de Mgr. de Laval* (Quebec: PUL, 1972), 122–24, describes four couples who, in 1680–82, gave themselves to the seminary. One couple had three little children, whose care and education became the institution's responsibility after it had received all of the couple's property. See AQ, Greffes, R. Becquet, 19 October 1680. This pair, Michel Buisson and his wife Suzanne, were motivated more by religious zeal than by a concern for material security. In AQ, Montreal, Greffes, F. Simonnet, 7 October 1738, Pierre Borloton and his wife gave all their assets to the Charon Brethren, who were to pay their debts and assure the couple lifetime maintenance.

26. AQ, Montreal, Greffes, A. Adhémar, 5 April 1709 and 18 May 1713. See a 10 December 1700 deed in the same file by which René Renaud, carpenter, retired to the hospice of the Charon Brethren on similar terms, with the promise of "a drink of brandy every day," after an initial payment of forty livres to the institution.

27. AQ, Greffes, G. Rageot, 20 April 1690: Marché Jolly—Thibierge, which was not carried out, in the end; AQ, Montreal, Greffes, A. Adhémar, 28 February 1704: Perpetual indenture of René Danot to Gérard Barsalou, tanner. See also ibid., J. B. Adhémar, 1 August 1754: transfer of a farm's title to someone outside the family in return for a lifelong allowance for a couple.

28. An early example is AQ, Montreal, Greffes, A. Adhémar, 24 January 1695: reciprocal deed of gift be-tween Gilles Bourgau and Marie Gazaille of Contrecoeur, "in consideration of the good love and recipro-cal affection that there is between them," with the proviso that it would not take effect if there were living children at the time of the first partner's death.

29. AQ, Montreal, Juridiction royale, Pièces judiciaires, 30 October 1711.

30. Article 334 was invoked in an April 1749 judgment of Quebec's Superior Council to compel the heirs and children to contribute to a widow's pension viagère. See G. Roy, *Inventaire des jugements et délibérations du Conseil supérieur de la Nouvelle-France de 1717 à 1760* (IJDCS), 7 vols. (Beaucevillle: l'Éclaireur, 1932–35), 5:104. Article 165 of the 1866 text of the Province of Quebec's Civil Code states, "Children are bound to maintain their father, mother and other ascendants, who are in want."

31. This observation about the domestic care of the mentally disturbed by rural families was made by Guy Boisclair in "Les fous et la perception de la folie au 18e siècle," in A. Lachance, ed., *Les marginaux, les exclus et l'autre au Canada aux 17e et 18e siècles* (Montreal: Fides, 1996), 134–36.

32. See, for example, AQ, Greffes, L. Chambalon, 26 June 1706: Agreement of Jancien Amiot, Quebec locksmith, and of his wife Marguerite with their twenty-seven-year-old son Jean-Baptiste Amiot or AQ, Montreal, Greffes, J. Lalanne, 26 September 1754: *Abandon* by André Roy, toolmaker, and his wife of their buildings and land to their children in return for lifetime maintenance in food, firewood, and a cash allowance. Deeds of gift to a child to ensure a comfortable retirement were primarily a rural practice. In occupations that did not demand physical strength, such as commerce, they were extremely rare.

33. This possibility is sketched out by Allan Greer, *in Peasant, Lord and Merchant: Rural Society in Three Quebec Parishes 1740–1840* (Toronto: University of Toronto Press, 1985), 84–87, and figure 7 is an ingenious map showing the geographic distribution of farms owned by people sharing four surnames. The pattern shows a tendency of members with a common family name to cluster in one area.

34. The distribution of an aristocratic family's estate was not egalitarian, and favored the oldest son.

35. AQ, Greffes, L. Chambalon, 12 July 1694. See also 1 July 1701 for a similar arrangement between a couple and their son. Such arrangements were made in the British colonies: in a 1723 contract made at Yarmouth, Massachusetts Bay, Elisha Hall gave his son his house and land in return for lifetime mainte-nance, "as to house Room fires meat drink clothing washing, lodging and tendance." This contract was lot 705 in the 18 January 1997 auction of the Early American Numismatic Auctions, Inc.

36. AQ, Montreal, Greffes, J. B. Adhémar, 28 January 1716 (date of registration). In the same file is a 30 July 1715 deed of gift of an eight-arpent-wide concession from Paul Hu to his son Louis. An early example of a special reward for a dutiful son from his mother is in ibid., C. Maugue, 2 April 1683. When her second husband failed to provide for her needs, her son François Prudhomme helped her. For this aid she gave him twenty acres of forested land from her patrimony.

37. AQ, Montreal, Greffes, J. B. Adhémar, 31 December 1743: Division of the lands of Marie Adhémar, widow of Jacques Tessier, between her children, voided 19 January 1744.

38. AQ, Greffes, F. Genaple, 8 March 1690: Agreement between the Poor Board directors and Marc Antoine Canard transferring responsibility for Widow Barreau to the board for one hundred livres a year as well as a cow or thirty livres deliverable in the following year.

39. German-speaking families in nineteenth-century Waterloo County, Ontario, built houses with a wing designated "the doddy house," in which retired parents lived after a child had taken over their farm and the principal residence. The transmission of the farm to a descendant, and care for the aged, were pro-vided for in advance.

40. AQ, Montreal, F. Simonnet, 2 October 1738. In this case, the couple's eight children were collectively responsible for this annual living allowance. Religious provisions appeared in about a quarter of the deeds of gift made in contemplation of retirement. Food allowances for retired parents in the Richelieu Valley during the late eighteenth century are described in Greer, *Peasant, Lord and Merchant* 34–37.

41. AQ, NF 23, vol. 13, ff.157–157vo. The widow was evidently Jeanne Boissoneau, aged eighty-three, with seven living descendants in 1755.

42. G. Roy, *Inventaire des ordonnances des Intendants de la Nouvelle-France {1705–1759},* 4 vols. (Beauceville: l'Éclaireur, 1919), 1:46, 57, 90, 93, 114, 117, 118–19, 122, 186, 198, 206–7, 243, 246, and passim. Quebec's Superior Council also enforced this obligation. See IJDCS, 1:25–26; 2:223; 5:104.

43. J. F. Perrault, *Extraits ou Précédents tirés des Registres de la Prévôté de Québec* (Quebec: T. Cary, 1824), 77.

44. Gérard Pelletier, "La Donation entre vifs sous le régime français: Etude de la donation entre parents et enfants, fondé sur l'analyse de quelques cas dans le gouvernement de Québec" (master's thesis, University of Ottawa, 1983), and Daniel Léveillé, "Vieillards et vieillesse dans le gouvernement de Montréal aux 17e et 18e siècles (1660–1800)" (master's thesis, Université de Sherbrooke, 1992), provided the general background to the forty or so retirement accords that I examined.

45. These social rules are stated in De Ferrière, *Dictionnaire de Droit,* 1:452–53: "Deuil." He admitted that it was not a legal requirement under the Coutume de Paris, but a "bienséance" (civility).

46. Charbonneau and others, *First French Canadians,* 108.

47. H. Têtu and C. O. Gagnon, eds., *Mandements, lettres pastorales et circulaires des Evêques de Québec,* 6 vols. (Quebec: Côté, 1887–90), 1:114–15. The background for this pastoral letter and examples of postconquest charivaris in the Montreal region are provided by E. Z. Massicotte, "Le Charivari au Canada," in BRH, 32 (1926): 712–25.

48. AQ, NF 25 (Collection de pi(ces judiciaires et notariales), liasse 20, #803: Instance de Claude Barolet (1728). A violent charivari by the governor's servants against M. de Pontise, a surgeon at Port Royal, Acadia, was reported in ANF, AC, série C11D, vol. 4, ff.191–206. In the 1830s rural supporters of Lower Canada's liberal-democratic Patriotes used charivaris to intimidate royalist supporters of the provincial government. In the mid-twentieth century Irish-Canadians near Valcartier, Quebec, were still stopping couples on their way to church to be married and exacting a toll in a ritual called a "shivaree." Noise was made by firing shotguns into the air.

49. The popular belief in mercantile conspiracies as the cause for shortages or for high prices is discussed in L. Dechêne, *Le Partage des Subsistances au Canada sous le régime français* (Montreal: Boréal, 1994), chap. 9: "Agitations et Discours."

50. *Jugements et Délibérations du Conseil souverain,* 6 vols. (Quebec: Côté and Dussault, 1885–91), 6:997.

51. T. Crowley, "Thunder Gusts: Popular Disturbances in Early French Canada," Canadian Historical Association, *Historical Papers for 1979* (Ottawa: C. H. A., 1979), 11–31. The English crowds' sense of a just price and their conservative protests against economic change are the subject of E. Thompson, "The Moral Economy of the English Crowd in the Eighteenth Century," in *Past and Present* 50 (1971): 76–136.

52. A. H. Clark, *Acadia: The Geography of Early Nova Scotia to 1760* (Madison: University of Wisconsin Press, 1968), 375–76, and passim.

53. A. B. Benson, trans. and ed., *Peter Kalm's Travels in North America,* 2 vols. (New York, Dover, 1966), 2:423. Kalm's description of Canadian garden vegetables is borne out by a 1716 court case at Trois-Rivières over pigs that had destroyed or damaged cabbages, pumpkins, corn, fruit trees, and "les gadelles" in a kitchen garden. See AQ, NF 23, vol. 8, 14 December 1716: Dufaut vs. Augustin.

54. Ibid, Benson, *Peter Kalm's Travels,* 2:438.

55. "Lettres de Mère Marie-Andrée Duplessis de Sainte-Hélène," *Nova Francia* (1927–28) 3:229: Letter of 17 October 1737.

56. Sylvie Savoie, "Les couples en difficulté aux XVIIe et XVIIIe siècles: Les Demandes en séparation en Nouvelle-France" (master's thesis, Université de Sherbrooke, 1986). My observations about legal separation were originallly based on sixteen petitions presented to courts at Montreal (8), Trois-Rivières (1), Quebec (5), and Louisbourg (2) and were impressionistic. Ms. Savoie's thesis describes the overall pattern in Canada with precision. Specific rulings in France's courts are given in Guy du Rousseaud de la Combe, *Recueil de Jurisprudence civile du Pays de Droit écrit et coutumier* (Paris: Le Gras, 1746), 613–17.

57. NAC, MG 8, C5, vol. 5, 427–29: Jeanne Roussin vs. Jean La Croix, 23 August 1697. See also 646–48 for the plea of an indebted man's wife for separation to save her and her children from "beggary."

58. NAC, MG 8, B1, vol. 10, 191–96: Marie Charlotte Arnault vs. André Spénard, 7 June 1708.

59. De Ferrière, *Dictionnaire de Droit et de Pratique,* 2:609–12.

60. Ibid., 1:50–54 ("Adultère"); 2:611. The writer explained this double standard by pointing out that a wife's adultery was a greater crime because it cast doubt on the legitimacy of her children. The frequent accusations of sexual promiscuity or infidelity in libels against married women, even by other women, indicate that this double standard was well rooted in popular values.

61. EOR, 2:431–32.

62. ANF, AC, série G2, vol. 180, ff.877–888: Petition of Jeanne Cromé, March 1731. The document was written by someone other than the petitioner, and the author clearly knew what evidence would be most effective in meeting the legal prerequisites for a separation order. We do not have Laumonier's reply to these charges. See also vol. 198, dossier 183, ff.28vo–30vo, for the 1743 petition of Marie-Louise Cruchon, the wife of a bankrupt merchant, for separation of goods.

63. AQ, NF 19 (Prév(té de Québec), vol. 7, f.28: 10 April 1674: Marie Regnouard's petition.

64. Information from the Louisbourg parish records on her children and husband came from ANF, AC, série G1, vol. 406, ff.3, 8vo, 9, 11, 18vo, 24, 35, 36; vol. 407, ff.12vo, 81vo.

65. For this supplementary information on the Laumonier family, its property, and history, I am indebted to A. John B. Johnston, and Eric Krause, Parks Canada historians working at the Fortress of Louisbourg National Historic Park, who responded to my inquiries in April 1991 and June 1995.

C H A P T E R   9

1. Public Record Office, High Court of Admiralty, Series 30 (PRO HCA 30), box 264, bundle 2, letter 26: 28 March 1757, F. Barrete dit La Hayette to Pierre Barrete at Louisbourg.

2. PRO, HCA 30, box 240, 15 August 1744 letter to Father Alemant S. J. at Cap Français from his sister in Bordeaux.

3. PRO, HCA 30, box 657, 1736–57 Mss. book, possibly owned by Charles-Marie Pereau, pilot (no pagination).

4. *Jugements et Délibérations du Conseil souverain de la Nouvelle-France* (JDCS), 6 vols. (Quebec: Côté and Dussault, 1885–91), 4:265, 275–76, 283–84, 285, 304–5.

5. Peter Kalm, *The America of 1750: Peter Kalm's Travels in North America,* trans. A. B. Benson, 2 vols. (New York: Dover, 1966), 2:422.

6. Ibid., "Lettres de Mère Marie-Andrée Duplessis de Sainte-Hélène," 2:541. Sister de Sainte-Hélène, in her visits to the countryfolk, observed "the attention and respect of these poor people in the recitation of their prayers." See *Nova Francia* 3 (1927–28): 281.

7. Montreal Superior Court, Paroisse Notre-Dame de Montréal, Registre des mariages, 1643–1670, 235, 267.

8. Peter Moogk, "GADOIS, Pierre," in *Dictionary of Canadian Biography,* vol. 2 (Toronto: University of Toronto Press, 1969), 233–34; R. L. Séguin, *La Sorcellerie au Québec du XVIIe au XIXe siècle* (Montreal: Lemeac, 1971), 49–62.

9. Kalm, *America of 1750,* 2:416.

10. Thomas Anburey, *With Bourgoyne to Quebec,* ed. S. Jackman (Toronto: Macmillan, 1963), 58.

11. Soeur [Marie] Morin, *Annales de l'Hôtel-Dieu de Montréal* (Montreal: Société historique de Montréal, 1921), 152–53.

12. E. Richard, *Supplement to Dr. Brymner's Report on Canadian Archives, . . . 1899* (Ottawa: Dawson, 1901), 7. This account dates from 1722 or later and she does not mention this appeal in a short 1699 narrative of the events of 1692. The plea is credible, although it would not be as composed as this one.

13. J. Marshall, trans. and ed., *Word from New France* (Toronto: Oxford University Press, 1967), 312.

14. Archives du Séminaire de Québec, Paroisses diverses, no.71: Testimony of Father F. M. Le Veyer, May 1700.

15. H. Têtu and C. O. Gagnon, *Mandements, lettres pastorales et circulaires,* 6 vols. (Quebec: Côté, 1887–90), 2:31–33.

16. R. G. Thwaites, ed., *The Jesuit Relations and Allied Documents,* 73 vols. (Cleveland: Burrows Brothers, 1890–1901), 18:84–85.

17. Archives du Québec (AQ), Montreal, Greffes des notaires, C. J. Porlier, 25 July 1743 act deposited with the royal court at Montreal on 1 August 1743.

18. Archives du Monastère des Ursulines de Québec, Actes des assemblées capitulaires de 1686 à 1802, 1.

19. PRO, HCA 30, box 240, 6 March 1745 letter to M. Berty at Grande Rivière, Cap Français, on St. Domingue, from his nephew at Sainte.

20. National Archives of Canada (NAC), MG 24, L3, vol. 2, 597, 632, 637. See also vol. 2, pp. 1400–1, M. de Vitré's letter from France of March 1755, to Mme. D'Argenteuil at Montreal, which describes the Lisbon earthquakes as "the punishments that God sends to make us aware that one must do penance for the sins one commits every day and to prepare ourselves to appear [before God] in the hope of mercy, when we will be judged and He will decide our [fate for] eternity."

21. Marshall, *Word from New France,* 263–64, 287–88, 290. The nuns observed comets, a celestial dart, and a "black vapor . . . from the sun" in the winter of 1664–65. See ibid., 308–9. The same belief in heavenly portents and providential causation was expressed by a contemporary cloth worker in Lille described by Alain Lottin in *Chavatte, ouvrier lillois: Un contemporain de Louis XIV* (Paris: Flammarion, 1979).

22. J. B. de La Croix de Chevrières de Saint-Vallier, *Rituel du Diocèse de Québec, publié par l'ordre de Monseigneur l'Evêque de Québec* (Paris: Simon Langlois, 1703), 590.

23. F. E. Rameau de Saint-Père, *Une colonie féodale en Amérique (L'Acadie, 1604–1710),* 2 vols. (Paris and Montreal: Plon and Granger frères, 1889), 2:304–7. Raymond Boyer, *Les Crimes et les Châtiments au Canada français du XVIIe au XXe siècle* (Montreal: Le Cercle du Livre de France, 1966), 300–301.

24. André Lachance, in his examination of the St. Lawrence Valley settlements' court records, found fourteen prosecutions for blasphemy in the seventeenth century and just one in the next century. See A. Lachance, *Crimes et Criminels en Nouvelle-France* (Montreal: Boréal, 1984), 63, 129. There are some gaps in the records of the law courts, but the trend is clear. The last case, in 1753, involved arson and theft as well as blasphemy. See E. Z. Massicotte, "Le Blasphème dans le bon vieux temps," *Bulletin des Recherches historiques* (BRH) 37 (1931): 169–73.

25. Guy du Rousseaud de la Combe, *Traité des Matières Criminelles* (Paris: Le Gras, 1753), 538–41.

26. F. Dareau, *Traité des Injures dans l'ordre judiciaire,* 2 vols. (Paris: Nyon l'aîné, 1785), 1:249. This is a later edition of a work that was in print, at least, since 1775.

27. AQ, NF 21, vol. 17 (no pagination), 30 August 1742 (37); and A. Lachance, "HAVARD de Beaufort, François-Charles," in *Dictionary of Canadian Biography,* vol. 3 (Toronto: University of Toronto, 1974), 278–79. The "outraged crucifix" is now encased, under glass, in the high altar of Quebec City's Hôtel-Dieu chapel, as an atonement for its profanation.

28. R. L. Séguin, *La Vie libertine en Nouvelle-France au dix-septième siècle,* 2 vols. (Montreal: Lemeac, 1972), 1:115–39.

29. Marshall, *Word from New France,* 264–65, 366. Identification of the girl and the miller was provided by Paul Ragueneau, *La Vie de la Mère Catherine de Saint Augustin* (Paris: Lambert, 1671), 163–65. Father Ragueneau's account confirms and supplements all that Marie de l'Incarnation reported to her son in her letter of September 1661. In nineteenth-century Montreal Marie Brault was a religious visionary who was also tormented by Satan. See Louis Bouhier, *The Extraordinary Life of Marie-Louise Brault* (1941).

30. C. H. Laverdière and H. R. Casgrain, eds., *Le Journal des Jésuites* (Montreal: Valois, 1892), 292, 295, 303. The same book identifies the bewitched girl as "Barbe Halé," who was "infestée d'un démon folet." The writer concluded that the girl was mentally disturbed. The journal is translated in Thwaites, *Jesuit Relations,* 45:167; 46:165, 171–73, and 187. While the journal says that Will was "hanged or rather shot (pendu ou plustost arquebuzé)" for selling liquor to the Indians, Father Ragueneau, in *La Vie de la Mère Catherine de Saint-Augustin,* 163–64, claims that Will was hanged for offenses against morality and Roman Catholicism. With only the Jesuits' journal as evidence, Gustave Lanctot exculpated Bishop Laval for Will's death. See Lanctot's *Une Nouvelle-France Inconnue* (Montreal: Ducharme, 1955), 89–117. For-

getting that continental French rarely uses the letter *w* and that seventeenth-century writers and printers employed a double *v* to represent this letter, later scholars have rendered Will's name as "Vvill" or "Voil."

31. J. C. Dupont, *Le Monde fantasque de la Beauce québécoise* (Ottawa: Collection Mercure, 1972). A thematic compendium of folk beliefs and sayings, including those on the French-held islands of Saint-Pierre and Miquelon and those of Acadia, is Pierre Des Ruisseaux's *Croyances et Pratiques populaires au Canada français* (Montreal: Editions du Jour, 1973).

32. Claude Aubry, *The Magic Fiddler and other Legends of French Canada* (Toronto: Clarke Irwin, 1968), 79.

33. Aubry, *The Magic Fiddler;* C. H. Carpenter, ed., *Explorations in Canadian Folklore* (Toronto: McClelland and Stewart, 1985); Dupont, *Le Monde fantasque;* E. Fowke, *Folktales of French Canada* (Toronto: NC Press, 1979); A. Wallace, *Baptiste Larocque: Legends of French Canada* (Toronto: Musson, 1923); E. Woodley, *Legends of French Canada* (Toronto: Nelson and Sons, 1931).

34. "Lettres de Mère Marie-Andrée Duplessis de Sainte-Hélène," *Nova Francia* 3 (1927–28): 229, 235.

35. "Les Mariages à la gaumine," *Rapport de l'Archiviste de la Province de Québec,* 1920–1921, 366–407. This entire article is devoted to this one case and cites no others. G. Roy, in BRH, 2 (1897): 46, lists four cases.

36. Archives nationales de France (ANF), Archives des Colonies (AC), série G2, vol. 184, ff.430–53: Extrait des Registres du Conseil Supérieur de Louisbourg, Isle Royale (12 February 1737). This case is also described in A. J. B. Johnston, *Religion and Life at Louisbourg, 1713–1758* (Kingston and Montreal: McGill-Queen's Press, 1984), 120–21, and in Christopher Moore's *Louisbourg Portraits: Life in an Eighteenth-Century Garrison Town* (Toronto: Macmillan, 1982), 179–89.

37. AQ, Montreal, Juridiction royale de Montréal, feuillets séparés, 9 April 1711: Ordinance of Intendant Raudot against Champagne and Widow Dionet. See also BRH 25 (1919): 120–22.

38. Têtu and Gagnon, *Mandements, lettres pastorales,* 1:333.

39. W. H. Lewis, *The Splendid Century: Life in the France of Louis XIV* (Garden City: Doubleday, 1957), 77. Mme. de Sevigné was the source of this tale.

40. Johnston, *Religion and Life at Louisbourg,* 118.

41. AQ, Greffes des notaires, G. Audouart, 14 May 1663; C. H. Dulaurent, 15 June 1752; F. Genaple, 8 September 1687; J. Jacob, 1 November 1739, 22 September 1740; J. C. Panet, 25 October 1771; AQ, Montreal, J. B. Adhémar, 18 December 1723, 28 December 1733; B. Basset, 24 August 1691; L. C. Danré de Blanzy, 12 December 1757.

42. Têtu and Gagnon, *Mandements, lettres pastorales,* 1:333.

43. AQ, Greffes, F. Genaple, 27 June 1703: Joseph Maillou; NF 23 (Juridiction de Trois-Rivières), vol. 3, ff.111–111vo (a joiner demands the return of a borrowed "histoire de la bible"); AQ, Montreal, Greffes, J. B. Adhémar, 13 June 1724: Prudhomme; Cameron Nish, *François-Étienne Cugnet: Entrepreneur et Entreprises en Nouvelle-France* (Montreal: Fides, 1975), 148. The 1727 gift from a sickly widow to her son of a two-volume edition of the saints' lives is described in "Le trésor d'une mère," BRH 38 (1932): 425–26.

44. AQ, Greffes, J. C. Louet, 13 August 1722: J. F. Martin de Lino; C. Barolet, 26 July 1752: N. de Rainville; AQ, Montreal, Greffes, L. C. Danré de Blanzy, 2 June 1760; A. Doughty and N. Dionne, *Quebec under Two Flags* (Quebec: n.p. 1903), appendix, no.3, vii (inventory of Jacquin Philibert, Quebec merchant, murdered in 1748); and E. Z. Massicotte, "Tableaux, portraits et images d'autrefois," BRH 40 (1934): 117–20.

45. AQ, Greffes, J. C. Louet, 16 December 1721: inventory of Gauvreau's estate, made four years after his death, when his wife was about to remarry.

46. AQ, Greffes, F. Genaple, 20 January 1706: J. Minet; and AQ, Montreal, 20 August 1708: LeMoyne de Maricourt. Montreal merchant Jean-Baptiste Neveu had a dozen "rings with a large seal" with a total value of ten sols, according to AQ, Montreal, Greffes, J. B. Adhémar, 20 March 1720.

47. Thwaites, *Jesuit Relations,* 8:188–89.

48. Marshall, *Word from New France,* 83–84.

49. "Lettres de Mère Marie-Andrée Duplessis de Sainte-Hélène," 50.

50. Ragueneau, *La Vie de la Mère Catherine de Saint Augustin,* 73–74. Although her behavior was, as her

biographer admits, an extreme example of self-mortification, Marie-Catherine was much admired in New France during her lifetime and after her death in 1668.

51. Hubert Deschamps, ed., *Les Voyages de Samuel Champlain, saintongeais, père du Canada* (Paris: PUF, 1951), 175, 270–71.

52. Thwaites, *Jesuit Relations*, 18:82–89 (my translation).

53. E. R. Adair, "France and the Beginnings of New France," *Canadian Historical Review* 25, no.3 (September 1944): 246–78.

54. Morin, *Annales de l'Hôtel-Dieu de Montréal*, 5, 102, 146, 157.

55. C. Le Roy Bacqueville de la Potherie, *Histoire de l'Amérique septentrionale*, 4 vols. (Paris: Nion and Didot, 1722), 1:308.

56. C. Tanguay, *A Travers les Registres* (Montreal: Librairie Saint-Joseph, 1886), 80–81.

57. Marshall, *Word from New France*, 355.

58. Morin, *Annales de l'Hôtel-Dieu*, 114–15.

59. "Lettres de Mère Marie-Andrée Duplessis de Sainte-Hélène," Nova Francia, vol. 3 (1927–28), 54, 172.

60. Têtu and Gagnon, *Mandements, lettres pastorales*, 1:106–7. His successor, Bishop Saint-Vallier, continued the attack on "the criminal fashions of the age" in 1686 and 1691. See ibid., 1: 185–86, 268–70. He was also offended by the fact that many women dressed in a style proper to a higher social rank.

61. Ibid., 1:169–74.

62. Ibid., 1:183–86, 267–74, 275–87, 328–31, 359–66, 368–77, 390–98, 491–92.

63. *Édits, ordonnances royaux, déclarations et arrêts . . . concernant le Canada* (EOR), 3 vols. (Quebec: Fréchette, 1854–56), 2:270, 286, 291–92, 346–47, 348–49, 396–97, 435–36, 443, 465, 474, 484–85, 507–8, 513, 516–17, 527–28, 543, 551–52, 576, 588–89; 3:158–59, 174, 421–22, 424–25, 426, 430–31.

64. EOR, 2:425.

65. Y. F. Zoltvany, ed., *The French Tradition in North America* (New York: Harper and Row, 1972), 83–84.

66. AQ, Montreal, Juridiction royale de Montréal, Feuillets séparés, 18 March 1710.

67. NAC, MG 8, B1 (Prévôté de Québec), vol. 20–1, 82–92, 94–96.

68. C. J. Jaenen, *The Role of the Church in New France* (Ottawa: Canadian Historical Association, 1985), 15.

69. Phileas Gagnon, "Le curé Lefèbvre et l'héroine de Verchères," BRH 6 (1900): 340–45; R. L. Séguin, *La Vie libertine en Nouvelle-France*, 2:534–35; A. Vachon, "JARRET DE VERCHÈRES, Marie-Madeleine," in DCB, vol. 3 (Toronto: University of Toronto Press, 1974), 308–13. Colin M. Coates, "Authority and Illegitimacy in New France," *Histoire sociale/Social History* 22, no.3 (May 1989): 65–90, provides a well-researched reconstruction of this episode, which, with one other event, is cited to demonstrate that there was a crisis of authority in New France. One can accept the evidence without assenting to the argument. In 1700 the censorious Bishop Saint-Vallier had instructed priests to stay away from gatherings where liquor was being served and never to utter "railleries et les paroles buffonnes, les airs profanes, les chansons mondaines." See Têtu and Gagnon, *Mandements, lettres pastorales*, 1:415.

70. Johnston, *Religion and Life at Louisbourg*, 38–41.

71. NAC, MG 17, A10 (Hôtel-Dieu de Québec: Registres, 1689–1774), vol. 2–5, part 3, 372.

72. EOR, 2:71–72.

73. JDCS, 2:613–14.

74. AQ, NF 25 (Collection de pièces judiciaires et notariales), 2e liasse, no.137: "Confrontation . . . A lencontre de Charles Catignon."

75. Thirty percent of the Quebec hospital's nuns came from the colony's social elite; there was a higher cachet to a religious vocation with the Ursulines or at Quebec's Hôpital-Général. See Micheline d'Allaire, *L'Hôpital-Général de Québec, 1692–1764* (Montreal: Fides, 1971), 220.

76. C. J. Jaenen, "JUCHEREAU DE LA FERTÉ, Jeanne-Françoise," in DCB, vol. 2 (Toronto: University of Toronto Press, 1969), 303–4.

77. NAC, MG 24, L3, dated letters, vol. 3, 1558: Meynardie to Etienne Augé, 27 June 1757.

78. Ibid., 1653–54: M. de Seville at Paris to Louis Perrault in Canada, 29 January 1759.

79. Ibid., 1699–700: Havy to the Bâby brothers at Montreal, 12 February 1759.

80. Ibid., 1744–46.

81. *L'Hôpital-Général des Soeurs Grises de la Charité,* 2 vols. (Montreal: n.p., n.d.), 1:238–40, quoted in K. A. MacKirdy, J. S. Moir, and Y. F. Zoltvany, eds., *Changing Perspectives in Canadian History: Selected Problems,* 2d ed. (Don Mills, Ont.: Dent and sons, 1971), 65. Only after the French Revolution of 1789–93 did the Roman Catholic clergy see God's logic in letting New France fall to the British: it was to preserve the Canadians from the anticlerical and regicidal excesses of the Jacobins, which would have spread to Canada had it still been a part of France's empire. The French Canadians were still God's people and He had not failed them.

CONCLUSION

1. Archives nationales de France, Archives des Colonies, série F3, vol. 2, f.198: De Meulles to the king, c.1684.

2. The theme of racial purity has now been superseded by an emphasis on the present generation's personal link with settlers from France. Thus Marcel Fournier, in *Les Européens au Canada, des origines à 1765* (Montreal: Editions du Fleuve, 1989), 32, writes, "all serious authors . . . are in agreement in saying that 97 percent of Quebec and Canada's French population comes from France." It is equally certain that most French-speakers have ancestors from countries other than France.

3. Apart from the circumstantial differences of being in a province with a French-speaking majority and being subject to a civil code rooted in French jurisprudence, there are few outward differences to set French-speakers within Quebec apart from French-speaking Canadians in other provinces. The lack of tangible or visible differences is not critical to one's outlook. The wonderful thing about cultural nationalism is that if enough people believe that they belong to a group whose interests are incompatible with those of other peoples, then they will be a nationality, whatever the external evidence indicates. Nationalism is, after all, a state of mind.

4. Claude Bergeron, *Architecture du XXe siècle au Québec* (Montreal: Editions du Méridien, 1989), 58–61, provides floor plans of this urban, low-income housing, which is still plentiful in Quebec's cities.

5. Philippe Garigue, "French-Canadian Kinship and Urban life," in Marcel Rioux and Yves Martin, eds., *French-Canadian Society* (Toronto: McClelland and Stewart, 1964), 358–72.

6. G. M. Wrong, ed., "Louisbourg in 1745: The Anonymous lettre d'un Habitant de Louisbourg," *University of Toronto Studies—History,* 2d ser., 1 (1897): 2–74. The original reads, "Les Anglais sont les seuls peuples capables de ces bisarreries, qui font cependant partie de cette précieuse liberté dont ils se montrent si jaloux."

7. See the opposing petitions from the two language groups, for and against an elected assembly, reprinted in A. Shortt and A. G. Doughty, eds., *Documents relating to the Consitutional History of Canada, 1759–1791* (Ottawa: Dawson, 1907), 502–20, 524–27, 541–47.

8. N. W. Taylor, "French Canadians as Industrial Entrepreneurs," *Journal of Political Economy* 68 (February 1960): 37–52.

9. In 1999, when the proposition "respect for authority is important" was presented to Candians, those who were most likely to agree were residents in areas with a preponderance of French-speakers, such as southern Manitoba, northern New Brunswick, and the Province of Quebec. See *Saturday Night* 114, no. 4 (1May 1999), 22.

10. One can see the consequences of relying on one family's labor and of subsistence farming with few animals in the size of Quebec barns built in the early 1800s: they are much smaller than contemporary barns constructed in the adjoining Province of Ontario.

11. Shortt and Doughty, *Documents,* 189.

12. Ibid., 294.

13. Ibid., 197–98.

14. Ibid., 121.

15. Ibid., 203.

16. Philip Lawson, *The Imperial Challenge: Quebec and Britain in the Age of the American Revolution* (Montreal and Kingston: McGill-Queen's University Press, 1989), has put to rest the claim, contained in the 1776 Declaration of Independence and endorsed by historian Chester Martin, about the counterrevolutionary aims of the Quebec Act. The late Professor Lawson showed that abandonment of the 1763 Royal Proclamation was considered, as was a compromise with French legal and administrative traditions, well before the outbreak of violence in New England. Lawson also diminished the role of Sir Guy Carleton in effecting this reversal of British administrative policy for Canada.

17. Shortt and Doughty, *Documents,* 404.

18. Ibid., 420. Elizabeth Arthur, "French-Canadian Participation in the Government of Canada, 1775–85," *Canadian Historical Review* 32 (1951): 303–14, suggested that these appointees were compliant "yes-men" who could never be independent spokesmen for French Canada.

19. F. Ouellet, *Louis-Joseph Papineau: A Divided Soul* (Ottawa: Canadian Historical Association, 1961).

20. A coincidental rebellion in Upper Canada in 1837 also suffered from a lack of coordination because of poor communication, but its leadership was indigenous and the plan of William Lyon Mackenzie's followers to seize the provincial capital in a surprise attack showed enterprise and daring.

21. Allan Greer, *The Patriots and the People: Rebellion of 1837 in Rural Lower Canada* (Toronto: University of Toronto Press, 1993), 100–107, 229–33.

22. The masculine prejudices of the Patriotes are discussed in Greer, *The Patriots and the People,* 197–210.

23. L. A. Paquet, "Le féminisme, un mouvement pervers," from the December 1918 issue of *Le Canada français,* reprinted in G. R. Cook and W. Mitchinson, eds., *The Proper Sphere: Woman's Place in Canadian Society* (Toronto: Macmillan, 1976), 84–91.

24. The expansion and extent of these services are described in A. Beaudoin, ed., *Services sociaux à l'enfance, à la famille, aux personnes âgées et dans le domaine de la santé: État de la situation au Québec* (Sillery: École de service social, Université Laval, 1988). The limitations and problems within this system are discussed by the Commission d'Enquête sur les Services de Santé et les Services sociaux, *Les services de santé et les services sociaux: Problématiques et enjeux* (Quebec: Gouvernement du Québec, 1987).

25. Marc Renaud, "Quebec's Middle Class in Search of Social Hegemony: Causes and Political Consequences," *International Review of Community Development,* n.s., 39/40 (1978): 1–36; reprinted in A. D. Gilbert, C. M. Wallace, and R. M. Bray, eds., *Reappraisals in Canadian History: Post-Confederation* (Scarborough: Prentice Hall, 1992), 451–87.

26. Under Bill 101, passed by Quebec's Parti Québécois government in 1977, English and bilingual signs were made illegal and all commercial enterprises with fifty or more employees were obliged to conduct their business in French. Even the international "stop" sign must read "arrêt," which reveals the nationalist antipathy to English. Quebec's linguistic minorities opposed the law on the grounds that it violated freedom of expression, guaranteed by the federal Charter of Rights and Freedoms. The Quebec Superior Court and the Supreme Court of Canada agreed, but the provincial government exercised the "notwithstanding clause" in the Canadian constitution to override these decisions.

The absence of a populist tradition among French-speakers raises the question of other missing elements, in comparison with the rest of Canada. Political separation from France in 1760 and a period of cultural isolation during the Anglo-French wars from 1793 to 1815 meant that French Canada was scarcely touched by eighteenth-century Romanticism, which celebrated nature as a source of spiritual renewal. Later, French historical romanticism did inspire paintings of past military glories and poems that nostalgically recalled the French Regime. Landscape painting was a late development in French Canada, as was literature in praise of natural beauty. Joseph Légaré (1795–1855) was called by Barry Lord "the father of Quebec landscape painting." Légaré's views contain figures or some manmade structure, and this "father" had few children. In the 1800s unpopulated scenes of Quebec's countryside were painted by English-speakers such as Lucius O'Brien, Homer Watson, and John A. Fraser. The charming landscapes produced by Clarence Gagnon (1881–1942), a French Canadian, show picturesque country villages, purged of telephone poles and wires, automobiles, and power lines. His paintings were a visual expression of the idealization of rural life among French Canadians in a postindustrial era. Symmetrical and formal private gardens were part of the French tradition. Naturalistic public parks, such as Montreal's Mount Royal Park or Quebec City's Battlefield Park, were introduced to Quebec by English-speakers in the 1800s. The botanical garden was so closely associated with British Canadians that, during the nineteenth century, many French Canadians referred to Montreal's botanical garden (*jardin botanique*) as the "jardin britannique." The absence of romantic naturalism in French-Canada's past explains the slow acceptance of the ecology movement in that province.

27. I realize that anyone who knows the nature of Canada will find this claim that all the other peoples of the country form a single cultural nation bizarre. Canada has a political nationality; it is not a single cultural entity, even if one subtracts Quebec from the equation. Talking about "Canada" and "Quebec" as mutually exclusive entities, when one comprises the other, presents another intellectual challenge.

28. Parti Québécois, *Programme du Parti Québécois: Édition 1989* (n.p., 1989).

Index